Susan Burke

Public Space

Public Space reveals the ways people actually use and value public space, focusing on the social basis for its design and management. The authors – an architect/environmental designer, a landscape architect, an environmental psychologist, and an open-space administrator – offer a well-conceived perspective on how to integrate public space and public life. They contend that three critical human dimensions should guide the process of design and management of public space: the users' essential needs, their spatial rights, and the meanings they seek. To develop and explain these three dimensions, the authors draw on the history of public life and public space, evidence from recent social research, their own professional design and planning experience, and a series of original case studies, all amply illustrated.

Cambridge Series in Environment and Behavior

General Editors: Daniel Stokols
             Irwin Altman

Public Space

Stephen Carr
Carr, Lynch, Hack and Sandell,
Architects, Landscape Architects and Planners

Mark Francis
University of California, Davis
CoDesign Inc., Landscape Architects and Architects

Leanne G. Rivlin
City University of New York Graduate School

Andrew M. Stone
Trust for Public Land

CAMBRIDGE
UNIVERSITY PRESS

Published by the Press Syndicate of the University of Cambridge
The Pitt Building, Trumpington Street, Cambridge CB2 1RP
40 West 20th Street, New York, NY 10011-4211, USA
10 Stamford Road, Oakleigh, Victoria 3166, Australia

First published 1992

Printed in the United States of America

Library of Congress Cataloging-in-Publication Data

Public space / Stephen Carr . . . [et al.]
p.   cm. – (Cambridge series in environment and behavior)
Includes bibliographical references and indexes.
ISBN 0-521-35148-0. – ISBN 0-521-35960-0 (pbk.)
1. Public spaces. 2. Public spaces – United States – Planning – Case
studies. 3. City and town life – United States. I. Carr, Stephen,
1935– . II. Series.
HT153.P83 1992
307.1'216'0973 – dc20   92-4909
A catalog record for this book is available from the British Library.

ISBN 0–521–35148–0 hardback
ISBN 0–521–35960–0 paperback

CONTENTS

Contents

CASE STUDIES

Case studies

SERIES FOREWORD

In recent decades the relationship between human behavior and the physical environment has attracted researchers from the social sciences – psychology, sociology, geography, and anthropology – and from the environmental-design disciplines – architecture, urban and regional planning, and interior design. What is in many respects a new and exciting field of study has developed rapidly. Its multidisciplinary character has led to stimulation and cross-fertilization, on the one hand, and to confusion and difficulty in communication, on the other. Those involved have diverse intellectual styles and goals. Some are concerned with basic and theoretical issues; some, with applied real-world problems of environmental design.

This series offers a common meeting ground. It consists of short books on different topics of interest to all those who analyze environment-behavior links. We hope that the series will provide a useful introduction to the field for students, researchers, and practitioners alike, and will facilitate its evolutionary growth as well.

Our goals are as follows: (1) to represent problems the study of which is relatively well established, with a reasonably substantial body of research and knowledge generated; (2) to recruit authors from a variety of disciplines with a variety of perspectives; (3) to ensure that they not only summarize work on their topic but also set forth a "point of view," if not a theoretical orientation; and (4) to produce books useful to a broad range of students, professionals, and scholars from different disciplines in the social sciences and environmental design fields.

Irwin Altman
Daniel Stokols

*In memory of Kevin Lynch and Harold M. Proshansky —
teachers, colleagues, friends, and inspirations*

PREFACE

This book is about public space and the life it supports. We see public space as the common ground where people carry out the functional and ritual activities that bind a community, whether in the normal routines of daily life or in periodic festivities. We recognize that in much of the rest of the world, and increasingly in the West, public space is also used for "private" purposes – for buying or selling things, for gardening, for self-improvement through exercise, or for simply finding a place to exist. It can also be the setting for activities that threaten communities, such as crime and protest. As public life evolves with the culture, new types of spaces may be needed and old ones discarded or revived. We need to learn how to create and maintain places that are appropriate to their users and context and are well used over time.

Public Space offers guidance for improving the design, management, and use of public places. We intend the book to be helpful to users, whose needs are not always met in existing spaces; to politicians, public administrators, or private developers, with responsibility for creating or improving spaces, as well as to designers and managers. Our sources include historic and social scientific studies of public space, professional design and planning experience, and the direct observation of many spaces. We propose a specific set of values to organize this information, and an approach and working process for using it in design and management.

Part I provides a critical perspective on public space and public life based on a historical review with an emphasis on our time. In the first chapter, we review the key motives for making public space and the main criticisms of the results. We propose that good public space should be supportive, democratic, and meaningful. In Chapter 2, we analyze public life in historical perspective, examine the forces that shape it, and ask how public space can help create a more humane culture. We conclude Part I by showing how the evolution of public life has produced the many types that we have today, including those specifically designed to support public life, such as parks, plazas, and playgrounds, and those appropriated for that purpose, such as street corners, steps to public buildings, or vacant lots.

In Part II, with the aid of existing environmental and social research and many case studies, we describe the human dimensions of public space. Our review of research is supplemented by case studies of public spaces in the United States and Europe. These are drawn primarily from our own site visits and evaluations and occasionally from studies by other researchers and designers. Our approach assumes that any good analysis of a public space must begin by spending time there, watching how the place is used, and recording how it feels. Taken together, these chapters provide a framework for identifying and evaluating people's needs in public space, for securing and protecting their rights, and for enabling spaces to become meaningful.

Part II does not present a comprehensive review of people–environment research on public space. More complete reviews already exist in the two-volume *Handbook of Environmental Psychology* by Altman and Stokols (1987); the multiple-volume series *Human Behavior and Environment,* including as its tenth volume the excellent *Public Spaces and Places* edited by Altman and Zube (1989); and the multiple-volume *Advances in Environment, Behavior and Design* edited by Zube and Moore (1987, 1989, 1991). Our intent is also not to provide another set of guidelines as can be found in *A Pattern Language,* by Christopher Alexander and others (1977); *People Places,* edited by Clare Cooper Marcus and Carolyn Francis (1990); and Geoffrey Broadbent's *Emerging Concepts in Urban Space Design* (1990). Instead, Part II is intended to provide the understanding of fundamentals – the "human dimensions" of public space – that is needed to design and manage spaces more creatively and effectively.

In Part III, we present our approach to design and management. Chapter 7 shows how the dimensions defined in Part II can be used to guide the processes in the context of our polycultural, changing society. We then analyze how design and management are typically carried out and propose a more effective process for our complex culture. We conclude with a discussion of the key social issues we believe must be addressed in the future evolution of public space.

Although our primary purpose is to assist the producers and users of public space to make and manage better spaces, the book also has three other agendas. First, we hope that this compendium of research and case studies will be useful to environmental psychologists and the other social researchers concerned with public life and public space. To aid future research, we include a bibliography on past research, theory, and design. We hope our review will help promote long-term case studies, because we have found few of these in the literature. We understand that the time and support required to do this well is often difficult to secure. A good postoccupancy evaluation, which includes extensive interviews of all those involved in the design process, as well as observation and interviews of managers and users, can approximate the in-depth understanding that could be gained from fully observed cases. However, it is our strong conviction that public spaces overall will only be as good as the processes by which they are created and managed and that, therefore, process as well as product needs to be studied. Is it too much to hope that designers and managers might take the lead in creating opportunities for social scientists to observe their work processes?

Our second desire is to inspire increased opportunities for collaboration among social scientists, sponsors, users, designers, and managers in the creation and tending of public spaces. The book attempts to demonstrate the value of this approach. Designers and managers need to provide leadership, but understanding and financial support from clients and users is also needed. The involvement of social scientists is no panacea for the many pitfalls of public space design and management, but the knowledge and perspective they can offer will greatly enrich the social art of making public space.

Finally, we want the education of designers and managers to be significantly broadened. We believe there should be more focus on the human and cultural dimensions of design and management as well as training in group process skills. Design education should not only include lectures and seminars on the social basis of design, but also bring environmentally aware social scientists into the studio to work with students on their design projects, challenging them to investigate the fit between their designs and people's needs. Although most design programs try to provide the experience of working in teams, only a few include learning how to work with groups of users and communities. Real world projects on which students can help can provide this experience, which will be most meaningful if it is guided by someone who is expert in group process. Management training may err in the opposite direction, with too much attention on the techniques of working with people and not enough on the social value of the products of this work.

More research, increased collaboration across disciplines, and broadened training for designers and managers will all contribute to making better public spaces. We are convinced, however, that enough is now known to improve dramatically the typical process and product of space making. This book is devoted to that task.

When we began, we were intrigued by the large amount of social research that had been done on public space and, even more, by how little of it was known and applied by designers and managers. As we examined this body of knowledge, looked at many existing public spaces, and reviewed our own experience as designers and planners, we reached some definite conclusions. The result of this collaborative exploration, *Public Space,* takes a firm position on the most important values that public space can serve, and on the processes of design and management that can best further those values. We intend that the book go beyond a scholarly presentation of what is currently known to provide inspiration to all those involved in creating, improving, and managing public spaces.

The particular blend of historical, social scientific, and practical knowledge evident in *Public Space* mirrors the interdisciplinary skills and experiences of its authors. Rivlin and Stone are environmental psychologists. Rivlin has consulted on design projects, and Stone is also a practicing planner. Carr is an architect and an urban and landscape designer. Francis is a landscape architect, researcher, and teacher. All four share a long-standing interest in environmental psychology. The book was conceived while the authors were engaged in collaborative teaching and research at the City University of New York doctoral program in environmental psychology.

The overall theory, purpose, structure, and content of the book were jointly determined, with each author taking responsibility for particular chapters. In general, Leanne Rivlin, Andrew Stone, and Mark Francis surveyed the social scientific research and historical studies that form the basis of Chapters 2 through 6. Stephen Carr and Mark Francis collaborated on the critique of present practice, which informs Chapter 1, and on the ideas for a better approach in Chapters 7 and 8. Rivlin, Stone, and Carr jointly worked out ideas presented in Chapter 6.

While working together over a long period of time there has been ample opportunity for cross-fertilization and, by now, there are bits of all of us in all chapters. In final form, Chapter 1 was written by Francis and Carr; Chapter 2 by Rivlin; Chapter 3 by Stone with contributions from Francis and Rivlin; Chapters 4 and 5 by Stone and Rivlin with input from Francis; Chapter 6 by Rivlin and Stone, with contributions from Carr; and Chapter 7, 8, and 9 by Carr, with suggestions from all. Illustrations were jointly selected by Carr and Francis. Final production was coordinated by Francis.

This book would not have been possible without the support and assistance of many organizations and individuals. The National Endowment for the Arts provided funding for our background research and the documentation of case studies. Our own institutions – the Cambridge, Massachusetts, design firm of Carr, Lynch, Hack and Sandell; the Department of Environmental Design at the University of California, Davis; the Environmental Psychology Program at the City University of New York; and the Trust for Public Land were generous in providing free time for this pursuit and in other significant ways. Lyn Lofland reviewed an early draft of the manuscript and made useful suggestions for improvements. The editors for this Cambridge University Press series, Irwin Altman and Daniel Stokols, were encouraging, thoughtful, and challenging in their most valuable comments on a late draft of the manuscript. Elizabeth March assisted with the case studies in Boston and Washington, D.C., helped us greatly with our early definitions of the dimensions, and, in the process, sharpened our thinking. Mary Naki, Marti Martino, Joe Fajen, Anne Marie Sadowski, and Beth Meres typed the many manuscript drafts with skill and good humor. Tom Frye assisted with preparing the illustrations.

We appreciate our readers' interest and invite their comments. We know that this would have been a better work if carried out in dialogue with you, and we hope to learn from your responses. In the continuing process of making and remaking the human environment, many conversations are needed and many voices must be heard.

PUBLIC SPACE AND PUBLIC LIFE

Part I examines the origins and current realities of public life and public space in America. Although there has been much discussion of the apparent decline in public life, we suggest that the recent public space renaissance demonstrates that it is simply taking new forms. The expansion in the number and types of public places seen today, including new commercial spaces, community gardens, greenways, and preserved natural areas, shows how changes in the ways we live together continue to shape the design and management of places. However, some motives for making public space do not adequately reflect user needs. As a result, there have been failures in design and management and much criticism. In the opening chapter, we discuss these issues and outline the essential values to consider in making public spaces.

Chapter 2 reviews the changing historical balance between public and private life, showing that important public life still occurs in public spaces. The key forces shaping public life are discussed, together with their effects on public space. Public life and public space change in response to these forces and, through its various transformations, public life continues to be central to our sense of community and culture.

In Chapter 3, we trace the evolution of specific types of public spaces such as streets, squares, playgrounds, malls, and community open spaces. The emphasis is on recent developments in public space as they have opened up and dispersed, with specialized types for different groups. The chapter concludes with a typology of the major public spaces that exist today.

THE VALUE OF PUBLIC SPACE

Public space is the stage upon which the drama of communal life unfolds. The streets, squares, and parks of a city give form to the ebb and flow of human exchange. These dynamic spaces are an essential counterpart to the more settled places and routines of work and home life, providing the channels for movement, the nodes of communication, and the common grounds for play and relaxation. There are pressing needs that public space can help people to satisfy, significant human rights that it can be shaped to define and protect, and special cultural meanings that it can best convey. These themes, to be explored and developed in this book, reveal the value of public space and lay the groundwork for improved design and management.

In all communal life there is a dynamic balance between public and private activities. Within this balance, different cultures place differing emphases on public space. Compare the Latin cultures of southern Europe, with their display of wealth and civic and religious power in palaces, town halls, and churches that face on main streets and squares, with the Muslim cultures of North Africa, with their limited number of public spaces apart from markets and shopping streets and yet rich design and expression in the more private domains of home, mosque, and Koranic school. Although the public–private balance is unique to each culture, it will shift under the influence of cultural exchange, technology, changing political and economic systems, and the ethos of the time.

interesting

In the relatively brief history of the United States, several such shifts have already occurred. In the seventeenth and eighteenth centuries, the functional needs of town and city required the building of roads and later paved streets, often laid out for convenience on a grid pattern. These simple spaces were the primary settings for public life, focused on daily commerce. Streets were complemented in New England by the common green

The New England common with its communal symbols: church, town hall, band-stand, and monument to the Revolutionary War. (Stephen Carr)

and elsewhere by town squares and public markets, taking their inspiration from London prototypes or, in the Southwest, from Spain. These commons and squares were, as in Europe, fronted by town halls and churches and, together with markets, became natural meeting grounds for the populace. In the nineteenth century, again influenced by European developments, Americans imported the boulevard and the landscaped public park, both to celebrate the growing wealth and leisure of the upper classes and to bring more beautiful and healthful settings to the working class, confined in our growing and crowded industrial cities. Later came the reform movement, with its emphasis on play settings for the children of the working poor, and still later the spread of small sports parks and playgrounds to serve the growing recreational needs of the middle classes, with their increased leisure time.

As middle-class and working-class people have moved to the suburbs, where they have private outdoor spaces, their way of living and use of public space has changed. On the functional side, isolated travel in automobiles and an obsession with traffic flow have diminished and degraded the life of the street. The impersonal shopping center and commercial strip have replaced downtown as a setting for communal life. For these suburbanites, the backyard, the high school playfield or tennis court, and the remaining undeveloped countryside have replaced the public park as settings for family relaxation, while the television and the video cassette recorder have tended to keep the family at home, even for entertainment.

This suburbanization, together with the increasing difficulties of the city for those who remained, have led some social scientists to lament a decline in public life, suggesting that the balance in our society is shifting strongly toward the security and pleasures of private life (Fischer, 1981;

Social realists identify the shopping mall as the new center of communal life. (Stephen Carr)

Lofland, 1973; Sennett, 1977). Even among the inner-city poor, known in the past for a vigorous public life, the home – when there is one – can become a haven against the threats of increasingly dangerous streets. More recently, views of absolute decline have been tempered by the idea of a transformation of public life into new forms of association and communication that do not depend on primary relationships in traditional public places (Brill, 1989a; Lofland, 1983). Socializing at the PTA or the local church or temple and communicating through local newspapers or cable television might be seen as replacing dialogue in the public square. Even middle-class teenagers hang out at the shopping center, rather than the neighborhood street corner, where they could meet familiar adults.

A RESURGENCE IN PUBLIC LIFE AND PUBLIC SPACE?

If one looks away from these particular social trends and examines the urban environment itself, a strikingly different picture comes into focus. Since World War II, there has been a proliferation of public space types to meet the needs of an increasingly stratified and specialized public life. Not only are public spaces proliferating under the demands of different subgroups in our society, but most of these new spaces seem to be well

Since World War II, successful new spaces have often had commercial purposes. Ghirardelli Square, San Francisco, developed in the 1960s. (Stephen Carr)

A fine fall day brings people to the Church Street Marketplace, in the center of Burlington, Vermont. (Stephen Carr)

used (Glazer & Lilla, 1987; Lennard & Lennard, 1984). In the past thirty years hundreds of new parks, pedestrian malls, plazas, atria, and community gardens have been built in all parts of the country with very large public and private investments (Brambilla & Longo, 1977; Heckscher & Robinson, 1977; Whyte, 1988). Older parks, playgrounds, and public squares, allowed to deteriorate in the latter part of this century, are now being renewed and revived in many cities. Farmers markets are increasingly popular and, in a few vanguard cities, public market structures have been renewed or created to house them. Street vending and performing are back, and not only in the contrived settings of "festive marketplaces." Outdoor cafés are enormously popular.

Beginning with the pedestrian mall movement in the late 1950s, most American cities have been striving to improve their downtown retail and office areas by creating new walking streets, parks, and plazas, and adding trees where possible. Although some of these malls have been economic failures, evidence from San Francisco, New York, Boston, Seattle, Portland, Chicago, and many other cities suggests that people are using downtown parks and plazas in increasing numbers (Cooper Marcus & Francis, 1990; Frieden & Sagalyn, 1989; Whyte, 1988). The most recent development in this renewal effort is the so-called festival marketplace, a kind of in-town shopping center with an emphasis on boutiques, eating, and entertainment, supporting a new form of public life known as recreational shopping.

Many cities are struggling to reclaim old industrial waterfronts for public access and use. Some, including Boston, Baltimore, Seattle, and Philadelphia have already accomplished major transformations. Often these efforts start with annual waterfront fairs and festivals, drawing thousands to experience the magic of light, water, and people enjoying themselves. Many localities are also attempting to capture remaining "urban wilds," unbuilt wetlands and other areas, that can become nature reserves, opened to walkers and wildlife. In a few towns, efforts are under way to link such areas with town trails for jogging and cycling enthusiasts (Goodey, 1979). In the older neighborhoods, the community garden movement is booming. Record attendance at arboretums, garden fairs, neighborhood fairs, and festivals provides further evidence of people's desire to gather in enjoyable settings (Francis, 1987c).

What seem contradictory trends, the decline of older forms of public life and the resurgence in public space, instead may be complementary. At least for the middle classes of our society, nearby public space is no longer so necessary as a relief from crowded living and working environments nor as an essential setting for the social exchange that helped to hold

Detroit's Hart Plaza was designed as a festival space on the river. (Stephen Carr)

The resurgence of public space, where different people rub elbows. Gallery Place, Washington, D.C. (Stephen Carr)

together the old "urban villages" with their social support systems (Gans, 1962). Instead, public spaces supporting particular types of public life become freely chosen settings for family and group enjoyment and for individual development and discovery. In the process of choosing the spaces for their public lives, people can also choose to experience other groups in settings that are conducive to relaxed exchange. Successful multicultural spaces add to the richness of the city as a learning environment and give hope to the American dream of cultural integration, or at the very least cultural understanding.

REASONS AND RESULTS IN PUBLIC SPACE DEVELOPMENT

The primary motives for making or remaking public spaces should be viewed against this changing panorama of public life in urban America. Goals most often cited by the producers and managers of public spaces include public welfare, visual enhancement, environmental enhancement, and economic development. Not always stated but also key in many settings is enhancement of the public image of the corporate or government producers and managers. The relative importance of these goals for the producers has shifted in response to the changing demands of various publics and to political and economic changes in cities. From the user's perspective, the resulting space may create a different set of benefits, some of which may not have been intended.

Public welfare has always been a primary motivation for creating or improving public space. The Greeks and Romans first paved and straightened streets to provide for movement and safety and they built their agoras and forums to provide convenient and noble centers for public life (Mumford, 1970). Still today these are the purposes most often used to justify street and plaza improvements. Parks, from their origins, have been seen as "the lungs of the city," substitute countryside where exposure to fresh air and sunlight, with the opportunity to stroll freely and relax, would serve as an antidote to the oppressive physical and psychological conditions of city life (Cranz, 1982; Heckscher & Robinson, 1977). Later, in the reform movement of the late nineteenth and early early twentieth centuries, this motive became even more explicit and we still build our parks and playgrounds to provide "recreational opportunities." Now advocacy groups often seek to define the dimensions of public welfare more narrowly.

Visual enhancement is also an ancient and honorable motive that raises new questions in our own social context. Roman emperors sought to outdo their predecessors in the provision of more and grander forums, basilicas, and baths to support public life in high style. In the Renaissance, Italian

The perfect urban setting for grand entrances also works for just hanging out.
Spanish Steps, Rome. (Stephen Carr)

architects and sculptors, when given the opportunity, created straight streets and piazzas, like outdoor rooms, as grand settings for the life of the times, perhaps reaching an apex in Rome at the end of the sixteenth century. Americans have tried their hand at such urban enhancement, seeking to beautify central cities and major streets through unified designs of public space coupled, sometimes, with controls over adjacent private development. How to achieve broad aesthetic appeal in a democratic and culturally diverse society is a question to be explored in later chapters.

The goal of environmental enhancement is closely related, because trees and greenery are also considered by most people to be aesthetically as well as psychologically important (Kaplan & Kaplan, 1989). This objective is more often used for larger-scale intervention, such as the acquisition of land for nature reserves, the creation of town trails, or widespread tree planting. It is likely that the growing public consciousness of environmental degradation, and of how human settlements relate to the larger ecosystems of which they are a part, will create political and economic support for more sensitive urban development, emphasizing preservation and enhancement of natural landscape, as well as the creation of new open space and the "greening" of existing environments (Hough, 1984; Sale, 1990; Spirn, 1984). The threat of global warming has already led to proposals for urban forests, with millions of trees to be planted in the coming decades (Schroeder, 1989).

Economic development is another common motivation for creating open space. Spaces designed for enjoyment and relaxation, with supports for informal performances and other interesting activity, can attract people who may then become good customers for retail business. Small plazas and atria are built to provide for relaxation at lunch and social relief from isolating office work. These spaces also can be used to encourage new commercial development. There are often tensions between the motive of serving the public and the desire to enhance the corporate or government image, but there are some useful guides for reconciling these goals (Whyte, 1980, 1988).

Indeed, image enhancement is normally an unstated goal of most producers of public space. It is natural that government sponsors would wish costly public spaces to reflect well upon themselves. Most corporations undertaking new buildings or developments in cities want to be, and to be seen as, good public citizens. Adjacent successful public spaces will also increase and protect the value of building investments. Local government can benefit from projects that help improve the image of the city and create points of pride, especially when private development or some other branch of government can be induced to pay for them. For these reasons, this quiet motive can be among the most important in determining the design of spaces.

In the past twenty years there have been numerous attempts to assess the actual performance of public spaces from the user's point of view. This research, reviewed in Part II of this book, points to the many social, psychological, and physical benefits that the broad goals of public space producers do not typically address. For the most part, these studies expand on the public welfare motive, revealing its true complexity. We will see how spaces can be made to serve human needs, from passive relaxation, through active engagement with others, to discovery of unknown worlds. Political dimensions will also be revealed, showing how public space can empower individuals and groups, while at the same time helping to manage potential conflicts among them. Beyond visual appeal, public space will be seen to convey meanings, from those that reinforce personal and group life to those that challenge the accepted world view of the culture and open the mind to new insights. Increased understanding of our place in natural ecosystems will be among the most important. By drawing upon these human dimensions in conceiving and managing spaces, governments, developers, and community groups can reach and satisfy the users. This achievement, in turn, will make it much more likely that goals such

The mall leading to the sunken skating rink at Rockefeller Center in Manhattan is
the prototype for corporate enhancement by means of public space. (Stephen Carr)

as economic development and image enhancement can actually be furthered by public spaces.

These same studies often highlight the human failures of public spaces, adding empirical weight to anecdotal evidence and critiques that appear from time to time in the press. Because the use of public space as a support for downtown retail development or as a setting for office towers has been much in the public eye, the resulting spaces are the ones most often criticized. For instance, pedestrian malls in many downtowns have not lived up to expectations, sometimes because of their contrived and overdone design, but more often because larger social and economic forces in the city have left downtown behind so decisively that no design could change the new patterns of shopping (Knack, 1982; Kowinski, 1985). Although it is tempting to point to the failure of the design, the real failure is likely to have been an inadequate economic and social analysis. Had the sponsors and designers understood that downtown retail would need to adjust to its new market of downtown office workers and nearby residents, then these potential users might have been consulted to help create appropriate spaces.

Criticism has also been focused on corporate plazas, often said to be inappropriately designed and managed for public use. Careful observation

One of the first downtown malls in the United States, in Fresno, California, could not reverse commercial decline, despite an abundance of design devices. (Stephen Carr)

of several of these spaces suggests that many are indeed underused or used in ways not intended (Chidister, 1986; Whyte, 1988). The lack of shelter from wind and sun and the shortage of seating all suggest that intensive public use was not a desired result. Sponsors often fear that their spaces will be taken over by "undesirable" or "deviant" users, such as drug dealers or teenagers, or by other people who will not be sufficiently dignified to reinforce the desired corporate image. As a result, these spaces have typically been treated as front yards, signs of status but not for use (for example, see the case of Grace Plaza in Chapter 5). When sponsors have actually wanted to provide usable spaces for their employees and others with whom they feel comfortable, they have sometimes been burdened with unwanted management problems in attempting to exclude other potential users.

Partly as a result of these conflicts, enclosed atria or gallerias are replacing open spaces at ground-floor level in new office developments. Such spaces can be surrounded by shops and restaurants, access controlled by guards, and use monitored by video cameras (see the Citicorp case in Chapter 5). Thus, although active use may be encouraged, public space

The corporate "front yard" is often a desolate place. Homeless person on Market Street in San Francisco. (Mark Francis)

The current trend is to put corporate "public" spaces under glass and to limit access by doors, signs, and guards. IBM Atrium, midtown Manhattan. (Mark Francis)

is made both private and commercial, severely limiting those who may enter. Several cities, including New York and San Francisco, have given developers benefits, usually the right to build larger buildings, in return for spatial amenities at ground level. Critics and advocacy groups have argued that such public largess requires that these spaces be opened to all members of the public, as was the intention when developers were allowed to enclose them (Whyte, 1988).

Similar criticisms have been launched against some festival marketplaces such as Baltimore's Harborplace or New York's South Street Seaport. These retail developments typically combine public outdoor spaces with semipublic space to which access is limited by design or management policy. They employ "social filters," uniformed service personnel, part of whose job is, unobtrusively, to keep undesirables moving along. Because these are expensive places to shop, offering few necessities, they tend not to attract lower-income users. They may offer free entertainment and some service jobs, but little else is within reach of poor people (Stephens, 1978b).

At a larger scale, developments like Philadelphia's Market Street East and Milwaukee's Grand Avenue complex replace shopping streets with controlled indoor environments. They often incorporate preexisting department stores within enclosed malls, spanning several blocks. Sometimes retail centers are embedded within even larger "megastructures," which include offices, hotels, and garages. While these enormous developments are sometimes less exclusive in their offerings than the festival marketplaces, access and use are much more restricted than in the old downtown streets that they replace, and the spaces that they provide are not fully public.

Publicly developed and managed spaces also have their critics (Heckscher & Robinson, 1977; Hitt, Fleming, Plater-Zyberk, Sennett, Wines, & Zimmerman, 1990). Many new parks and plazas have been built, often with elaborate and expensive designs, without adequate public funding to maintain and manage them. Capital funds, provided by various urban renewal programs, have been easier to secure than operating funds and in any case the expertise to manage public space creatively has not always been available to the public sector (see the Downtown Washington Streets for People case in Chapter 7). This has led both to overdesign, the attempt to create facilities to support all possible uses and also to make them vandal-proof, and to inflexible design where everything is bolted in place. Where good management is available, as in a few downtown malls (see the Church Street Marketplace Case in Chapter 6), simple demountable systems can be used to support changing activity. Even movable seating and tables are possible. At worst, where management is lacking, poor upkeep will soon produce spaces that are underused and neglected.

Designs for public places often are too constrained, not providing for basic human needs such as comfort, relaxation, and discovery. They may allow only for passive engagement with others or be structured only for predetermined actions, making them rigid and unchallenging. Little is left to the imagination of the user. The underlying natural qualities of a place may be suppressed or opportunities for creating rich local ecologies may be ignored (Hough, 1984). As a result, the space may be cold and uninteresting, out of context with its setting and not inviting to its intended users.

The visual identity of much contemporary public space has also been criticized (Laurie, 1978; Whyte, 1988). It is often said that designers rely too heavily on inappropriate models, lacking relevance to American life. Mark Chidister (1989) has argued that American designers have directly borrowed European plaza designs, especially from Italy, whereas the public life in this country is distinctly different. Michael Brill (1989a) has called this "Euro-urbanism." We are not a café society, and we lack the tradition of the evening promenade. Whether this is changing is an interesting question, but there certainly are some spaces based on obvious European prototypes that are not well used (see the Boston City Hall Plaza case in Chapter 4).

Designs that relentlessly advance an abstract concept or a particular formal style can sometimes create a hostile environment with no apparent social purpose. Freedom Plaza in Washington, D.C., is an example of a literary idea gone wrong as a human space (see this case in Chapter 6). The sculptor Richard Serra's controversial *Tilted Arc*, now removed from the Federal Plaza in downtown Manhattan, is an example of an artwork that created distinct problems for public movement through an important space, without striking a sympathetic chord in those who were inconvenienced (Storr, 1985). When designs are not grounded in social understanding, they may fall back on the relative certainties of geometry, in preference to the apparent vagaries of use and meaning. Both designers and clients may easily confuse their desire to make a strong visual statement with good design. Public space design has a special responsibility to understand and serve the public good, which is only partly a matter of aesthetics.

RESPONDING TO THE CHALLENGE

The rest of this book is intended to help sponsors, designers, and managers of public space understand this public good and how best to serve

Despite its attempt to mirror its context, or perhaps because of it, Freedom Plaza, in Washington, D.C., offers little to its users. (Elizabeth March)

Community involvement is the key to making responsive, democratic, and meaningful public spaces. A community garden project in Oakland, California. (Trust for Public Land)

it. Although we have begun by presenting motives for and criticisms of public space, we wish to broaden the discussion to include issues not often addressed. These issues, we believe, are even more important to the end results.

There are three primary values that guide the development of our perspective: We believe that public places should be *responsive, democratic, and meaningful.*

Responsive spaces are those that are designed and managed to serve the needs of their users. The primary needs that people seek to satisfy in public space are those for comfort, relaxation, active and passive engagement, and discovery. Relaxation provides relief from the stresses of daily life and both active and passive engagement with others promote individual well-being and community. Public space can also be a setting for physically and mentally rewarding activity, such as exercise, gardening, or conversation. It can be a place for discovery of self or others, a step into the larger world. Visual and physical contact with nature and plants can also result in important health (Ulrich, 1979, 1984) and restorative benefits for people (Kaplan & Kaplan, 1990).

Democratic spaces protect the rights of user groups. They are accessible to all groups and provide for freedom of action but also for temporary claim and ownership. A public space can be a place to act more freely than when under constraints of home or workplace. In most settings one can temporarily lay claim to a piece of turf even when one does not own it. Ultimately, public space can be changed by public action, because it is owned by all. It can offer a sense of power and control limited only by the rights of others. In public space, people can learn to live together.

Meaningful spaces are those that allow people to make strong connections between the place, their personal lives, and the larger world. They relate to their physical and social context. These connections may be to one's own history or future, to a valued group, to one's culture or relevant history, to biological and psychological realities, or even to other worlds. A continuously used public space with its many memories can help anchor one's sense of personal continuity in a rapidly changing world (Francis & Hester, 1990). By the buildup of overlapping memories of individual and shared experience, a place becomes sacred to a community.

These values can incorporate the public space motivations previously discussed. For instance, they define "public welfare." Visual and environmental motives come into play in satisfying people's needs for passive engagement, discovery, and meaning. Spaces that satisfy people's needs, protect their rights, and offer them meaning will be attractive, and are therefore quite likely to be economically successful. Corporate and government symbolism can be appropriate aspects of the meaning of certain spaces. Our central assertion is that public space values must grow out of an understanding of why people go to spaces, how they actually use them, and what they mean to their users over time.

We proceed from these three general values to a set of "human dimensions," as described in Part II, which we believe can be useful in analyzing, conceiving, designing, and managing spaces. The particular dimensions that will be important in any given situation are to be discovered through the processes of analysis, programming, design, and management. In Part III, we describe an approach to using these dimensions that is consistent with our values. It is based on the active involvement of users with producers, designers, and managers in the creation of good, durable spaces. User participation helps the sponsor, designers, and managers to understand fully the social context of a space, to strike the right balance among various claims on its use and meaning, to manage conflict, and to adjust to changing public life over time.

In the remainder of Part I, we will continue to lay the groundwork for the approach we advocate. We think that it is important to begin with a historical understanding of both public space and the life it supports, as well as with a more complete discussion of public life and the types of public space that exist in our society at this time. We are acutely aware of the quick pace of social change in an open society, and so we imagine that new forms of public life and new types of spaces are emerging as we write. This is why we insist on the necessity of a clear and strong set of values, while urging a method of work that can interpret these values in changing contexts and adjust to that change. A great public space will evolve and endure, well loved by the people in its reach, adding joy and meaning to their lives.

Chapter

2

THE NATURE OF PUBLIC LIFE

By studying the eighteenth-century painting of the Piazza San Marco by Canaletto (1697–1768), it is possible to identify clusters of people engaged in conversations, others crossing the piazza, some observing the activity, children running about and playing, dogs stretched out in the sun, and what appear to be vendors along the edges. The space is filled with life, with energy, and with a sense of the enjoyment of spending time in this public setting. This panoramic view conveys a picture of public life in this space in Venice, one in which everyone seems to have a place with ample room to engage in the varied activities that are captured by the artist. It is the public life that enriches the scene as well as the beautiful space in which it takes place.

The existence of some form of public life is a prerequisite to the development of public spaces. Although every society has some mixture of public and private, the emphasis given to each one and the values they express help to explain the differences across settings, across cultures, and across times. The public spaces created by societies serve as a mirror of their public and private values as can be seen in the Greek agora, the Roman forum, the New England common, and the contemporary plaza, as well as Canaletto's scene of Venice.

Examples of individuals living largely private or asocial lives throughout history have been exceptions rather than the rule. Most, if not all settlements of people establish public and private spheres, areas with differing degrees of privacy and publicness. These public and private domains are a product of the prevailing values of a society, and reflect different degrees of recognition of the needs, rights, and quest for meaning of their members.

Throughout history, communities have developed public spaces that support their needs, whether these are markets, places for sacred celebra-

The basic forms of public life in the Piazza San Marco, in Venice, still look much the same as in Canaletto's time. (Mark Francis)

tions, or sites for local rituals. Public spaces often come to symbolize the community and the larger society or culture in which it exists. Specific places acquire meanings through their functions, further deepening their roles in people's lives. The river used for laundering clothing can be a place for exchanging information. The market has long played a role in communicating local news, providing a context for political behavior. Public places have enabled the social exchange of a widely ranging nature covering individual as well as communal issues. They also provide the grounds for demanding personal and political rights. Although there are vast differences in the forms of communal life across societies, public life has been an integral part of the formation and continuation of social groups.

THE BALANCE OF PUBLIC AND PRIVATE LIFE

For most people, the various parts of a day are distributed over public and private spheres. What is striking, when examining culture and history, is the variety of forms of public and private life at different times and in different societies. Each culture has its own public–private profile, which emerges from a complex set of factors, the interaction of physical, social, political, and economic realities. This concept is beautifully illustrated in the volumes, under the general editorship of the late Phillipe Ariès and Georges Duby, *A History of Private Life*. Tracing the nature of privacy over twenty centuries beginning with the pagan Romans, the various authors of this monumental series have detailed the qualities of public and private life, and the ways they are supported by the values and mores of the various societies, including the design and uses of spaces. Paul Veyne's sections on the Roman Empire indicate that all wills had to be opened in a public place – a basilica or forum – and this had to be done during the day with witnesses present (Veyne, 1987, p. 30). On the other hand, marriage was a completely private activity requiring no public authority. Thus, we find a finely articulated balance, shaped by the nature of this society, defining the public and private domains and forming the choreography of people's lives.

Over the years changes in the nature of family life, especially the household, have contributed significantly to the public and private balance. The growth of domesticity by the seventeenth century, an outcome of the "gradual divorce of the home . . . from the workplace" (Mumford, 1961, p. 383), was a central factor when the three central domestic functions – producing, selling, and consuming – were uncoupled and placed in three distinct institutions located in three different buildings in three areas of the city. The concept of the "private house" emerged, in Mumford's words, "private from business, and spatially separated from any visible means of support. Every part of life came increasingly to share this privacy" (p. 383). Mumford considered this development of domesticity as a factor in the "weakening of public interest among the middle-class citizens" (p. 383). Privacy, formerly possible only for the upper classes, "a luxury of the well-to-do" (p. 384) up to the seventeenth century, slowly began to trickle down to the "lower" classes, stimulated by social and economic changes, although the wealthy always maintained an advantage in their control over their lives. In time, privacy became a sacred quality of modern life in Western society, carefully guarded by constitutional law and public policy.

Public spaces play a signal role in the process of defining what Forrest and Paxson (1979) have called the publicness and privateness of life. With changes over the years, the increasing size of cities, the privatization of life, and the filling up of public spaces formerly available for markets, play, and social intercourse, many of the grounds for public life have disappeared. There is much to be lost in these changes, because public life can support the essential communication system of cities, the linkage that holds them together, helping to orient people and enabling connections both to community and to preurban nature. Public life enables the transmission of important public messages for people, some of them the sym-

Political graffiti during the Vietnam War, Boston. (Tony Lob)

bolic messages of the power of the state or their own power, others the news of the local area. Through a robust public life people can voice their common and individual needs and petition for changes. But public life also can threaten governments and they may come to fear and repress the communication of information and the demands of their citizens. When public life and public spaces are missing from a community, residents can become isolated from each other, less likely to offer mutual help and support.

There have been many contemporary assessments of the balance between private and public life. Richard Sennett (1977) in *The Fall of Public Man* documents the social, political, and economic factors leading to the "end of public culture," the privatization of people's lives. This development toward an intimate society began, in large measure, in the nineteenth century and has continued, creating in Sennett's view, the "tyrannies of intimacy," "denials of the reality and worth of impersonal life" (p. 340). Contemporary social and political systems, especially as they affect cities, tend to encourage privatization as people are drawn inward by their work, their personal lives, and their political activities, if these exist at all.

A similar theme is found in Lyn Lofland's (1973) *A World of Strangers*. She has described the many ways that urban residents learn to order complex urban spaces, their mastery of the social and physical environment of the city. However, she has recognized that some people relish the adventures and encounters of the public scene, the fun in engaging in the various games and maneuvers that can be part of urban life. In a later work, Lofland (1983) challenged the view that city dwellers are alienated, suggesting instead that new forms of connections have developed that do not necessarily depend on primary relationships. This echoes a theme that has been expressed by a number of others (Brill, 1989a; Hitt et al., 1990; Webber, 1963), one that looks to new kinds of associations, especially in the dense and heterogeneous conditions of contemporary urban areas. Whether these associations are among people meeting in health clubs, as volunteers, as joggers sharing a path, as teenagers "hanging out" near a neighborhood corner, or in political and social organizations, they can provide satisfying relationships and a form of public life for the persons involved.

FORCES SHAPING PUBLIC LIFE

In considering the public–private spheres of people's lives, the origins of public spaces and their changes over time, physical, social, and political factors come into play. Climate and topography act as significant constraints on both the existence of an outdoor public life and the nature of the settings that develop. Although these may be factors, they are not sufficient causes for the kinds of places one can find in an area or the functions that they serve. Public life is generally more pronounced in warm areas, although the use of air conditioning has altered this pattern in some settings. However, there are public places in Canadian cities that are more heavily used in winter than some California public spaces in summer. Climate thus enters as a part of the story, but does not offer a full explanation. The existence of successful public places also depends on social and political milieus supportive of an active public life.

At least three cultural forces shape public life. The first is predominantly a social one, served by multipurpose spaces with various activities but mainly focused on the social life of the community. There may be areas to promenade, a bandstand with regular concerts, food vendors, and a generally festive air. Examples can be found in many places, especially in the Hispanic cultures of the New World (Low, 1988).

The second is a functional form of public life serving the basic needs of a society – flows of people on the paths and streets obtaining food for the household, providing shelter against the elements for themselves and other members of the group, and gathering together for the protection of the group members. This kind of group life can be found in the barn-raising and house-building activities that were seen as the public responsibilities

Public life is highly valued in San Miguel d'Allende, Mexico. (Stephen Carr)

of a community, the formation of marketplaces to sell produce and products, and delineation of grazing areas as in the early American commons, places in which military could parade or engage in their various exercises.

Symbolic public life, the third kind, develops out of the shared meanings people have for physical settings and rituals that occur in public. They are the spiritual and mystical experiences in a society, the celebrations of past events and memorable women and men that kindle bonds across people. National and religious holidays and historical events all create opportunities for a form of public life that goes beyond the individual household, offering a type of communication that transcends language. By observing other people and their activities and participating with them in shared tasks, the existence of a community can be confirmed, enabling people to feel that they are part of a larger group in an active manner. However temporary this may be, for the time it occurs there is a direct sense of sharing for some of those present, an immediate if short-lived participation in an event that can best be experienced with others.

Functional public life can also serve social needs. A market in Campo dei Fiori, Rome. (Stephen Carr)

Technology also enters as a factor defining the public–private balance and the use of public spaces in at least two ways. First, it sets out what can and cannot be accomplished in a particular society. The available technology provides limits to the nature of construction and transportation, shaping the form of the community by influencing the ability of residents to have access to available resources, including public spaces. If considerable parts of the day must be spent in pursuit of basic survival, the social functions of public spaces may not enter as significant aspects of daily life, creating an essentially functional public life. In fact, marketplaces, wells, and river banks all have taken on social functions as well as functional ones. If transportation to distant parts of the community is not available, or is only possible for the affluent, the life-world of the masses may be close to home.

Technology enters public life in another way, in its integration into the society. In this second sense, the availability of microcomputers for work at home provides a useful example. From research on people working at home using computers, Jamie Horwitz (1986) has speculated on new kinds of communications via the microcomputer and some new dimensions to local community life. There are opportunities for reaching out to others while remaining at home. This began with the development of the telegraph system and was further extended with the introduction of the telephone, raising some intriguing possibilities of an aspatial public arena, a privatized public life. The use of home computers for work is reminiscent of the medieval workshop that was part of the home. However, missing from this contemporary form of employment is the presence of a wide range of family members, apprentices, employees, and customers who no doubt created a form of public life. If this trend continues it may require the development of a social-symbolic life close to home as well as the settings to support it. It may be necessary to create the modern equivalent of the guildhall, the town hall, and other gathering places such as the churches, seen in medieval towns. The modern equivalents are likely to be recreational ones, for sports, shopping, and walking, but perhaps some spiritual settings or places for meditation and relaxation will emerge as well. With predictions that facsimile machines and computers will enable increasing numbers of people to work at home, away from the supportive professional contacts that characterize a job for most people, the existence of a public life in residential areas may be needed to moderate the isolation and alienation of home work. Although different forms of communication and mutual assistance will likely develop around the microcomputer, the local community may also come to serve new functions as homeworkers seek out contacts to replace the camaraderie of an office (Rivlin, 1987). At the very least, with the increasing incidence of home microcomputer

Symbolic public life in Bali where villagers carry the gods to the sea for ritual purification on the day before their New Year's celebration. (Stephen Carr)

work, as well as use of computers for personal accounts, electronic mail, and recreation, it is important to consider the isolating effects of these activities and the impacts on public and private life.

The physical structure of places can strongly affect their public–private balance and the nature of public life. This is especially apparent in looking at cities. For example, streets are components of the urban communication system – the means of moving objects, people, and information from one sector to another (Anderson, 1986; Vernez-Moudon, 1987). As arteries of the city they enable contacts, both planned and serendipitous ones, that can draw people together. Because streets, also, are the context for crime and fear, both the positive and negative functions are written in urban history. Jane Jacobs (1961) was an early advocate of street life, with diverse uses and activities filling the streets with people, making them

Toronto inner city
keep it alive
people live &c
business

The inequitable space provided for autos and pedestrians in American cities is a barrier to the creation of public life. Third Avenue, New York City. (Mark Francis)

exciting places and safe ones. The impact of the automobile, on the other hand, was seen as a reason for the decline of street life (Appleyard, 1981; Rudofsky, 1969). Appleyard's study of streets with differing degrees of traffic revealed an inverse relationship between the intensity of vehicles and the residents' sense of public life. But the qualities of streets in the past should not be romanticized. Streets were dirty, noisy, and chaotic in the nineteenth century. In a book originally published in 1882, James D. McCabe, Jr. (1984), a journalist, examined New York with the fine eye of a travel writer and historian and provided a guided tour through the city, including its dark sides. His portrait of Broadway described a rush-hour "crush of vehicles" that delayed movement for "for ten minutes or more" (p. 143). It required considerable efforts on the part of the police to "disentangle the dense, chaotic mess and set it in progress again" (p. 143). This traffic, made up of street cars, wagons, trucks, omnibuses, and peddlers' carts "made the place a very Babel" (p. 269).

By the turn of the century, writers complained of the noise, with trolleys, motorcars, bicycles, and ambulances replete with gongs and whistles and the tendency to blow or ring them "on the slightest provocation" (Van Dyke, 1909, p. 181). But the automobile was singled out as the major villain in producing congestion, smoke, and dangers from the "careless and speed-mad" drivers. In looking at Fifth Avenue at four o'clock in the afternoon, Van Dyke (1909) found smoke contaminating the streets in ways prohibited in European cities, creating conditions that forced the wealthy residents of the avenue to move further uptown. What the effects were on the poor populations left behind can only be imagined.

Comparing these conditions with the gridlock and pollutions in contemporary times is impossible, but these descriptions offer a critique of traffic that has a long history. What is most apparent is the failure to include the separation and movement of traffic as an important design consideration in the interest of a healthy and enjoyable public life. Although streets were dirty, noisy, and chaotic in the nineteenth century as well, the automobile has resulted in the privatization of many streets. Some recent efforts have been made to alter this pattern with many cities attempting to recover streets for pedestrians, especially in dense residential areas and downtowns.

The nature of the community, its size and heterogeneity, also affects the balance between the public and private. In highly diverse communities it can be difficult to make contacts in the public realm unless people are able to identify others with similar interests or backgrounds. Heterogeneity can lead to withdrawal to the private realm. Large communities, where residents are unknown to each other, encourage private behavior and retreat into private spaces. Unlike the preindustrial city, where people were identifiable to each other by the clothing that they wore, modern urbanites are largely unknown quantities. They cannot be distinguished as easily through the indicators of earlier times when dress defined the occupations in which people were engaged, signifying their social status as well (Lofland, 1973). Although clothing still offers some clues as to the wearer, styles are subtler than earlier times and change from year to year.

Stanley Milgram (1970) has described the condition of "overload," a term taken from systems analysis, where the person has too much stimulation to process and must prioritize and select from alternatives in order to function. This adaptation process, which he identified with much of city life, leads people to turn inward toward their own concerns, disregarding much of the stimulation with which they cannot cope. There are many losses that accompany this process not the least of which are opportunities to connect up with others in a public realm. By being fearful of others or ignoring their problems, tuning out beggars, homeless persons, and individuals needing help, people move quickly through spaces with tunnel vision, narrowing their view and losing the richness, diversity, and humanity around them. They also lose the assistance of others when help is needed and contribute to the anonymity and facelessness of the city. However, this perspective on urban life has been challenged as deterministic

Street life in Boston's North End. (Mark Francis)

by sociologists – in particular, by Claude Fischer (1976), who has pointed to the development of urban subcultures that form the basis of people's lives. These subcultures, which develop around various combinations of ethnicity, occupation, and economic status, provide "meaningful environments for urban residents" (p. 36). Fischer's "subcultural theory" acknowledges the direct impacts of urbanism but does not see it creating "mental collapse, anomie, or interpersonal estrangement" (p. 38). These concerns raise questions about the ability of people to identify enclaves of common interests and the degree to which they can locate places for themselves in contemporary cities, towns, and suburban areas. If public life now is dependent upon existing subgroups, this may be a fragile relationship difficult to sustain. Although urban villages of the kind that Gans (1962) described still exist, not everyone relates to the ethnic or religious qualities that sustain them. There is a need to acknowledge and nurture new ideas for the formation and development of the grounds for public life, perhaps around people's interests, needs, and stages in the life cycle.

Although it is important to acknowledge the dangers present in contemporary urban life, especially in the larger cities – the impacts of the drug culture, threats to person and property, and criminal behavior directed against women – a balanced view is essential. This means that efforts must be made to make the streets safer at the same time that we recognize the supportive side of life, the ways people extend themselves to offer help, and the risks taken to provide assistance. It is the crime in the public space that receives attention while the examples of courtesy and concern are ignored. Yet people continue to go to public spaces and to enjoy a public life. They can be found in parks and beaches; they join the crowds watching marathon races (and participate in them as well); they sun themselves on the steps of public buildings or rest on a piece of street furniture to view the pedestrian flow – all indicators of public life. Although people are more cautious in public, in their home and work neighborhoods as well as in recreational places, public life has not disappeared even though changes have occurred.

The public–private balance also is influenced by the social, political, and economic system. One of the first rights to be lost under a totalitarian government is the right to gather in public, which implies controls on free speech. The outlawing of demonstrations by the Chinese government in 1989 is an example that shocked the world. However, the outpouring of protestors in a number of Eastern European countries and the scenes of public places filled with people demanding changes have reified the effectiveness of a public life. The presence of the Speaker's Corner in Hyde Park in London allows for the expression of personal views and ideas,

The beach is an important setting for seasonal public life. Coney Island, New York City. (Mark Francis)

some of which may threaten the existing system. Public spaces are channels for communication among members of a society that may be supported, tolerated, or abhorred by various political systems. Whereas many major political events have occurred in the back rooms of governments, others took place in the public places. Some of them had tragic consequences – the assassinations of leaders, the killings of protesting students at Kent State and in China. Others celebrated monumental events – the ends of wars, the accomplishment of spectacular feats from Lindbergh to the cosmonauts and astronauts. With the assembly of people, a sharing and unity are possible that can give expression to communal feelings and an exercise of rights, sometimes leading to political action.

When viewed against the course of history, the social values of communities either support or work against the development of a public life. The ethos of a time and place shape the opportunities for a healthy and well-balanced public–private life. In her study of life in Oneida County, New York, from 1790 to 1865, Mary Ryan (1981) describes the privatization of the middle classes. Events that had been widely shared across the classes including parades and public celebrations increasingly became the activities of the working class. Others retreated into "a private world" (p. 146) influenced by what she characterizes as the "cult of domesticity." The "ideology of domestic privacy" (p. 146) placed value on escape into the peace and sanctity of the home, first for women, but by the mid-nineteenth century it had extended to men and children, as well. The home no longer served as the place of production but rather became a haven and retreat for its members. Clearly, these are not supportive values for an active public life but still remain part of American attitudes toward public life given growing concerns over drugs, crime, kidnapping of children, and the presence of so-called "undesirables."

In contrast, evidence of a public life revival can be seen periodically. In the 1960s, the streets became grounds for public protest with campuses

Peddling in Manhattan, New York City. (Stephen Carr)

and parks all over the United States serving as settings for public demonstrations – against the war in Vietnam, against school authorities, against social injustices. The "Free Speech" movement in People's Park in Berkeley, California, stands out as a powerful example. In our view, these served a critical function at the time, placing value on the street, the square, and the park as forums for debate and public outcry. This period helped to create a new perspective on public life, one that has carried over into the present, albeit in different forms. Street performing and vending of merchandise, a revival of the nineteenth-century forms of public life, have become commonplace in towns and cities. Given the economic difficulties of the 1980s and early 1990s, these forms of alternative employment, peddling talents and goods, have helped many persons survive the loss of their jobs and the difficulties in obtaining work. The block and neighborhood associations and community gardens are examples of these new public activities (Francis, Cashdan, & Paxson, 1984). These efforts, which often involve the participation of local residents in neighborhood improvements, demonstrate that public strength and public life can be valuable to citizens as the twentieth century draws to a close.

The economics of the public–private balance have directly influenced public life. Economics determine the availability and accessibility of the public space and whether priorities exist for its development and maintenance. Unless there is commitment to create public spaces and to care for existing ones, public life is threatened. In the 1980s, many cities in the United States lost public spaces to private development. Many of the spaces created during this period were various forms of marketplaces, creating a particular commercial type of public life for a segment of the population. But there also has been considerable development of downtown public spaces, especially in the 1960s through the 1980s. Waterfront revival has created public access to these valuable resources. The unmet demands for more recreational spaces in cities have resulted in the appropriation of unused docks and other waterfront spaces for various activities as well as the continuing use of the streets for play, more evident in some neighborhoods than others. Without available and accessible spaces life turns inward or people are forced to appropriate their own places.

Writing in 1909, on the parks of New York City, John C. Van Dyke looked with some concern and accuracy to the future:

But some day business is to absorb the whole island of Manhattan, the residences will be converted into stores and offices, the streets will be for motor wagons only, business men will walk on second-story platforms, and the women and children will be housed beyond the thirty-mile circle. In that not-distant day what will

Ethnic "quick cuisine" is the big attraction in the new American festival market-places. South Street Seaport, New York City. (Mark Francis)

become of the parks and their growths? Will they be flattened into asphalt and swept by the vagrant winds or will they be built up with steel and stone structures? In New York everything keeps shifting, moving on, passing away. How shall the parks escape the swift transition and the general change? (pp. 355–6)

These questions resound with concerns voiced today about our open space priorities, the quality of our parks and other public places. People continue to worry but they also have risen to the defense of these spaces. In many cities and towns, threats to parks and recreational areas have rallied populations to their defense, in many cases, saving irreplaceable treasures.

In most parts of the world, and especially in the United States, economics have driven the design of towns and cities and influenced public life. Although there have been periods when people's energy and public finances greatly advanced the development of public places, there has been

An early photograph of New York's Lower East Side, Hester Street. (Courtesy of the New-York Historical Society, New York City)

a continuing struggle to maintain what is there and develop more. Although business has not "absorbed the whole island of Manhattan" as Van Dyke envisioned (Van Dyke, 1909, p. 356), some neighborhoods are losing their community gardens to the developer, and other communities are struggling against changes in the composition of local residents and the resources available in the area, including the availability of affordable housing. In midtown Manhattan, the sky has been lost to high-rise buildings blocking out sunlight to the sidewalks, street corners, and parks. Controversies over the human impact of high-rise development proposed for Times Square (Hiss, 1987, 1990) and the southwest corner adjacent to Central Park are examples of efforts to preserve New York's remaining open-sky space. The general shortage of low-cost housing also has threatened many areas as available housing stock is upgraded out of the pocketbooks of the poor and middle classes, and communities are rendered unfamiliar to those long-time residents able to remain. This process of gentrification, the transformation of neighborhoods through upgrading local shops and housing, has created crises for many of the residents affected. The Lower East Side of Manhattan, long a refuge for immigrant and poor populations and an epitome of street life and public space use, went through a period of deterioration and abandonment, now replaced with growing gentrification.

At the same time, economics also can encourage a positive public life. Street markets and farmer's markets are returning to small towns and large cities in increasing numbers. Vancouver, British Columbia, has three large, recently built public food markets devoid of the teddy bears, rainbows, and balloons that signal some of the contemporary recreational shopping places seen all over the world. This suggests that the desire for fresh, high-quality food can support the public market movement in North America. Although these markets do not automatically guarantee public life or a good public space, they do move people out in public. While the marketplace is a well-established part of European towns and cities, it has not been commonplace in the United States in contemporary times and is a recently established or, to be more accurate, reestablished public space type. Some of the new American markets, such as Rouse's Festival Marketplaces, represent costly ways to shop but others bring the farm closer to the city and enable people to purchase high-quality if not inexpensive produce. Seattle's Pike Place Market is a prime example. In other areas street peddlers, flea markets, and garage and stoop sales provide public ways of selling or recycling goods at low cost. Most are small efforts that go against the larger movement toward shopping malls, supermarkets, and other forms of large-scale, commercial sales. However, they can be quite important to the public life and image of a city.

Markets combine social and economic purposes. They can be centers for both social exchange and commerce, attraction points that serve essential functions with a social overlay that can draw people out for more than the commodities offered (Sommer, 1989). Across cultures, geographies, and time, the marketplace has served a central role in the public life of communities. We believe that this role will expand in the future and give rise to increased public life.

Heckscher captures the quality of the marketplace:

That shopping should be more than a chore, and should have about it something of recreation and even celebration, has been recognized since markets and bazaars first took form. The marketplace became in the European cities an open space coequal with those of the city hall and the cathedral; and it was, like them, a scene of animation, a point of meetings, a stage for the dramas and entertainments of civic life. (Heckscher & Robinson, 1977, pp. 337–8)

In Heckscher and Robinson's view, market streets have been defiled with "wheeled traffic," and the efforts to recapture some of the potential qualities in suburban malls and new downtown developments show "contempt for the surrounding community" and failure to recognize that "the shopping center must be in some way a continuation of the street" (p. 339).

Other forces are influencing the existence of a public life. The strong interests of the new young middle-class urbanites in active sports and fitness combine with the environmental movement to create new de-

Pike Place in Seattle, Washington, is a true public market, created and revived over the years. (Mark Francis)

Cyclists and joggers compete for the narrow sidewalk space at Magazine Beach park on the Charles River in Cambridge, Massachusetts. (Stephen Carr)

mands for open space and more nature provided close to where people live and work. City governments have been pressured to revive older parks, playgrounds, and other central spaces and to make them useful again. The enthusiasm for running, jogging, bicycling, and other active sports has drawn many persons into public spaces to exercise. Whether the public presence of sports-minded people reflects a genuine interest in public life, a self-centered and hedonistic preoccupation with personal vanity, or a concern with the health-related benefits of strenuous activity, those involved are out in the public spheres and open to public encounters. Not all of these contacts are positive ones; recent history provides frightening examples of threats to many in public – rapes and robberies that discourage public behavior. However, if the desire to engage in these activities is strong, it may encourage demands for safe public areas.

These changes suggest an emerging form of public life that combines urban and suburban elements. Vancouver, again, offers an example with walking streets in high-density residential areas, a delightful public esplanade and beach within minutes walk of downtown, and a huge park with a wild forest just next to the center, along with the three markets. These all suggest a strong and blossoming public life.

People's attraction to natural features also supports a public life. Vegetation, street trees, and gardens are highly valued parts of cities (Francis, 1987b; Spirn, 1984; Ulrich, 1979). Contemporary plazas, streets, and squares are designed to include various combinations of trees, flowers, plants, and grass because these elements soften the quality of the spaces and attract the passerby. In many societies, parks invite people into the public space through designs that evoke natural qualities. In many ways they are idealized nature, tamed, cultivated, and predictable, based on romantic images borrowed from eighteenth-century English parks and estates. They are not part of the usual necessities of life, although they can be important for their restorative qualities (Kaplan & Kaplan, 1989). They may recall the natural setting of the city, but they are physical constructions of a particular society at specific points in time. Nonetheless, they are important to public life because they offer opportunities for different groups to encounter each other in positive ways.

Rivers, streams, and waterfronts are often edges to communities, lining and bordering them with the splendor of water, long a powerful need and attraction for all species. When the water serves central functions of life, places to bathe and wash clothing, to fish, to fill containers for use at home, it also creates opportunities to be in a public place open to social contacts where local news and survival strategies can be shared. Towns and cities have used their water edges in strikingly different ways. In the best examples, the river or lake bordering or cutting through a city provides opportunities for a vista, a view of what lies ahead, drawing people

San Antonio's beautiful Paseo del Rio turned a forgotten stream into the city's greatest attraction. (Stephen Carr)

to the water. In others, conscious development of water boundaries has offered panoramic scenes, recreational facilities, and comfortable resting places for the urban inhabitants. Chicago, Budapest, Paris, and Seattle come to mind as exemplars of the creative use of waterways. The Seine not only is bordered by magnificent architecture and green areas, it integrates the city with a series of bridges carrying traffic, including pedestrians, each one providing a glimpse into the past and an essential function for the present. In fine weather, its quays also serve as a kind of city beach for Parisians, adding another dimension to the public life of that city. In contrast, some cities and towns fail to develop their waterways in any manner other than commercial ones while others literally turn their backs on them so that they become sewerage systems and depositories for contamination rather than amenities. For years New York City's waterfront, two broad rivers and an entry to the Atlantic Ocean, was a vibrant commercial and passenger center with small sections developed for public access and recreation. As in the case of many cities, lack of access to the waterfront was counterbalanced by the development of public parks toward the center with creation of a park system that was largely inland (Heckscher & Robinson, 1977). (There are some notable exceptions in New York, including Riverside Park and The Battery.) With the decline of their commercial use, many of the piers edging the rivers fell into decay and were abandoned but became found spaces used by creative appropriators for fishing, sunning, and relaxing with a water view. In New York, and many other cities, elaborate highway systems have further isolated the water edges, obscuring them from view and public use (Heckscher & Robinson, 1977). Only in recent years has there been some consciousness of the need to reclaim the declining waterfront. Because commercial and residential development in the form of high-rise buildings has begun to cover the landfill areas of lower Manhattan, further isolating the water from view, the public waterfront areas being created must be critically assessed from the perspective of public access.

If waterfront areas are acknowledged to be valuable to people, and are valued by them, the successful examples offered by cities like Paris and Vancouver warrant serious reflection. Although the topography, form, and culture of each place is individual to its own area, there is much to be learned. It is possible to identify the elements that support a pleasing waterfront experience, not the least of which is easy public access to the area, a basic requirement for public life.

PUBLIC LIFE: A KEY SOCIAL BINDER

Inherent in these pages is an assumption reflecting our view that public life in public spaces is desirable for people, good for societies. We do not

On the Hudson River waterfront, the dangerous physical condition of piers does
not prevent their recreational use. (Betsy Haggerty)

want to romanticize public life, but it is important to acknowledge its value.
At the same time, the need for privacy must be recognized as well. Our
perspective is that a healthy life contains a balance of private and public
experiences and that people need opportunities to engage in each domain.

Public places afford casual encounters in the course of daily life that can bind people together and give their lives meaning and power. They also can be the source of disagreements and conflict. Open disagreements, however, may be healthier and easier to resolve than those kept in private. Public spaces not only can serve daily needs but also can be places to gather for special occasions. In her study of Oneida County, Ryan (1981) recalled a period in which parades attracted many local citizens, something that changed over the years. Whether it is the Fourth of July festivities or the celebration of the return of a local hero, these moments of relief from daily chores can lighten, distract, and draw people together. They can enrich their lives.

Public life also offers relief from the stresses of work, providing opportunities for relaxation, entertainment, and social contact. People can discover new things and learn from others (Carr & Lynch, 1968; Ward, 1978). Some of the early parks developed in cities were seen as places where the lower classes could view and imitate the activities and postures of the more affluent. Even without this biased and elitist view, it is important to recognize the educational opportunities offered by public places where music and other entertainment can be programmed into their functioning. A public life has the potential of bringing diverse groups together so that they learn from each other, perhaps the richest quality of a multi-class, multicultural, heterogeneous society.

It is impossible to understand public life and the spaces in which it takes place without recognizing the political nature of public activities. As indicated earlier, the presence of citizens in public can be a threatening act to some, a liberating one to others. Governments can control the popular voice by limiting access to public places and by controlling the numbers permitted. Historically in the United States, discussions of politics and religion were generally kept out of parks. They were considered too heated to take place in areas that commissioners wanted to appear nonsectarian in order "to justify public spending" (Cranz, 1982, p. 23). On the other hand, the political voice of government was heard in public because arsenals and military parade grounds were common in large parks. In the 1890s, Golden Gate Park in San Francisco was used for military drills and New York's Central Park included an arsenal building. During World War II, many parks were adapted for various military activities (Cranz, 1982).

Governments and private owners also can restrict the creation of public places and control access to them. This may explain why many demonstrations take place in the less-controllable streets. For it is in the public area that people can join together to protest injustices, to demand their rights, to proclaim their freedom. In this sense, a public life is one of our

Labor Day Parade, Union Square, New York City, 1887. (Museum of the City of
New York, with permission)

most democratic rights, facilitating free society civility and public resolve
(Carr & Lynch, 1981). It is in public spaces that political struggles and
democratic actions become visible as in numerous recent examples in
China, Korea, Eastern Europe, Central America, and the United States.

History offers us many examples of people exercising their rights using
the power of their numbers to communicate their messages. We can see
these efforts from the protests initiating the American Revolution to the
storming of the Bastille. In contemporary times we have memorable im-

phillipines

ages of civil rights demonstrations occurring, rallies on behalf of the rights
of minorities, including women and homosexuals. Youths protesting university activities and the war in Vietnam extended from Telegraph Avenue in Berkeley to upper Broadway in New York, from Kent State University to the campus of Columbia University. In Europe, the Parisian student
protests of the late 1960s provided the model for many others, document-
ing dissatisfactions through political posters and mass action taking place
on the streets. More recently, the tragic massacre of student demonstrators in Tiananmen Square in Beijing and demonstrations in the streets of
Eastern Europe offer remarkable pictures of the power of public protests
and the politics of public life.

Public life in public space also serves as a social binder on the scale of
a group's history and culture. One level, that we will explore later, is that
of public historical places and monuments: Bunker Hill and Lexington in
Massachusetts, the Boston Common, the Lincoln Memorial and the Vietnam Memorial in Washington, D.C. These places evoke connections to
past events that stimulate feelings of national pride, of a sense of belonging, of concern for an entity outside of one's primary associations with

On the Charles River Esplanade, Boston's people come together for public concerts. (Carr, Lynch, Hack and Sandell)

family and friends. They define people's membership in groups – national ones such as citizenship, local ones such as residents of a town or neighborhood. People also engage in public life through cultural, social, and interest groups, by attending meetings and other public events. The parades of Hispanic, Polish, Caribbean, and other national groups, the marches of gays and lesbians, the marathons and other running events – all make political and social statements while enabling groups to join with others to display their numbers and sense their unity and power. The spirit and comradeship that can result from these signs of connection strengthen groups, attract members, and define both the mandate and meaning of the groups. They are the essence of a pluralistic, diverse society displayed through its public life in streets, parks, and other public spaces.

Michael Brill (1989a) has argued that public life in the United States and Europe "has gone through a transformation, but it is not a decline" (p. 8). This transformation, he suggests, has taken three hundred years and will continue into the future. But Brill echoes concerns reflected in this volume, including issues of impoverishment of street life and the privatizing of public space through changes and management policies that remove people from public places. Brill views neighborhood or community social life as different from public life. "Public life," he says, "is with strangers," which involves "spectating and observation while neighborhood life is much about verbal interaction" (p. 20). Some questions can be raised about this distinction. Much of contemporary neighborhood life takes place in the presence of strangers, but it can be in a context that makes these people more available for social exchange and sometimes (but not always) safer to encounter than in other areas. This qualification acknowledges that for many persons their home neighborhoods are dangerous and deteriorated, places where residents are fearful of contacts with others and where they retreat to the relative safety of their homes.

It is the quality of public life and the purposes it serves that in the end are most important. A public life in the interests of oppressing people, the kind that can be seen in the public displays of Nazi Germany, revealing militaristic power and contempt for particular citizens, is reprehensible and intolerable. Public life that is restrictive, that makes it difficult and dangerous for children, for women, for the elderly, for the physically challenged, or for particular minorities, commonplace in many areas today, is a source of serious concern.

We can take encouragement from the increasing consciousness of the value of positive public life experiences and the efforts of many to ensure that such opportunities continue and increase. Many recent events have fostered this awareness – the consumer movement, the work of public space activists, and the advocates for parks, local gardens, and other community spaces. Public life that leads to increased beneficial contacts between different cultural groups and greater tolerance and understanding is much to be desired. It is toward a rich, diverse, and open public life that we should be striving. How the proper balance of private life and safe public life can be encouraged is a complex and difficult mission for contemporary times, and a design and management challenge that these pages will address.

Chapter

3

PUBLIC SPACE EVOLVING

Against the historical backdrop of public life, public spaces have arisen out of many different forces. Some were the consequence of the creeping encroachment of a society bent on finishing and filling up spaces, especially in urban areas. Some were the products of a heterogeneous society with many and differing needs, interests, and aesthetics. Others were products of a desire for careful planning, whatever the priorities guiding their forms and functions. Still others just happened without formal planning procedures.

For the purposes of this book, we define public spaces as open, publicly accessible places where people go for group or individual activities. While public spaces can take many forms and may assume various names such as plazas, malls, and playgrounds, they all share common ingredients. Public spaces generally contain public amenities such as walkways, benches, and water; physical and visual elements, such as paving or lawn, and vegetation that support activities. Whether planned or found, they are usually open and accessible to the public. Some are under public ownership and management, whereas others are privately owned but open to the public. (s poor gardens)

Public spaces are formed by at least two different processes. Some have developed naturally – that is, in an ad hoc way without deliberate planning – through appropriation, by repeated use in a particular way, or by the concentration of people because of an attraction. Each of these results in a place that accommodates people for specific purposes and becomes, over time, a site that people rely on to meet, relax, protest, or market. This may take place on a street corner, some steps in front of a building, or on an undeveloped lot in a neighborhood. The bustling Djemaa-el-Fna square in Marrakech, Morocco, more a triangle in shape, is one such example with its smorgasbord of offerings: food vendors, performing animals, letter

The Djemaa-el-Fna square in Marrakech: a traditional medieval marketplace, outside the walls.

writers, fortune-tellers, and storytellers, all pieces in a bustling mosaic of activity.

Planned public places have different origins, although the functions they serve may be similar to unplanned or evolving sites. Planned spaces frequently emerge from the offices of city planners, architects, and landscape architects, commissioned by public or private clients. They may be the result of laying out an urban area – the deliberate or "accidental" consequences of constructing housing, offices, or public buildings. A town or neighborhood may be organized around a square, or the space around a monumental building may be planned as a public place with other buildings arranged around, or a space may be the leftover result of setback rules in a zoning ordinance. Still other places, such as parks, may require the acquisition of unused land or even the clearance of former uses to create a space. This book covers all of these types of planned spaces, which range from the formal, national public places in a city such as Washington, D.C., to the plazas that may be the result of bonus-encouraged planning of high-rise office buildings.

We have made a distinction between planned and naturally evolving places, but there is actually a continuum in the formation of sites, that is, degrees of naturalness and planning in their development. Many places are combinations of both. One such site is the steps of the New York Public Library, an area that we will describe in a later case study. Originally planned as an essential part of a building, the steps were designed as a grand entrance way. Over the years they have evolved into a popular public place attracting many different kinds of users and uses.

OPEN SPACE AS PART OF THE URBAN FABRIC

Greek Agora and Roman Forum

While some form of public marketplace can be traced back to the Mesopotamian cities of 2000 B.C. (Mumford, 1961), the major precursors of latter-day public spaces occurred in the cities of Ancient Greece and Rome. The acropolis, a fortified area containing the temple precinct, served as the nucleus of early Greek towns. But as this civilization developed, the agora – the secular market and meeting place – assumed increasing prominence. Mumford (1961) stresses that the most important function of the agora was for daily communications and formal and informal assembly.

For the one-seventh of the population fortunate enough to be citizens during the height of Greek civilization, public life – centered around the

One of the earliest broad avenues in the late Greek city of Ephesus, today in western Turkey. (Stephen Carr)

agora – was extremely rich. By the sixth century B.C., with the growth of Greek cities, new public institutions also emerged. Dramatic performances and sports, which in smaller communities had occurred within the context of the marketplace, now were held in open air gymnasia and the theaters on the outskirts of cities (Mumford, 1961, pp. 138–9).

The relative richness of public life in the cities of mainland Greece was not encompassed within a particularly formal or planned spatial order. These cities, including Athens, developed in a spontaneous, organic fashion, lacked coherent street systems, and contained "only the beginnings of arcaded public promenades" (Mumford, 1961, p. 163). Yet, in Asia Minor, starting in the sixth century B.C. and culminating in the third century B.C., new Greek cities emerged that were based on a systematic plan. The basic form of these cities was a gridiron – with standardized blocks, long wide avenues, and a rectangular agora, surrounded by colonnaded streets. Ironically, the greater formal structure and architectural grandeur of the late Greek city corresponded with an increase in despotism and a more regimented public life – a pattern extended by the Romans (Mumford, 1961).

The cities of the Roman Empire were centered around the forum – which combined the functions of the Greek acropolis and agora. In large cities, the forum constituted "a whole precinct," incorporating enclosed, semi-enclosed, and open spaces for commerce, religious congregation, political assembly, athletics, and informal meetings (Mumford, 1961).

The forum and the surrounding center of cities like Rome reflected a rigorous spatial order and grandeur beyond that of the Greeks. It has been estimated that, under Emperor Augustus, thirteen miles of colonnaded streets were built in Rome (Mumford, 1961). While the center of Rome was designed to aggrandize the emperor, "the main population of the city . . . lived in cramped, noisy, airless quarters . . . undergoing daily indignities and terrors that coarsened and brutalized them" (Mumford, 1961, p. 221).

The Medieval Market Square

With the fall of the Roman Empire, people fled from Europe's cities to defensible spots in the countryside. Between about the fifth and tenth centuries, cities ceased to play any significant roles as centers of production and trade (Mumford, 1961). Then around the tenth century, the two islands of safety against invaders – the castle and the abbey – increasingly extended their walls to encircle growing settlements. The walled town provided the security necessary for the revival of the marketplace – at

In Sarlat, France, the weekly market still takes place in front of City Hall. (Stephen Carr)

first, a weekly event just outside the wall. The reemergence of the marketplace, in turn, encouraged the growth of towns.

The cathedral was the central institution in the growing city of the Middle Ages, and the marketplace could often be found in an adjacent space, to take advantage of the constant activity. Initially a single marketplace accommodated most cities' commerce, but market activities became increasingly decentralized as medieval cities expanded. The growing prosperity of those holding market stalls, combined with the congestion of the original marketplace as a medieval city grew, caused merchants to develop individual shops, and also led to the emergence of covered markets and multiple marketplaces (both open and indoor) in most cities (Girouard, 1985).

In addition to market squares, a number of medieval European cities contained civic squares or piazzas adjacent to their town halls. According to Girouard, by the mid-fifteenth century "the idea of a piazza expressing civic dignity and therefore unsuitable for commercial activities had clearly crystalized" (p. 55). One such space, Piazza San Marco in Venice, began its life as a small medieval square "filled with market stalls" and gradually was changed into a grand Renaissance civic plaza (Mumford, 1961, p. 322).

Despite its grandeur, San Marco, like most medieval squares accommodated a wide variety of activities, and special events, "from bullfights and tournaments to processions . . . [and] great religious feasts. . . . At all times of crisis the people gathered in the piazza in enormous numbers . . . victories were celebrated with bonfires on the piazza" (Girouard, 1985, p. 108).

The Renaissance Square

The great plazas of the Renaissance, carefully planned and formally designed, were a departure from the more organic, naturally evolving public spaces of the Middle Ages. Starting in Livorno, Italy, in the late sixteenth century, main squares began to be constructed as a unity, based on a fully symmetrical design (Girouard, 1985, p. 128). Whereas some of these grand

Place des Vosges in the Marais district of Paris remains one of the world's great residential squares. (Stephen Carr)

central spaces, like St. Peter's Square in Rome, were emblems of civic and religious pride, others – like the Place de la Concorde in Paris – are arguably too large and lacking in connections to the surrounding city.

In the first years of the 1600s, two smaller squares of unified design were developed in Paris – Place Dauphine and Place Royale (now Place des Vosges). The latter was tremendously important, the first exclusively residential square of integrated design (Girouard, 1985).

This tradition of designing residential quarters (primarily for the wealthy) around squares blossomed in central London, where over two dozen such spaces were developed between 1630 and 1827 – epitomized by the quiet squares of Bloomsbury (Mumford, 1961). The greater proliferation of these residential squares in London than on the continent is partially due to their frequently semipublic character. In England, "the idea that a square was necessarily a place for public assembly" and noise and activities was less strong than elsewhere in Europe (Girouard, 1985, p. 224). Apparently, the ability to restrict public access to and use of these London squares made them more popular among developers of new residential districts.

This 1768 view shows a British military encampment sharing the Boston Common with grazing cattle and a wide variety of strollers. (New York Public Library, Stokes Collection, with permission)

The Plaza and Square in the New World

Many of the most prominent early settlements in the New World were established by the Spanish. The towns, modeled after settlements in Spain, were centered around a main plaza used as a marketplace and for a variety of other purposes, including celebrations, tournaments, and even bullfights (Girouard, 1985). Typically, the plaza was surrounded by an arcaded street containing the town's major buildings – the main church, town halls, and shops. In America, towns throughout the Southwest and California retain this prominent central square, with that of Santa Fe perhaps the best known.

The English towns of the Northeast were also generally established around a central green or common, often – as in Boston – quite large in size (Mumford, 1961; Reps, 1965). The common served diverse purposes, from cattle grazing to militia drills. The church or meetinghouse and civic buildings were sited either on the common or directly adjacent to it. In

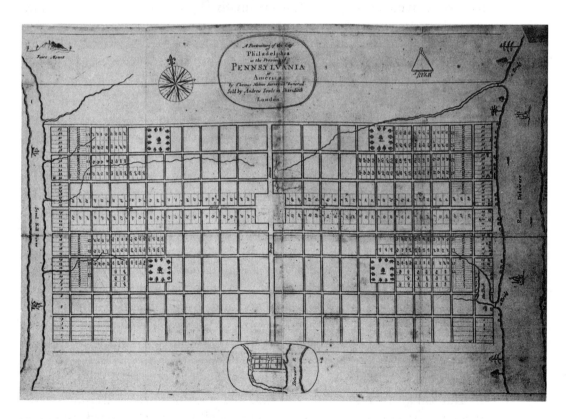

The 1682 Philadelphia plan by Thomas Holme, under the guidance of William Penn, was widely influential. (New York Public Library, Stokes Collection, with permission)

Boston, the Common has remained the city's most significant public space, almost sacred to Bostonians.

The enormously influential Penn and Holme plan of 1682 for Philadelphia, which featured a central square and four equidistant public residential squares (Rittenhouse, Washington, Franklin, and Logan) was apparently influenced by the squares of London (Reps, 1965). The Philadelphia model of a planned street grid containing one or more squares was adopted by many cities. Whereas some cities, like Savannah, were organized around a series of squares, Reps (1965) states that "the single open square in the center of town became the typical expression of the Philadelphia plan as it was transplanted west" (p. 174).

Among the many American squares that continue to function as vital downtown open spaces are Jackson Square in New Orleans, Pershing Square in Los Angeles, and Mount Vernon Square in Baltimore. These squares at the center of a city or town are often closely linked to local history and identity. Typically, they accommodate a variety of relatively passive activities such as sitting, sunbathing, socializing, and watching special events.

The Street as Public Space

The streets of a typical medieval city were narrow and heavily used. Considerable conflict occurred between residents and shopkeepers who wished to encroach on streets, and city governments who wished to prevent this (Girouard, 1985).

At the same time, Mumford (1961, p. 370) argues that "In the medieval town, the upper classes and the lower classes had jostled together on the street, in the marketplace, as they did in the cathedral: the rich might ride on horseback, but they must wait for . . . the blind beggar groping with his stick to get out of the way." In the sixteenth century, straight, wide avenues and a formal spatial order harkening back to the Romans changed the shape of many cities, beginning in Italy. This can be attributed to several factors, ranging from the acceptance by architects of a new spatial perspective, to a practical need to move commercial vehicles more easily through increasingly dense cities, to a political desire to ease military movement through the cities (Girouard, 1985; Mumford, 1961).

These new boulevards that emerged throughout Europe – culminating in Haussmann's nineteenth-century redesign of Paris – frequently became major gathering points for people of all classes (Girouard, 1985). At the same time, in many places a dissociation occurred, with the rich driving back and forth on the boulevards in the carriages, and the poor relegated to the gutter or, eventually, the sidewalk (Mumford, 1961, p. 370).

Florence was one of the first cities in the Renaissance to build straight streets, initially to facilitate the movement of goods. (Mark Francis)

The most important attempt to transplant the European boulevard to America was L'Enfant's plan of the 1790s, for Washington, D.C. L'Enfant's intention was that both the mall and the many radiating boulevards with their tree-lined walkways would be filled with strollers and people promenading in carriages. However, Washington's commerce and population expanded more slowly than anticipated, and these spaces never fully served their intended functions as public gathering places.

The boulevard also emerged as an important component of the City Beautiful movement of the late nineteenth century. This movement put America's new industrial wealth on display, with great civic buildings – city halls, libraries, museums, and courthouses – often placed on carefully landscaped boulevards, such as Philadelphia's Benjamin Franklin Parkway. Although City Beautiful was very much a product of the industrial age, its goal was to bring classical beauty into an urban scene that was rejected as being chaotic and untidy. The movement's boulevards and grand spaces, such as Philadelphia's Parkway and the San Francisco Civic

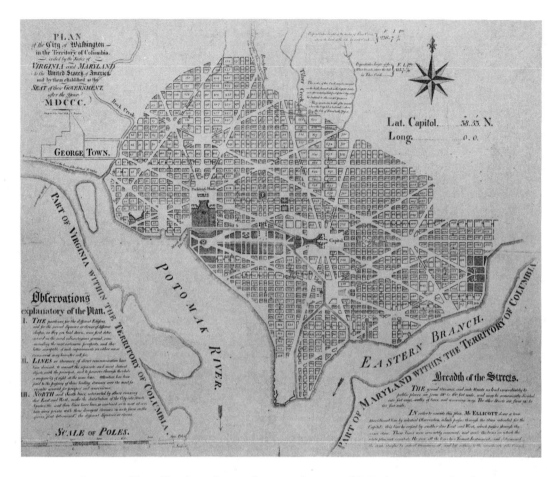

A series of broad boulevards was the central aspect of L'Enfant's 1792 plan for Washington, D.C. (New York Public Library, Stokes Collection with permission)

Center, lack the connection to dense adjacent areas that made some of Paris' boulevards vibrant with public life.

THE EMERGENCE OF THE PARK AND PLAYGROUND

The Nineteenth-Century Parks Movement and Its Forerunners

The major public spaces in European and American cities prior to the industrial revolution were the centrally located squares. The public provision of sizable green spaces and recreation areas was limited prior to the emergence of the parks movement in the mid 1800s.

Yet, the contemporary park has several major forerunners. First of all, most European cities, from the Middle Ages on, had "an area informally

Boston's Commonwealth Avenue was an early boulevard built in the United States.
(Stephen Carr)

set aside for sports and games" (Jackson, 1981, p. 34). Such spaces were generally at the edge of town. Although they were just open areas, without plantings or structures, these spaces typically "were much valued by the citizens, and attempts to reduce or intrude on them were bitterly resented" (Girouard, 1985, p. 82).

In the New World, this pattern of active recreation in various odd spaces continued. According to J. B. Jackson (1981, p. 34):

New Englanders, despite the disapproval of the Puritan clergy, hunted, fished, played football on the beach, competed in violent sports with neighboring villages and even frolicked on the common. As for the Southern passion for non-establishment competitive sports, either in the backyard of taverns or along the road in the open country, there is ample historical evidence of its existence.

A more formal outdoor recreation area, catering especially to the affluent, was the pleasure ground. Pleasure grounds, which appeared starting in the late 1600s throughout Europe and later America, were commercial enterprises combining diverse elements such as intricately landscaped gardens, small waterbodies, outdoor concert grounds, restaurants, and elaborate architectural features (Girouard, 1985). The major remaining example of this form is Copenhagen's Tivoli Gardens, although twentieth-century amusement parks, from Coney Island to Epcot Center, retain some aspects of the pleasure ground.

The most direct forerunners of the public park are probably the royal gardens and grounds of France and England dating back to the sixteenth century. The word *parc* or *park* originally meant an enclosed area containing animals for the hunt (Whitaker & Browne, 1971). These royal parks were set aside for members of the court, although they were "on occasion open to a limited element of the public" (Jackson, 1981, p. 34). Although the earliest of these royal parks were highly formal and geometric in design, the eighteenth century saw the emergence of the more informal, picturesque "landscape gardening school" in England (Newton, 1971). The royal parks that are still such an important part of central London, such as St. James, Hyde, and Green parks, epitomize this school. These parks are characterized by meandering pathways and bodies of water, expansive lawns, and gently undulating topography; they are designed landscapes modeled on a vision of a romantic countryside scene.

In late seventeenth- and early eighteenth-century England, there was a growing enthusiasm for developing fine urban neighborhoods in conjunction with new spacious landscaped parks. Yet such parks, including London's Regent Park, were thought of as an adjunct and amenity for the houses around them, rather than for the city or town, and access into these parks was generally limited (Girouard, 1985).

Among the first parks specifically set aside for public use was the Friedrich-Wilhelmsgarten in Magdeburg, Germany, started in 1824 (Olmsted, Jr. & Kimball, 1973). Other public parks opened in German cities such as Berlin, Frankfurt, and Munich beginning in 1840. The first British park developed solely for public use was Birkenhead Park, opened in 1845. This park had an important influence, in 1850, on the visiting Fredrick Law Olmsted (Olmsted, Jr. & Kimball, 1973), soon to become the pivotal figure in America's emerging public parks movement.

In the second half of the nineteenth century, most American cities established large, landscaped central parks. Many were designed by Olmsted and nearly all were influenced by him. These parks, designed primarily for passive pursuits, were intended as a civilizing influence on what was viewed as an increasingly dense and chaotic urban society. Olmsted, speaking of Central Park, wrote:

> The main object and justification (of the park) is simply to produce a certain influence in the minds of people and through this to make life in the city healthier and happier. The character of this influence is a poetic one and it is to be produced by means of scenes, through observation of which the mind may be more or less lifted out of moods and habits into which it is, under the ordinary conditions of life in the city, likely to fall. (from Barlow, 1987, p. 25)

Landscape architecture was born in the mid-nineteenth century as a specialized profession and offices such as Olmsted's prospered. Because the poor, the working class, and the well-to-do typically lived in close proximity, these new parks were welcomed and put to use by the lower classes as well as the gentry. In many parks, including New York's Central Park, controversy immediately developed over the rules of use (Olmsted, Jr. & Kimball, 1973). The rough and tumble manners of street life spilled over into these new public spaces, leading to attempts to restrict the use of lawns, restrain crowds, fence off plantings, and the like. As Cranz (1982) and others have noted, public space became an arena for socializing poor immigrants to the values of the gentry.

The Playground and Park of the Reform Era

The Reform movement of the late nineteenth and early twentieth centuries led to a major shift in the provision of public space in America. During this period a great surge in immigration and the subsequent growth of slum districts in the largest cities led to the emergence of settlement houses and vigorous efforts to ameliorate conditions in their districts. One idea advocated by the settlement houses was the provision of small active play

The Conservatory Water, Central Park (Boat Pond). New York City. (Museum of the City of New York, with permission)

spaces, primarily for children, within the most densely populated districts (Cranz, 1982). In 1897, a New York City mayoral committee, with Jacob Riis as secretary, stated that a lack of such recreation space "has been the most efficient cause of the growth of crime and pauperism in our midst" (City of New York, 1897, p. 2). Yet, according to the committee, "since the city has secured the larger parks there has been a strange oversight of the necessity of providing, first of all, for the children the opportunity to use these public grounds for games and recreative sports" (p. 2).

With the reformers, "children became a distinct and important focus of park planning" for the first time (Cranz, 1982, p. 63). Examples of children's playgrounds existed during the final decades of the nineteenth century in cities such as Chicago, Boston, New York, and San Francisco. Yet the playground movement was not fully embraced by municipal governments until the early 1900s. Most of the early public playgrounds were located in dense, immigrant neighborhoods – either as additions to existing small parks or as wholly new open spaces. In 1903, New York opened its first playgrounds at nine sites, five of them on the Lower East Side. A typical New York playground of this era contained both an outdoor gymnasium for older children and a playground for younger children, each amply supplied with gymnastic apparatus and play equipment. Separate play areas for boys and girls were common.

Organized play, involving trained play leaders and the "teaching and learning of social content through games," was a key focus of the playground movement (Cranz, 1982, p. 66). A report of the New York City Department of Parks from 1906 indicates that one or two play leaders were assigned to each playground. Over time, professional play leaders introduced a wide range of activities, including Americanization and naturalization classes, and crafts and pageants – all aimed toward the assimilation of middle-class, mainstream values.

These reform era activities, although apparently responding to the needs of the working classes, were themselves a form of social control. By channeling the energies of the people, by providing services defined by another class, and by ignoring the value and vitality of ethnic recreational habits, the sanitized set of resources shaped rather than reflected the needs of the users. But this was exactly the intention of the reformers. Anxious to develop a set of "American" values in the poor and immigrant groups, all aspects of their lives were seen as appropriate channels for education. Home life received the attention of the newly developed profession of home economics. Kindergartens, schools, playgrounds, and settlement houses became systems for educating children and their parents to attitudes and practices that were considered healthy and patriotic ones, essential to new citizens of the country.

Early playground in New York City. Tompkins Square, 1904. (The Byron Collection, Museum of the City of New York, with permission)

An additional aspect of the reform-era park was the widespread introduction of large athletic fields and courts. As previously mentioned, for centuries people had utilized open spaces – frequently areas on the edge of neighborhoods and towns – for sports and active games. Cranz (1982) points out that the large landscaped parks of the late nineteenth century were extensively used for various games and sports. However, these activities often were unstructured and generally occurred in open areas with few physical facilities supporting them. During the reform era, administrators greatly increased the number of officially designated ball fields and game courts at parks both large and small, new and old. For example, between 1907 and 1913, twenty-eight baseball fields were laid out at Van Cortlandt Park in the Bronx (City of New York, 1914, p. 195). In the reform-era spirit of highly structured activity and the promotion of social assimilation, tournaments and other athletic competitions were a major focus of municipal parks departments during the period.

Recreation Facilities for the Growing Middle Class

The aftermath of World War I brought a substantial decline in the social reform efforts of the early twentieth century. The social climate in America was conservative, with reformers susceptible to "official and unofficial Red-hunts" (Goldman, 1955, p. 220).

Galen Cranz (1982) characterizes the years from 1930 to 1965 as the era of the recreation facility. During this period, public facilities for active recreation – both outdoor and indoor – were developed at a level far exceeding that of the reform era. Yet the provision of these resources was not influenced by the kind of overarching social philosophy that guided the mid to late nineteenth-century parks movement or the reform-era playground movement. Rather, parks and recreation officials viewed facilities like ball fields, playgrounds, pools, and beaches as public services that were demanded and expected by a growing middle class confronted with substantial leisure time.

The person epitomizing this period was Robert Moses. In addition to simultaneously heading many other public works agencies, Moses was New York City's parks commissioner from 1934 to 1960. Greatly aided by the availability of New Deal relief workers, Moses immediately set about transforming New York's parks system. From 1934 to 1940, the number of playgrounds in New York increased from 119 to 441 (City of New York, 1960), and the city's inventory of pools, tennis courts, and ball fields expanded dramatically. Vastly extending a reform-era practice, many of these

Many playgrounds like this one was built by Robert Moses when he was the New York City commissioner. (Mark Francis)

recreation areas were grafted onto the great landscaped parks of the mid-to-late 1800s, including Central Park.

Design during this period was marked by "the standardization of . . . elements into a basic municipal package, one that was used repeatedly without regard to local site conditions" (Cranz, 1982, p. 122). This was particularly true for playgrounds, where a standard design – consisting of swings, slides, seesaws, a jungle gym, and benches, on an asphalt surface – became the norm in cities and towns across America.

With the emphasis during this period on active recreation, nature was kept within very narrow confines. Out of a desire to accommodate multiple, active recreational uses and to simplify maintenance, hard surfaces proliferated.

By the late 1950s, with the widespread purchase of automobiles, increasing numbers of the middle class were able to realize their dream of owning a small "country estate," a parcel of land providing private outdoor green space. One result was the decline of middle-class interest in and support for parks and existing ones, like the inner cities around them, became more and more the domain of the working class and the poor. By midcentury, many working-class people as well were able to buy a piece of the American dream in the new higher-density suburbs, aided by Veterans Administration loans and massive federal highway funding. There began to be widespread concern about the "flight" to the suburbs and "abandonment" of the center cities to poor minorities. There is little doubt that the severe financial problems of many cities and the resulting lack of attention to public space were due, in part, to this exodus. Without middle-class political support, the growth of open space systems was halted and they began to go into decline as other social demands on scarce public funds came to the fore. Rules of use in existing spaces were relaxed, and sometimes, as in the infamous case of Detroit's Belle Isle in the 1950s, public spaces became battlegrounds in the growing social and racial conflict between less successful members of the white ethnic working class and people of color.

THE PROLIFERATION OF PUBLIC SPACE TYPES

Since the late 1950s, America has witnessed the emergence of new public space forms – the downtown pedestrian mall, the corporate plaza, the festival marketplace, the adventure playground, the town trail, and the vest-pocket park – as well as the revival of older forms, such as the farmers' market, the community garden, and the waterfront esplanade. Although this multiplicity of spaces suggests the persistence of public life in America, it is also indicative of a highly stratified society. Different spaces

serve different social groups, and public spaces play increasingly specialized roles in most people's lives.

Demographic forces have shaped the nature of American public space
during the past thirty-five years. Perhaps the pivotal influence was the
tremendous growth of the suburbs starting in the 1950s. This population
shift brought to prominence a significant new forum for public life – the
shopping mall – and also greatly altered the shape of center cities. Cities,
increasingly the domain of the least affluent and most disenfranchised,
experienced a demand for public spaces more responsive to local residents. In addition, the success of the suburban malls encouraged various
attempts to revitalize downtown shopping areas and introduce new types
of public spaces in city centers. Beginning around the mid-1970s, a modest return of young professionals to older urban neighborhoods contributed somewhat to the emergence and revitalization of public spaces in
numerous cities.

gentrification

Social Activism, Community Participation, and Open Space

During the 1960s, social and political turmoils were frequently played out
in public spaces, ranging from the Mall in Washington, D.C., to Berkeley's
Sproul Plaza, to the streets of Chicago. Public places were decorated with

Community gardens, such as Kleingarten in Munich, Germany, have long been a
part of city life in Europe. (Mark Francis)

the language of protests – banners, murals, and graffiti. Protestors frequently appropriated public spaces, and sometimes private ones, to voice their dissent.

Fostered by the turmoil of the 1960s, the recognition that people could take over the public arena had an impact on the provision and use of public spaces in the next two decades. On one hand, starting in the late 1960s, new college campuses and other facilities were sometimes designed without large central spaces in which major demonstrations and assemblies could occur. On the other hand, the notion that citizens can and should take control of open spaces became a significant focus of the community self-help movement of the 1970s. Community gardens represent one widespread fulfillment of this trend.

Community gardens have a fairly long and continuous history in Europe, where allotment gardens – large groups of individual plots for vegetables and flowers – are frequently found along railroad tracks and at the edges of cities. The history of community gardens in America is much more intermittent. As Bassett (1981) points out, vacant lot gardening in this country has primarily been associated with crises. During economic depressions in the 1890s and 1930s, considerable vacant land was made available for the poor to grow vegetables. During the two world wars, liberty gardens and victory gardens were established on vacant lots to enable urban dwellers without yards to do their patriotic duty by producing a portion of their own food. Bassett stresses that outside of these crises, urban residents have remained interested in gardening but property owners (with more lucrative options) have not made land available for this purpose.

The community garden regained prominence in the early 1970s when environmental and grassroots community activism, coupled with building abandonment and demolition in inner city areas, led to the creation of vegetable and flower gardens and informal local gathering places on vacant lots (Francis, Cashdan, & Paxson, 1984; Warner, 1987).

This movement has been most prominent in the Northeast and Midwest, where cities like New York, Philadelphia, and Chicago each contain hundreds of community gardens. But cities throughout every region of America are involved; the newer, less dense cities of the South and West often accommodate gardens of several acres, containing plots for hundreds of families. By the 1980s, the community gardening concept became more pervasive, even somewhat "mainstream," with additional sites developed at hospitals, workplaces, schools, public parks, and elsewhere (Francis, 1989b). One large challenge to the future of these spaces is the tendency of many municipal governments to view them as solely an interim use of land.

Another public space form, equally expressive of the ideals of user participation and control but less widespread in America, is the adventure playground. (A discussion of this setting in Chapter 5 will address its qualities in detail.) This type of playground, which emerged in Europe and is common in England and Scandinavia, engages children in the planning and construction of play features, which change over time. A variety of resources, equipment, and building elements along with adult play leaders are on the site; and children, usually from the neighborhood, are participants in the construction and destruction of on-site components. The site itself may be an empty lot, a square block, or the location of what previously had been a traditional playground. An essential physical component of the adventure playground is what Simon Nicholson (1971) has termed "loose parts," natural elements such as sand, earth, plants and seeds, and building components such as wood, nails, tools, and paint. "Loose rules" and shared responsibility are equally important partners in this play form. Adventure playgrounds have been more frequently adopted in Europe than in America, particularly in large cities. Although American children generally have responded enthusiastically to these playgrounds, adults have often opposed them, viewing them as disorderly and aesthetically unappealing. City bureaucracies have been bothered by their failure to correspond with conventional construction specifications and safety standards (Spivack, 1969). As a result of these concerns, very few true adventure playgrounds exist today in the United States, and most innovation has been taken out of playground design due to the concerns over liability.

Social activism also led to the concept of "play streets." Influenced by efforts in Europe such as the Dutch "woonerf" (see Chapter 5), planners restricted traffic on some residential streets to reduce the volume of traffic and its speed and to encourage socializing and play. Based on resident initiative and concerns, cities such as Berkeley put up barricades to block through traffic (Appleyard, 1981). Unfortunately, these efforts have not been widely accepted because of the strong attachment to and love of the automobile.

The Suburban Shopping Mall

The spread of the suburbs and the proliferation of the suburban shopping mall have greatly affected the shape of North America's public spaces in the second half of the twentieth century. Many examples of clearly bounded shopping areas existed prior to the twentieth century, from the medieval marketplace to the Victorian arcade. However, forms like the nineteenth-century arcade – best represented in America by the Cleveland Arcade of 1890 – fit directly within the existing urban grid. The suburban mall, typically set in the midst of a large parking area, bears no such relationship with its surroundings.

The most commonly cited precursors of the suburban mall are planned shopping districts such as Market Square built in 1916 in the Chicago suburb of Lake Forest, and Kansas City's Country Club Plaza of 1922. These shopping areas were "developed and managed as a unit, often with a special parking area but always with a street designated for the exclusive use of pedestrians" (Kowinski, 1985, p. 104). In 1931, at Highland Park Shopping Village in Dallas, a shopping center was developed for the first time around a central courtyard rather than a street (Kowinski, 1985).

But the widespread development of shopping centers did not occur until the 1950s, accompanying the construction of superhighways and the explosion of suburbia. Whereas the shopping centers of the early 1950s were primarily linear highway strip developments, the "concept of creating the interior world was (quickly) rediscovered" (Kowinski, 1985, p. 105), and the shopping center consisting of two parallel rows of stores facing each other across an outdoor pedestrian area became common.

With the emergence of the first fully enclosed shopping center – Victor Gruen's Southdale Mall in Edina, Minnesota, built in 1956 – malls began

A "woonerf" play street. Delft, the Netherlands. (Mark Francis)

to truly dominate public life in suburbia. Once it was enclosed, the mall became "a major source of attraction in its own right, rather than simply a gap between stores" (Maitland, 1985, p. 12), and could host a wide variety of informal eating areas, exhibitions, and special events throughout the year. By the early 1970s, many of the new suburban malls being developed throughout North America bore little resemblance to the early centers, which were essentially parallel-sided covered streets. Malls like Eastridge Center in San Jose and Fox Hills Mall in Los Angeles contained a variety of differently scaled subareas, and "squares" or "courts," often with different design themes and distinct vegetation and art works (Maitland, 1985). Inevitably, the line between the suburban shopping mall and the "theme park" has become somewhat blurred. Canada's West Edmonton Mall, opened in 1986, contains 836 stores and also includes "a copy of the Versailles fountains, a re-creation of New Orleans' Bourbon Street, a miniature golf course modeled on Pebble Beach . . . an indoor amusement park, Canada Fantasyland . . . and a five acre wave pool that will be used for surfing championships" (Martin, 1987, p. 19).

The Urban Mall and Center City Revitalization

Pedestrian Malls

By the late 1950s, the downtown shopping districts of many North American cities and towns were losing much of their business to suburban shopping malls. Inspired by successful efforts in Europe, American planners set out to revitalize these declining downtowns by eliminating or restricting traffic on main streets and constructing elaborate pedestrian malls. Following the lead of Kalamazoo, Michigan, in 1959, about 150 such malls were developed during the 1960s and 1970s (Knack, 1982). While many of these pedestrian malls have met with success, few have been the panacea for downtown decline that planners and officials hoped for, and a number have been removed.

In response to the lack of activity in many of the early pedestrian malls, the late 1960s saw the emergence of malls that incorporated a public transit function. This was spurred by the availability of Federal Urban Mass Transit Administration Funds for transit malls (Knack, 1982). Several cities, such as Sacramento, have replaced strictly pedestrian malls with transit malls where other forms of traffic such as buses and "light rail" lines are accommodated. Other cities, such as Philadelphia, Chicago, Denver, and Burlington, Vermont, developed their downtown malls to incorporate public transit.

A successful downtown "auto-restricted zone." Downtown Crossing, Boston. (Mark Francis)

One variation, emerging in the mid 1970s, is the auto-restricted zone, where whole sections of downtown are to be restricted primarily to buses and pedestrians (Vernez-Moudon, 1987). This concept has been successfully applied to the historic centers of European cities such as Rome. Although much discussed and planned for, it has yet to be tried in the United States, although partial and quite successful variants exist in Portland, Oregon, and Boston, Massachusetts. *Burlington — N. Ireland by necessity —*

The best urban malls are often those that are truly part of an overall downtown plan. According to August Hecksher and Phyllis Robinson (1977), the prime example of this is Minneapolis's Nicollet Mall. The mall grew out of a downtown master planning process that started in the mid 1950s but was not fully opened until 1967 (Hecksher & Robinson, 1977). Nicollet runs the full length of downtown, accommodating pedestrians and buses, and serves as the core of Minneapolis. As Hecksher and Robinson describe it, the mall is

a sensitively landscaped street, shaped to a gentle curve through much of its extent. . . . Separate blocks are designed to be different in their street furniture and planting, giving almost the appearance of a series of plazas. . . . The mall is crossed at various points by second-level skywalks, and it ties in with the enclosed spaces of the IDS Center (a popular shopping complex). (pp. 130–1)

Hecksher and Robinson (1977) stress that the success of the mall is dependent on its continuing ability to evolve and connect with new downtown developments. One problem with the Minneapolis case is that increasingly activity is occurring in the second-level skywalks, rather than at street level. In cities that face extreme temperatures (like Montreal and Dallas), systems of aboveground and underground enclosed walkways have become popular. In Dallas they contribute to an unfortunate segregation, with the white middle-class population using the cool underground walkways, and less affluent minority residents using the hot sidewalks.

Urban Malls Move Indoors

While variations on the downtown pedestrian mall persisted throughout the 1970s and 1980s, planners and developers increasingly sought to bring the controlled environment of the indoor mall to the center city. Large scale developments like Philadelphia's Market Street East and Milwaukee's Grand Avenue complex incorporate preexisting department stores within new enclosed malls spanning blocks at the very heart of old downtown areas. Although these malls are at street level and easily accessible from the sidewalk, the main action is clearly inside. Some stores at Milwaukee's Grand Avenue mall were designed with windows and secondary doors facing the city streets, but the doors of several are now blocked and the windows crammed with empty boxes and packing materials.

Even more separated from the street is what William H. Whyte (1988, p. 206) calls the "megastructure" – a "huge multipurpose complex combining offices, stores, hotels, and garages, and enclosed in a great carapace of concrete and glass." Some of the large complexes, like Detroit's Renaissance Center, Atlanta's Omni International, Toronto's Eaton Place, and Houston Center provide little more than a blank wall to the street, and offer suburbanites and out-of-towners the opportunity to visit downtown without being aware of the city's streets and inhabitants.

Corporate Plazas and Atria

In the largest American cities, particularly New York and Chicago, the transformation of downtown sections generally occurred in a more piecemeal, block-by-block fashion, due to high land values and existing dense development. In these two cities, starting in the 1960s, the development of new office buildings began to change the look of downtown.

In New York, starting in 1961, "incentive zoning" regulations allowed office developers to add significant height or bulk to their buildings in exchange for ground floor plazas. These corporate plazas often bear little resemblance to their historical namesake. Unlike the medieval plaza, which was integrally connected to its surroundings, too many corporate plazas function primarily as impressive foregrounds for an adjacent building. The largely architectural and visual quality of many of these plazas is demonstrated by their frequent use as settings for very large public artworks. In the case of Chicago, where three plazas in close proximity host huge works by Chagall, Calder, and Picasso, the effect can be quite impressive.

In response to the barren, windswept quality of most of New York City's plazas developed in connection with the 1961 incentive zoning provision, William H. Whyte was hired to overhaul the city's plaza requirements. Guidelines adopted in 1975 stated specific requirements for public seating, vegetation, connection to the street, and various amenities. Although this has resulted in some busier plazas, New York's office developers have increasingly chosen to incorporate indoor atria and concourses, rather than outdoor spaces.

Some of these atria, such as "The Market" at Citicorp Center in New York, serve as lively, well-used public gathering places, but most are rather dull and fail to attract the public. Whyte (1988) argues that the key to success for these indoor spaces is their relationship to the street. As examples, he cites the sculpture garden at the Phillip Morris Building on East Forty-second Street and the IBM Building's indoor garden on Madi-

Atrium – the plaza moves indoors. IDS Center, Minneapolis. (Stephen Carr)

son Avenue – both glass-enclosed atria where an intriguing and visible indoor space draws in pedestrians, and the life of the street provides diversion from within.

The Marketplace in the City

In the mid-1960s a new type of shopping mall emerged – this time from the city rather than the suburbs. This form, most frequently referred to as the "festival marketplace," is characterized by an absence of department store anchors and emphasis on upscale, often offbeat, specialty stores; a preponderance of eating places and entertainments; reuse of historic structures or emphasis on historical associations and themes; and, generally, a location in a waterfront or warehouse district. They have been most successful in cities with large numbers of tourists and business visitors, and where they are proximate to large populations of office workers. In locations lacking one or both of these supports, they have been economic failures.

The forerunner of the festival marketplace is San Francisco's Ghirardelli Square, developed in 1964, and shortly followed by its neighbor, the Cannery. These two represent one physical prototype for the festival mar-

The private marketplace as public space. Faneuil Hall Marketplace, Boston. (Mark Francis)

ketplace, with all the activity contained within one large city block and occurring inside buildings or in building courtyards, which often emulate village squares (Maitland, 1985). The other prototype incorporates one or more pedestrianized "main streets" as a focal point. Representative of this prototype is Boston's Faneuil Hall Marketplace.

The Faneuil Hall complex, opened in the mid 1970s, has become America's most successful retail center (Whyte, 1988), attracting sixteen million visitors each year – "three times as many as Hawaii" (Frieden & Sagalyn, 1989, p. 176). Emanating from a ten-year planning process aimed at saving historic market buildings, the Faneuil marketplace has brought life and vitality to Boston's waterfront. Its developer James Rouse and designer Benjamin Thompson went on to collaborate on several other large festival marketplaces, most notably Baltimore's Harborplace and New York's South Street Seaport. The Rouse/Thompson marketplaces, while praised by most planners and many commentators on urban life, are not without their detractors. One criticism of both Faneuil and South Street is that they supplanted commercial districts that still had long-established businesses and authentic links to their cities' histories. Yet, many policy makers in both cities argued that the upscale, somewhat artificial festival marketplace approach was the only economically feasible way to save historic structures.

Despite the popularity and continued spread of the festival marketplace, a few American cities have preserved or revived sites that have a strong and genuine connection to the historical tradition of the marketplace. Perhaps best known is Seattle's Pike Place Market – a large semienclosed market overlooking Puget Sound that has been in operation since 1907. When the marketplace declined and fell into disrepair after World War II, citizens rallied to prevent destructive urban renewal schemes and started a multiyear renovation (Frieden & Sagalyn, 1989). This rehabilitation minimized changes to the old form of the marketplace, and retained – very much out in the open – daily operations that suburban malls and festival marketplaces conceal (such as delivery, unpacking, and hosing down fish stands). In addition, policies were established that strongly favor local produce and other foods; independent merchants; and unusual, obscure, and generally moderately priced stores. Vancouver, British Columbia, now has three new public markets based on Seattle's Pike Place that serve different parts of the city.

Less well known, but equally distinct from the expensive, self-consciously designed festival marketplace are two long-established Philadelphia institutions – the Reading Terminal Market (beneath a downtown train station) and the Italian Market in South Philadelphia. Both provide fresh produce and other local specialties to a clientele that includes peo-

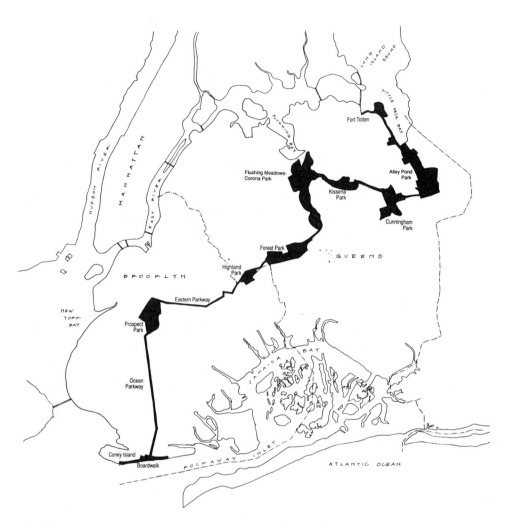

An interconnected urban greenway system – the forty-mile Brooklyn–Queens Greenway links waterfronts, parks, and cultural institutions. (New York Neighborhood Open Space Coalition)

ple of every income from all over the metropolitan area. A more modest variation on the Seattle and Philadelphia markets – generally referred to as "the farmers' market" – has made a comeback in many cities since the 1970s. One model program is "Greenmarket," sponsored by the Council on the Environment of New York City, which brings the region's farmers and other independent food producers each week to sites in neighborhoods throughout the city. Many towns and cities around the country now have weekly farmers' markets.

Urban Nature in the Metropolitan Area

Since the environmental movement in the 1960s, there has been an increase in public interest and advocacy for preserving open spaces. This interest has focused on existing natural areas as well as introducing natural systems and habitat into cities (Spirn, 1984). Emphasis has been placed in many communities on acquisition and preservation of natural areas including wetlands, wildlife habitat, and last bits of undeveloped land in cities. Bond issues for open space have met with success in many communities and a large amount of land has been purchased or donated for undeveloped, natural open space.

More recently, there has been interest in creating interconnected open space systems for recreation or nature conservation. In the late 1980s, "greenways" became a widely used term to designate citywide or rural-scale open space systems (Little, 1990). Examples include the Brooklyn/Queens Greenway in New York City, the Capital Area Greenway in Raleigh, North Carolina, and the Davis (California) Greenway. Greenways attempt to link together existing open spaces into a publicly accessible network joined by trails, paths, and greenbelts.

SUMMARY

The historical evolution of public space has given us the wide variety of overlapping types existing today. This diversity of public space types is shown in Table 3.1. They reflect the multiple uses and great importance of public spaces in American life. We now turn to the human dimensions of these physical spaces and the qualities that make them successful.

Table 3.1: *A typology of contemporary urban public spaces*

Type	Characteristics	Case study examples presented in book (chapter)
Public parks		
Public/central park	Publicly developed and managed open space as part of zoned open space system of city; open space of citywide importance; often located near center of city; often larger than neighborhood park	Central Park, New York (7)

Table 3.1 *(cont.)*

Type	Characteristics	Case study examples presented in book (chapter)
Downtown parks	Green parks with grass and trees located in downtown areas; can be traditional, historic parks or newly developed open spaces	Bryant Park, New York (5); Pershing Park, Washington, D.C. (4)
Commons	A large green area developed in older New England cities and towns; once pasture area for common use; now used for leisure activities	Boston Common and the Public Garden (5)
Neighborhood park	Open space developed in residential environments; publicly developed and managed as part of the zoned open space of cities, or as part of new private residential development; may include playgrounds, sport facilities, etc.	Gas Works Park, Seattle (4); North Park, Battery Park City, New York (8)
Mini/vest-pocket park	Small urban park bounded by buildings; may include fountain or water feature	Greenacre Park, New York (4)
Squares and plazas		
Central square	Square or plaza; often part of historic development of city center; may be formally planned or exist as a meeting place of streets; frequently publicly developed and managed	Boston City Hall Plaza (4); Entrance Plazas – Lowell Heritage State Park, Massachusetts (6); Freedom Plaza, Washington, D.C. (6); Lovejoy and Forecourt Fountains, Portland, Oregon (4); Square of the Centre Georges Pompidou, Paris, France (4); Times Square, New York (6)

Corporate plaza	Plaza developed as part of new office or commercial building(s), often in downtown area but increasingly part of suburban office park development; built and managed by building owners or managers; some publicly developed examples but primarily privately developed and funded	Grace Plaza, New York (5)
Memorial	Public place that memorializes people or events of local and national importance	Vietnam Veterans Memorial, Washington, D.C. (6)
Markets		
Farmers' markets	Open space or streets used for farmers' markets or flea markets; often temporary or occur only during certain times in existing space such as parks, downtown streets or parking lots	Farmers' Market, Davis, California; Haymarket, Boston (6)
Streets		
Pedestrian sidewalks	Part of cities where people move on foot; most commonly along sidewalks and paths, planned or found, that connect one destination with another	Examples include pedestrian sidewalk widening projects
Pedestrian mall	Street closed to auto traffic; pedestrian amenities provided such as benches, planting; often located along main street in downtown area	Church Street Market Place, Burlington, Vermont (6)
Transit mall	Development of improved transit access to downtown areas; replacement of traditional pedestrian malls with	Examples include Nicollet Mall, Minneapolis; Minnesota; Portland, Oregon, transit mall; K Street Transit

Table 3.1 *(cont.)*

Type	Characteristics	Case study examples presented in book (chapter)
	bus and "light rail" malls	Mall, Sacramento, California
Traffic restricted streets	Streets used as public open space; traffic and vehicle restriction can include pedestrian improvements and sidewalk widening, street tree planting	Downtown Washington "Streets for People," D.C. (7); Gågate Walking Street, Røros, Norway (5); Woonerf, Delft, The Netherlands (5)
Town trails	Connect parts of cities through integrated urban trails; use of streets and open spaces planned as setting for environmental learning; some are designed and marked trails	Examples include Freedom Trail, Boston; Town Trails, Britain
Playgrounds		
Playground	Play area located in neighborhood; frequently includes traditional play equipment such as slides and swings; sometimes include amenities for adults such as benches; can also include innovative designs such as Adventure Playgrounds	Tranehytten Adventure Playground, Denmark (5); Village Homes Playground, Davis, California (8)
Schoolyard	Schoolyard as play area; some developed as place for environmental learning or as community use spaces	Examples include Washington Environmental Yard, Berkeley, California
Community open spaces		
Community garden/ park	Neighborhood spaces designed, developed, or managed by local residents on vacant land; may include viewing	Barretto Street Park, New York (5); People's Park, Berkeley, California (6)

	gardens, play areas, and community gardens; often developed on private land; not officially viewed as part of open space system of cities; often vulnerable to displacement by other uses such as housing and commercial development	
Greenways and parkways		
Interconnected recreational and natural areas	Natural areas and recreational spaces connected by pedestrian and bicycle paths	Examples include Davis Greenway, California; Raleigh Greenway, North Carolina; neighborhood greenbelts; natural areas
Atrium/indoor marketplace		
Atrium	Interior private space developed as indoor atrium space; an indoor, lockable plaza or pedestrian street; counted by many cities as part of open space system; privately developed and managed as part of new office or commercial development	The Market at Citicorp Center, New York (5)
Marketplace/downtown shopping center	Interior, private shopping areas, usually freestanding or rehabilitation of older building(s); may include both interior and exterior spaces; sometimes called "Festival marketplaces"; privately developed and managed as part of new office or commercial development	Faneuil Hall Marketplace, Boston (6)

Table 3.1 *(cont.)*

Type	Characteristics	Case study examples presented in book (chapter)
Found/neighborhood spaces		
Found spaces/everyday open spaces	Publicly accessible open space such as street corners; steps to buildings, etc., which people claim and use; also can be vacant or undeveloped space located in neighborhood including vacant lots and future building sites; often used by children and teenagers, and local residents	New York Public Library Steps (4); Manteo Neighborhood and Waterfront Plan, North Carolina (7)
Waterfronts		
Waterfronts, harbors, beaches, riverfronts, piers, lakefronts	Open space along waterways in cities; increased public access to waterfront areas; development of waterfront parks	Boston Waterfront Park (6); Grand Street Waterfront Park, New York (7)

HUMAN DIMENSIONS OF PUBLIC SPACE

Three critical dimensions emerge from our values and form the foundation of our perspective on public spaces: needs, rights, and meanings. Although these are not the only important qualities, we believe they often are not addressed when public spaces are developed.

This perspective offsets the frequent tendency to emphasize the physical qualities of a site to the exclusion of other qualities, a view that is unidimensional and fails to cover the full array of factors that are critical to successful public places. An emphasis on physical attributes alone gives a simplistic, deterministic conception of the functioning of public places, one that has turned out to be limiting in many respects.

Our view is centered on understanding the interaction of people and places and how this affects the ways settings function. It considers a range of factors including the natural qualities of the environment, the users and potential users, their cultural and demographic backgrounds, and their economic status. It encompasses the context of settings, the people, resources, and structures in the area, including other public settings. Most important, it places public settings and their analysis in a framework that examines the history of the site, the tradition of the users, and the relationship of both to the context.

We do not view people–environment relationships in a deterministic or simplistic manner. These relationships are interactive and complex, and attempts to simplify them cannot lead to successful design or management policies. Recipes for public places will not reflect the complicated mix of the personal qualities of people, their life histories, and the significance of places to them. The limited, single focus views that emphasize specific features alone, the physical or aesthetic qualities of settings or management policies, bring little of value to an understanding of public space and behavior.

The dimensions that we will describe outline some of the essential human qualities of public spaces, qualities that distinguish the places that support and stimulate the needs and activities of users. How this occurs can be understood through an analysis of each of the dimensions presented in the next three chapters.

NEEDS IN PUBLIC SPACE

In order to have effective design and management of public spaces it is essential to understand the role that those places play in people's lives, and why spaces are used or ignored. In our view, the human perspective has been neglected in both public space design and management. Places are proposed, built, and assessed with assumptions about what *should* be done in them. Much of this is based on the goals of space designers, their clients, and space managers and does not address people's needs or the ways that public places can function to serve these needs. All kinds of purposes have influenced the qualities of public spaces. For example, plazas often are designed for commercial reasons, to act as corporate emblems, to give builders and developers bonuses in the form of additional floors and space. Parks have taken their form from the past, acting as city emblems, often making statements about the city rather than its citizens. An understanding of the purposes of public places and their use by people is essential to any speculation about their qualities.

Using an open space may be the result of a deliberate plan, or it may be accidental and serendipitous, for example, stopping in a plaza that happens to be along a route, or pausing in one that is a shortcut to a destination. Chance discovery can uncover places worth a stop, and a brief pause may provide a new resource for future use. But the opposite effect also is possible. An uninviting or threatening setting may repel potential users, depositing an unfriendly memory of a place to be avoided in the future.

These incidental users probably make up a minority of the people we find in public places, although they cannot be ignored. Most people go to public open spaces for specific reasons. Some involve immediate needs – to get a drink of water, to eat lunch in a sunny area, or to rest. Others are long-range purposes and may be less obvious, for example, the need for a change or the opportunity to exercise.

BOSTON CITY HALL PLAZA
Boston, Massachusetts

Located at intersection of Cambridge and Court streets in downtown Boston adjacent to Government Center; designed by Kallman, McKinnel and Knowles, Architects; managed by City of Boston; completed in 1968.

City Hall Plaza is one of Boston's most monumental and least-used public open spaces. Designed to serve primarily as a dramatic forecourt to the new City Hall, the plaza's vast expanse and sweeping simplicity raise a number of questions about its intent and function as a public space. Although the plaza heightens the drama of Kallman and McKinnel's unusual building and successfully ties the surrounding buildings together in a coherent scheme, it is less successful in meeting basic human needs or in sustaining a truly symbolic significance.

Historically, civic plazas have been linked to sentiments of civic power and pride. The Italian plazas, such as the elegant, shell-shaped Piazza del Campo in Siena after which the City Hall Plaza is modeled, were and still remain truly civic spaces. They function not only as monumental forecourts to city hall but as the marketplace and as a space for festivals, tournaments, and civic celebrations. Today, often rimmed with cafés and shops, Italian plazas remain the heart of the city.

Aerial view of Boston City Hall Plaza. (Stephen Carr)

The Boston City Hall Plaza is primarily a circulation space. (Elizabeth March)

Unlike these activity-filled plazas, Boston's City Hall Plaza is almost always empty. Although its design borrows extensively from the Piazza del Campo, City Hall Plaza lacks the activities and symbolic significance that give the Campo its vitality.

Although the design was said to represent the ideals of openness and accessibility in government, the great barren plaza seems to speak instead of the government's inaccessibility and of the insignificance of the individual citizen.

Planned as part of the Government Center Urban Renewal Project, City Hall Plaza is surrounded almost entirely by government buildings and reflects the 1960s planning philosophy of separating activities and functions. With no retail stores and only two restaurants immediately adjacent to the plaza, anyone without government business has little reason to be in the area, especially in the evenings or on weekends. As City Hall provides only a limited canteen for its employees, the lack of restaurants is a particular problem. At lunch, one of the few times when employees might use the plaza, most people go elsewhere.

City Hall Plaza was clearly designed to fulfill architectural rather than human needs, as many of the most basic aspects of comfort have been ignored. Although the allée lined with trees and benches on the western edge of the plaza is one of the few shaded places to sit, it is far from inviting. The massive, concrete benches, once described by a critic as "designed to withstand nuclear attack," are immovable, uncomfortable, and oriented inward, away from any activity that might be occurring on the plaza.

In the southwest corner is a sunken sitting area with a fountain, which, like many recessed sitting areas, is rarely used. As the work of William Whyte (1980, 1988) has shown, it is the connection to the street and the opportunity for people watching that so often spells the success of urban plazas. As Whyte might have predicted, one of the favorite sitting areas in City Hall Plaza is along the street edge, although no formal provisions for seating were made. The back wall of the subway station is one of the most popular places for the simple reason that it is one of the best people-watching spots. Located at the intersection of the two main streets that bound the plaza, it is always a hub of activity. While hardly comfortable, the concrete bollards that line the street are also a popular spot because of the view they provide both into the street and into the plaza. Although people often put up with major discomforts in attempts to enjoy themselves, there are limits to what can be tolerated. As the design offers no protection from the high winds that sweep across the plaza, the space becomes almost impassable on windy days.

People cluster at the street edge, where concrete bollards are the only available seating. (Elizabeth March)

Although the vast central expanse of the plaza demands to be filled with people and activity, the city makes little effort outside of scheduling summer concerts to fill the plaza with the events that would give it life. One senses a concern that potential activities such as flea markets might denigrate the intended ceremonial and monumental aspects of the space. Unfortunately, the people of Boston are left with little more than a space to be crossed uncomfortably on their way to somewhere else.

Related cases: Grace Plaza, Plaza of the Centre Georges Pompidou, Freedom Plaza.

SOUTH MALL
SKATING, CONCERTS, EVENTS

———

The specific reasons drawing people to public areas reflect many aspects of life, especially urban life. A stop in a public place may enable a person to rest and escape from the confusion, noise, crowds and "overload" (Milgram, 1970) in the surroundings – a common need in complex, urban settings. In this instance the place becomes a haven, a "stimulus shelter" (Wachs, 1979), providing a contrast to the outside. It satisfies the periodic need people have to regroup their resources before moving on. In their study of Bryant Park, Nager and Wentworth (1976) classify a series of reasons users gave for coming to the park under the heading of "park as retreat." People used such words as "relaxing and comfortable," "tranquil, peaceful urban oasis, sanctuary" – words that we also have heard in our own interviews with users in Greenacre Park, another Manhattan green area. These same places also offer a contrast to the daily routine or a transition from the world of work to that of leisure, however brief the stop may be.

There are other reasons to stop, reflecting the need *to go to* rather than the need *to get away from*. Public areas also enable people to connect with others, to affiliate in some way with other people. This may occur in a very passive mode, as in cases where people position themselves to watch the passing scene, content to have their eyes follow the flow of strangers moving by. In other cases a more active participation is desired, where a place is used to meet friends.

Some users may seek specific activities hoping or certain that they will be available in a site. These may be bicyclers going to use paths in parks, people going to the beach to sun or swim, or the elderly in search of a bench. The intensity and nature of the activity may vary but there is an expectation that specific experiences will be possible in the place and that particular resources will be available.

Based on our review of past research and the case study sites, five types of reasons seem to account for people's needs in public spaces: comfort, relaxation, passive engagement with the environment, active engagement with the environment, and discovery. Any one encounter with a place may satisfy more than one purpose. It is important to examine needs, not only

On the Boardwalk at Brighton Beach, elderly people gather with their friends to talk and watch. (Mark Francis)

because they explain the use of places but also because use is important to success. Places that do not meet people's needs or that serve no important functions for people will be underused and unsuccessful.

COMFORT

Comfort is a basic need. The need for food, drink, shelter from the elements, or a place to rest when tired all require some degree of comfort to be satisfied. Without comfort it is difficult to perceive how other needs can be met, although people sometimes will endure major discomforts in attempts to enjoy themselves.

Relief from sun or access to sun is a major factor in the use of specific places, as indicated by our review of past research. Studies conducted in cool cities such as Seattle (Project for Public Spaces, 1978) and San Francisco (Bosselmann, 1983a, 1983b; Linday, 1978), with many overcast days, indicate that design of an outdoor space to allow maximum sunlight may be one of the most crucial factors in the success of the space. The San Francisco Downtown Plan (San Francisco Department of City Planning, 1985), heralded as a model for other cities, uses solar access to public spaces as a basis for controlling new development projects downtown. A film that included time-lapse footage made by Jamie Horwitz and Stephan Klein in 1977 traced the pattern of people sitting on the steps of the New York Public Library. The moving path of the January sun defined the places where people were sitting and the film caught this remarkable choreography.

Research in other parts of the country often stresses the need for some escape from the sun. A study of the Chicago First National Bank (Rutledge, 1976) indicates that lack of relief from the sun was a major source of user dissatisfaction; this situation is said to be "aggravated by the glare which rebounded from the Plaza's unyielding reaches of granite" (p. 59). Research at Riis Park, a beach and landscaped shore in New York City (Madden & Bussard, 1977), suggests that even at a seaside recreation place, certain segments of the population may not value maximum exposure to sunlight. For these people, shade from trees, umbrellas, or some form of shelter is required. As people become more aware of the hazardous

The best spaces provide attractive choices in sun and shade. The Esplanade at Battery Park City, New York City. (Stephen Carr)

effects of the sun, the provision of shade will become essential. Shelter, whether from the sun, the rain, or inclement weather, is an important but frequently neglected element of open space design. Becker (1973, p. 453), in his evaluation of Sacramento's former downtown pedestrian mall, suggests that people who used the mall for extended periods of time were particularly bothered by the lack of "protection from the weather." An excellent but expensive form of multipurpose outdoor shelter is provided at New York's Greenacre Park, where a covered terrace on a section of the site provides shade and also contains an overhead heating element for cold days.

Comfortable and sufficient seating also is an important aspect of nearly any successful open space. Particularly important features of physically comfortable seating include the orientation of the seating, its proximity to areas of access, seating that is movable, seating for individuals and groups, seating that enables reading, eating, talking, resting and privacy, seats with backs, and, in the case of adults with children, seating in the sight line of play areas.

Comfort is also a function of the length of time people are to remain in a site. The steps of the New York Public Library (see its case in this chapter) or the Metropolitan Museum in New York could be adequate seating for the time it takes for a friend to arrive or for a view of the street performers below, but might not comfortably support an afternoon of sitting. A

The best orientation for seating is not always obvious. (Elizabeth March)

dramatic example of seating that does not accommodate users is provided by Clare Cooper Marcus (1978b) in her observations of Minneapolis' Federal Reserve Plaza. During an observation session she found seven of the nine people in the plaza seated on the concrete floor instead of on the sculptural, rounded "sausage benches" that fill the plaza. It seems likely that other potential users chose not to go to the plaza at all.

In addition to physical comfort, seating should be designed so as to offer social and psychological comfort. For some years, William Whyte has been studying people in public places and he has been a careful documenter of the qualities of places that stimulate or frustrate people's needs. A major finding of his work, reported in *The Social Life of Small Urban Spaces* (1980) and in *City* (1988), calls attention to the need for "sittable space" that is comfortable and properly oriented, spaces that have access to sunlight, trees, water, and food, among other amenities. In stressing this point, he states that it is particularly related to choice: "sitting up front, in back, to the side, in the sun, in the shade, in groups, off alone" (1980, p. 28).

————

PERSHING PARK
Washington, D.C.

Located on Pennsylvania Avenue between East Fourteenth and Fifteenth streets; designed by M. Paul Friedberg and Partners/Jerome Lindsey Associates, Joint Venture, with later revisions to planting by Ohme van Sweden Associates; managed by National Park Service; completed in 1981 as part of the Pennsylvania Avenue Redevelopment Plan.

Pershing Park is named in honor of General John J. Pershing and dedicated to the men who fought on the western front in World War I. Designed around a central pool and waterfall, the multilevel park exemplifies many of the best attributes of open space design and provides a striking contrast to its stark neighbor, Western Plaza (see the Freedom Plaza case in Chapter 6). Screened from the street on the three sides with most vehicular traffic by earth berms, the park provides a green oasis in the middle of the city, which is removed from, yet easily accessible to the street and entirely from the pedestrian-oriented side. The waterfall and naturalistic planting scheme around the pool are the most important elements in creating an atmosphere of relaxation and retreat. Both features help to reduce noise from Pennsylvania Avenue and Fourteenth and Fifteenth streets, while also providing visual contrast, cooling the park on hot days.

A wide variety of seating choices and arrangements – movable tables and chairs, picnic tables, benches, and stairs – allows for both physical and psychological comfort, as well as access to both sun and shade. The variety of levels on which the park is developed – each of which has a distinctly different character – allows the park to accommodate a wide range of activities and experiences from quiet contemplation to the more lively café scene. The café/kiosk that is open until early evening provides an added element of

Pershing Park in Washington, D.C., is a green oasis with movable seating and a food kiosk. (Elizabeth March)

comfort and safety in the park. Although the park is used primarily for passive recreation in the summer, the pool has been designed to allow for skating in the winter, thereby fulfilling the additional human purpose of active engagement with the environment.

Given the park's success at meeting a wide variety of human needs, it is little wonder that it has become such a popular spot.

Related cases: Greenacre Park, Lovejoy and Forecourt Fountains, Bryant Park, Boston Waterfront Park.

Some of these points will be further discussed later in this chapter in a section dealing with the way spaces are used. A useful finding from the research of Project for Public Spaces (Madden & Bussard, 1977) is that the people they studied preferred to be seated facing pedestrian flow and avoided seating where their backs were turned to all or part of this traffic.

Social and psychological comfort is a deep and pervasive need that extends to people's experiences in public places. It is a sense of security, a feeling that one's person and possessions are not vulnerable. Crime is a common concern and a reality in many public places and cannot be ignored in an analysis of their qualities. Across many cultures and times women have been threatened in public spaces, making them less comfortable to use. In a study of found or informal spaces, local neighborhood sites were especially noted by women to be places where they felt safe, surrounded by familiar faces in a neighborhood they could trust (Rivlin & Windsor, 1986). But for many women the streets in their home neighborhoods are dangerous and local parks cannot be used. Their range of movement is constrained by the challenges to their safety, a condition little changed over the years.

Attention to features that reduce threats to safety are likely to increase comfort in settings (Franck & Paxson, 1989). In some cases this may involve space management policies, the use of personnel to ensure the security of users. In other cases design features can enhance the openness, providing visual access into the site. Concern for safety is one of the reasons why people avoid parks or plazas that have barriers to visibility. In their study of Bryant Park in New York, Nager and Wentworth (1976) found that the very features that helped to make the park a pleasant sanctuary from the midtown noise and crowding, the ornamental wall, fence, and shrubbery, obstructed visual access, creating safety problems and discouraging some people from going into the park.

There is another kind of comfort uniformly ignored in the creation of public spaces in this country – the need for toilets. Even in cases where public toilets were part of the original designs, they have been systematically removed or locked. Bryant Park in New York and playgrounds across the country are examples. Some places, including Bryant Park, are incorporating new toilet designs into their plans for changes. For years city management cited long lists of reasons why removal of toilets was necessary. Yet many cities have devised innovative ways to maintain clean public restrooms, such as painting over graffiti on a daily basis. As far back as 1909, Karl Baedeker's guide to the United States reported the disgraceful inadequacy of public conveniences (cited in Rudofsky, 1969). This shameful neglect of public comfort has persisted and increased. Meeting the public need for comfort has not been a priority in public design. Consistent maintenance, careful design, and the presence of caretakers should be viewed as essential components of public spaces rather than as expendable and unnecessary frills.

RELAXATION

Relaxation is distinguished from comfort by the level of release it describes. It is a more developed state with body and mind at ease. A sense of psychological comfort may be a prerequisite of relaxation – a lifting of physical strains, moving the person to a sense of repose. Relaxation frequently is cited by designers as their intent in planning space, and the description of a site as "relaxing" defines the experience possible in the place more than the physical setting, although the two are clearly interrelated.

Urban open spaces, particularly parks, traditionally have been viewed in the United States as places of relaxation and respite for the harried city dweller. However, some authors have argued that this perspective has been overstressed. J. B. Jackson (1981) claims that American designers and policy makers have devoted too much attention to landscaped parks, designed for relaxation and contemplation, and have overlooked the public's need for active recreation areas. Whyte (1980, 1988) has demonstrated convincingly that many users of small urban parks and plazas seek liveliness and some form of engagement with the life of a city, rather than retreat from it. The growing interest in community gardening also points

The ultimate in public space relaxation. The Boston Common. (Kathryn Madden)

to the need for the public landscape to accommodate active recreation. Despite the validity of these arguments, there is evidence that people also look for spaces that accommodate repose and relaxation and offer a brief pause from the routines and demands of city life.

Research in a variety of public spaces indicates that urbanites do frequently seek out settings for relaxation. Becker (1973, p. 453) reports that a large proportion of the users of Sacramento's downtown pedestrian mall liked its "quiet relaxing atmosphere," although this was not what the retailers had desired. In another dense and active context, Nager and Wentworth (1976) found that interview respondents in Bryant Park reported their most frequent activities as relaxing and resting. Users of Greenacre Park, a Manhattan vest-pocket park (cited both by Burden, 1977, and in our own research), viewed the space primarily as a place for relaxation.

GREENACRE PARK
New York, New York

Located on the northside of Fifty-first Street between Second and Third Avenues, Manhattan; designed by Sasaki Associates, Landscape Architects, with Harmon Goldstone as consultant; managed by Greenacre Foundation; completed in 1971.

Greenacre Park, like Paley Park, is a small, in-block park, a so-called vest-pocket park, that attracts a large number of users in Manhattan's dense, commercial midtown. The most basic, and probably most important, reason for the success and popularity of Greenacre is that it fulfills several important purposes. First and foremost, it satisfies the need of many of its users for a place of retreat and relaxation amid the noise and concrete of midtown.

One study of Greenacre (Burden, 1977), based on careful observations, notes a wide variety of activities but concludes that they are all "things one would choose or be able to do only in an environment which was removed, relaxed and tranquil" (p. 21). This is confirmed by interviews in a study of Greenacre conducted by one of the authors. The majority of users reported that they came to the park to relax, rest, "collect their thoughts," or get some sun and fresh air.

The major element contributing to this sense of relaxation and retreat is the dramatic waterfall that dominates the site visually and aurally. Almost all users interviewed stressed the appeal of the waterfall, many of them emphasizing its relaxing quality or noting that it cools them off on a hot day. At any given time, a large proportion of the people in the park can be seen gazing directly at the falls.

On the other hand, users frequently refer to one quality that seems to detract from the relaxing nature of Greenacre. When asked "are there things about this place that you'd like to see changed," nine out of twenty-two of those interviewed in the park responded that they would like the park to be bigger or to have more seating and tables. Complaints about crowding and lack of seating came from people interviewed at different times of the day,

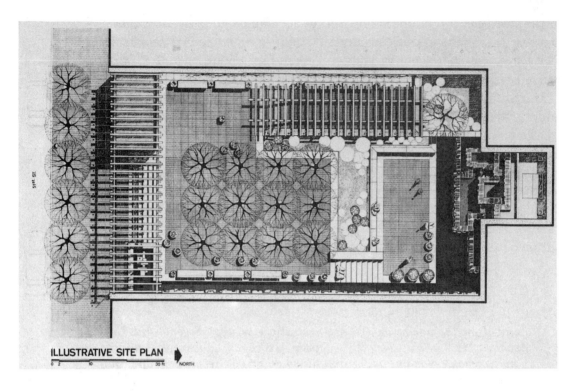

ILLUSTRATIVE SITE PLAN

Site plan of Greenacre Park, New York City. (Golstone, Dearborn and Hinz, Architects; Sasaki, Dawson and Demay, Landscape Architects)

but especially at lunch hour, when people were observed standing, sitting in very uncomfortable places, and leaving the park due to the difficulty of finding a seat. It seems clear that a small park like Greenacre cannot function optimally, offering a relaxing stop for all who seek it at peak times, because it is the only open space in the eastern section of midtown that adequately fulfills this purpose. When Greenacre Park users were asked "are there any other public places in this area that you go to when you have free time," only 10 percent of them named other outdoor spaces in midtown – Paley Park, two blocks north and four blocks west is the closest competitor. The inability of the many office-building developers and designers in this area to produce any outdoor space of comparable quality should be something of an embarrassment.

While it seems clear that users of Greenacre primarily seek relaxation or a brief respite from the surrounding urban environment, the park, in fact, is able to accommodate a variety of activities and experiences. Greenacre's design divides the space into three distinct levels. Each level attracts a slightly different range of activities, except at the peak lunchtime hour when users generally locate themselves "wherever I can find a seat," as many of them told us, rather than in a preferred location.

The park's main level is adjacent to the street but set back from and elevated over the sidewalk by a series of steps. This level constitutes about half the floor area of the park and is open to the sky but shaded by honey locust

Lunchtime activity at Greenacre Park, New York City. (Stephen Carr)

trees for much of the day. A wide range of behavior can be observed on this level, but on the whole it is distinctly more sociable than the other two levels. This is largely attributable to the "constant core of elderly people," mostly residents of nearby apartment buildings, usually seated near the entrance to the park, facing the street in anticipation of the arrival of friends (Burden,

1977, p. 22). This main level also contains the largest number and density of movable tables and chairs, creating a situation where casual interaction is more likely.

The park's lower level, at the foot of the waterfall, can be reached by crossing the main level and descending some stairs. This area is character-ized by its relative visual seclusion from the rest of the park, and its expo-sure to the direct rays of the sun and the full aural impact of the waterfall. Because of these environmental factors, it tends to attract people seeking privacy: couples engaged in intimate conversation, and individuals reading, meditating, or sunning themselves. Many of the users of this section are young; perhaps the powerful sensory stimulation of the falls and the sun are most appealing to people in this age group.

Greenacre's third level is a covered raised platform, to the side of the main level and overlooking the waterfall and the rest of the park. This level is primarily used for observing the waterfall and the activities in the park. The area generally contains a lower density of people and less cross-traffic than the main level. Many users of this raised level seem to be seeking the seclu-sion of the lower deck, while remaining somewhat removed from the direct impact of the water and the sun.

The success of Greenacre as a vest-pocket park offering a welcome con-trast to the midtown Manhattan setting is due, in large part, to its design. However, management also plays a role; a guard or maintenance person is visible in the park at most times of the day. This person generally maintains a low profile, frequently socializing with the park users, but occasionally approaching people to remind them of the park rules, asking children not to run or stand on the benches, expelling people for drinking or smoking mar-ijuana, or admonishing someone who feeds the pigeons. The frequent en-forcement of these and other regulations makes Greenacre a more restricted setting than most urban public places. However, very few of the users we interviewed were bothered by the rules, or felt that they personally were restricted from carrying out any desired activity. It seems reasonable to con-clude that the freedom of most Greenacre users to use the park as they wish, primarily for relaxation and subdued activity, is protected rather than in-fringed upon by the park's rules. In fact, Burden (1977) points out that regular users are so respectful of the park and the way it is run that they frequently can be seen enforcing the rules themselves.

In examining the factors that support relaxation, the element of respite from or contrast to the adjacent urban context appears to be prominent. Separation from vehicular traffic, as in the case of pedestrian malls, often makes it easier to be relaxed, although it also may increase user concern about safety and security during low use times.

However, as we have noted, setting off a space from adjacent streets and sidewalks can present safety problems as well as benefits. Indeed, the Paseo del Rio was generally considered unsafe in San Antonio until, in the

1960s, commercial activities – especially cafés and restaurants – began to appear along the river and it became a tourist attraction, greatly increasing the user population.

The importance of natural elements, especially water, in accentuating a contrast to the urban setting is a frequent theme in open space research. Studies of New York's Exxon Minipark and Greenacre Park have demonstrated the drawing power of simulated waterfalls for people seeking "a respite from the 'hustle-bustle' of the city" (Project for Public Spaces, 1978, p. 15). In her Greenacre Park study, Burden (1977) underscores the significance of the park's waterfall by describing what happens when it is turned off: "People halt conversations abruptly and make ready to leave. The sounds of the city suddenly fill the park, absorbing it and transforming an oasis into an adjunct of the street" (p. 33).

Natural features, such as trees and other greenery, were found to be the dominant factor in Bryant Park offering opportunities for retreat and relaxation (Nager & Wentworth, 1976). This is a view echoed in people's reactions to many open spaces. The opportunities to sit on grass, bask in the shade cast by a tree, or enjoy the greenery and flowers are greatly appreciated.

Water is highly valued in public space. (Byron McCulley)

Although research bears out the importance of providing opportunities for relaxation in urban public spaces, not all spaces should be designed and managed with this in mind. Some sites should accommodate persons seeking liveliness and engagement with the city and its people. The Lovejoy and Forecourt case study describes fairly similar sites that differ substantially – one primarily accommodating relaxation, and the other primarily engagement of various kinds.

LOVEJOY AND FORECOURT FOUNTAINS
Portland, Oregon

Lovejoy Fountain located between Fourth and Harrison, Forecourt located in front of Municipal Auditorium between Market and Clay, Third, and Fourth; both designed by Lawrence Halprin & Associates, Landscape Architects.

Ruth Love (1973) conducted systematic observations and interviews at two small parks in downtown Portland, each of which is centered on a large, complex fountain. These spaces are located within a five-minute walk of each other and thus draw from the same population. Despite similarities in size, context, and general nature, these fountains accommodate different types of activities, and their users view them quite differently. Love found that "Lovejoy projects an atmosphere of solitude, contemplation and serenity, while Forecourt projects one of action and sociability" (p. 197). These contrasting "atmospheres" are a result of the design and siting of each fountain and also of the activities and uses attracted by each design. Love describes two major physical differences between the fountains that have important effects on atmosphere and, in turn, use:

1. *Noise and stimulation levels.* Lovejoy is located in an auto-free zone, unlike Forecourt, which is surrounded by vehicular traffic. Lovejoy Falls has a "relatively muted" sound with the water rolling down a series of steps. The wider Forecourt Falls "tumble freely for eighteen feet, producing a roar that muffles conversation in the immediate vicinity" (pp. 200–1).

2. *Design of the fountains and their surroundings.* The design of Forecourt permits more people to engage in a greater variety of activities than Lovejoy, due to the large number of pools and waterfalls, which accommodate "more waders without crowding" (p. 199).

As a result of these differences in design and use, Lovejoy and Forecourt attract people seeking different types of experiences.

Sixty-five percent of the respondents who prefer Lovejoy do so, among other reasons, because there are fewer people and the atmosphere is more tranquil and relaxing. Sixty-two percent of the respondents who like Forecourt better do so because there are more and a greater variety of people present, and because more is happening than at Lovejoy (p. 197).

Love aptly concludes that "Neither fountain, then, by itself, is sufficiently versatile to satisfy both those seeking serenity and quiet, and those seeking hubbub and excitement" (p. 197).

Forecourt Fountain in Portland, Oregon, offers opportunities for people-watching as well as frolicking in the water. (Mark Francis)

PASSIVE ENGAGEMENT

Passive engagement with the environment could lead to a sense of relaxation but it differs in that it involves the need for an encounter with the setting, albeit without becoming actively involved. This category includes the frequently observed interest and enjoyment people derive from watching the passing scene. This kind of encounter is indirect or passive, because it involves looking rather than talking or doing. There are many examples of places that serve this function and a popularity that testifies to this need.

People-watching is a frequently reported activity in small urban spaces. Whyte (1980, 1988) and his associates (Linday, 1978) indicate that it is

Watching the scene is a popular form of passive engagement. Downtown Crossing, Boston. (Carr, Lynch, Hack and Sandell)

the most popular activity in downtown plazas. According to Whyte (1980, p. 13), "What attracts people most, it would appear, is other people." In a study of San Francisco plazas, Linday (1978) found that the favorite sitting places were adjacent to the pedestrian flow, in particular, near street corners. Similarly, R. L. Love found that the most frequently mentioned activity at two Portland fountains was "watching other people." She concludes, somewhat optimistically, that "The popularity of people watching, in conjunction with the heterogeneity of fountain visitors, points to the conclusion that through their visits to the fountains people do partake of the city's urbanity by being in contact with all the social types that contribute to it" (p. 193).

Other writers suggest that physical separations can facilitate visual contacts with people. Cooper Marcus (1978b) states that observing others is the most popular activity at Minneapolis's Crystal Court, and that the provision of an upper balcony from which to look down at the crowd is particularly important. This elevated vantage point allows the observer to "watch people while avoiding eye contact" (p. 39). The terrace overlooking Rockefeller Center's skating rink is another heavily frequented viewing spot, especially in cool weather when skaters are below. Even when the recessed level is a restaurant, people look down into the space below. Cascades of steps leading to public buildings such as the Metropolitan Museum of Art in New York are popular if unplanned places for watching an array of city sights.

The open cafés of European cities, especially in France, are enjoyed as much for the opportunity to watch pedestrian traffic as for their refreshments. In the open cafés in mild weather and glass-enclosed ones in the cold seasons, patrons linger for hours over a drink or a coffee cup, which provides the excuse to observe the street scenes. This form of public activity has increased in popularity in the United States as restaurants have obtained permits to spill over onto the streets.

Another important attraction of public spaces is the opportunity to observe performers and formal activities. The scheduling of special events has become a popular management approach in many urban plazas and

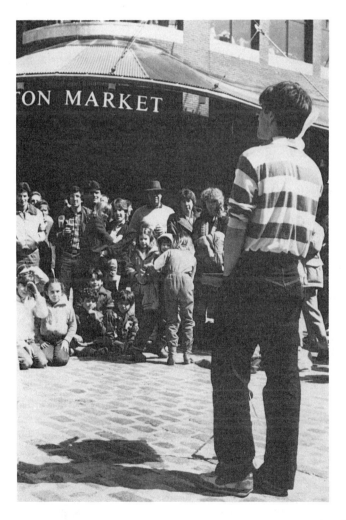

The opportunity to observe performers is an attraction for developments such as the South Street Seaport in Lower Manhattan, New York City. (Mark Francis)

parks. In addition to the now commonplace scheduling of concerts and other formal events, several of the larger downtown complexes such as Boston's Faneuil Market (see Chapter 6), New York's South Street Seaport and San Francisco's Ghirardelli Square feature regular performances by street entertainers throughout the day. Although these events may strike some visitors as spontaneous, the artists generally are auditioned and issued permits by the management (Project for Public Spaces, 1984).

According to the Project for Public Spaces, programmed events in outdoor public spaces have been used to improve the public's image and awareness of downtown areas. For example, the Greater Cleveland Association has sponsored a summertime "Party in the Park" in a different section of downtown every Friday night and the Downtown Seattle Development Association has sponsored daily noontime and evening events in fourteen public spaces throughout downtown. Eighty-seven percent of the people surveyed at four of these Seattle events described being introduced to areas of the city that they had never visited before the special occasion (Project for Public Spaces, 1984). Unscheduled performances, generally occurring near pedestrian paths, are also a natural part of the public life of large cities. The grand steps up to the New York Public Library and the Metropolitan Museum of Art are favorite spots for both scheduled and impromptu performances, which always attract large crowds.

STEPS OF THE NEW YORK PUBLIC LIBRARY
New York, New York

Located on Fifth Avenue between Fortieth and Forty-second streets, Manhattan; designed by Carrere and Hastings (Thomas Hastings, architect), redesigned by Hanna/Olin, Landscape Architects; managed by a partnership between New York City and private philanthropy; original project completed in 1911, redesign in early 1980s; cost of entire building, approximately $9 million.

The monumental neoclassic white marble building of the New York Public Library in mid-Manhattan, its forecourt flanked by two reclining "guardian lions" sculpted by Edward C. Potter, is known for its extraordinary research collections, serving as a major library resource for the city. This architectural landmark owes its existence to nineteenth-century philanthropists – John Jacob Astor, James Lenox, and Samuel Tilden – and now represents a partnership of private contributors and New York City, with private funds providing 80 percent of its support.

For many years the grand staircase that leads to the main entrance on Fifth Avenue has been a highly popular gathering place in this midtown location. Consisting of a cascade of steps, platform areas (one of which has stone benches on either side of the steps), and planted areas in the porticoes extending around the building's facade, its different sectors serve a variety of functions for this commercial neighborhood. Behind the library is Bryant

Public life in a found space: the steps to the New York Public Library. (Mark Francis)

Park, which has had the reputation of being a major place for drug dealing in recent years, some of which once spilled over onto the south side of the steps. During the mild weather these upper porticoes now have outdoor cafés with food kiosks, chairs, and tables with umbrellas on either side, available weekdays and Saturdays.

Even before the library took commercial advantage of its impressive entrance, people were there in large numbers – on the steps, the porticoes, the plazas, on the stone benches and fences, where they could be seen leaning, sitting, standing, or reclining. The major activity was the people-watching that Whyte (1980) has identified as a popular pastime in other urban public spaces, suggesting that the design of the steps and adjacent areas – the amphitheater they create with the street – offers a particularly good vantage point for this activity. Although the predominant activities identified in observations of the steps are on the passive end of the continuum – watching the passing scene, looking at entertainers, reading, sleeping, sunning – there were some active behaviors. They provide an indication of what can occur when people are given the freedom to play out their lives on a public territory that accommodates variety. There was evidence of people talking to each other or eating, or engaging in both activities. Some ate from brown bags brought to the site while others ate the urban foods purchased from nearby vendors – frankfurters, sodas, pretzels, and ice cream.

People could be seen feeding the local pigeons, playing instruments, photographing the scene (some clearly tourists); others sat on the steps to look at their belongings or to rearrange or remove pieces of clothing. Many came to the steps prepared for their stay with food, books, newspapers, writing materials, and audio equipment in hand. There were few instances of people doing or saying peculiar or "inappropriate" things and these users tended to be in the side areas of the site.

Interviews revealed that those using the library steps typically had made many prior visits to the site. People explained their choice of a spot on the site as either an effort to have a good view of what was going on or their attempts to find some privacy — to get away from people — and indeed, observations revealed people absorbed in their own thoughts. Others were searching for sun, or shade, or a corner, a clean place, a central place. There was a range of personal needs reflected in the search for a spot, and a recognition that this space could accommodate the needs. The array of alternatives that the library steps provide offers users various places that can support active engagement with the setting and other people there or quiet reflection and rest. These options were appreciated by users.

Thus, the steps of the New York Public Library have places in which to linger, a variety of physical supports on which to stand, sit, or lean and various entertainments from people-watching to viewing professional performers. Set at a crossroads, it draws passersby and people who work in the vicinity, many of whom can be found there on a regular basis. It enjoys the dual status of a landmark building and a work-neighborhood haunt. In both of these roles the steps attract large numbers of users, over the year, including the cold, winter months.

Along with other found spaces, the New York Public Library steps serve people's needs by offering them choices involving minimal commitment, although they can and do remain there for significant periods of time. Found spaces fit into people's lives in an easy, casual manner, providing amenities that people can enjoy with an immediacy and spontaneity that is rare in conventional sites. The found space may be discovered serendipitously because it is located in a convenient place, often a crossroad that is part of a network of places near the workplace, shopping areas, tourist areas, or residences. Many, like the steps, require little or no extra effort to use, as they are so much a part of daily life. But while the steps also have a reputation that draws people there, as evidenced by the tourists present, they remain and return because the steps are a satisfying, comfortable and safe place in which to spend time.

PLAZA OF THE CENTRE GEORGES POMPIDOU
Paris, France

Located in the fourth arrondissement; designed by Piano and Rogers, architects, Ovre Arup, engineers.

In the center of historic Paris, near the Marais and close to the redeveloped site of the old food market, Les Halles, is a large, modern building, "high tech" in its design. This new national monument to the modern arts is the

Overview of the Plaza of the Centre Georges Pompidou, Paris. (Stephen Carr)

Pompidou Centre, popularly called "Beaubourg." According to the prospectus on the building, this construction was to be "a live center of information, entertainment and culture" (Global Architecture, 1977, p. 3).

In planning the building, half of the site was left as an open square sloping down to the entrance – a grand entrance to the Centre and an arena for various public activities. In addition, streets in the surrounding area were closed to traffic, creating a large pedestrian network. Small shops and boutiques cater to the people in the vicinity and their users spill out into the lively pedestrian flow.

Place de Beaubourg presents a huge sweep of public plaza that attracts an extraordinary array of street performers. The result is a mosaic of events on this vast square that creates an amphitheater for people to watch the activities both on the street and on the ground, and from the many viewing places within the building. From its early days, the square has attracted a wide variety of activities and huge numbers of visitors, some people on their way into the Centre, others remaining in the large open space.

Two of the authors observed the square on occasions in the summers of 1982 and 1988 and the winters of 1985 and 1987, and reviewed the available literature on the project. Discussions were held with Centre staff and members of various planning offices in Paris in order to identify the policies and planning guiding the site's functioning.

The plaza has attracted a variety of spontaneous events. On one July weekday afternoon there were two mimes, a group playing classical music, a jazz band, a bagpiper, a Middle Eastern musical group, a magician, a lineup of artists sketching portraits and caricatures, an environmental group, and a fire eater. In addition to the audiences for these performers, there were people sunning themselves, eating, talking, reading, sleeping, and resting. Often people joined in, dancing and singing to the music, actively a part of the scene.

Pompidou Centre has become a Paris attraction, and it would seem that people are drawn to the activity out front as much as to the building itself. The plaza illustrates the various forms of meeting people's needs, integrated most effectively, reflecting opportunities to relax, to observe the activity in a passive manner, to participate in activities, and to discover new amusements. Even though it is largely a concrete pavement, the square seems to be a comfortable place for people to watch what is going on, and it is common to see people stretched out on the incline of the ground, sleeping, resting, or reading.

The panoply of activity in front of the Centre, impressive on a summer weekday and compounded on weekends, draws audiences in a magnetic fashion. The artists display great variety and professionalism, and it is clear that poor quality is quickly perceived. On one day an inferior mime was consistently ignored as people moved toward the more skilled performers.

How this space evolved to its present state as the arena for interesting action is somewhat difficult to unravel from a distance in time and space. People were attracted to the site from its inception, but performers and peddlers are to be seen all over Paris – in subway stations (where it is illegal), in arcades, on the streets. It is very much a street culture of people selling their wares or their talents, a phenomenon common to many urban areas.

However, the enduring quality of these displays is testimony to their interest as people are drawn to the pageantry and distraction that these activ-

The Pompidou Centre Plaza has become the premier stage for the street performers of Paris. (Leanne Rivlin)

ities provide. The Pompidou Centre square is a magnificent stage enabling the various acts to attract their audiences without conflicting with each other. In its periods of high use, it is much like the great markets of North Africa, with people drawn there because they know that they will find things to entertain them and things that they need. Perhaps a circus arena is a more accurate analogy than a market. What is available at the Beaubourg is a colorful pageant, an array of performers that satisfy the need for drama, amusement, and novelty, all for a few coins if one wants to contribute. There is also something attractive about the contrast between the "high tech" Centre Pompidou facade and the more medieval show in the square. It is inexpensive entertainment in a time of rising costs, appealing to the audience's desire to discover new things, to find the unexpected, and be relieved of life's pressures for a time.

Critics may attack the architecture of the Beaubourg and the exhibits, but the plaza activity has been praised by the judges of artistic work as well as the general public (Schonberg, 1982). Beaubourg is similar in size to Boston City Hall Plaza but is highly successful, whereas Boston's Plaza is void of life and activities because commercial activity has been discouraged. The lesson one can learn from the success of Beaubourg is that a combination of the centrality of place, the physical supports of surrounding pedestrian streets, and the drawing power of a structure of interest can create a context – but only a context – for use. It must be further supported by an appropriate physical arena and open-minded management policies. In this case the square was wisely left in rather simple form and not overdesigned. A critical mass of people and a variety of interesting events, not necessarily programmed ones, can provide expected and unexpected stimulation to the audience. In this respect, the Pompidou Plaza appears to be successful.

In parks outside downtown areas, observing games and sporting events offers a kind of passive engagement that often is sought. For example, baseball and basketball games in neighborhood parks may be surrounded by clusters of spectators. Designs for active recreation areas sometimes overlook this, failing to account for people who enjoy watching games in progress. Researchers at Riis Park in New York City (Madden & Bussard, 1977) found a lack of seating for spectators of handball and other games and noted that fences and bushes frequently blocked the view of such activities from adjacent areas.

People also are attracted to public spaces by various physical features. Fountains often function as a particular focus of interest. Rutledge (1976) observed that many people will walk down a flight of stairs to the sunken plaza, at Chicago's First National Bank, just to look at the large fountain there. Similarly, our research at Greenacre Park in New York indicates that viewing the dramatic waterfall was a major reason for coming to the park. This is also true for both Lovejoy and Forecourt Fountains in Portland, Oregon. In a study of the qualities people prefer in outdoor spaces,

Buker and Montarzino (1983) found that water was the single most desired feature, mentioned by 98 percent of their interviewees.

Another type of passive engagement that concerns the physical and aesthetic qualities of a site involves viewing public art or a compelling landscape. It would be unfortunate to ignore this function, because it is an important aspect of the enjoyment of the public scene. The scenery and the panoramic views are features that draw people to national parks, but even users of vest-pocket parks speak of the pleasure of watching cascades of water.

The conception of what constitutes public art both in contemporary times and in the past has a wide range (Beardsley, 1981). It covers public monuments that are meant to inspire patriotic feelings and awe, such as the Lincoln Memorial, and monuments that dot the public squares and commons of cities and towns. It also includes places that delight or surprise the viewer, for example, Claes Oldenburg's *Clothespin* across from Philadelphia's City Hall or Jean Dubuffet's *Group of Four Trees* in New York's Chase Manhattan Plaza. The art object itself may incorporate practical, functional features as in the street furniture of Paris, the kiosks that are public bulletin boards, or in the grand designs of bridges that became more than connections between the two places – the magnificent Brooklyn Bridge, or the many bridges crossing the Seine. Buildings themselves, their forms and external decoration, have been art objects for thousands of years.

A good deal of the public art in contemporary times has been the subject of controversy on aesthetic and "moral" grounds. Whether it is Eero Saarinen's dramatic arch proclaiming St. Louis as the "Gateway to the West," described in a brochure as "our country's tallest National Monument" (cited by Greenbie, 1981, p. 171); the much-debated *Tilted Arc* (Storr, 1985), a 12-foot high, 112-foot long steel wall by the sculptor Richard Serra now removed from its site; or the murals decorating building facades, especially in poor neighborhoods, proclaiming social rather than aesthetic messages, such as the City Arts Workshop projects described by Filler (1981) – all have been criticized by some part of the public. Most rancorous are the debates over the aesthetic value of graffiti, prominent decoration on many public places and vehicles. There have been studies of the social significance of graffiti and the nature of graffiti writers, and we are beginning to understand some of the meanings behind this controversial form of public art and the teenage subculture that has formed around the writing (Feiner & Klein, 1982).

There is a formal type of wall decoration, what Filler (1981) calls "high-style wall activity." He describes two such examples, a mural and vest-pocket park in Philadelphia designed by the artist Herbert Bayer, and

Richard Haas's mural wall on Boston's Architectural Center. The Philadelphia mural, called *Horizons,* was designed to integrate into the setting, whereas the Boston painting "depicts an imaginary sectional cutaway view of a grand, neo-classical edifice, and has become a distinctive visual landmark on the Boston skyline" (p. 87).

For each of the art forms, whether community or stylized murals, sculpture, monuments, or even graffiti, there is evidence that there is a public appetite for outdoor art. In a study in which she observed and interviewed people in the immediate vicinity of murals and sculpture, Degnore (1987) found general enthusiasm for public art. However, people were discriminating in their tastes and capable of incorporating the public art into their experience of the place. They often were intrigued by abstract sculpture,

With the best public art, engagement can become more active. Fountain at the entrance to Parc Guell, Barcelona, Spain, designed by Antonio Gaudi. (Mark Francis)

even though they were uncertain about the artist's intent. Whereas some public art blended into the background, barely noticed by pedestrians and people who lingered nearby, other art leaped out and drew an audience of people, some of whom admired the piece, while others disliked it. Neutrality seemed impossible for some pieces. Why this is so and how this information can be used to enhance the public scene is an area much in need of further thought and documentation. Empirical research on public art such as that of Degnore (1977) and Israel (1988) may prove to be useful in anticipating the qualities of public art that are likely to be noticed and enjoyed. Many cities now require that 1 percent of new construction costs be relegated to some form of art that will be placed outside the building (Filler, 1981). Though tastes may vary, and one would expect this in a country as varied as the United States, there seems to be a realization that art lends interest and excitement to the experience in public places and an identity to the setting.

Natural features, particularly vegetation, seem to attract people to urban places. In a linear park in downtown Yokohama, Japan, which offers three distinct types of settings, a "forest plaza" is "greatly enjoyed by the city dwellers" (Iwasaki & Tyrwhitt, 1978, p. 439). In our own study of Greenacre Park, the greenery and water were mentioned frequently by users as enjoyable qualities of the site. The opportunity to be close to plants, trees, flowers, and water is strongly desired by people and there is some evidence that these elements may have relaxing and "restorative" qualities (Hartig, Mang, & Evans, 1991; Kaplan, 1983, 1985; Kaplan & Kaplan, 1990).

Some urban spaces attract users because they offer splendid views. Francis and his associates (1984) report that many people came to Brooklyn's "drive-in" Grand Street Waterfront Park primarily to enjoy the panorama of the East River and Manhattan across the river.

———

GRAND STREET WATERFRONT PARK
Brooklyn, New York

Located at the end of Grand Street at the East River, Williamsburg neighborhood; designed by Philip Winslow, Landscape Architect; managed by the Parks Council and neighborhood residents; completed in 1979; size, approximately .75 acre; cost, $35,000.

A vacant lot on the Brooklyn waterfront was slowly transformed by local residents into a passive neighborhood park (Heritage Conservation and Recreation Service, 1979). Working with a landscape architect and the Parks Council, residents constructed the park in phases from 1976 to 1979 with $35,000 in public and private funds. Designed as a "drive-in park," Grand Street Park was programmed to allow local residents to drive their cars into

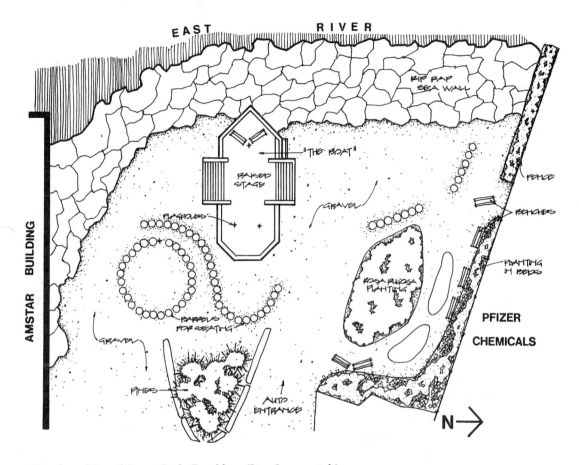

Site plan of Grand Street Park, Brooklyn. (Lisa Jovanowich)

the park to view the Manhattan skyline, and relax (Francis, Cashdan, & Paxson, 1984).

The design grew out of observations made by the project initiator, Norm Cohen of the Parks Council, and the landscape architect, Philip Winslow, hired to prepare a site design. Early in the design phase, the designers realized that the vacant lot already was used heavily by local residents. Human needs were an important guideline that informed the parks design.

The next step was to observe. Though much of the street-ending was heaped with refuse, visitors were coming, and we spent hours watching what they did. The results were extremely useful. We discovered that most of the visitors were children ages 6 to 16 who invariably headed straight for the water's edge to explore, throw stones in the river, etc. Adults on foot usually went to the point with the highest elevation where they stood quietly for a few minutes while enjoying the view. We learned that many visitors, in cold weather or warm, during the day or at night, drove as close to the water as possible and stayed in their cars, looking at the river. We saw no reason to disrupt these existing uses by construction of the park; rather, we would seek to preserve and enhance them. They were activities we could expect to be popular after the site was improved. (Cited in Francis et al. 1984, p. 103)

Possible activities included "throwing things into the water, sitting, group conversation," and, as one park user reported, "getting away from the hustle and bustle of the neighborhood" (Francis et al. 1984, p. 104). During the evening, the park was designed to be a lovers' lane, complete with trash cans and benches, along with the good view of the East River.

The park, one of the few places along the northern Brooklyn waterfront where residents can gain access to the river, has remained actively used since its creation. Neighborhood residents and employees of adjacent manufacturing plants visit regularly, and special events occur at the park. However, maintenance of a fully accessible public park has proved challenging for neighborhood volunteers and the nonprofit Parks Council. Dumping and litter are regular problems, and vegetation has become overgrown. The park's location, several blocks from residential streets, also results in nighttime drug use and prostitution.

The city's Department of Parks and Recreation has agreed to map the site as parkland and provide regular maintenance and trash removal, following a restoration funded by the Parks Council. The proposed restoration will not change the basic layout of the park, but will address basic infrastructure issues.

Related cases: Barretto Street Neighborhood Park, Boston Waterfront Park.

Similarly, in their study of downtown Vancouver, Joardar and Neill (1978) found that waterfront places have a strong drawing power because of the vistas they offer. Unfortunately, until very recently, waterfronts in many cities have been largely ignored as public, open space resources. Mooney (1979) summarizes some of the problems in an article about the Mississippi River: "All too frequently locations for simple visual linkage with river activities have been usurped by marinas, parking lots, industrial blight and warehouses. With few exceptions, the urban edge of the Mississippi is uninviting to pedestrians" (p. 49).

With the development of waterfront parks such as the esplanade stretching along Battery Park City in Lower Manhattan, there is some hope that these policies are changing. New York City is planning the creation of an esplanade park from the Battery to Fifty-ninth Street, and other cities are building waterfront parks. However, one could complain that what is being done is too little and too late.

ACTIVE ENGAGEMENT

Active engagement represents a more direct experience with a place and the people within it. This function has a number of components. First, although some people find satisfaction in people-watching, others desire more direct contact with people – whether they are strangers in a site or members of their own group. Based on considerable research, primarily

Las Ramblas in Barcelona is one of the world's great promenades. (Mark Francis)

in New York City, William Whyte concluded that plazas in downtown areas "are not ideal places for striking up acquaintances, and even on the most sociable of them, there is not much mingling" (Whyte, 1980, p. 19). Yet Whyte notes that unusual features or occurrences in a plaza, such as an entertainer or a fine sculpture, will often result in what he calls "triangulation" whereby that special feature "provides a linkage between people and prompts strangers to talk to each other" (p. 94). In places other than the plazas of large, urban downtown areas, some degree of interaction between strangers may be more common. Christopher Alexander has pointed out the importance of the promenades, often centrally located shopping streets, common in older neighborhoods and small cities in Europe and Latin America where "people with a shared way of life gather together to rub shoulders and confirm their community" (Alexander et al.,

1977, p. 169). Although Alexander suggests that promenades are used mainly by people who live within ten minutes' walking distance, some readers may be familiar with a variation of the promenade where teenagers and young adults with similar interests converge on a street and interact while driving cars slowly, sitting in cars, sitting on cars, and strolling.

Another type of space that is important in facilitating interaction between strangers is the small square or piazza, most commonly found in the old residential districts of Mediterranean cities. Alexander argues that with a few exceptions, such as Venice's Piazza San Marco and London's Trafalgar Square, such squares are most successful when they are under seventy feet in diameter (Alexander et al., 1977). In a plaza of this size people are able to "make out the faces and half hear the talk" (Alexander et al. 1977, p. 313) of those around them, which encourages a sense of social connection, increasing opportunities for interaction.

Public spaces also play a crucial role as a setting for socializing with relatives, neighbors, acquaintances, and friends. Although public space activities such as picnics and Sunday outings cut across class, less affluent people, particularly in cities, are clearly more dependent upon outdoor spaces close to home. The public spaces that play the most important social function in many older, working-class, and low-income neighborhoods are the streets and sidewalks (Fried & Gleicher, 1961; Jacobs, 1961). In fact, streets and sidewalks abound as public spaces supporting a range of child and adult activities. But some streets are more successful settings than others. In a study of informal or "found" public spaces we have observed places that are popular ones for street peddlers. The traffic of people is critical to drawing vendors to a site, but the width of the pavement and the attitudes of local shopkeepers are important factors as well.

The life of the street that Jane Jacobs (1961) has described so well as a complex mélange of tolerance, friendliness, mutual concern, and resources. However, young people are not necessarily welcome users of either commercial or residential streets. Whether it is casual "hanging out" by teenagers or the lively ball playing of younger children, complaints are commonplace. It may be easy to romanticize the streets as natural playgrounds for children as they are growing up but the reality often is less ideal. In the inner city the street is filled with dangers – vehicular and drug traffic, broken glass, and filth. In affluent areas the streets rarely are used for play. Children are transported to special play facilities – parks, gymnasiums, and the like – or they remain within their own homes. In both settings, the slum and the high-priced residential area, parents' fears for their children's safety make the street as a context for play and development an ideal rather than a reality.

But we can question whether this situation could be changed. The complex cultural and economic factors that underlie it cannot be ignored, but there are design and management alternatives that can alleviate some of the difficulties. The work of Appleyard (1981) has demonstrated that when residents were able to control the speed and volume of traffic on their streets, their use of the streets and attachments to them increased. Similarly, through the introduction of *woonerven*, zones where traffic is slowed down and play and planting areas introduced, many towns and cities in the Netherlands have made their streets safer and more pleasant. This approach has been adopted in other countries, as well, including in selected new developments in the United States (see Woonerf case in Chapter 5).

During different stages in the life cycle, spaces assume a particular importance as a setting for interaction with friends and acquaintances. Parents caring for young children depend on nearby parks and playgrounds not only as facilities to occupy their children but also as places to enjoy contact with others, particularly other parents. Play areas that can accommodate a long social visit by parents supervising their children require comfortable seating arranged to enable face-to-face interaction, tables, running water, and ideally, restrooms.

Parent socializing appears to be as important as child play. Jefferson Market Park, Manhattan, New York City. (Stephen Carr)

Another group whose social life often centers around public spaces is the elderly. Brown, Sijpkes, and MacLean (1986) report that a number of elderly welfare recipients who frequent Complexe Desjardins, an indoor shopping center in downtown Montreal, "have refused to be moved further than a reasonable walking distance" (p. 170) away from the center. Groups of elderly people often are most concentrated in sitting areas around the perimeters of parks and other public areas. At this location there is a feeling of safety provided by passersby, and friends and acquaintances are most likely to be spotted.

In New York City's vest-pocket Greenacre Park, while the majority of users position their seats to view the waterfall at the back of the space, the elderly regulars are an exception. They seat themselves near the entrance, generally facing the street, so as to watch the pedestrian flow and greet acquaintances.

For adults, particularly young adults, considerable socializing occurs in the context of recreation. A study of a small park adjacent to a Delaware campus (Ulrich & Addoms, 1981) found that although students visited the park primarily to engage in sports activities, considerable socializing occurred there. The study did not reveal a strong connection between socializing and recreation at facilities such as the school gymnasium where, it can be assumed, athletic activities are pursued more for their own sakes.

In a comparative study of parks in Paris and Los Angeles, Lyle (1970) found large group activities such as picnics more common in Los Angeles. Linday's (1977) study of Central Park suggested that some Hispanics seek intense high-energy activities (such as dancing) while others seem to be seeking a "pastoral retreat."

Providing for active recreational needs is a predominant aspect of public place design. In recreation we also find regional, geographic, cultural, and age differences, both within and across spaces. People go to parks because ball playing, tennis, boating, and hiking are available and, although the public does vary in its preferences for these activities, they are generally popular. O'Donnell (1981) found that when youths were given the opportunity to select from among different amenities for a new park, as might be expected, they were strongly in favor of the development of recreational facilities in contrast with more passive options preferred by adults. Yet adults, too, are involved in active pursuits; jogging has become a popular exercise as enthusiasts find appropriate paths in likely and unlikely places. Bicycling also has increased and many parks provide paths for this active recreation.

Other cultural differences appeared in the contrast between parks in Los Angeles and Paris (Lyle, 1970). Active sports and games were spread over the parks in Los Angeles, whereas in Paris they were restricted to specific portions of the space. In addition, large group activities were more frequent in Los Angeles. Lyle also found considerably more variety of use in the local parks in Los Angeles when compared with those in Paris.

In some cases, activities enable participants to exercise both their bodies and their competitive desires. In other cases there seem to be other needs – for adventure, challenge, mastery, and perhaps even risk. Certainly the popularity of wilderness areas such as those frequented in Outward Bound courses attests to this quality. At the very least, they offer an extreme contrast to daily life, although risks are not necessarily unique to the wilderness.

Vigorous encounters with physical elements of a setting represent another dimension of active engagement. Here we are describing direct physical contact rather than just being within or moving across a place. One example can be found in the wading and frolicking found in some fountains – for example, Lovejoy and Forecourt in Portland (Love, 1973). This contact with water also formed part of the most frequent activities

Children often make their own opportunities for challenge. Children in Parisian plaza. (Mark Francis)

on the original Sacramento Mall in California, now replaced by a more open transit mall (Becker, 1973). In his cross-city comparison, Lyle (1970) found people were actively involved with natural elements in Los Angeles, whereas Parisians were more apt to be viewers of the scene. From our own observations, the use of large, public fountains by children to float toy boats and feed fish, although common in Paris, is rare in the United States.

One can argue, as Kevin Lynch does, that our cities reinforce the passive, inactive mode of life despite the fact that we recognize the threats that this may have for health.

While popular interest in daily exercise is rising, traditional settlement design has always sought to reduce physical effort: to shorten distances, avoid human portage, abolish level changes, introduce mechanical lifts and vehicles, multiply labor-saving devices. The memory of hard human labor has been too fresh. Recent studies in one North American suburb have shown that the average adult there moves his or her body somewhat less than someone permanently bed-ridden. Designing to promote rather than avoid the use of the body may be on its way: not simply by providing space for athletics, which are indulged in by no more than a minor portion of the population, but by arrangements which encourage bodily action in everyday life, or even compel it. (Lynch, 1981, p. 127)

Although it is important to respect the needs of people with physical disabilities, public places could, and should, promote vigorous energetic use of the human body, something lacking in most present-day designs. The jogging paths, bicycle lanes, gardening plots, horseback riding paths, ice-skating rinks, and tennis courts are examples of some forms of active uses, and reflect the growing interest in exercise and health. But they are the exceptions rather than the rule in most public parks and are limited to a small portion of the public.

Another aspect of physical engagement involves manipulation of elements such as sculpture. There are examples of public art encouraging this activity, for example, the Calder sculpture in a Chicago plaza (Goldstein, 1975). In other cases, users may manipulate or alter fixed elements as a kind of protest against the lack of responsiveness of public places. This is especially apparent in the provision of seating, most of which is rigid and unyielding. Where movable chairs are available, they are used and appreciated.

Challenge and mastery are qualities that stimulate interest and use and are human needs that explain much of the use of public places. Yet most of the time this need is not acknowledged as sites are designed to minimize dangers and reduce the risks of liability of the space managers. People need to be able to test themselves, intellectually and physically, or they

Disney is the master of safe challenges for all ages. Tom Sawyer Island, Disneyland. (Mark Francis)

lose interest. These opportunities are especially critical to children because they are the foundation of the development of their cognitive abilities and their sense of competence (White, 1959). Florence Ladd has identified another developmental need. In an article entitled "City Kids in the Absence of . . ." she argues that adventure should be provided for city teenagers (Ladd, 1975). These issues are major concerns in the design of children's play spaces, especially adventure playgrounds (Cooper, 1970; Nicholson, 1971). However, opportunities for healthy challenge and mastery are needed across the life cycle. Psychologists have shown that stimulation is essential throughout the years, including the later ones. Some of the deterioration of the elderly appears to come from the limited, uninteresting lives of many, due to physical problems, poverty, and restricted participation in the outside world. Yet most positive challenge has been removed from our public environment, although it may be one of the key reasons to have public space.

Their active qualities may be among the most important influences on the staying power of places, separating the ones that are boring and not worth a second visit from those of enduring interest. There are risks that are unnecessary and frightening and others that are stimulating and growth-producing, and it is the latter that should be identified and incorporated into public sites.

GAS WORKS PARK
Seattle, Washington

Located on North Lake Place at northern tip of Lake Union; designed by Richard Haag and Associates, Inc., Landscape Architects; managed by City of Seattle Department of Parks and Recreation; completed in 1978; cost, $900,000; size, 20.5 acres.

Designed as a multiuse neighborhood open space, Gas Works Park has attracted citywide use and national attention as an innovative public space purposely designed for a diversity of users and activities. An important early design decision was to preserve old gas generator towers on the site, which were determined by the designer Rich Haag to be historic and symbolic "sacred" structures. A key decision was made to maintain continuity of the site and people's connections to it by using the historic gas structures and

Richard Haag explains his vision in Gas Works Park, Seattle. (Mark Francis)

the existing building as major elements in the park. Haag (1982, p. 3) reports on how he reached this conclusion:

In 1970, I was asked to design a public park for the site. I brought with me all the baggage and preconceptions of most landscape architects. Then I began with the site. I haunted the buildings and let the spirit of the place enjoin mine. I began seeing what I like and then I liked what I saw – new eyes for old. Permanent oil slicks become plains with outcroppings of concrete, industrial middens were drumlins, the towers were ferro-forests and their brooding presence became the most sacred of symbols. I accepted these gifts, and decided to absolve the community's vindictive feelings towards the gas plant. This vanishing species of the industrial revolution was saved from extinction through adaptive use.

This idea was not an easy one for many people to accept. Many preferred a more traditional, passive park with open space and trees. Rich Haag persisted and fought to recycle the site into an "urban, intensely used pleasure ground" (Gas Works Park, 1981, p. 3). Eventually Haag's view prevailed and the master plan was approved in 1975. The park was completed and opened to the public in 1978. In 1981, Gas Works Park received the President's Award of Excellence from the American Society of Landscape Architects, its highest award, as a "most commendable piece of constructive city improvement."

Gas Works Park gains part of its success from careful attention to people's needs. The park is unique in providing for a wide variety of purposes including comfort, relaxation, passive and active engagement with the environment, and discovery that opens up new experiences over time. People's needs were met through careful programming of a variety of spaces. Included in the park is an old boiler house, which has been converted into a picnic shelter with tables, an open dance floor, and a stage for musical events. Nearby is the former exhauster-compressor building, which has been transformed into a play-barn where children and parents can climb over old but freshly painted machines, pipes, and equipment. The barn provides needed shelter and comfort from the frequent rainy days in Seattle. In the large outdoor area is "The Great Mound," formed by stockpiling contaminated soil on the site, an idea that later closed the park for some time until toxic material could be removed. The mound provides a place to sunbathe, fly a kite, or enjoy a good view of downtown Seattle across the lake. On top of the mound is a bronze sundial, designed by local artist Chuck Greening. Near the lake is "The Prow," a lakeside platform that serves as a stage for outdoor concerts, as well as a dock for swimming and diving. On a sunny day, a visitor is struck with the range of uses of the park by diverse users and age groups. The 1981 ASLA award jury comments stated that, "Gas Works Park is Seattle's foremost play experience. It is a place to show out-of-town guests, watch a sunset, fly a kite, hold a concert, a place to play and picnic, rain or shine" (Gas Works Park, 1981, p. 596).

In addition to providing for many human needs, the park was designed and managed to be flexible enough to offer users substantial freedom of use and for people to claim symbolic ownership over the park (Hester, 1983). Haag says his approach to designing Gas Works Park was "as an open space to encompass and allow for continual change and adaptations" (C. Camp-

The Play Barn is a place where parents and children together can experience challenge and adventures. Gas Works Park, Seattle. (Mark Francis)

bell, 1973). A critique of Gas Works Park by landscape architect Randy Hester attributes Haag's commitment to the project as a "labor of love" (Hester, 1983). Hester argues that because they are open-ended to invite participation, public labors of love have less clearly articulated edges than more traditional designs. Haag's attitude toward the design of the waterfront edge reflects how flexibility of design and activity worked at Gas Works Park (Hester, 1983): "The traditional design would have bulk-headed the entire waterfront to create a clean, well-defined edge, but we have all sorts of edges, some hard, some muddy, some sloppy, and look how the people use it" (p. 20).

What Haag was creating, Hester points out, was a different aesthetic, which allowed people to adapt the place to their desired activities.

Related cases: People's Park, Boston Common, North Park, Central Park.

Ceremony, celebration, and festivity are other qualities that people often seek in urban public places. People require joyousness to refresh their lives. We speak here of a distinctive quality of life – the pleasure in engaging in a multifaceted activity that encompasses people-watching, socializing, being entertained, and consuming or buying food and other goods. The popularity of flea markets is one sign of this need where affordable merchandising and carnival spirit combine to draw crowds. Public places can become the stage of gatherings, special events and performances

(Brower, 1977b). For many decades this type of activity was characteristic of the market areas and entertainment strips of most American cities. With the growth of suburbs, the invention of television, and the increasing prominence of supermarkets and shopping centers, celebration became less a characteristic of American cities, while remaining prominent in many other parts of the world. The periodic events that attract large numbers, such as the yearly street fair in Brooklyn called "Atlantic Antic," the Italian saint day festivities, and the carnivals for which New Orleans is so noted, suggest that the capacity to enjoy is there, given the opportunity and the place. In these instances city streets become the fairgrounds for a wide range of pleasures.

Market areas providing the festivity of an earlier era still persist in many places. Philadelphians of all types gravitate to the Italian Market where vendors sell fresh produce, meat, poultry, and fish of all varieties, other foods, and bargain merchandise. In Seattle, for eighty years Pike Place Market has withstood many threats to its survival to retain its variety of shops and stalls in a seven-acre area overlooking Elliot Bay. New Yorkers still flock to the Lower East Side, especially on Sundays, to streets like Orchard, Delancey, and Essex, which specialize in discounted clothing and a wide variety of foods associated with this neighborhood. In many

Festivals change the spaces in which they occur, providing a counterpoint to ordinary public life. A street parade in San Antonio, Texas. (Stephen Carr)

small towns residents visit weekend farmers' markets, which serve as a town center or gathering place (Sommer, 1981, 1989).

——————

DAVIS FARMERS' MARKET
Davis, California

Located on C Street between Third and Fifth streets along Davis's Central Park; redesign and plaza by CoDesign Inc.; managed by Board of Directors of Davis Farmers' Market with permits from City Public Works and Fire Department.

In this university town of some fifty thousand, the Farmers' Market brings people in the community together on Wednesday afternoons and Saturday mornings throughout the year. Along with the needs to buy fresh fruits and vegetables grown by local farmers, the market satisfies many other community needs. It is a place to bump into friends and neighbors, share news, gossip, and lobby local officials. People are more likely to see neighbors at the Farmers' Market than to meet them on their own block in this rural town.

The Farmers' Market in Davis is part of a growing national movement to provide good-quality, low-cost produce in towns and cities. The markets are called by different names in different places – Community Farm Markets in Illinois, Food Fairs in Alabama, Curb Markets and Trade Fairs in the Northeast, and Certified Farmers' Markets in California. Eleven years ago in California, there was only one public market where farmers could sell their produce directly to consumers; by 1980, over fifty certified farmers' markets were in operation (Sommer, 1980).

The effect of farmers' markets on human needs has been systematically studied by Sommer and his colleagues. One of the most direct benefits of the markets studied was lower cost to the consumer than in traditional supermarkets (Sommer, Wing, & Aitkins, 1980). In their research in fifteen California cities, they found farmers' market prices to be 34 percent lower than those at supermarkets. Other human benefits of the markets documented include a higher quality and flavor of farmers' market produce (Sommer, Stumpf, & Bennett, 1981) and a positive social climate of the market (Sommer, Herrick, & Sommer, 1981). It is this "social climate" that is so striking in one's first visit to the Davis Farmers' Market. Sommer (1981) described some of these human qualities: "Farmers' markets are among the most social spaces in America today. People are there to buy, barter, converse, and watch the spectacle. In designing and modifying urban parks, there is a need to provide space and facilities for such gatherings to help build and preserve a sense of community" (p. 31).

Jason Tyburczy (1982) has evaluated the effect of a farmers' market on downtown revitalization in Tracy and Stockton, California. He found that trips to a farmers' market are frequently tied to other trips to nearby businesses, thus having a positive spin-off effect on downtown sales. In surveys, he found that over 70 percent of people interviewed would not have been downtown if it had not been for the farmers' market. Also, 45 percent of those interviewed in the three downtowns reported having a more positive image of the downtown as a result of the farmers' market.

The Davis Farmers' Market is a simple affair with great community value. Davis, California. (Mark Francis)

Many merchants and planners are picking up on this public design solution to revitalize areas of towns and cities. As discussed elsewhere, new public commercial areas such as Quincy Market and Harborplace gain their attention and financial success from taking maximum advantage of the human-needs qualities of farmers' markets. Yet there are major differences in these more commercial markets. Cost of food is much higher than in farmers' markets and there is less social diversity than at places like Davis Farmers' Market.

One of the key qualities of the Davis Farmers' Market is its informal and temporary design. A small community park near the downtown is quickly transformed for the market. Farmers start backing their trucks up to the curb early in the morning and set out simple tables or use their tailgates to display produce. Sommer describes how the design and layout of the Farmers' Market works in Davis:

Produce is sold directly from the tailgate without the need for unloading except for display purposes. Empty crates and baskets are piled alongside the cab and later in front of the storage bed as the produce is sold off. The area around the cab is seller's turf, the sidewalk belongs to the customers, and the space at the tailgate is the meeting ground between buyer and seller. (Sommer, 1980, p. 16)

The economic value of farmers' markets has been discovered by downtown Davis merchants, who cosponsor an evening market in the downtown during summer months. (Davis Farmers' Market)

The market is a complex and diverse social space. Other sellers set up on the side of the sidewalk offering, for example, fresh bagels, cut flowers, and political information. A three-piece country band joins the festivities. A table displaying information on the Farmers' Market and selling calendars is set up by the Market Board of Directors to help pay for maintenance and management costs. As customers arrive, the sidewalk becomes a block-long promenade. The play area in the park quickly becomes filled with small children dropped off by parents who go on to do their shopping. The children are always within close shouting range or eye contact of their parents. As people walk along doing their shopping, they bump into old and new friends making the sidewalk a congested but lively bazaar.

> Although some additional comforts are needed, such as protection from rain and shelter in winter, the Davis Farmers' Market illustrates how public design and management can cheaply, quickly, and even temporarily satisfy many human purposes. It provides a successful alternative to more expensive and permanent public spaces.
>
> *Related case: Haymarket.*

———

Farmers' markets have been returning to cities, as well. In New York City, eighteen locations host Greenmarkets that enable produce from regional farms to be sold by the people who grow it. Many visitors to these market areas are primarily in search of bargains or particular wares, but others are seeking engagement with the diversity of sights, sounds, and smells of these quintessential urban areas. In comparing the "behavioral ecology" of farmers' markets with that of supermarkets, Sommer (1981) finds the former friendlier, with more contacts with people.

Many merchants and planners are interested in this public design solution to revitalize areas of towns and cities. As discussed elsewhere, new retail spaces such as the Faneuil Hall Marketplace and Harborplace use prominent display of produce near entries to attract customers. However, these are not farmers' markets and the cost of food is much higher. These markets have much less social diversity and exchange than places like the Davis Farmers' Market.

While a handful of the old markets persist, a new phenomenon has recently arisen: a sort of in-town shopping mall, which nevertheless is quite different from the suburban prototype. Many of these places have adopted the name "market" – the Market at Citicorp in New York, Boston's Quincy Market, the Newmarket and Reading Station Market in Philadelphia – suggesting a parallel with the diverse, colorful, often chaotic marketplaces of an earlier era. Some of these "new markets" do bear similarities to their predecessors. For example, Quincy Market provides a wide variety of attractions, and on a busy day it is full of energy. Others, like the Market at Citicorp, are pleasant places to linger or pass through, but offer little that resembles the variety, excitement, and spontaneity of the old markets. In general, these contemporary, highly designed, largely artificial and costly to use "marketplaces" lack the liveliness, disorderliness, and unexpected possibilities of places like Philadelphia's Italian Market and New York's Lower East Side. It is odd to realize that pushcarts have largely disappeared from the Lower East Side but can be found in the South Street Seaport development in New York. One commentator (R. Campbell, 1980) accurately described these new markets as reflecting a yearning for the marketplaces and main streets of America's past but representing a very self-conscious re-creation of these prototypes. As Campbell states, these developments cater to people "who yearn for town life but who are not quite ready for the real city" (p. 48).

There is another kind of festivity common to public spaces that also seems to have considerable appeal, one that can be called ritual celebration. This is embodied in the convergence on Times Square to greet the New Year, the Fourth of July celebration in a town square, Chinese New Year in San Francisco, the Mardi Gras in New Orleans. The satisfaction here is in the predictable, shared experience that binds people together in the present and also allows them to feel part of history. Periodic communal celebration can be facilitated through environmental management. Some ritual celebrations, less geared toward a particular moment, can occur in settings that encourage more diffuse and varied forms of activity. Bacon (1981, p. 3) describes one such event, a day-long Fourth of July celebration that was designed as "a rambling, lazy family picnic day," spent in lower Manhattan.

DISCOVERY

Discovery is the fifth reason for people's presence in public spaces and represents the desire for stimulation (Lynch, 1963) and the delight we all have in new, pleasurable experiences. Exploration is a human need. Forcing people to remain in confined, bare settings is a form of torture or punishment. For children, being deprived of stimulation can permanently stunt their intellectual and social development, as dramatically documented by Spitz (1945) and Goldfarb (1945).

In the context of urban public spaces, discovery has some specific meanings. It is the opportunity to observe the different things that people are doing when moving through a site, a quality that has been associated with San Francisco's Cannery (Burns, 1978). The visitor is able to move around and discover parts of the place – balconies that jut out, escalators, elevators, flags, strange or interesting people. In this example, the major aspects of discovery appear to be the diversity in the physical design and the changing vistas. Greenacre Park in New York often is cited as having a sense of discovery through its use of levels and the various sectors that visitors can find (Burden, 1977). It is very likely that these are unexpected vistas for the visitor only the first time in the park, although repeated use may uncover other things of interest. For discovery to continue to be part of someone's experience of familiar places, it would be essential to have changing physical qualities and changing human activity as well. Either people must bring the components of an interesting stay with them (in the form of equipment, books, or thoughts) or the place itself must provide the stimulation that enables users' interests to endure.

The Cannery in San Francisco provides a dimension of discovery to a retail setting.
(Stephen Carr)

A sense of discovery can be enhanced by the design, as is clearly evident
in the case of the Cannery in San Francisco where changes in perspective
offer a succession of vistas to enjoy. Lynch (1963) suggests that contrast
and juxtaposition of elements can provide a sense of pleasurable surprise
that people enjoy, a quality that is epitomized by the Pompidou Centre.
The management also can contribute by programming activities in a creative way. The streets in front of New York's Public Library on Fifth Avenue and along Bryant Park on Forty-second Street have been used for
crafts fairs. Concerts have enlivened many moribund plazas. The experience of discovery can also contain a sense of mystery, as a photograph in
Cullen's *Townscape* (1961) suggests. The caption reads: "From the matter-
of-fact pavement of the busy world we glimpse the unknown mystery of a

city where anything could happen or exist, the noble or the sordid, genius or lunacy" (p. 51).

The need for discovery often is met by travel, going to new places to discover their special qualities, to meet new people, to find new challenges from landscapes that contrast with familiar ones. Some places have been designed to create a sense of discovery as reflected in Tony Hiss's (1987, 1990) description of the entrance to Prospect Park, Olmsted's creative design for the borough of Brooklyn, New York. But discovery also can occur at home under conditions in which elements of known places change. A concert or flea market can transform a well-used plaza or park. Toys brought to a playground can introduce new opportunities for amusement. Some of these can be initiated by users, but most depend upon the support and instigation of space managers who can extend the opportunities for discovery beyond any individual user. Ultimately, the readiness for discovery lies within each of us, waiting to be evoked in public places by enlightened designs and management policies.

SUMMARY

The various public space needs cover many aspects of human functioning. They include the physical comforts involved in relief from the elements, rest, and seating. Social needs address the stimulation surrounding people, escape from urban overload, and protection from the threats from others. People need to relax, to enjoy the respite offered by public places and have opportunities to enjoy natural elements with public places functioning as oases. While some persons seek out settings in which to relax, others gravitate toward physical and social challenges, active engagement with the public place and its occupants including interaction with others, shopping, participation in street life, and vigorous encounters such as sports, wading, and jogging. Other challenges can be found in places that support discovery, enabling opportunities for new experiences, new vistas that excite, educate, and delight.

This array of human needs, which no doubt could be supplemented by others, also should include opportunities for pure joy and fun, qualities missing from many places. The descriptions provide clues as to why some sites are filled whereas others are empty. Functionality, the usefulness of a site, provides a simple explanation of its success. But needs alone are not a sufficient reason for vitality. There are other qualities that constrain or facilitate open space experiences, and the different uses and rights of users of areas are essential ones.

RIGHTS IN PUBLIC SPACE

A central question is whether people are free to achieve the types of experiences they desire in public spaces. The rights to use a public space and have a sense of control within it are basic and overarching requirements.

Spatial rights involve freedom of use, most simply, the feeling that it is possible to use the space in a way that draws on its resources and satisfies personal needs. Obviously, it is more complex than the statement implies. As social beings we live in a world with others, with norms, rule systems, and supervisors, all potential constraints, along with environmental ones, on an individual's freedom. Moreover, life in communities is based on some form of social order, and that order inhibits the freedom of particular individuals either in the interest of the larger group or the owners and managers of settings. A good deal of the conflict over what public space should offer, both in the past and in contemporary times, revolves around differences in viewpoint between the dominant group and minority users, whether they are the working class in Olmsted's pristine parks or the drug dealers in modern-day plazas.

In examining a variety of parks, plazas, and other spaces, it becomes apparent that different degrees of freedom and control exist in different situations. The precise balance between these two factors at a particular time is dependent on a number of factors, including the norms and behaviors of the individuals and groups using the space, and the design and management of the space (Carr & Lynch, 1981).

To guide us in the discussion of freedom of use and control we have adapted Kevin Lynch's (1981) delineation of five dimensions of spatial rights, which he described as presence, use and action, appropriation, modification, and disposition. Retitled access, freedom of action, claim, change, and ownership and disposition, we view them as essential com-

Freedom of use is an important spatial right. (Elizabeth March)

ponents of control over use. Although there are other aspects to people's rights, the five qualities that we propose provide the opportunity for an environmentally based analysis of freedom of use. Here, as in the case of needs, the five dimensions represent degrees of freedom, with rights of access fundamental to the attainment of other rights.

ACCESS

The ability to enter spaces is basic to their use. A simple way of conceptualizing access is in terms of its three major components. First there is *physical access*. Is the space physically available to the public? To provide an extreme example, some New York City plazas, designed by developers as public spaces in exchange for increases in building height or bulk, have, at times, been closed to the public by means of fences or guards who prohibit or discourage entry. City regulations now require that new spaces of this kind have signs indicating that they are open to the public and listing their hours. In many cities spaces such as public schoolyards are freely accessible during so few hours of the day that their status as public space is doubtful even though the public owns them. There is a real question, in many instances, whether open space is, indeed, open to the public. When limits to access exist in the form of gates or gatekeepers,

This downtown park in Sausalito, California, is permanently closed and locked with a sign that reads, "This historic park is for your viewing pleasure, please do not enter." (Mark Francis)

the use of a space is severely restricted, the site privatized, and people's rights are limited.

Other spaces may present barriers to the physical access of particular groups. For example, sunken plazas that must be approached by way of stairs (like Chicago's First National Plaza; see Rutledge, 1976) may be inaccessible to persons pushing carriages, people in wheelchairs, and some elderly people. In a similar vein, the predominance of automobiles on residential streets can be seen as a barrier in residential areas (Appleyard & Lintell, 1977). Recently, communities throughout the world have made attempts to limit the dominance of the automobile in residential areas (Appleyard, 1981). A notable example described in the preceding chapter, is the Dutch *woonerf,* where streets are designed to control traffic and enable play and pedestrian access.

————

WOONERF
Delft, The Netherlands

Located in Delft, The Netherlands (several examples in both older and new neighborhoods); designed by Planners of Municipality of Delft; managed by Municipality of Delft; completed in phases, since the 1960s; size, approximately .25 to 1.0 mile in diameter per woonerf.

Overview of a woonerf in a new residential area in Delft, the Netherlands. (Mark Francis)

Residents and officials in many countries have become concerned with making neighborhood streets more usable and accessible for predestrians. One of the oldest and most active efforts to restrict automobiles in favor of people has occurred in the Netherlands. Here the woonerf concept has been extensively developed and tested. Today woonerven are a part of the neighborhood landscape in most Dutch towns and cities (Appleyard, 1981).

The woonerf was described in a 1977 publication intended to inform other countries of the Dutch experience with neighborhood traffic management (Royal Dutch Touring Club, 1978). It is a traffic-restricted section of a residential area with street furniture emphasizing its functions as a home setting.

Donald Appleyard, an American urban designer who studied the Dutch woonerf in detail, summarizes the concept by identifying two principal characteristics (Appleyard, 1981). The street, Appleyard points out, becomes a space shared between the pedestrian and the automobile. Furthermore, pedestrians have the legal right-of-way over motorized vehicles. Through extensive redesign of the street, automobile traffic is slowed down in favor of a landscaped pedestrian environment.

According to Poulton (1982), over eight hundred woonerven have been developed in the Netherlands. Such a large number is also a result of the Dutch government's attempt to provide specific legislation and design guidelines for woonerven in 1976. These guidelines (Royal Dutch Touring Club, 1978) have been revised to incorporate evaluations of the effects of the woonerf on neighborhood life and residents' attitudes in Holland. The interest in increasing pedestrian accessibility to neighborhoods has spread to many other countries such as Britain, Denmark, and Germany, where numerous examples have been constructed (Appleyard, 1981).

According to Appleyard (1981), accessibility is provided in the woonerf by five basic traffic management rules. First, you may walk anywhere on a road within a woonerf and children may play anywhere. Second, cars are driven at a walking pace, as are mopeds and cycles. Third, anyone who drives a car or rides a bike or moped within a woonerf must not impede pedestrians, but pedestrians and children at play should not obstruct or unnecessarily impede drivers. Fourth, parking is forbidden except where P is painted on the street. Fifth, within a woonerf, traffic from the right always has priority.

The street space is redesigned and reconstructed to emphasize these rules. As Appleyard points out in *Livable Streets* (1981), path direction, vertical features, surface changes, planting, and street furniture are all designed as obstacles to vehicular travel and to create a residential atmosphere. There is a sensitivity on the part of the planners of the woonerf to design traffic control devices as usable elements. As one Dutch planner pointed out, "a tree is an obstacle but is also part of the greenery; a small hill can force cars to the side, but it is also an object for children's play; a pillar in front of your door prevents cars from passing too close, but it also marks your entrance, and it is easy to put your bike up against" (Appleyard, 1981, p. 307).

Delft has become a frequent stop for planners and officials eager to learn more about the Dutch experience with woonerven. Delft has some of the oldest and newest examples of woonerven design. The application of woonerven to different types of neighborhood environments can be viewed all in one visit. As an outsider, it is not difficult to find one. A stop at the bicycle rental shop at the train station finds several local residents willing to point you in the direction of nearby woonerven. The one closest to the train station in the older area of Delft is also one of the oldest examples of woonerf design.

Several design devices are used effectively to inform a newcomer that you are entering a different kind of neighborhood. A sign with the universal woonerf symbol greets you at the entrance and an abrupt change in paving informs you that this is not a typical street. One is struck by the lack of a curb to divide vehicle space from pedestrian space. The street becomes a paved and landscaped area where pedestrians and children can move freely. Cars must slow down and move carefully to avoid numerous new trees, bumps, benches and posts.

Several other features added to the street make it different from traditional streets and also help explain its social success. Planters and landscaping have been extended into the street by some residents. Children play freely in the street using it for activity such as gardening, not commonly seen in more traditional Dutch residential streets.

Further to the north in Delft, an extensive new residential area has incorporated woonerf as a major circulation element. Here the streets are wider and more private open space is provided around walk-up apartments and duplexes. Some of the same uses can be observed in this new area with children playing in the street in parking areas, and parents stopping to talk to friends and neighbors.

The woonerf concept has not been without problems and criticism. One critique of the woonerf idea (Poulton, 1982) notes problems such as the additional maintenance and construction costs over more traditional street design. The Dutch planners point out that in their experience the woonerf can cost about 150 percent more than typical residential streets (Royal Dutch Touring Club, 1978). Other problems cited by Poulton include overall circulation problems, parking problems for service vans, and the difficulty strangers have finding their way around a woonerf. Because additional traffic is placed on adjacent through streets, observers, such as Appleyard, have indicated that the concept can have a negative impact on adjacent residents. Appleyard (1981) argues that residents on streets that gain additional traffic as part of a traffic management plan should be compensated by decreased property taxes or other means for these negative effects. A further problem with the Dutch woonerf concept is that some drivers fail to respect the speed limits. This can be fatal for those children who use the street space regularly because they may develop a false sense of security.

The goals of increasing accessibility of residents to their streets and fostering a greater attachment to that street appear to have been successfully met. One study by V. A. Guttinger of both a traditional neighborhood street and a new woonerf in Delft reveals striking effects on children's accessibility to the neighborhood (Verwer, 1980). The study found that children's use of the public street space was much greater in the woonerf and covered a wider territory than on conventional streets. In addition, the researcher found less supervision by parents of child play in the woonerf streets, indicating that adults consider the streets safe enough to children to play on their own.

Most planners and researchers who have studied the woonerf concept agree that another dimension of spatial rights is essential to their potential success. Where resident participation and consensus is a driving force in initiating a woonerf, the potential success may be greater (Appleyard, 1981; Poulton, 1982; Royal Dutch Touring Club, 1978). A participatory model has been used in transferring this street redesign concept to other towns, such as Stavanger, Norway. Here an entire neighborhood street system was redesigned, reconstructed, and is now managed by the local resident association. Poulton points out that planners must be careful not to raise unreasonable expectations from residents whose streets may be unsuitable for woonerven. Where appropriate, increased user accessibility resulting from active resident participation in the design and management of local streets appears a realistic possibility in urban neighborhoods in the United States and elsewhere.

Related cases: Davis Farmers' Market, Gågate Walking Street, Tranehytten Adventure Playground, Church Street Marketplace.

GÅGATE WALKING STREET
Røros, Norway

Located on Bergmannsgate (small commercial street); managed by Town of Røros and adjacent merchants; 2 blocks long.

In this small (population thirty-three hundred) historic town in central Norway, one of the downtown streets is closed during summer days to create a gågate, or "walking street." A common feature of most Scandinavian towns

A Gågate or walking street in Rorøs, Norway. The street returns to traffic during the evening and winter months. (Mark Francis)

and cities, the gågate can be used by auto and trucks only during the evenings or in harsh winters. Limited vehicle use has enabled the street to keep much of its local character. Neighborhood shops are located along the street, including a restaurant that sets out picnic tables in the middle of the street for outdoor eating. Some displays on wooden tables placed by adjacent shops also occupy the street during sunny days. Here hand-crafted Norwegian goods are sold to tourists. Locals gather in the street chatting as tourists stroll, looking at the displays. The local recreation department has placed inexpensive and portable play equipment in the street for use by children. As one strolls along the street, the historic wooden Røros church is visible in the distance. When not closed to traffic, the street looks like most streets in town, with narrow sidewalks, parking, and moving vehicles.

Related cases: Woonerf, Haymarket, Downtown Washington Streets for People, Church Street Marketplace.

———

For a space to be physically accessible, it should not only be without barriers to entry, it should also be well connected to paths of circulation. The connection of a plaza or small park to adjacent sidewalks is an important aspect of this access (Whyte, 1980). Before renovations, the lack of connections from one side of New York's Bryant Park to another and the failure of its paths to connect can be viewed as serious obstacles to its use. Two Seattle plazas studied by the Project for Public Spaces (1978) have very different relationships to adjacent pathways. The First National Bank Plaza can be entered from only one side; "as a result it tends to be viewed as a private space and is almost exclusively used by building tenants" (pp. 17–18). In contrast, the nearby Federal Building Plaza is open to the sidewalk on three sides and is used by a more diverse population. Similarly, Cooper Marcus (1978b) contrasts two Minneapolis public spaces with differing degrees of physical access: the popular indoor space, Crystal Court, which has numerous entrances at grade level and one flight up; and the poorly used Federal Reserve Plaza, which can only be entered from one side. Some designers and managers have used information on limited access through limited entrances as a design device to reduce use in their spaces. This can be seen in some of the new atrium spaces in midtown Manhattan. While numerous factors account for the degree of use of such spaces, physical accessibility seems to play an important role.

In addition to physical access, *visual access* or visibility is important in order for people to feel free to enter a space. The question to ask here is: Can potential users easily see into the space from outside, so that they know that it is a public space where they can enter safely and will be welcome? Clear visibility seems to be particularly important in judgments of the safety of a space. In many large cities, the public's perception that a space is free of drug dealers, muggers, and other persons who threaten users is an important consideration for its use. For fragile elderly persons, a park with too much activity – bike riding or ball playing – may be difficult to tolerate and thus may reduce their use by this group. The ability to check out these potential threats before entering is a critical requirement. The three-foot walls and bushes that surrounded Bryant Park for many

Although there is a fence and gate at Redwood Park in downtown San Francisco, this corporate park reveals itself prior to entry. (Mark Francis)

years made it difficult for passersby to see into the space and thereby discouraged entry. This is also the case for Union Square in San Francisco, which is raised and visually secluded. In contrast, New York's Washington Square and Philadelphia's Rittenhouse Square are at street level and clear views into them are possible from all adjacent sidewalks. Potential users of these spaces have much more information about what is going on inside, and so are more likely to enter.

Visual access to a site must be viewed against people's needs for privacy and their desire for places that provide a retreat – a hidden corner in which to escape the pressures, stimulation, and crowding of urban life. There is an inherent dilemma in providing both opportunities for privacy and a sense of security, but it is critical to recognize that the two can be accommodated by sensitive design.

Crime statistics show a wide gap between perception and the reality of safety in cities. But the perception of danger can be an important deterrent to use of urban public places especially for women. Hidden places and screens from the street's view may support the desire for privacy or retreat, but they also reduce the perceived safety of the site. In New York, both Bryant Park and Greenacre Park offer users places to withdraw, but with different consequences. For many years, Bryant Park's size, relative isolation from the street, and absence of supervision have limited its use. It has attracted drug dealing and other socially unsanctioned activities.

Now, after extensive renovation, its more open design is drawing many users. Greenacre, on the other hand, is small, has an on-site staff, and is perceived as secure. It is therefore enjoyed for its opportunities for privacy (see Chapter 4). In contrast with both are many of the open plazas whose activities are clearly visible and safe but do not satisfy privacy needs, thus restricting their use.

BRYANT PARK
New York, New York

Located between Avenue of the Americas between Fortieth and Forty-second streets behind the New York Public Library, Manhattan; redesign by Hanna/ Olin, Landscape Architects; managed by New York City Department of Parks and Bryant Park Restoration Corporation (BPRC); original park completed in 1934; redesigned and reconstructed 1990–2; size, 4.6 acres.

Bryant Park, located one block from Times Square and behind the main branch of the New York Public Library, is the major open space in Manhattan's bustling midtown. The recent history of the park graphically demonstrates some of the conflicts inherent in managing public spaces in dense urban centers.

Bryant Park's great lawn in Midtown Manhattan was intensively used at midday. (Stephen Carr)

The raised and well-shaded terraces in New York City's Bryant Park became areas
for drug dealing. (Stephen Carr)

While the site has served as a public open space since 1858, its present
configuration was established in 1934. In that year, Parks Commissioner
Robert Moses supervised the redesign of the park into a classically influenced formal space, surrounded by a stone fence and laid out in a symmetrical fashion. Moses intended the park to be a place of "restful beauty," with
ample trees and hedges, rather than a space for active recreation (Biederman & Nager, 1981).

Considering its location, the notion of Bryant Park as a place for relaxation
can be viewed as appropriate on one hand and rather unrealistic on the
other. Clearly many urbanites seek a place of retreat from the activity of the
city, and Bryant Park is one of the few places in central Manhattan that
could conceivably offer this respite. Indeed, in their 1976 study, Nager and
Wentworth found that relaxing or resting was the most frequent activity
engaged in by the park users they interviewed.

However, as these same researchers suggest, some of the very factors that
made the park a place for retreat and relaxation, such as its ample vegetation and the stone fences separating it from the street, also encouraged its
intensive use by drug dealers, who operated easily in the semiseclusion of
the park. During the 1970s it became clear that some design or management changes were necessary in order to counteract the appropriation of
the park by dealers and their clients and to increase its use by a wider range
of people, including local office workers and shoppers.

To achieve this goal the Bryant Park Restoration Corporation, a private
nonprofit group funded primarily by corporations located near the park and

the Rockefeller Brothers' Fund, was founded in 1980. While the corporation dealt extensively with maintenance and security issues in cooperation with the city's parks and police departments, its major goal was "to fill Bryant Park with activity, to attract to the park as many legitimate users as possible" (Bryant Park Restoration Corporation, 1981, p. 1). In the years it has operated, the restoration group in conjunction with the Parks Council, the Public Art Fund, and other organizations was responsible for an array of events and new activities in the park. These included several concert series, an artists-in-residence program, arts and crafts shows, a booth selling half-price tickets to musical and dance events, book and flower stalls, and, in the summer, a small café. It is generally agreed that these activities, along with improvements in policing and maintenance, significantly increased park use and reduced crime (Fowler, 1982). However, it was clear that more had to be done to restore and refresh the park.

Landscape architectural consultant Laurie Olin of Hanna/Olin proposed $6 million of physical changes, including adding more seating, increasing access points, refurbishing hedges, lawns, and flower beds, restoring the fountains and the Bryant statue, and expanding the library's central book stacks underneath the Great Lawn (Program on Public Space Partnerships, 1987). The addition of a new restaurant was proposed with Warner Leroy, owner of the famous Tavern on the Green restaurant in Central Park, as developer. Leroy pledged $12 million to construct a large privately operated conservatory/restaurant behind the New York Public Library building. In addition, he offered $2 million for renovation of the park. The office of Hardy, Holtzman, Pfieffer Associates, a firm known for being sensitive to historical landmarks, was selected as architect for the restaurant addition. The proposal to encroach into the public park with a private development received considerable opposition, including objections from the influential private advocacy group, the Parks Council. After three years of public debate and review, Leroy withdrew his proposal. A current, scaled-down proposal calls for two smaller buildings on the upper terrace, one housing an upgrade, moderately priced restaurant, the other concessions for low-cost food. Public restrooms long closed in the park have been renovated and reopened. The plan remains controversial. Bryant Park, closed while the renovations and construction were underway, opened in the spring of 1992.

The efforts of the Restoration Corporation and its design plans raise two important questions. First, considering the issue of spatial rights, can Bryant Park accommodate all of these new activities and still serve as a place of retreat and relaxation for some of its users? The Bryant Park Restoration Corporation has leaned primarily toward improved management and increased programming and has not significantly altered the park's 1934 design, which, despite its problems, did provide many subspaces. Intense activity can be occurring in certain locations – for example, adjacent to the fountain or on the balcony adjoining the library – while more passive activities occur in other areas.

Another issue, that of who has ultimate control over public parks, is raised by the situation at Bryant Park. In spring 1983, the Restoration Corporation, in cooperation with the New York Public Library, entered into a thirty-five-year agreement with the City Parks Department whereby the corporation would be responsible for all aspects of the park's maintenance, management, and renovation, under the overall supervision of the city's parks commissioner. Responding to the original café proposal and the overall management plan, Peter Berle, then president of the Parks Council, said, "I'm concerned about taking public land, removing it from the protections of public park status and turning it over to a private entity. . . . If you have a private entity running a public park, who is to say that you and I may not be the undesirables next year?" (Carmody, 1983, p. B3). Berle's concerns are crucial. Although the efforts of the Restoration Corporation have opened Bryant Park up to a wider range of purposes and a greater number of users, in the long run the ideal of maximum access to public parks may not be well served by city government turning over considerable control to private agencies.

Related cases: Pershing Park, Greenacre Park, Steps of the New York City Public Library, Boston Common and the Public Gardens, People's Park.

A final type of access is *symbolic access,* which involves the presence of cues, in the form of people or design elements, suggesting who is and is not welcome in the space. Individuals and groups perceived either as threatening, or comforting or inviting may affect entry into a public space. The clearest examples of this are "gatekeepers" located near the entry points who subtly or conspicuously control those coming into the space. For example, a study in New York's Exxon Park reported that the visibility of drug dealers at the two gates to the space "often makes it uncomfortable for people to even enter" (Project for Public Spaces, 1978, p. 14). Changes to the space made in 1979 by the building managers such as adding programmed events, food vendors, and more security have altered the situation. Security guards present at entrances to many of the newest corporate sponsored public plazas may suggest order and safety from harassment to most middle-class adults, but may present a less welcoming image to others.

Various nonhuman factors also are related to social-symbolic access. Certain facilities or design elements may act as cues regarding the type of people who are desired. In particular, the presence of shops and vendors may signal the "publicness" of a space and the type of people who are welcome there. On the one hand, the expensive shops and cafés that dominate indoor malls and atria such as Manhattan's Trump Tower provide clear signs as to the intended users. On the other hand, the presence of simple, affordable eating places and shops can suggest to passersby that the management of a plaza or atrium welcomes the public. This perspective is reinforced by a study of two Baltimore neighborhoods (Brower, 1988) where residents and visitors rated local shopping streets as more "public" than two local parks. According to Brower (personal communication, 1987) this is because shops, more than parks, depend on public patronage and clearly cater to residents and passersby.

Some barriers in settings act to define a space as belonging to a particular group, signaling that outsiders are unwelcome. Oscar Newman's (1973) controversial idea of defensible space is a way of excluding threatening outsiders by providing an identity for an area that facilitates surveillance and discourages entry by those who do not belong there. These environmental barriers, which can include limited entrance points, visibility to people, and signage are alternatives to the presence of guards who are associated with security. There are many subtle ways designs can provide a sense of safety instead of using security people. In fact, the presence of guards not only signals ownership of an area and a "keep out unless you belong here" message, it also suggests that the site is a risky one for the insiders. This message communicates the potential dangers to a setting and this may be as unsettling to insiders as it is threatening to those outside.

These three types of access – physical, visual, and symbolic – frequently interact, and can present a strong or ambiguous picture of who is free to enter a space and who has control over "the right of access." "The Market" at New York's Citicorp Building illustrates all three categories of access.

THE MARKET AT CITICORP
New York, New York

Located on Lexington Avenue at Fifty-third Street, Manhattan; designed by Hugh Stubbins Associates, Architects; managed by building owners; size, 1 block square.

The Market at Citicorp is an example of a public space where free access is limited in a number of ways although the space is considered to be one of the most successful indoor public spaces in the city.

In terms of physical access, the main entrance is set back several hundred feet from the sidewalk. The outdoor space is designed in a way that discourages easy pass through (Forrest & Paxson, 1979). The Market also provides limited visual access from the surrounding sidewalks. As Stephens (1978b, p. 57) points out, "not much of the exterior gives a clue to the offerings within." There is little transparency into the space, a lack of clearly visible signage, and no display of wares on three of the four exterior sides.

In a broad sense, the public space at Citicorp also is limited in terms of social-symbolic access. Security guards are frequently present at entry points and throughout the space, implicitly if not explicitly suggesting that this is a controlled space. The restaurants and food stores that dominate the Market appeal largely to an affluent clientele. The management may feel that by limiting access they are ensuring the success of the business enterprises.

However, there is heavy use of the indoor and outdoor spaces by a cadre of regulars who make up a diverse group. For elderly people who can linger over a cup of coffee or an ice cream in the seats provided or for those who come for the program of concerts, the Citicorp is a desirable urban resource.

Citicorp Center in New York City offers comfortable access to those who can pay to sit down at its cafés. (Mark Francis)

However, the homeless person carrying bags of personal possessions may find it difficult to go past the security posted at entrances. These restrictions to free access led one writer to suggest that "the mall owes its popularity in large measure to what it keeps out as well as what it offers within. Whether this isolationism should occur in 'public' spaces created through the city's incentive zoning measures should be addressed at the city planning level" (Stephens, 1978b, p. 54).

Related cases: Faneuil Hall Marketplace.

FREEDOM OF ACTION

Freedom of action reflects Lynch's (1981) second category of spatial rights, "the right of use and action, of behaving freely in a place or using its facilities" (p. 205). It involves the ability to carry out the activities that one desires, to use a place as one wishes but with the recognition that a public space is a shared space. Responsible freedom enables personal satisfaction without abusing the rights of others – yet this is frequently as difficult to achieve in public spaces as it is in the political arena.

The difficulties come from a number of directions. The competing interests of a heterogeneous society sometimes make the freedoms for one group potential threats to the freedoms of others. In many instances the public spaces provided by commercial developers primarily serve their own interests and the needs and rights of the public may receive little attention. Private property acts to constrain the public's use of areas it needs. In other cases the strength or numbers of a group may dominate an area, eliminating the possibility that others can be there. This is a familiar pattern, one that begins with the older children dominating a schoolyard or playground, limiting its use for younger age groups, and it occurs particularly when the space and resources are limited.

The existence or lack of rules and regulations is important to the achievement of this freedom. Research conducted at Sacramento's earlier

Freedom of action is easily achieved in spaces with malleable materials like water and sand. Village Homes, Davis, California. (Mark Francis)

Cities in the United States also have their traditional spots for speechmaking. The corner of Wall and Broad streets, New York City. (Stephen Carr)

Downtown Mall (Becker, 1973) indicated that children wished to play on the concrete sculptures and in fountains but were prohibited from doing so by police and merchants. In contrast, Love (1973) reports that the managers of Lovejoy and Forecourt Fountains in Portland actually encourage wading, and a large number of children and adults engage in this activity.

Demonstrations, rallies, distributing leaflets, and speechmaking have long been an important component of the life of many parks and squares. At London's Hyde Park, residents and tourists flock to the Speaker's Corner to hear speeches on a variety of topics, political and nonpolitical. On the other hand, shopping malls, private spaces that serve as the most important gathering places in many U.S. and Canadian communities, often strictly regulate political activity. Currently, restrictions on activities such as leafletting and petitioning in malls have become what some civil libertarians regard as "the most significant free speech issues of the day" (*New York Times*, February 10, 1986). In 1980 the United States Supreme Court allowed states to rule on this issue, under their own constitutions. Courts in over a dozen states have addressed the issue. Some states, such as California, have ruled that free-speech clauses in their constitutions give political petitioners access to privately owned malls (*New York Times*, February 10, 1986). Other courts, including those in New York and in

Canada, have ruled that constitutional free-speech guarantees do not apply to private property. Although this issue is currently most significant in suburbs and small cities where shopping malls have eclipsed main streets as civic centers, it may become increasingly important in large cities where privately owned shopping complexes have proliferated since the mid-1970s. Stephens (1978b, p. 50) reports that at one such space, the Galleria in downtown Philadelphia, controversy over the exclusion of political demonstrators focused on the fact that the mall had been in part publicly funded.

In addition to rules and prohibitions, the physical layout of a public space can have a substantial impact on people's ability to carry out desired activities. Different spaces offer different degrees of choices and opportunities for use. Wurman, Levy, and Katz (1972) speak of the "specificity" of a space – whether it can accommodate primarily one activity (e.g., a tennis court), a moderate range of activities (e.g., a path through the woods), or a wide variety of activities (e.g., a grassy meadow). A study of Riis Park in New York City (Madden & Bussard, 1977), contrasts two types of spaces, of similar size, in terms of opportunities for use. Several large lawn areas, sprinkled with trees, were among the most popular sections of the park. They were used for various types of games and by families who picnic there and used these areas as a "base camp" from which to visit other parts of the park. In contrast to these rather "nonspecific" spaces were two ball fields with fences, bleachers, and a few trees. These fields were little used, except for occasional organized baseball games. Although highly "specific" spaces such as the fields are often an integral part of parks and recreation areas, it is important to offer free access to sufficient additional spaces where freedom of choice is greater.

Settings that are internally differentiated into a number of subspaces are particularly well suited to a wide variety of activities. In comparing Lovejoy and Forecourt Fountains in Portland, Love (1973) points out that although these large fountains have much in common, Forecourt encourages more of a diversity of activities due to its greater number and variety of pools, waterfalls, and seating platforms (see Chapter 4).

At the level of freedom of action, psychological comfort again emerges as an important consideration. In the preceding chapter, we suggested that comfort, including psychological comfort, is a basic human need. We find that many public spaces have been designed to be uncomfortable, to encourage people to look at or move through space rather than use it. The presence of gatekeepers may also restrict use by discouraging lingering. Psychological comfort or ease implies freedom from worry and concern. People need to feel at ease if they are to use a space as they wish.

Three special groups whose freedom of action in the public environment is often restricted by a lack of comfortable, well-managed spaces are women, the elderly, and the physically disabled. The restricted freedom of women in many cities is well described in a magazine article:

A woman in New York City dresses up as a man to find out what it would be like to act as a man. Her boyfriend strongly advises her: "Take your time as you walk. Women always seem to move as if they need a reason to be here; as if they need to reach a certain destination. As a man you simply occupy the space. It's yours." (Wiedermann, 1985, p. 27, from *Stern*, May 11, 1983)

This restricted right to public space is a common experience of women who have had limits on their use of open spaces for thousands of years. What is most striking is the fact that despite the rhetoric of change, women continue to feel vulnerable in the public setting and, indeed, their fears are supported by statistics on victimization. Women continue to be open to harassment and intrusion, experiences that discourage enthusiastic use of public areas, including the streets. They have had limits on their *freedom to* participate in public life and activities and constraints on their *freedom from* the unwelcome advances and threats of others. As Franck and Paxson (1989) point out: "As in the nineteenth century, when women are in public spaces they are still defined and perceived in terms of their sexuality, which is a private role. They are never free of this role as men are" (p. 130).

A woman alone may feel safer on an uncomfortable concrete block, big enough for only one, than on a nearby bench. Boston Common. (Elizabeth March)

In our studies of public spaces we have found places with gatekeepers like the vest-pocket Greenacre Park appreciated by women because they felt safe there. Some of the "found" neighborhood spaces also were places where women felt comfortable. In other places, for example, on street corners or lingering in front of shops, women either were not present in any significant numbers or were positioned in areas that were close to the flow of traffic. On the steps of the New York Public Library women were commonly found in the central or high density areas, less often in the side sections where the view was obscured from the street and where drug dealing and other urban negotiations took place.

Women often avoid using certain urban parks and plazas (Franck & Paxson, 1989; Stoks, 1983). A study of women's attitudes toward West Berlin's Jungfernheide Park (Wiedermann, 1985) found that less than 10 percent of younger women interviewed would enter the park unescorted, while 70 percent of women who did use the park reported feeling insecure. In their 1976 study of New York's Bryant Park, Wentworth and Nager found that in no section of this park, where safety was a significant concern, did women constitute more than one-third of total users. The two park areas where women were best represented among total users were a sitting area directly adjoining the sidewalk and the ledge of a fountain, a location that eliminated the fear of being approached from behind and which also was adjacent to a park exit.

In addition to a clear concern with personal safety, Whyte (1980) reports that with regard to the use of plazas, "women are more discriminatory than men as to where they will sit, more sensitive to annoyances, and women spend more time casting the various possibilities. . . . Where there is a higher than average proportion of women, the plaza is probably a good one and has been chosen as such" (p. 18).

Similar considerations of safety and comfort apply for elderly persons. A study by Godbey and Blazey (1983) of the use of parks in five American cities by the elderly stresses the frequent, routine nature of park use by this group, and the important role that parks play in their lives. Yet, according to the authors, the frequency and nature of this use is greatly affected by how a park is managed. Elderly users are said to schedule park visits based on considerations such as availability of desired programs and hours when the park environment is safest and most comfortable. Older people in the five cities used parks most heavily in the morning and early afternoon; these periods generally offer the most available sunshine and the least competition with older children, teens, and adults.

The failure of public spaces to accommodate people with physical disabilities is a tremendous constraint. Although increasing numbers of places have been providing access for wheelchairs, the other needs of disabled persons rarely are addressed beyond the ramp, limiting their access to these settings. For disabled people, physical constraints as well as threatening persons make the public space unwelcoming and out of bounds. With most designs based on the hypothetical average-sized, mobile person, many potential users are excluded.

The presence of activities and people perceived as unpleasant or threatening often places severe limits on free use of a space. The alcoholics who are habitués of some public spaces, the disheveled urban nomads, or the unfortunate homeless people with their shopping bags of personal possessions may make a site unappealing to others, especially if they dominate the setting. Clusters of young men, some dealing in or consuming drugs,

By increased management and increased signs of care, such as the hanging plants and movable chairs, Exxon Plaza in New York City is now perceived as safe. (Stephen Carr)

found in many parks and plazas in cities throughout the United States restrict the activity of other users and potential users. Considerable redesign and increased management efforts have addressed this problem in places such as Exxon Minipark in midtown Manhattan (Project for Public Spaces, 1984).

There is a clear need for a balance of users and activities in public spaces. It is possible to encourage diverse activities so that no one group dominates a space to the exclusion of others. The risk of diversity is that the individual needs and activities of the various users groups may collide unless skillful design and timing of uses and users help to provide sufficient space and resources. There is a real challenge to design spaces so that compatible diversity is possible. A major issue here is the claim over a public space by one user group to the exclusion of others. While claiming an area may enhance one group's experience of a setting, it also can restrict the freedom of other groups, as in the cases that have been cited. This issue of individual and group control is important to address.

A park designed in the early 1980s in Los Angeles's downtown "Skid Row," seems to have been successful in accommodating an array of alcoholics, derelicts, and transients in addition to local Latino families (Johnson, 1982). At least partially as a result of a participatory design process that involved potential users, derelicts sleeping on the grass were reported as coexisting with children playing. One by-product of the participatory design process was that some of the men who frequented the park were assisting with maintenance because "they feel proud of the park and their role in helping to design an important part of their environment" (p. 87).

Freedom of action, thus, is a product of conditions and designs that maximize people's freedom to engage in satisfying activities in public spaces while assured of freedom from disturbance, interference, or threats. It is a product of reasonable rules, adequate choices, opportunities for use, and designs that support the needs of users.

CLAIM

Claim to a space goes beyond access and freedom of action in stating a proprietary interest over space. In discussing the claims to a space, we will be suggesting that a degree of spatial *control* is sometimes necessary for people to achieve their goals in public spaces. By acknowledging this, we confront a significant dilemma: In claiming a space in order to fulfill its own needs, one group or individual may be restricting the freedom of others.

In considering the act of claiming – an individual or a group asserting control over a space – we are dealing with two frequently discussed behavioral science concepts: privacy and territoriality. Our perspective is that privacy and territoriality are not basic human needs or instincts, nor are they generally ends in themselves. Rather, these forms of spatial appropriation "seem always to be instrumental to the achievement of more primary goals" (Proshansky, Ittelson, & Rivlin, 1970, p. 180). Privacy and territoriality are "mechanisms" whereby people "can increase the range of options open to them and maximize their freedom of choice in the given situation" (Proshansky, Ittelson, & Rivlin, 1970, p. 180).

Individuals may wish to appropriate sections of a public setting for several different reasons. Alan Westin's (1967) distinction between four states of privacy – solitude, intimacy, anonymity, and reserve – suggests that there are a variety of reasons why an individual needs to control a setting. Two of these states are particularly relevant to urban public spaces. While it may be difficult to achieve genuine solitude in an urban space, anonymity – freedom from interaction and close observation within a public setting – is frequently sought. Such a state of privacy may be necessary for reflection, relaxation, or quiet activity. Another sort of privacy often sought in an urban public area is what Westin calls intimacy: engaging in close communication with another person or small group, activities that are visible in a range of places, including parks, plazas, and found spaces.

Washington Market Park in Lower Manhattan, New York City, has been successfully, if restrictively, managed by the community that claimed it as open space. (Mark Francis)

Research in public spaces suggests that both anonymity and intimacy can be facilitated by designs that incorporate small, well-differentiated subspaces and elements. For example, Love notes that Forecourt Fountain in Portland (see Chapter 4) can easily accommodate large numbers of people while affording a reasonable degree of privacy, due to the many "nooks, crannies, and stepped platforms" built into the fountain structure (Love, 1973, p. 199).

Individuals and small groups seeking privacy are frequently found in the section of a public setting that is farthest from the pedestrian flow and the direct observation of others. For example, a sunken platform at the base of a waterfall in Greenacre Park (see Chapter 4) – a visually and aurally separated section of the space – is the place most frequented by couples engaged in intimate conversation.

One value of control is that it provides evidence that someone cares for the place, that it belongs to someone, and that people, even nonusers, respect it and value its presence. In studies of community open spaces (Francis, Cashdan, & Paxson, 1984), the critical issue identified is the development of a sense of control, a sense of territoriality over a space that enhances its use and serves the local residents' needs. There are indications that nonusers of community-controlled spaces recognize and place value on the fact that the place is "cared for" by local residents (Francis, 1987b). However, there is a fine balance between territorial rights of the community or some members of the community, and the denial of the rights of others to use and enjoy a space.

The type of seating provided in a public space is a particularly important factor in facilitating spatial claims by an individual or intimate group. This is borne out by the comments of Cooper Marcus (1978b) concerning the "seating cubes" that then existed at Minneapolis's Crystal Court: "unlike the usual plaza benches, these seem like individual seats . . . you can lay claim to the whole cube, or you can share it with one or two others" (p. 38). Large decklike benches at San Francisco's Transamerica Redwood Park provided groups of users with an opportunity to claim and arrange space to fit their behavioral needs. Movable seating also facilitates the achievement of spatial control by individuals and small groups in urban parks and plazas. Research at Greenacre Park (Burden, 1977) indicated that the park's movable chairs and tables allowed individuals and small groups to be in very close proximity but to be physically aligned in a way that ensured an adequate degree of privacy. In contrast, in studies of a number of spaces, including Exxon Minipark and Seattle Bank Plaza (Project for Public Spaces, 1978) and Chicago First National Bank Plaza (Rutledge, 1976), it was found that fixed seating made it difficult for many users to engage in group conversations or find a secluded spot for themselves.

Movable chairs in the Metropolitan Museum plaza in New York City allow people
to claim their own space. (Stephen Carr)

Another form of claim can be found in community open spaces where
local people take over a vacant lot, developing it as a passive park or community garden, taking responsibility for the ongoing management or
stewardship of the land. These community-controlled projects have become permanent parts of the open spaces of neighborhoods, forming an
alternative park system designed, built, managed, and owned by those
who use them. An example of this kind of project is Barretto Street Neighborhood Park in the South Bronx. Numerous technical assistance organizations have been started to provide needed horticultural, design, or legal expertise for these efforts. A national one, the Trust for Public Land,
assists groups in becoming owners of their projects by forming a neighborhood land trust. Local control of neighborhood land is becoming an
important means toward providing recreational space across the country.

BARRETTO STREET NEIGHBORHOOD PARK
Bronx, New York

*Located at 636 Barretto Street, South Bronx; designed by Harry Dodson,
Landscape Architect, working with Bronx Frontier Development Corpora-*

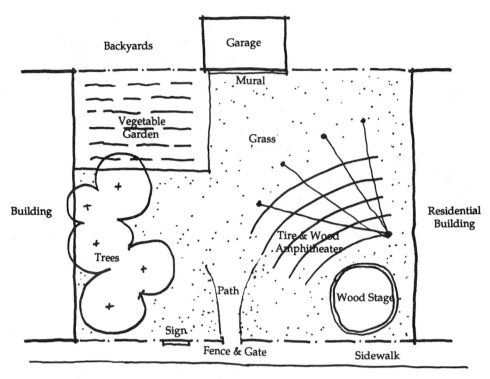

Site plan of Barretto Street Neighborhood Park, South Bronx, New York City.

tion and South Bronx Open Space Task Force; managed by Barretto Street Community Association Incorporated; completed in phases ending in 1980; size, about .3 acre.

In 1975, an abandoned building at 636 Barretto Street in the South Bronx burned and left a dangerous building and a lot filled with debris (Francis, Cashdan, & Paxson, 1984). Unfortunately, abandonment and rubble is not unusual in places like the South Bronx. The residents of Barretto Street decided not to sit back and allow their block to continue to deteriorate. In 1976, Joan Pipolo organized a group of seven people who agreed that something should be done. Together they convinced the Housing, Preservation and Development Department of the City of New York to demolish what was left of the abandoned building. In its place was a rubble-strewn lot, but succeeding in getting the building demolished was important for the group's spirit because "people felt they could accomplish things" by working together.

An initial group then organized in the neighborhood and later formed a larger group willing to help clean out the lot. They planned a carnival fundraising event to provide the money necessary to start a crime prevention program in the neighborhood. The local merchants had requested assistance in preventing crime in the area. For their local "block watch" scheme, they needed walkie-talkies with which to patrol the neighborhood. They raised $1,800 from the carnival and again felt a sense of pride in what they had done.

In the spring of 1976, a bulldozer arrived to clean off the rubbled lots. Later the group learned that the owner was planning to develop a parking lot for his oil trucks. Through collective action, the Barretto Street Block Association was successful in getting the zoning change required to deny a parking lot in a residential block.

During this time, a member of the block association suggested that the site be used for a community garden. When the other members in the group agreed that a garden was a good idea, they began developing plans. Several local organizations were contacted for assistance including the Bronx Frontier Development Corporation, which provides greening technical assistance to community groups in the Bronx.

Development of the garden park was started by local residents and summer youth workers during the summer of 1977. The final design included a vegetable garden, amphitheater and stage, cornucopia mural, and sitting area with trees. One and one-half years after the project was first initiated, the South Bronx Open Space Task Force was incorporated by the Bronx Frontier Development Corporation, People's Development Corporation, and Community School District 10 to assist in organizing and financing a total of fourteen open space projects including Barretto Street in the South Bronx (Fox & Huxley, 1978). The Task Force was established as the entity through which federal funding allocated by the Department of Interior could be channeled through the state and city Department of Parks to local groups

Entry to community-built Barretto Street Neighborhood Park in New York City during its early stage of development. (Trust for Public Land)

involved in developing community and small-scale neighborhood open space projects. The grant of $1.1 million was matched by the $1.1 million worth of sweat equity, donated compost, and in-kind services and approximately $100,000 of Community Development Block Grant monies provided by the city.

Barretto Street Park is part of a growing open space movement in cities across the United States and Europe, where residents are attempting to turn vacant urban land into community parks, playgrounds, and gardens (Francis, Cashdan, & Paxson, 1984). Several common features of these community-controlled open spaces can be seen in the Barretto Street Park. The site is owned by the residents, functioning as a land trust, so the group does not have to worry about the land being sold for development or some purpose other than open space use. The park is managed and maintained by residents. All park decisions are made by park users who govern the park, not by the city or outside professionals. The park is fenced, and a gate and lock restrict use to association members except during specific times when open to the public. The design changes and evolves to fit the changing needs of its users.

In 1990 and 1991 after twelve years of relative stability, the block association that owns and manages the garden suffered the loss of its two major leaders. The garden continues to be well maintained and actively used, but the leadership situation is unclear. The Trust for Public Land, which helped the Barretto residents acquire their garden and provides regular assistance with organizational issues, has met with key members including residents of a tenant-owned building across from the garden, and is optimistic that new leaders will emerge.

Despite the challenges inherent in management by volunteers, Barretto Street provides a unique approach to public open space design that is community generated and controlled. The tension between freedom and control is carefully balanced by residents and users.

Related cases: Grand Street Waterfront Park, Woonerf, Tranehytten Adventure Playground, People's Park, Village Homes Community Playground.

We have so far been discussing the appropriation of space by individuals or small groups attempting to achieve a degree of control in order to carry out desired activities. Individuals and small groups of friends or family members do not ordinarily appropriate more than a small piece of public space. In this sense, their attempts at control do not generally represent a threat to the freedom of the rest of the public to use the space. However, spaces are frequently appropriated by larger groups. Such groups may transform a public setting into a kind of "home territory" (Lyman & Scott, 1972), where rights to access and use by members of other groups may be limited. For example, Linday (1977) reports that the area around Bethesda Fountain, a landmark of New York's Central Park, was appropriated by Hispanic teenagers and young adults during the early 1970s. The intense activities and music of this group apparently established their

Young men claim the balustrade in New York City's Bryant Park. (Stephen Carr)

"claim" to this area, discouraging use by most other members of the public. Another example is the section of the beach at Riis Park in New York that is used largely by homosexuals. Over the years this group has converged on the area, giving it a distinctive quality. The construction of "casitas," small structures that function as clubhouses, represents a form of appropriation and control exerted by Hispanic males. Built on empty lots and other found spaces in East Harlem, the Lower East Side of Manhattan, Brooklyn, and the Bronx, they serve as gathering places for members.

Although claims by one segment of the population may limit the freedom of other groups, it is important to recognize that such spatial control also may be necessary in order for the claiming group to achieve its own goals. For example, youths from particular age or culture groups may view the presence of a critical mass of their peers, engaged in particular activities, as essential to the creation of the atmosphere that is sought.

Sometimes areas are subject to time sharing, with different groups claiming the space and establishing their territories at different hours. A playground used by young children and their parents during the day may become a teen hangout at night. The commercial street filled with business people on weekdays may be a shopping promenade on weekends. Groups with different needs, norms, and paces may use time rather than space as a means of separating activities that might collide or create conflict. An example of the way a public space can accommodate different

Old men gathering to talk at the Bergen Fishmarket, Norway. (Mark Francis)

users and activities at different times can be seen by observing the cycle of activities that take place at the Bergen Fish Market, an open area along the central waterfront in this Norwegian city. In the morning the market is filled with fish vendors and people buying fresh fish. Elderly people gather in small groups discussing politics and local gossip. In midafternoon, the vendors pack up, leaving the place empty and deserted, except for occasional tourists, during the dinner hours. In early evening a truck selling hot dogs pulls up into the center of the space followed by teenagers parking and displaying their cars, many of them vintage American models, and making the space a crowded hang-out. In some cases the presence of other groups, however physically separate they may be, discourages users who require exclusivity in a setting.

R. G. Lee (1972) suggests that middle-income people possess norms and expectations about control of outdoor space that are frequently different from those of lower income people. The values of middle-income groups, coupled with the frequency of home ownership among these groups, leads to a "mode of belonging" to places, which he calls "belonging through possession" (p. 75). These people rely on formalized rules of ownership, viewing spaces that are not owned by private parties as belonging to everyone and thus not available for appropriation by any single group. In addition, Lee claims that middle-income people tend to believe in "formal modes of social control." An idealized type of public morality is expected, which coincides with the expectations of the law and its enforcers. The result is that middle-income people expect parks and other public spaces to be "free" spaces, open to all and not the special province or concern of any particular segment of the public.

In contrast, according to Lee, among lower-income groups the feeling of "belonging" or "at homeness" in any public place is based on knowledge of the place and its inhabitants. The formal ownership of a place, whether it is public or private is less an issue. In addition, formal modes of social control are less subscribed to; people are expected to watch out for their own interests, and little reliance is placed on outside agents of control, such as police. The result is that, among lower-income groups, the expectation is often that public spaces such as parks (or parts of them) are the province or "territory" of a particular ethnic, age, or other group. Such appropriation is viewed as acceptable and even necessary. It is felt that people can only use a space freely and consistently if they are among others whose behavior is familiar and predictable.

If there is a strong fear that a particular group will take over a space, the predominant group or the space managers may deny access or comforts to that group. This is found in some small towns, such as those in the Sacramento Valley in California that have significant numbers of migrant workers. By not placing benches in their downtown spaces, these towns discourage such groups from hanging out.

One additional factor contributing to this class-based pattern of open space use is the experience of being a low-income person. The inability to own property and the necessity to live in rented, often small apartments combine to reinforce the need to use public spaces for recreation and socialization. Although middle-class people may, in fact, rely on formal ownership rules, they do so because it is an extension of their economic status and social norms, a result of socialization to these values. They have many available places open to them by virtue of their ability to pay. The limited buying power of the poor makes it necessary for them to rely on public spaces because other alternatives do not exist, and they use these spaces for many more functions than do middle-class persons. Broad and frequent uses are likely to create personal attachments between people and places, hence the "at homeness" of the working-class people that Lee describes and the reliance on informal rather than formal modes of control.

These claims to a space by particular groups may be necessary in order for them to act freely and comfortably in the space. Claims also may promote feelings of concern for the place and identification with it that are positive and worth fostering. The challenge is to recognize where this form of spatial control is necessary and even desirable and where it unduly restricts the freedom of other groups.

Public space management and policy can be very significant in promoting group claims where they are deemed beneficial while limiting or tempering them where they clearly restrict the freedom of others. Park officials in cities such as New York are attempting to encourage local residents to take a greater concern for their neighborhood parks by forming "Friends of the Park" groups (Francis, Cashdan, & Paxson, 1984). In a sense, such efforts are aimed at encouraging claims to an area, without sanctioning the exclusion of other people and without granting local groups the right to modify, own, or dispose of the space. One interesting finding, from a study by Perla Korosec-Serfaty (1982), is that strict local regulations and highly formal municipal management of a public square resulted in limited concern and identification with the square on the part of local residents. This contrasts with a square that was less controlled by local government and showed numerous signs of claims by local residents.

Both design and management policies can help or hinder control. In some cases the best solution may be no management. However, in other cases the presence of management expands the opportunities for groups and individuals, as in the vest-pocket parks.

One group that has been frequently denied its claim to public spaces is homeless people. Whereas some cities ignore their presence, others sweep them out of the public arena, ostensibly for their own protection. For many homeless persons the public space is far safer and more comfortable than the enormous congregate shelters provided for them, yet they often are not welcome as users.

In cases where the claims to a site by one group seriously restrict the freedom of others, management may need to intervene. An important means of doing this is through programming of activities that appeal to a variety of people. Managers of many urban parks and plazas have used this approach on a "special event" basis, programming events a few times each year (Project for Public Spaces, 1984). Although the intent may be to alter public perceptions of the site through well-publicized occurrences, the net result is generally that the user population is only transformed on the event days. A more useful programming strategy is that of much more frequent activities and events that are modest in scale (single performers or small groups) but diverse in appeal, a shifting schedule of singers, mimes, dancers, and musicians.

In some cases, the presence of site managers or guards may be necessary to promote the free and comfortable use of a space. In a study of a Chicago neighborhood where interethnic tensions were high, Gerald Suttles (1968, p. 56) noted that successful recreational events involving members of different groups can occur only "if street workers and policemen are present to keep the peace."

Whether through programming or active supervision, the managers of public spaces are capable of encouraging use by a diversity of people. Linday (1977) suggests that when managers abdicate their responsibility by failing to play any kind of "host" role, claims to a site by a particular group are especially likely to happen.

The design and planning of public space can also play a role with respect to the claims of groups. One important function that physical design can serve is to allow different groups to coexist in a public area through provision of subspaces. In some cases, this may require an ample amount of space, such as that provided by a large meadow or beach so that different groups can each take over their own section. Regular users of two large New York beaches, Jones Beach and Riis Park, are well aware that particular sections of these beaches are frequented by different groups based on life-style, age, ethnicity, and sexual preferences. In other cases this would require the inclusion of bounded and qualitatively different subspaces within a setting.

We have indicated that individuals and groups frequently claim spaces in order to carry out desired activities or achieve a desired state. In some cases, the type of control or regulation of a space involved in claims may not be sufficient to enable users to achieve their goals. Some sort of changes to the site may be necessary.

CHANGE

Change is an important dimension of successful public spaces. The ability of a place to evolve and change over time is an important quality of good environments (Lynch, 1972b). A large-scale example is the neighborhoods of San Francisco, which Vernez-Moudon (1986) has shown to have been able to change over time. This has allowed residents to develop an enduring image of their area's physical and social qualities.

Change has a complex meaning because it can occur in many different ways. Elements may be added both temporarily and permanently. People may bring decorations, picnic tables, or badminton nets to a site to alter its appearance and functions. But once their visit ends, the "loose parts" (Nicholson, 1971) are removed. At other times changes may be more permanent as in the cases of graffiti, community murals, or participatory projects such as the reconstruction of a playground (R. Moore, 1978).

When we consider the issue of change, it is essential to determine the degree to which a site is modifiable or adaptable. Two important questions are suggested by Lynch (1981, p. 171). First, how manipulable is the site? How difficult is it to alter? Second, how reversible are the changes once they are made? How difficult and costly is it to return the site to its original state? In a sense, manipulability refers to the freedom of present users: Can they alter the setting to fulfill their purposes? Reversibility relates to the freedom of future users: Can they undo changes made by earlier users or have these changes been forced upon them?

An elementary example of change, referred to earlier, is the manipulation of movable tables and chairs in increasing numbers of sites such as downtown plazas across the country. Movable furniture allows users to go into the sun or shade and can facilitate either conversation or anonymity. Whyte (1980) suggests that even in a crowded area where there is little room to move, the ability to change the position of a chair even a few inches expresses respect for the privacy of adjacent users.

The moving of chairs and tables is a small, highly reversible modification; the furniture is generally returned to its original location at the end of each day. Another easily reversible change is exemplified by the per-

The opportunity to change a place to suit one's needs is rare in U.S. public space. Children building a play horse in a playground in Davis, California. (Mark Francis)

sonal memorials placed at the base and on the face of the Vietnam Veterans Memorial in lower Manhattan and also at the Vietnam Veterans Memorial in Washington, D.C. (see Chapter 6). The Manhattan memorial, consisting of opaque glass inscribed with writings, including diary selections and letters home, from soldiers fighting in Vietnam, has become a magnet for poems, tributes, political statements, and religious objects dedicated to individual veterans or involving the war experience. A similar phenomenon occurs at the Vietnam Memorial in Washington, D.C., although the more somber form of that memorial (consisting of the names of veterans who died in Vietnam, etched into black granite) brings forth a more limited array of objects.

Making a personal statement or dedication by adding something to the public environment is most commonly seen in graffiti. Despite the unattractive quality of much graffiti, well-placed, carefully conceived graffiti murals (both sanctioned and unsanctioned) add a sense of place and distinctiveness to many otherwise anonymous city playgrounds. It seems that other opportunities for users to constructively make their marks, either transient or permanent ones, on an open space are largely unexplored. One marvels at the intricate, still-visible carvings left by medieval prisoners at the Tower of London, but there are few visual examples of personal expression in the contemporary environment. A more substantial type of user modification of a public space would involve altering the physical form of the space. Such an alteration might, in turn, affect the type of activities that could be carried out in the setting.

An adventure playground is an example of a public space where extensive manipulation by users is permitted and often encouraged. Spivack (1969, p. 292) provides a rationale for the adventure playground: "Neighborhood play areas probably require the greatest setting adaptability of any designed environment anywhere. And manipulability of the environment appears to be the essential property for play behavior that is fluid, changing and unpredictable." Because of the simple materials, obtained at little or no expense, fairly large numbers of children can participate in building and altering their play environment. Also, whatever built forms emerge can be simply undone. At some adventure playgrounds observed in London, participants literally burn down old constructions in a ritualistic bonfire, in order to start anew.

TRANEHYTTEN ADVENTURE PLAYGROUND
Copenhagen, Denmark

Located at Tranevaegate 50A, Glostrup, Ballerup-Molov, suburb of Copenhagen; managed by Ballerup City Government; completed in 1968; size, approximately 2 acres.

A short train ride from downtown Copenhagen is Ballerup, a new town built after World War II to provide needed housing for Copenhagen. Walking from the Ballerup train station, one notices uniform three- and four-story housing blocks surrounded by manicured landscaping and designed playgrounds. Hidden behind a tall hedge and fence between two housing areas, the Tranehytten adventure playground (the translation from Danish is "children building playground") is a pleasant relief to the ordered Danish neighborhood landscape. Children are free here, with adult supervision and assistance, to build their own houses and manage their own playground.

Adventure playgrounds have been the subject of much interest in Europe and the United States (Sorenson, Larsson, & Ledet, 1973). Several countries such as Denmark (Scharnberg, 1973) and England (Lady Allen of Hurtwood, 1968) have developed ambitious publicly funded adventure playground programs.They are seen by parents, officials, and designers as an alternative to fixed traditional playgrounds, which allow little child manipulation or control. Reportedly discovered by a Danish landscape architect who found his traditional playground to be more heavily used during the construction phase than after completion, the children's building concept has emerged as a successful way to encourage child manipulation of the landscape (Hart, 1974; Ward, 1978).

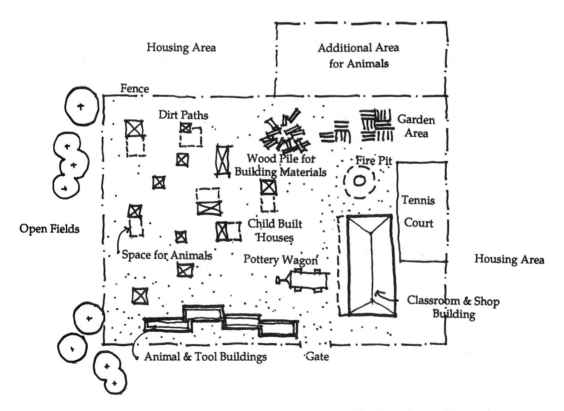

Site plan of Tranehytten Adventure Playground outside Copenhagen, Denmark.

Tranehytten is an example of how this concept has become a permanent public place for children in many Danish neighborhoods. The playground is run very much like a school with fixed hours and paid teachers. Children enter the two-acre playground from one gate passing a new building that serves as a day care center, classroom, and shop. Most of the site is devoted to a play yard where children build, remodel, and tear down houses. Also included in the play yard is a common area for animals such as the playground horse, rabbits, and pigs. Animals are an important part of the Danish playgrounds providing a unique opportunity for city children to interact and care for them on a daily basis. A pottery studio, tool room, and even a tennis court are resources in this diverse playground.

Children's manipulation and building in Tranehytten occurs in structured ways. First, the child must become a member of the playground, paying a fee of thirty-five crowns (about four dollars) a month. For example, in 1973 there were 138 children enrolled as members with a waiting list of about 250 (Sorensen, Larsson, & Ledet, 1973). A child needs to take a carpentry class from one of six paid play leaders. After gaining basic building skills, children are free to apply their skills to remodel or build on one of approximately thirty building sites in the playground. There is a complex system of passing building sites from child to child and generation to generation. Unlike the English adventure playgrounds, which are rebuilt annually, the houses remain year after year going through many phases of reconstruction and transformation. Off to an edge of the playground is a large pile of scrap wood, which becomes the building materials used by children. When a house is torn down, old wood is burned in a central fire pit. Extra space is set aside for garden plots, which are tended by members of the playground. Children are provided numerous opportunities to manipulate and control many types of natural elements including animals, fire, plants, and wood.

One of the earliest and most comprehensive surveys of adventure playgrounds, by Clare Cooper (1970), discusses the reasons why this concept has been slow to be adopted in the United States. Issues such as the "junky" character of child-built playgrounds, safety concerns of parents, and requirements for adult supervision are barriers to the acceptance of this concept in the United States. There has been a small but active group of people in the United States and Canada who have been involved in developing adventure playgrounds and evaluating their effects (cf. *Childhood City Newsletter*, now published as *Children's Environments Quarterly*). A review of adventure playgrounds in the United States (Vance, 1982) found them in seven states, with Illinois, Wisconsin, and California being the most active. Current examples in California include the Berkeley Adventure-Playground located next to the Berkeley marina; the Huntington Beach Adventure Playground sited in an old sand and gravel quarry; and Irvine, where park officials have dug a two and one-half acre pit in an existing public park to create an adventure play area.

The concept has not caught on in the United States due to continued resistance from parks officials, parents, and designers. A combination of concern over the appearance and the current liability climate have discouraged their development. Attempts have combined some of the elements of

Fire pit with child-built houses at Tranehytten Adventure Playground, Copenhagen. (Mark Francis)

traditional playgrounds with child-built playgrounds to satisfy the desires of both parents and children (Francis, 1988b). Child building and manipulation of the landscape is now recognized as an important part of childhood. Adventure playgrounds, such as Tranehytten in Copenhagen, provide a successful design model for public design that allows for both freedom and control.

Related cases: Lovejoy and Forecourt Fountains, Village Homes Community Playground.

Some of the most common examples of user change to public places involve large, relatively undifferentiated spaces. In what Seamon and Nordin (1980) call "place ballet," public spaces can allow their users to continually add and take back elements that facilitate desired activities. For example, in the large meadows in New York's Central and Prospect parks users frequently can be seen setting up large barbecues, hammocks, volleyball nets, and tents to accommodate their needs. The "Mudflats" on the Berkeley waterfront is a setting for handcrafted signs and sculptures, which change weekly. Similarly, many of Italy's squares and the open plazas in both Italy and Mexico experience regular modification by their users, in the service of diverse activities.

Although open, unarticulated spaces often allow for user changes and a diversity of activities, such spaces are not always appropriate. This is particularly the case in downtown areas where plazas offering a variety of seating options and other amenities are frequently most successful. Downtown plazas that are largely open and unarticulated are often "mere concourses for random pedestrian movement" (Joardar & Neill, 1978, p. 489). Equally problematical are plazas or other open spaces that are overdesigned, providing built-in supports for every activity imagined at the time they were designed. While unarticulated spaces may be devoid of interest, overdesign may eliminate the opportunities for modification and personal use, a quality important to satisfying users' public space rights.

Public spaces also can be altered for special occasions, events, or celebrations. Plazas in several Italian cities are transformed periodically for horse racing or soccer matches. For these events bleachers are created and new surfaces may be added – a significantly different type of space is created. In American cities, streets and parks are periodically used for street fairs, block parties, or exhibitions. The street in front of the New York Public Library regularly accommodates a grandstand for viewing parades, set up for the occasion. These periodic changes generally are organized and carried out by policy makers and space managers as opposed to users, although there are some exceptions. The alterations to the ordinary state of a public setting facilitate new activities and transform users' perceptions of the site. Indeed, transformations implemented by officials and managers may encourage ordinary users to see the potential for carrying out their own modifications of a space. In Prospect Park in Brooklyn, many different kinds of "official" changes including fishing contests in the lake, concerts, activities sponsored by the Park Rangers and the Friends of the Park, as well as some renovation and rebuilding of structures and monuments have instilled an active image of the place. The heightened activity

In many modest urban neighborhoods the sense of home can be extended into the street. A block party in Queens, New York. (Mark Francis)

is reflected in what users are doing too, with more picnicking evident than in past years and badminton and volleyball nets set up along with tents and creative shelters built out of blankets and branches.

Programming activities has been discovered by space managers as one of the most effective ways to add activity to public spaces. Many downtown malls now have management organizations that direct changes and program activities and events in the space. An example is the Memphis Mall, advertised as the longest in the United States, which was extensively remodeled in the mid 1970s to accommodate increased activity programming.

However, it may be the case that when users are involved in the development of a space, they are most likely to see opportunities for changes. Based on their study of locally developed open spaces, Francis, Cashdan, and Paxson (1984) found that designs for community-developed projects were constantly evolving and changing to fit the needs of the groups. A garden plot one year became a sitting area the next. The group decided a shelter was needed and a shed was erected. Furthermore, the authors concluded that when community groups own their sites, they are more likely to consider making changes a regular feature of the site.

OWNERSHIP AND DISPOSITION

All truly public space is, in fact, owned by the public even though the control implied may not be exercised. Disposition of a site may be the ultimate right of possession. It is implicit in our society's definition of ownership, which offers owners the permanent right to do with a property as they see fit (albeit with limits defined by building codes and zoning restriction). However, legal ownership is actually "a bundle of rights." Owners may sell or be legally obliged to forfeit development rights, mineral rights, and various rights of use. In these cases, the right of disposition is retained but may involve little more than the right to sell or transfer legal ownership.

In many cases, the right of disposition represents a form of ultimate control, encompassing and transcending the rights inherent in access, action, claim, and change. In dense urban neighborhoods, the owners of large apartment buildings may deny public access to spaces that frequently represent a large proportion of the available local open space. Municipal parks departments, often without public input, close off large sections of their facilities for long periods of time to do renovation. Office building owners frequently restrict public access to ground-level plazas, or close these plazas entirely during certain times of the year. This practice is particularly controversial in cases where the public plazas were included in exchange for a variance or bonus allowing for greater building height or bulk.

———

GRACE PLAZA
New York, New York

Located at corner of Avenue of the Americas and Forty-third Street, Manhattan, adjacent to the Grace Building; designed by Skidmore, Owings and Merrill, Architects; managed by Swig-Weiler and Arnow; completed in 1973; size, 20,000 square feet.

Grace Plaza was developed as part of incentive zoning, the system of bonuses given to developers when they provided public space in Manhattan in the 1960s and 1970s. This zoning system allowed builders of new corporate offices an additional ten square feet of floor area for every square foot of plaza (Whyte, 1980). The 1961 resolution generated a series of urban plazas, and an amendment in 1975 specified guidelines for making them "amenable" to the public (Whyte, 1980). There was also provision for the leasing of space for commercial activities.

Grace Plaza initially was leased by the Grace Company, a major tenant in the building. The Grace Corporation has relocated its operations to another state but the name remains until new tenants arrive. Grace sponsored a student competition to redesign the plaza from its original, bare design, with a single bench and tree. However, the ideas were not directly used in the final designs, which included a simple combination of two rows of trees raised in pots and a series of benches. On the southern boundary along a wall shared with the building next door is a long row of benches. A liquid plastic kinetic sculpture box was installed in 1980, and was removed a few years later. The plaza serves as the official entrance to the building at 1114 Avenue of the Americas (originally, and still unofficially, known as Sixth Avenue). It also has an entry to the underground garage. Under the plaza is space rented to the Graduate School and University Center of the City University of New York for its library. Because this space is occupied, there are limitations to the development of the plaza. Since the waterproof membrane beneath the surface of the open space cannot be penetrated, potential leakages constrain what can be done on the site.

Information on this case is based in part on a design analysis of the plaza undertaken in 1980 – by some students and faculty of the Environmental Psychology Program at the Graduate School of the City University of New York, as well as periodic updates by them. As neighbors, the group had been observing the site for some time. The assessment provided an opportunity to do systematic observations and examine other studies of the site, including an analysis in conjunction with a study of Bryant Park (Nager & Wentworth, 1976), and one by the Project for Public Spaces (1979).

Grace Plaza is a good example of the difficulties faced by many urban open spaces, especially those in the incentive zoning category. Because these plazas grow out of developers' desires to increase commercial space in adjacent structures, rather than user needs, they often end up with unexpected users, serious problems, and questions regarding their appropriateness.

From the time of its dedication in March 1974 to today, Grace Plaza has been the subject of serious questioning. In the beginning, the criticism was

Grace Plaza in New York City is an urban void. The plaza has remained unchanged since this photo was taken in 1979, but at times the security guard has a trained guard dog. (Mark Francis)

directed toward the bareness of the site and the absence of any features that might attract users. A large expanse relieved only by some trees and benches for most of its life, the changes made over time merely rearranged the vegetation and seating, adding some additional trees and benches as well as the liquid plastic sculpture. It has been considered by architectural critics such as Paul Goldberger of the *New York Times* as one of the less successful plazas in New York City.

Qualities of the site appeared to repel local office workers but attract a small group of "undesirables." Among these users were "spillovers" from nearby Bryant Park, after efforts were made to "clean up" and renovate that area. The plaza management complained of some incidents involving violence and, despite an attempt to attract people through occasional summer concerts, the plaza continued to be dominated by one user group to the exclusion of others.

The solution, in the summer of 1981, was the construction of a six-foot high spiked iron fence, open at both ends. The explanation offered at the time it was put up was that it offered protection from the debris of the adjoining building that was being extensively renovated. The fence violated the city's zoning laws, and, after being in place for less than one year, was finally removed the following June.

After observing the site, the study group found limited use, lack of variety in the users, and little that would attract people to the plaza. The windy, sunless corner was comfortable only during hot days when people might be searching out a shady spot. But even then, few users could be found, other than people walking through the plaza and "street people" who were there selling drugs or "hanging out."

Clearly this site lacks a strong purpose apart from summer concerts, and offers little control for the casual user. It has been described as having low "activity versatility" (Nager & Wentworth, 1976). Its limited resources are useful only for a narrow range of functions: the passive activities of people-watching along Forty-third Street and the Avenue of the Americas and the possibility of finding shade from the sun. In winter, the winds and absence of sun and shelter make the site difficult for all but the most hardy. In fact, the tiny section of the corner of Forty-third Street that does have direct sun is the one place in which people other than pedestrians can be found. Beyond that there is nothing – no vendors, no shops, no comfort or interest. The liquid plastic sculpture that was put up may have been of some interest the first time it was seen, but the general reaction to it was less than enthusiastic. It was not a sufficiently strong element to attract more than a few passersby.

One of the recommendations of the design analysis group was that a redesign include amenities that would be useful to the local office workers – shops or kiosks that would provide food, books, clothing, flowers, fruit, newspapers, and the like, all of which were difficult to obtain in the area. To make the plaza even more attractive, it was suggested that a strong element be integrated into the design, one that would not only add to the color and interest of the place but be useful to people as well. The incorporation of a giant mosaic map of Manhattan into the ground or wall was offered as one possibility, although there were many other alternatives. This design feature would add to the distinctiveness or imageability of the plaza, giving a focal point now sorely lacking (Nager & Wentworth, 1976). It was anticipated that with a reason to use the plaza, people might be drawn there, mitigating the effects of the single kind of users presently thought to repel the broader group.

Plans were developed by the plaza management to enclose the space and create a shopping arcade. This proposal attracted a public debate over the potential privatization of the publicness of the space. The further development of this proposal would also require a variance from the zoning codes. The project has now been abandoned.

The domination of a site by people considered "undesirables" by the management, and perhaps by potential users, raises the issue of control. Access is a fundamental requisite of a public place and its restriction either by a particular user group or by management is a violation of this right. We would argue for a mix of people in a site, with designs that encourage a mosaic of people, each satisfying their own needs without violating those of others. Similarly, the responsibilities of management must be evaluated against its violation of the public's rights, and the Grace Plaza fence was one such violation. Interestingly, the fence moved the "undesirables" to the outer edge of the plaza where they perched on the street side of the barrier. The later addition of a security guard who patrolled the site with a dog during mild weather broadened the range of users and removed much of the drug dealing, at least during the day.

The problems of control in this plaza mirror the experiences of many other cities. It is especially true of urban areas where there is a social, ethnic, and economic mix, and the interests of people differ. In a large park people can find their own places and activities can vary without necessarily colliding. However, in a small site such as Grace Plaza, it is critical that the place itself support the users in their efforts to sit peacefully alone, to mingle, to find comfort, or to enjoy something of interest. In this, it has largely failed.

Related cases: Boston City Hall Plaza, Bryant Park, Plaza of the Centre Georges Pompidou, Freedom Plaza, Pershing Park, Entrance Plazas – Lowell Heritage State Park.

Some of the traditional forms of ownership enable the owner to retain absolute control, for the good of a small group (office building executives and employees, apartment building residents) or the general public (park users who will eventually enjoy an improved renovated facility). These lockable parks leave little doubt regarding freedom of access and reflect the ultimate rights of ownership. An example of corporate controlled ownership is Transamerica's Redwood Park, a "lockable park" in San Francisco that is open to the public during the day and closed off during the evening.

Recently, another form of ownership has become prominent: community ownership of open space. Ownership of a site by local residents has been found to be associated with greater responsiveness to community needs, lower maintenance costs, less vandalism, and frequent modification and changes when compared with other open spaces (Francis, 1989b; Francis, Cashdan, & Paxson, 1984).

There are several distinct types of control associated with community ownership. The first type limits access and use to a small group of community residents. One prototype for this is New York's Gramercy Park, where only tenants of the apartment buildings that surround it have keys to enter, and others can only gaze into the park from outside. Some recently developed community-owned gardens have followed this model. Examples in New York are the Jefferson Market Garden in Greenwich Village and the Clinton Garden in the Clinton neighborhood, which has several hundred keys checked out to residents who use the garden.

Wykoff Bond Garden is a community-built and owned open space created upon a former rubble-filled lot in Brooklyn, New York. (Mark Francis)

A second type of control exists in the case of numerous community-owned gardens and parks that are open to the public when a member of the community is present on the site, but are fenced off and closed at other times. In these cases, any limitation on access is usually due to the fear of vandalism or the fragility of the sites.

A third category covers a number of community-owned sites that are totally open to the public at all hours. Examples of this are Grand Street Waterfront Park (see chapter 4) and a large section of the Westside Community Garden, both in New York City. Community control thus has many dimensions and its application to public spaces can be made in diverse ways.

There is a strong link between change and ownership. If we acknowledge that people own a public space, they have the right to make changes when the site no longer meets their needs. This can be compared with the right to change elected representatives when they no longer serve the public, or the ultimate right of revolution, even in a democracy, when rulers become intolerable and resist relinquishing their power. In a milder form, the many "friends of" organizations, the advocates for particular public spaces, have successfully lobbied for changes and then controlled the renovations to central parks.

Although it may be easier to obtain this form of political activism for large parks and local neighborhood spaces, many other kinds of public places fall between the cracks, however much they require changes. This suggests the need for increased consciousness on the part of users and a new structure in the interests of these places. With greater concern by public space advocates and the media, efforts toward change may extend to a broader range of settings than presently exists.

BOSTON COMMON AND THE PUBLIC GARDEN
Boston, Massachusetts

Located between Boylston, Tremont, Arlington and Beacon streets; managed by Boston Parks Department.

Side by side in the center of the city, yet established nearly two centuries apart, the Boston Common and the Public Garden have each played important, yet distinctly different roles in the life of the city. Whereas the Boston Common, long associated with ideals of civic and political freedom, continues to be the city's most popular site for political protests, the Public Garden has remained the grande dame of public open spaces in Boston – a quiet, elegant oasis in the middle of the city. Despite Boston's vast transformation, the parks have maintained a symbolic and historic significance that has proved to be critical in establishing the limits of freedom and control under which each is used, managed, and maintained.

The Boston Public Garden with its famous swan boats. (Elizabeth March)

Established in 1640 by colonial decree, the Boston Common originally served as a military training ground and common grazing field. Later, as the city began to develop and the land was no longer appropriate for grazing, the Common became the site of a number of important historic events and civic celebrations, each of which added to its symbolic significance. As Walter Firey pointed out in *Land Use in Central Boston* (1968), this significance eventually transcended the actual events and came to be associated not with the British encampment or the celebration of Cornwallis's surrender, but instead with more generalized sentiments of nationhood and civic freedom.

The Common has remained the most public of the city's public open spaces. Citizens feel that their right to gather and express their opinions there is historically sanctioned and the Common lends symbolic significance to almost any demonstration. Its openness and accessibility to the street also provide a sense of comfort and safety to those who choose to participate.

However, as Boston society has become increasingly diverse, there are those for whom the Common has little symbolic significance. For these people its value lies not in its history but in the facilities and opportunities it affords today. Increasingly, the Common has come to be used for a variety of activities – both legal and illegal – that many consider inappropriate to its historic character and detrimental to its long-term health. Of particular concern are activities such as vandalism, drug dealing, and sidewalk gambling that affect the public's perception of safety in the park. Many people view these activities and the presence of "undesirables" as limitations on their right to use the park safely, comfortably, and for its intended use.

The Common is subject to significantly less control than its well-manicured neighbor, the Public Garden, and its often shabby condition is at least partially a reflection of the wider variety of users it attracts and the broader range of activities and behaviors it permits. Although park regulations clearly define inappropriate activities, the police are often unable or unwilling to concern themselves with what they view as minor infractions of the law.

The bandstand is a focal point for large gatherings in the Boston Common. (Elizabeth March)

Unfortunately, it can be difficult to achieve a satisfactory balance between the public's freedom to use a space and the necessity of imposing certain limitations and controls. It raises such questions as who should pay the cost of damages that large gatherings on the Common can cause. In recent years, the city began requiring a deposit that could be withheld if a gathering caused significant damage or undue litter. Although the legality of this has been successfully challenged in court, most groups still comply with the request. While there is a growing sense that the public must begin to share the responsibility of controlling and maintaining public open space, the Common's history and symbolic significance demand that the city take particular care to safeguard and advocate its citizens' historically sanctioned freedoms.

In contrast to the Common, the significance of the Public Garden is dependent on maintaining a high degree of control. Established in 1838, Boston's Public Garden was the nation's first public botanic garden. Today, with its ancient trees and seasonal flower displays, the Public Garden is one of the city's most elegant and well-maintained public open spaces. Although the Public Garden, like the Common, is managed by the city's Department of Parks and Recreation, the Friends of the Public Garden, a private, nonprofit citizens group, has been working closely with the city in maintaining and upgrading the park since the early 1970s. Interested in preserving the garden as "a place of quiet beauty, free from encroachment and exploitation," the organization has initiated a number of fund-raising events and has acted as horticultural consultants to the city. Maintaining the original character and intent of the Public Garden clearly requires limiting certain activities, particularly as funds for maintenance are cut back.

The Public Garden displays a number of messages, both implicit and explicit, about the types of behavior considered appropriate. Posted at the main entrance is a list of rules: no bike riding; no roller skating; no playing in the water; no dogs, no frisbees; and no walking on the grass where designated. The rules, however, can be read not only at the entrance but in the design and maintenance of the park, as well. Set off behind a wrought iron fence, the Garden's formal design and high level of maintenance are strong indications that certain activities, such as touch football, would not be appropriate. An equally important means of control is the behavior of the majority of visitors who choose to follow most of the rules. Of course, not everyone does. People frequently sit on the lawns (their well-maintained condition makes them an almost impossible temptation to resist), climb the trees, play in the water, or curl up for a nap on a bench. As in the Common, the police do little to enforce the regulations.

Minor though the infractions may seem, they are of great concern to the Friends of the Public Garden who see the damaging effect to plant materials and to the public's perception of comfort and safety in the Garden. Although they are not interested in controlling who enters the Garden, they are concerned with limiting the activities that occur there. Their goal is both to maintain the Public Garden as an important historic resource and to preserve the public's freedom to enjoy it for its intended use. Following the successful example of the Central Park Conservancy, the Friends of the Public Garden are raising funds to hire urban park rangers for both the Common and the Public Garden. It is felt that rangers could provide the consistent and concerned, but quite different, levels of surveillance that each of the parks requires.

While it is important to understand the capacity of a public space to withstand certain types of use and to assess correctly the funds and personnel available for maintenance, the examples of the Public Garden and the Boston Common clearly demonstrate the need to understand a site's symbolic and historic significance as well as changing conditions when analyzing and assessing the balance between freedom and control.

Related cases: Central Park, Bryant Park.

SUMMARY

The term public open space implies the freedom to use a place, but there are numerous constraints that prohibit or discourage members of the public from exercising their rights. We have identified a number of qualities essential to the promotion of these rights. Freedom of *access* is a basic requirement and physical, visual, and symbolic barriers can limit the availability of public settings. Freedom of *action,* the right to use a place, also is necessary, but it calls for a reconciliation among competing interests, rules, and regulations. The right includes both freedom from disturbance and interference and freedom to use a place in a desired manner. *Claim* represents the right of an individual or a group to appropriate spaces for personal use. In some cases the claim is made by a community retrieving spaces for its own needs. In other instances claims can be made for shared spaces that require a balance between the appropriation by one person or group and the rights of the remainder of users. The freedom to *change* settings, to add, remove, or alter elements either temporarily or permanently represents a way of making personal statements about a place with *ownership* and *disposition* the ultimate exercise of rights. But freedom and control are unevenly distributed, partly by cultural restrictions, partly by design and management policies. Understanding how and why people are excluded and the conditions under which public space users assume control is an important first step toward facilitating public space rights.

PUBLIC SPACE MEANINGS
AND CONNECTIONS

Reflecting on his influential book *Image of the City* (1963) some twenty years after its publication, Kevin Lynch (1984) offered a critique of his research and the methods that had been used. In hindsight he was uneasy with the emphasis that he had given the physical attributes of places: "the original study set the meaning of places aside and dealt only with their identity and their structuring into larger wholes. It did not succeed, of course. Meaning always crept in, in every sketch and comment. People could not help connecting their surroundings with the rest of their lives" (p. 158).

THE SIGNIFICANCE OF MEANING AND CONNECTIONS

People need links to the world, and some are provided by the spaces they inhabit and the activities occurring within these spaces. Public space experiences yield meanings that accrue over time, and if these are positive meanings they will lead to connections that go beyond the immediate experience of a setting (Appleyard, 1979; Rapoport, 1982). Links are established between that place and the life of an individual, links to a valued group, to a whole culture and its history, economics, and politics, or symbolically to the universe or other worlds through a person's biological and psychological reality, through nature, through growth, through sexuality. In discussing this level of place meaning, Lynch (1981, p. 142) states that "A good place is one which, in some way appropriate to the person and her culture, makes her aware of her community, her past, the web of life, and the universe of time and space in which these are contained."

For a space to become meaningful and for people to develop connections to it, a number of fundamental requirements must be met. First it must be "legible," borrowing the term from Lynch's analyses (Lynch, 1963).

For a public space to become meaningful it must be legible. The Washington Monument and the Reflecting Pool in Washington, D.C. (Mark Francis)

In order for a space to be legible, particularly in the case of public areas, it must have recognizable cues that are understood by potential users, cues that communicate what kind of place it is and whether they are welcome. This is a place that "would invite the eye and ear to greater attention and participation" (Lynch, 1963, p. 10). Although every setting does not invite all passersby, it should be expected to attract some. An empty lot may be read as a resource for youthful ballplayers while it may be a nuisance to local adults. Legibility is the ability of a place to communicate first that it is open to the user and then what is possible there, once the user is inside. But although legibility is necessary for the development of meaning, it is not sufficient.

In order for people to see some positive meaning in a place it must resonate with their lives and evoke patterns of use that create bonds with the space. If people see possibilities and share goals with others, their

The Imperial Palace in Tokyo resounds with the memories of the culture and thus becomes an important place to be photographed. (Mark Francis)

connections to that place will be enhanced. It is likely that the space will address the needs and the rights of the people in a way that enriches their lives. If it operates at a higher level, the site also will be an evocative one, a place that resounds with the memories and experiences of an individual, a family, a group, or a culture in ways that connect each one to a larger entity, a group memory, or experience. The place then can evoke strong feelings of concern, affiliation, and caring and become significant to people's lives.

But time and history do not deposit their stories in literal ways. They leave traces that communicate to the individual or group for whom that sign has meaning. Significant connections between people and places arise in various ways. For connections to emerge, a site must have relevance. Relevance operates on several levels. At the level of individual users, a place must satisfy needs (discussed in an earlier section). For example, a small park in a dense neighborhood that does not offer opportunities for active engagement – socializing or playing – may be lacking in relevance. At the level of a culture, a site must be congruent with cultural norms and practices. Jensen (1981) points out that the design of many contemporary American plazas is based on an image derived from Medieval and Renaissance Europe, which is largely irrelevant in contemporary American cities. Jensen claims that such irrelevance is due to the fact that the type of "public and political exchange" carried on in the European plazas of earlier centuries, has become increasingly privatized in contemporary America. A site that is incongruent with the life and thought of the culture in which it exists is unlikely to be well used and cannot foster the type of symbolic meaning we are describing as "connections."

Although we will emphasize social meanings and connections, this dimension also could be applied to the physical qualities of a site. Physical connections are based on the degree to which the location, design, resources, and arrangement of a place are reflective of the surrounding area, that is, the relationship between the site and its context. Powerful, evocative stimuli can encourage these connections but often designs are too complicated and so loaded with attempts at "contextualism" as to become merely a collection of clichés. Clearly this type of connection does not exist apart from the people in an area, for it is their judgment that defines the significance of the site and its relationship to their larger environment.

For a space to have meaning other qualities are necessary. First, the space must be comfortable enough to allow an experience with it to occur. If the steps of the New York Public Library did not invite seating or if management policies prohibited people from lingering there, it is unlikely that people would flock there in the numbers that presently are attracted. Second, positive meaning is created by positive connections to people, connections that create a sense of belonging, of safety, a feeling that personal rights will be protected. There are many public spaces that create negative meanings, that communicate messages that are likely to discourage use, at least by some portions of the public. A setting that appears to be dominated by unfriendly, dangerous, or unsympathetic persons – for example, drug dealers – may make other potential users apprehensive about entering. The meanings that they form will be unpleasant ones. They will not develop connections to that place which require positive meanings based on satisfying experiences. The connections to people can exist on many levels: the cultural connections of people with similar backgrounds; the shared experiences of members of an audience viewing a performance that is enhanced by the others present; the interpersonal connections of family, friends, or acquaintances who share the regular use of a public area.

The ability to claim and change a space also can encourage the development of connections, something that researchers on neighborhood participation have been saying for some time (see, e.g., Francis, Cashdan, & Paxson, 1984).

BOSTON WATERFRONT PARK
Boston, Massachusetts

Also known as Christopher Columbus Park; located at Atlantic Avenue between Long and Commercial wharfs; designed by Sasaki Associates, Inc., Landscape Architects; completed in 1976; cost, $2.5 million; size, 4.5 acres.

Since 1964, the city of Boston and private investors have spent millions of dollars to revitalize the Boston waterfront. As part of this effort, the city has publicly supported – although some would say not nearly strongly enough – a long-standing plan to allow public access along the water's edge. The goal has been to reconnect the city, both physically and symbolically, to the sea. Waterfront Park, the only large open space on the waterfront, is the cornerstone of the city's plan. As the terminus of Boston's Walk-to-the-Sea, a pedestrian pathway that extends from Beacon Hill to the waterfront, Waterfront Park was to play a central role in celebrating Boston's maritime connections.

The location of the park presented a number of obstacles to building a strong sense of connection between the park and the city. Atlantic Avenue, the major roadway that forms the park's western boundary, runs beneath the elevated Southeast Expressway. Together, the roadways make a formidable physical and visual barrier between the city and the waterfront site. Unfortunately, the new waterfront hotel has compounded this sense of isolation from the city by effectively creating a wall along the south side of the park. Although the hotel was to have been designed with a public walkway through its center, the walkway is nothing more than the hotel lobby itself. Most pedestrians walk back to Atlantic Avenue to reach the New England Aquarium that lies just on the other side of the hotel.

The design of the park is fairly complex and includes a number of separate activity areas. Immediately adjacent to the water's edge is a large, cobblestone-paved plaza. Behind the plaza is wide, sloping lawn that is bounded by seating walls and bisected by a stairway, which leads up to a trellis-

Aerial view of the Boston Waterfront Park and surrounding context. (Stephen Carr)

covered promenade. The park also includes a children's play area, a small formal plaza with a fountain, a rose garden, and a large lawn area along Atlantic Avenue.

Unfortunately, the design of Waterfront Park falls short of making the connections that would have most significantly enhanced its success. Given the limited amount of public open space on the waterfront and the obvious appeal of the water itself, building a strong physical and symbolic connection to the water was critical. The considerable use of planting, mounding, and changes in elevation, however, conspire to block views of the water from many points in the park as well as from Atlantic Avenue. This particular solution to screening the adjacent roadway sacrifices many important opportunities to make a strong visual connection to the site's most compelling feature.

Although the designers attempted to reinforce the connection to the sea by using building materials, bollards, light fixtures, and even a play structure that reflect a nautical theme, other elements such as the large lawn areas, mounding, heavy planting and wooden trellis, give the park an almost suburban character that is incongruent with the urban waterfront location. One senses that in trying to meet a wide variety of user needs – those of the North End's Italian community, the affluent residents of the waterfront, tourists following the Walk-to-the-Sea, and Bostonians looking for a glimpse of the water – the design failed to take advantage of the only opportunity Boston has had in recent years to reconnect powerfully the city to the sea. It was a site and a goal that demanded bold, even sweeping solutions; ones that would have expressed and celebrated both the urban and the natural qualities of the unique location. Unfortunately, the complex and cluttered Waterfront Park does neither.

In understanding how spaces develop personal meanings for people, it is essential to examine the nature of human development and the characteristics and conduct of daily life. All activity is place-based. Although contacts with other persons constitute the most powerful learning experiences, these relationships are grounded in settings that contribute to the interpersonal experiences. Most central are the experiences within the home but these are not the only important ones. As children grow, their play environments, schools, visits to the homes and offices of other persons, explorations of their local communities, and travel experiences all contribute to their development, their identity, and their senses of themselves. And this process continues over time to produce a rich array of environmental memories that become part of people, much as their family experiences, their intellectual abilities and talents, their personalities, and their physical appearance mark them as distinctive human beings. Not all interpersonal experiences are happy ones nor are all environmental experiences pleasant. Nonetheless, they are the ingredients of people's personalities, their preferences for settings, and their world view, including their connections to places (Rivlin & Wolfe, 1985).

INDIVIDUAL CONNECTIONS

Assuming a certain degree of "relevance" or congruence between users and a setting, symbolic connections can result from use. Such connections often exist at the level of the individual. Lynch (1972b) argues for the importance of such individual connections, which often are overlooked in discussions of preservation of the environment:

If we examine the feelings that accompany daily life, we find that historic monuments occupy a small place. Our strongest emotions concern our own lives and the lives of our families and friends. ... The crucial reminders of the past are therefore those connected with our own childhood, or with our parents' or perhaps our grandparents' lives. (pp. 60–61)

Connections of this type may be largely personal, involving, for example, links between a person's childhood or important life events and a particular outdoor space. Such spaces will come to have special meaning and may help to support a sense of continuity between different stages of a person's life. This special meaning is articulated by people in many ways including their nostalgic descriptions of childhood places. The significance of these memories is becoming increasingly apparent. Social scientists have used the terms "spatial identity" (M. Fried, 1963) and "place identity" (Proshansky, 1978) to describe the role that places play in the development of people's senses of themselves, their own personal identities.

Loved childhood places remain meaningful to people in later life and provide proto-types for good spaces. "Clover path," Jennie's favorite place. Village Homes, Davis, California. (Mark Francis)

ENTRANCE PLAZAS – LOWELL HERITAGE STATE PARK
Lowell, Massachusetts

Located on the Merrimack Canal between Shattuck, Market, and Button streets; designed by Carr, Lynch Associates; managed by Massachusetts Department of Environmental Management; completed in 1984; size, .5 acre.

Lowell was America's first planned industrial city and was recently designated as the first National Urban Heritage Park. Massachusetts and the federal government have cooperated in creating a series of exhibits and connected spaces that reveal and interpret the structure and history of Lowell. The Entrance Plazas are the first exterior spaces the visitor encounters. They are intended to introduce the themes of the park, as well as to help the visitor interpret the history and meaning of their particular site.

The designers intended to make an enduring urban space, appropriate to its place and to the needs of nearby residents as well as one-time park visitors. Four goals were set: to interpret the character and history of Lowell; to commemorate the unusual history of the site, including the Merrimack Canal, an existing set of locks, the importance of water power, and the former Huntington Hall, which served as the train station for waves of immigrants entering the city; to meet the visitors' needs for a place of rest and relaxation where both gatherings and individual retreats are possible; and to meet the needs of the citizens of Lowell, especially the residents of nearby housing for the elderly.

Faced with the challenge of creating two separate but closely linked plazas, the designers developed the two sites in distinction to one another but with common elements such as lamps, benches, and pavement. The West Plaza is intended as a reminder and celebration of Lowell's canal system, which was used to power the textile mills. The East Plaza recalls the millworkers, their arrival in the city, the proper Victorian scene that greeted them, and, in contrast, the reality of millwork with its long hours and oppressive conditions. These themes are developed further in the Mack Building, a historic structure lying between the plazas and housing an exhibit on water power and mill life.

The West Plaza is designed as a traditional urban place with brick paving, a bosque of trees, and a fountain. It is flanked to the north by the Merrimack Canal with a set of locks. It works well as a setting for groups of visitors to gather for a description of the canal system by a park ranger. The fountain itself, with its roughhewn granite blocks and sculpture of a canal builder, recalls these great engineering works and the labor that built them. The bosque is a pleasant shaded area for visitors to rest or eat lunch in sight of the canal and fountain. It is also a good place for nearby elderly residents to sit, in view of the visitor activity, but out of the flow of traffic.

The East Plaza is divided into two areas, both without extensive tree canopy. It was known that at the north side of the site, a brick barrel vault covered the canal where it passed under the former Huntington Hall. The designers convinced the client to uncover and preserve this remarkable, enigmatic piece of industrial archaeology. To complement and further explain the barrel vault, the outline of Huntington Hall was traced in granite across the East Plaza and around the vault. This line also passes through a

The fountain, in West Plaza, recalls the building of the canals. Lowell Heritage State Park, Massachusetts. (Stephen Carr)

The locks, the tracks with an old passenger car, and a reconstructed end wall of the former station all testify to former uses of this site. Lowell Heritage State Park, Massachusetts. (Stephen Carr)

corner of the plantings in the fenced garden. At the northeast corner, a screen wall was built as a replica of the first-floor facade of Huntington Hall. To the north, the first car of a restored two-car train has been placed on new tracks in the same location where trains had formerly waited outside Huntington Hall.

To the south, a fenced garden was designed in the former forecourt of Huntington Hall. An interpretation of the kind of garden prevalent in Victorian Lowell, it has typical elements such as beds of hosta, day lilies, and ferns set against a clipped lawn. The detailing of the fencing and site furnishing also recall the period. The garden creates a separate but visible setting for relaxation and contemplation.

In contrast to the tranquil garden and looming above its fence, an eighteen-foot belt pulley wheel was placed, at the end of a sight-line axis that begins at the arcade in the nearby Market Mills. Drawing the attention of park visitors as they emerge from the park orientation center, it is a reminder of the harshness of the working conditions in the mills. It marks the entrance to the Mack Building water power exhibit.

While needs and rights of both visitors and residents were important in shaping this design, the desire to create a meaningful place was the principal motive. The plazas illustrate how the specific history of a site can be recalled, as well as some techniques for evoking the larger historical context. In the setting of a historical park, this is a proper and effective design approach. In many other urban settings, an overemphasis on history can create the hollow feeling of a pastiche.

Connections to places require experiences that enable the development of a sense of rootedness, which Yi-Fu Tuan (1980, p. 6) has described as "an unreflected state of being in which the human personality merges with milieu." Tuan is pessimistic about this happening in contemporary American society, although he considers it an ideal state. While rootedness may be difficult to achieve today, there is evidence, from people's descriptions of the places in which they have lived, that it has not disappeared (M. Fried, 1963; Rivlin, 1982, 1987).

This process has been described by Proshansky and his associates as place identity, the environmental contribution to the development of self-identity (Proshansky, Fabrian, & Kaminoff, 1983). Largely a product of social relationships, it consists of

cognitions about the physical world in which the individual lives. These cognitions represent memories, ideas, feelings, attitudes, values, preferences, meanings, and conceptions of behavior and experience which relate to the variety and complexity of physical settings that define the day-to-day existence of every human being. (p.59)

Place identity is not conceived of as an integrated component of self-identity. Rather, it is "a potpourri of memories, conceptions, interpretations,

The belt pulley, in contrast to the fenced garden, recalls the harshness of mill life, while marking the entrance to the waterpower exhibit. Lowell Heritage State Park, Massachusetts. (Stephen Carr)

ideas, and related feelings about specific physical settings as well as types of settings" (Proshansky, Fabrian, & Kaminoff, 1983, p. 60). Place identity, according this formulation is both "enduring" and "changing" over the life cycle.

Proshansky (1978) includes experience in public spaces, especially social interaction in them, as a contribution to place identity. Coping with others in these settings and learning to find one's place within them, helps to define the sense of self. The playground, the schoolyard, the local park, and, of course, the streets are settings in which children and adolescents learn to negotiate their places, testing out their abilities of a widely ranging sort, but especially their social and physical prowess. This process continues for adults although the profile of places and activities changes, over time.

This contribution of places to people's personalities is reiterated in the work on environmental autobiographies, techniques that encourage people to provide accounts of places that are important to them. These descriptions, which sometimes include drawings, have identified the powerful ways that both the experiences in places and the memories that accumulate affect images of self and preferences for particular objects, housing types, and settings. The work of Clare Cooper Marcus (1978 a,c) Florence Ladd (1978), and Kenneth Helphand (1976) provides examples of these influences and the enduring effects they have on people's lives. If our memories, our sense of self, and our aspirations are enfused with environmental images, as the work on the autobiographies suggests, the quality of our environment is more than a pleasant amenity; it is an ingredient in the kinds of people we are.

Childhood spaces, especially found spaces, are a part of daily life for many children whether they live in rural, suburban, or urban settings. The vacant lot as a play area may be a stereotypical image but it provokes real memories for many contemporary adults. The street corner gathering place remains an adolescent "hangout" although in some areas it is being replaced by the shopping mall.

Personal spaces develop over time as places that appear along familiar paths. These can become a home away from home, a safe, secure spot that is a sanctuary in the outside world. Many different kinds of places can take on this function including the schoolyard that is the setting for daily games, the storefront of a shop that is used for family shopping, a neighborhood park that is central to the person's life experiences, the local street that becomes a playground, or the front porch or backyard of a house where predictable people and familiar activities are likely to be found. Appropriate location, protection, scale, and design of these ordinary spaces, with their potential for personal meaning, can do much to enhance this potential (see the Woonerf case in Chapter 5).

Digging up the street to plant shade trees in Davis, California, is a memorable experience, with both personal and symbolic meanings. (Mark Francis)

While safe, secure niches are one aspect of an individual's public life, there are other connections such as those to *nurturing spaces*, places providing sustenance and memories from the services and people located there. In the past, local shopping provided much of the experience, and it may continue to do so in many areas. But for increasing numbers of people, the supermarket and shopping mall have replaced the neighborhood grocery. Some of this experience has been regained in the rebirth of the farmers' market that has been celebrated by contemporary writers (Biesenthal & Wilson, 1980; Sommer, 1980). In her analysis of public markets in Canada, Biesenthal (1980) has described their essential qualities:

The market tradition has been passed down for thousands of years from one generation to the next and carried over thousands of miles by merchants and colonists. Markets throughout history have shared three essential features: they are open to all buyers, and sellers in the community; they handle local trade and mostly food; and they are regulated and supervised to ensure that consumers are protected from unscrupulous sellers. (p. 4)

Sommer, Herrick, and Sommer (1981) point out an additional quality of the public market – it is a gathering place for the community, a personal form of shopping where seller and buyer can take special interest in the interchange. It thus is more likely to become a meaningful experience than the expedition to the supermarket or shopping mall. The fact that nurturing items are purchased, food for the table and other necessities, enhances its qualities and its role in a person's life.

Personal connections also may be centered around activities or people in urban public spaces. For example, in a study of a weekly market that has been held for the past four hundred years in Varberg, Sweden (Seaman & Nordin, 1980), one older marketgoer said: "At the market, there are three or four vegetable sellers that I have known since childhood. . . . They're still at the same places they had when I was a child. That gives me a sense of continuity" (p. 40).

Special event spaces form another category of meaningful places that evolve as part of a person's life history. These are important for the particular experiences that have occurred there – ethnic celebrations, family picnics, weddings, funerals, places where good news or sad news was received or where a special person was first encountered. These settings carry important private memories that become part of the identity of a person, sometimes sharpened by photographs but always embedded within, ready to be evoked.

———

HAYMARKET
Boston, Massachusetts

Located on Blackstone Street between downtown and the North End; managed by City of Boston; size, 1.5 blocks long.

Every Friday and Saturday, Boston's open air food market comes alive as pushcarts and stands piled high with fruits, vegetables, and fish crowd the narrow confines of Blackstone Street in the city's Haymarket district. For many, the trip to Haymarket is a weekly ritual, and the market's delight is as much in its sights, sounds, smells as its reasonable prices. One need not be a regular customer to sense that its meaning extends beyond the simple economy of exchange to encompass the history of the site and the significance of the marketplace to urban life.

Whether or not one knows the history of the market, the area abounds with clues to its past. The narrow winding streets of the Blackstone block, the ribbed stone sidewalks, and the aging storefronts and signs provide even the most casual visitor with evidence of the area's long history. There is a sense of congruence between the old-fashioned market and the aging surroundings, which heightens both the experience and the meaning of the place and the activity. Unlike many of the modern urban marketplaces, Haymarket has maintained its connection to the marketplaces that throughout time have been the centers of urban life. This connection is especially

Public spaces can enhance the most meaningful events of life. Parc Guell, Barcelona, Spain. (Mark Francis)

evident when cars are banned on market days – the buildings and the street are bound together once again by a common purpose and activity. As people move freely between the stores, sidewalk and street, they may sense a connection to the city and to the marketplace as it was before the automobile.

Shopping for fresh fruits and vegetables provides the focus for public life at the Haymarket, Boston. (Elizabeth March)

> Coming to the market may also evoke memories of visiting it as a child or memories of markets in Asia, Europe, or South America.
>
> Haymarket provides a connection not only to the older forms and ways of the city but also to the nonurban world. The smells of fruits, vegetables, and meat, free from plastic wrap and freezer compartments, fill the air and inevitably bring the country to mind. It reminds users of the vital connection between the city and the farm and reaffirms, once again, our ancient ties to the nonurban world.
>
> *Related case: Davis Farmers' Market.*

GROUP CONNECTIONS

While important connections can derive from an individual's personal history, they may also stem from the history of a group in an area where connections to other members enhance and shape the experience of a place. Spatial identity is largely a product of social relationships with others. These others may be loosely affiliated groups or cultural, subcultural, or national ones.

Before its renovations in the mid-1980s the territory set down by young Hispanics around Central Park's Bethesda Fountain is one such example, and cities are dotted by places that have significance for particular groups.

Homosexual beaches, teenage sections of parks, dog runs of pet enthusiasts, jogging paths, hangout areas of the young or old, and community gardens are examples of these types of places where even a casual affiliation with others enhances the experience.

We find these loosely affiliated people in many different kinds of settings. The reasons why they are together vary from the regular visits of parents supervising their children in playgrounds to people who have come together to enjoy a concert in a park or a plaza where musical events are programmed into the setting. In other situations the reason for getting together may be around special interests. The participants in community gardening or players in local sports – baseball, basketball, and the like – are drawn together by common interests forming what Janowitz (1967) has termed a "community of limited liability."

Participation in planning and conducting local events can enhance the meaning of the setting to groups. Street and neighborhood fairs, community gardens, and ethnic festivals all may become part of group connections to places. An interesting example can be found in the plaza on the riverfront in downtown Detroit where, in the summer, a different ethnic festival each week makes use of food kiosks, stages, and other supports built into the space. In some cases the places themselves may be created out of the efforts of the group.

In the Church Street Marketplace in Burlington, the Christmas celebration brings people together in Vermont's bleak winter. (Carr, Lynch, Hack and Sandell)

Meaningful connections between people and places are promoted by user participation in design and management. In their study of community open space in New York City, Francis, Cashdan, and Paxson (1984) found that direct participation in decision making and site development enhanced the attachment to the place for persons involved. The type of caring for a space that develops among participants is in direct contrast to the alienation from community that seems to exist among those who vandalize public areas. One handbook on community garden management suggests that involving vandals or potential vandals in caring for the garden is a significant way of decreasing willful damage (Sommers, 1984).

For years, Lars Lende would take children in Stavanger, Norway, on a ride with his pony and cart. When he died, the children, now adults, commissioned this sculpture, which stands in a small park near the downtown, to help keep the memory alive. (Mark Francis)

Group ties also can be reinforced by activities, which may or may not be centered in specific places. Suzuki (1976) describes such an activity in his study of the public space behavior of Turkish immigrants in Germany. These immigrants engage in a somewhat ritualized, highly sociable, and decidedly non-German promenade or "procession" in areas near city centers. Suzuki claims that this "offers a visible means that lends continuity between what [the Turks] knew in their homeland and what confronts them in their new urban environment" (p. 399). It should be noted that this behavior drew critical responses from the German inhabitants.

As an area is used by a group, the repeated activities there can encourage ties to the site. The connections can be facilitated by physical attributes of the site – wall murals, signs in a group's language, the name given to the place. These physical details become symbols of group membership. For example, in the South Bronx a grass-roots group, the People's Development Corporation, developed a community site called Unity Park in the late 1970s. An important part was a mural on the adjacent building that depicts the local workers who rehabilitated that building and developed the open space. The mural seems to be a tangible symbol of the grass-roots revitalization efforts that occurred in the late 1970s in this devastated area. Most of the workers shown were community residents as were the users of the open space, suggesting that all were part of community revitalization. Another example of connections reflected in public art is a statue of a man and his pony and cart in a downtown park in Stavanger, Norway. The man used to give local children rides on his cart. When he died, adults with warm memories of this experience, had a statue placed there in his memory.

Perhaps the epitome of a group that relies on the physical environment to provide solidarity and reinforce shared meanings is the religious one. According to Halbwachs (1980, p. 151):

The believer entering a church, cemetery, or other consecration place knows he will recover a mental state he has experienced many times. Together with fellow believers he will re-establish, in addition to their visible community, a common thought and remembrance formed and maintained there through the ages.

Halbwachs stresses that because religious groups claim to be stable in their beliefs and practices, amid a changing world, they have a particular need for unchanging buildings and physical spaces that clearly represent this stability.

In the same way, a community or subculture may wish to preserve physical elements that have, over a period of decades or centuries, supported and symbolized a certain way of life and system of beliefs. In the small city of Manteo, North Carolina, landscape architect Randy Hester and his associates set out to pinpoint and preserve places in the community with which residents collectively identified (Hester, 1984). Through a process where residents ranked a long list of places in the city, a list of significant places was developed, which was dubbed "the Sacred Structure of Manteo" (see this case in Chapter 7). A number of the places on this list were outdoor public spaces, including a waterfront park, marshes near the center of town, front porches, an outdoor Christmas tree, and the town boat launch. According to Hester, these significant places have "become synonymous with residents' concepts and use of their town. The loss of such places would reorder or destroy something or some social process familiar to the community's collective being" (p. 15). Town officials have taken a number of actions to assure the preservation of "the Sacred Structure" in conjunction with new planning and development.

Although most of the "sacred" places of Manteo became significant to residents through their repeated use and association with community events over many years, one place, a waterfront park, was developed in the 1970s with the clear intention of incorporating individual and community meanings into the site design. This place, Bicentennial Park, was developed on a very low budget by town commissioner Jules Burrus with volunteer help and has come to be called "Jules Park" (Hester, 1985). Burrus utilized as the theme for the park "building from ruins" to symbolize the history of Manteo which, since 1584, has experienced several cycles of destruction or partial destruction and rebuilding (p. 20). More specific aspects of site design, aimed at infusing the site with symbolic associations, include the use of rubble from a demolished local high school, lamp posts endowed by residents as memorials to loved ones, and a twenty-foot statue of Sir Walter Raleigh, an important local historical figure, carved from a single cypress tree.

A different example of a contemporary space designed to be meaningful to the local community is Charles Moore's Piazza d'Italia in New Orleans. This ambitious, controversial, postmodernist plaza was sponsored by local Italian-Americans, and incorporates a raised map of Italy surrounded by water, numerous classical columns and arches, and references to the Trevi Fountain in Rome. It has become a source of pride for many local Italian-Americans and is utilized as a setting for festivals sponsored by local Italian-American associations. On the other hand, many commentators criticize the garishness of the plaza, question the authenticity of its references, and point out its limited use (Place Debate, 1984). Despite its possible flaws, Piazza d'Italia seems a refreshing departure from the typical modernist plaza, stripped down and devoid of meaning.

In this delightful design of the Piazza d'Italia in New Orleans, associations with Italy come through the pastiche of borrowed forms. (Stephen Carr)

CONNECTIONS TO THE LARGER SOCIETY

Public spaces also serve to foster connections at a larger scale, among members of a culture or subculture. Historically, common examples have been sacred places or ceremonial plazas that through repeated use by groups of people have instilled awe, reverence, and powerful feelings of connectedness for adherents of a particular faith or system of beliefs. In sacred forests, churches, synagogues, temples, mosques, and other settings that evoke the spiritual nature of people, these connections have drawn believers together, as they exclude others, creating a special experience for participants. One example can be seen in the Western Wall in Jerusalem which not only functions as a sacred place of prayer but also as a religious and political symbol for Jews throughout the world, albeit one that has engendered considerable political controversy. Other types of spaces are the historic sites or public monuments, places of political significance that can reinforce ties at a national or local level. These include town squares as well as capital grounds. Some monuments are created intentionally to foster solidarity or patriotism. Examples of this can be found in Washington, D.C., where nearly all of the monuments and shrines were designed to communicate to future visitors a sense of the grandeur and solidity of a nation through a combination of design elements and symbolic features. A recent attempt has been made to commemorate the city of Washington itself in the design of the Freedom Plaza on Pennsylvania Avenue (see this case elsewhere in this chapter).

VIETNAM VETERANS MEMORIAL
Washington, D.C.

Located on the Washington Mall; designed by Maya Ying Lin as national design competition; built and managed by the National Park Service; completed in 1982; size is two 240-foot-long walls located on a .5 acre site.

The Vietnam Memorial is a public place of great meaning. Subtle yet powerful, it quickly captures the full attention and emotions of the visitor. It is also a public space of great national importance, providing a connection for people to the historical memories of the Vietnam War and serving as a physical record of the pain and tragedy of this controversial war.

Located along the Mall in Washington, D.C., between the Lincoln Memorial and Washington Monument, just a short walk from the White House, the black polished wall is set into the ground with names of 57,692 killed in the war inscribed into the highly reflective granite. The two walls form a V with one pointing toward the Lincoln Memorial, the other toward the Wash-

The Vietnam Veterans Memorial in Washington, D.C., is a public place of great national meaning. (Mark Francis)

Visitors add to the power of the Vietnam Veterans Memorial by adding memorabilia
of their personal tragedies. (Mark Francis)

ington Monument. The design of the memorial is a work of landscape art
with the walls starting at grade, sloping down to a low point of ten feet at
the intersection of the two walls. It is at once simple yet complex.

The process for deciding on an appropriate design for the memorial was,
like the war, controversial. Howett (1985) summarizes the early history and
design selection process for the memorial:

Jan Scruggs served as an infantry corporal in Vietnam before being badly wounded
and sent home in 1969. Once home, he worked with a small group of Veterans in
Washington, D.C., who proposed that a national monument be erected to honor the
more than 57,000 Americans who died in the war. In 1979, Scruggs incorporated
the Vietnam Veterans Memorial Fund and enlisted the help of Charles Mathias,
Republican senator from Maryland. Mathias initiated the campaign in Congress that
led to the allocation of land for the site. . . . The VVMF decided to hold a national
competition to select a design for the memorial. . . . During a five-day period in May

1981 the jury examined more than 1,400 anonymous entries. At the end they chose the work of a young Chinese-American architecture student from Yale University, Maya Ying Lin. This young woman had submitted a sculptural solution formally integrated with the surrounding landscape, and hence more closely related to the work of many environmental artists of the late 1960s and 1970s, rather than the older tradition of monuments that became the dominant elements in the landscapes into which they were introduced. (pp. 3–4)

Considerable controversy followed the selection of Lin's design. Some Vietnam veterans responded negatively to the non-traditional design, labeling the depressed walls as "a degrading ditch." When it became clear that there was enough official support to build the monument as designed, a compromise was formulated allowing for the provision of a more traditional statue of three soldiers by artist Frederick E. Hart, located nearby.

Today, the Vietnam Memorial lives as a place in the mind and heart. Visiting it is a moving and powerful experience, so much so in fact, that some Vietnam vets visiting the wall have committed suicide, prompting veterans' groups to set up a twenty-four-hour watch. Relatives bring flowers, pictures of loved ones and family memorabilia, leaving them at the base of the wall below their lost family member's name. The National Park Service is keeping the offerings. Volunteers help visitors locate names in the wall with a thick guide book, and assist them with making a rubbing of the name to take home.

The Vietnam Memorial also exists as a meaningful place for millions of Americans who have never visited it. Like other significant national public places such as Times Square, the Golden Gate Bridge, and other public monuments in Washington, D.C., the Vietnam Veterans Memorial holds meaning for millions of Americans as a national public place. It has established itself in less than a decade as one of America's most significant and powerful public spaces, a means of confronting painful feelings and memories of a controversial war.

Related Cases: People's Park, Freedom Plaza.

While some connections may be made at a time when the experience in a setting stirs civic or national pride, these specific meanings tied to human history can lose their power over time, as the events they commemorate pass from consciousness. Those that are truly powerful seem to evoke meanings on a more visceral level, perhaps by their associations with natural, biological, evolutionary, and cosmic forces.

The selection of subjects for public monuments is yet another area in which women have been excluded from public places. Rarely do the images used in these monuments include women. Rather, it is the male figure that is omnipresent in park statuary and around public buildings. Women do not appear except in symbolic forms – as models for justice or freedom, as in the Statue of Liberty. Their historic contributions and roles are not reflected in monuments (Franck & Paxson, 1989). The public scene in the United States is masculine, largely Anglo-Saxon, and of the upper classes. It is hardly a setting with which women and minorities easily can identify. While the addition of statues of Martin Luther King, Jr., in public places represents a recent change, there is a distance to go before there is equal representation of the minority or female presence.

FREEDOM PLAZA
Washington, D.C.

Located on Pennsylvania Avenue between Fourteenth and Fifteenth streets; designed by George E. Patton and Venturi, Rauch and Scott Brown, Joint Venture; managed by the National Park Service.

An elegant composition in black and white stone, Freedom Plaza (formerly called "Western Plaza") depicts an 1887 plan of Washington at an unusually monumental scale. Lawn areas on the terrace represent the mall and the ellipse, while bronze floor plans designate the location of the White House and the Capitol. Historic quotations about the city are inscribed in the pavement on both the raised terrace and the surrounding walkway. While the map/terrace is the plaza's central feature, there is also a sitting area around the equestrian statue of General Casimir Pulaski at the plaza's east end and a reflecting pool at the west end.

Raised above the street level and set behind low granite walls, the plaza has effectively been disconnected from the street and, unlike many plazas of its size, has no particular relationship to the surrounding buildings. More

Overview of Freedom Plaza along Pennsylvania Avenue near the White House in Washington, D.C., shows the pavement map. (Mark Francis)

a monument than a plaza in the traditional sense, Freedom Plaza makes few concessions to human needs and can be a shimmering wasteland in summer or midwinter. The effectiveness of the stark, almost abstract design depends instead on the plaza's ability to function both as a symbol and as a tool for understanding the city. As with most monuments, its success depends on maintaining a delicate balance between abstract and concrete associations.

By combining the plan rendering with the historic quotations, a connection begins to be made between the physical city and the historic or symbolic city. The plan of the city can suggest the expression of the people's will and be seen as a vehicle through which their ideas of nationhood are expressed. For some visitors, the historic quotations may also elicit a feeling of patriotism – a sense of connection between themselves and their nation as represented by the capital city.

As a map, the terrace also should function as a means of orienting users to the city and as a tool for helping them understand the relationship of the plaza site to the city as a whole. A small model of the plaza, placed at the east entrance, explains that the plan of Washington represents two orders of scale: the grand federal order of diagonal avenues and the smaller rectangular order of the city's local structure.

Although the initial design included large scale models of key buildings such as the White House and the Capitol, the final design represents the city only through a highly abstract plan, and in doing so, weakened many of the connections that might have been made. In order to cover the plaza, the plan was reproduced at a scale that makes it extremely difficult to understand. There are few means of orienting oneself on the map since only major features such as Pennsylvania Avenue, the White House, and the Capitol are labeled. Because there are no public vantage points from which one can see the entire plan, it functions more as an elegant, abstract composition than as a map. With the exception of a small bronze model, there are no interpretive graphics that might help visitors understand such features of the plan as the two orders of Washington streets.

Unlike the streets, which themselves express a federal and a local purpose, the plaza seems to have only a national and, inevitably, a touristic purpose. There is little reason to return after a first visit, which raises the question of whether such a plaza is an appropriate use of a major large, open space.

Connecting people to the physical city – both to its immediate surroundings and to its symbolic and historic implications – is a laudable and important goal. Unfortunately, Freedom Plaza sacrifices the possibilities of building a strong sense of connectedness to the goals of elegance and monumentality and an abstract idea.

Related cases: Pershing Park, Boston City Hall Plaza, Square of the Centre Georges Pompidou, Grace Plaza, Lowell Entrance Plazas.

Other monuments and sites gradually come to have symbolic associations, taking on this value in a more natural, unplanned way. Firey (1968) demonstrates how, over time, the Boston Common has come to symbolize important community values and sentiments for many generations of Bostonians. Interestingly, Firey points out that these sentiments do not specifically involve "the dramatic events [of the Revolution] which originally gave the Common its symbolic character" (p. 142). These events "have receded into the background and the Common, already established as a symbol and having become an end value in its own right, now serves as the focus of a vague cluster of sentiments referring to national and civic identity" (p. 143). (See the Boston Common case in Chapter 5.) A more recent example of an open space that has come to take on important symbolic values is discussed in the case of People's Park in Berkeley, California.

PEOPLE'S PARK
Berkeley, California

Located between Bowditch Street, Haste Way, Dwight Way, and Telegraph Avenue; designed by University of California at Berkeley with modifications by users; owned and managed by the Regents of the University of California.

A square block known as People's Park, in a dense residential section of Berkeley, California, exemplifies the symbolic power of open space. The associations and meanings connected with this bit of land go well beyond the functional value of the space and are quite contrary to the wishes and designs of its owner, the University of California.

People's Park was created in April 1969, on land that had been acquired and cleared by the University in 1968, as part of a plan for expansion into an old neighborhood adjacent to the campus. In late April and early May of 1969, gardens and a play area emerged on this site, as a result of sponta-

The symbolic meaning of People's Park, Berkeley, has not waned, even though the park itself has deteriorated. University officials' response has been to "clean it up": by adding a sand volleyball court for students. (Mark Francis)

neous efforts by a loosely organized collection of students, hippies, activists, and local residents (Scheer, 1969). In response to this act of appropriation and in an apparent attempt to dampen the growth of student and community activism, the university erected a fence around the site on May 14. The following day, a large rally, called in response to the university's action, turned into a march toward the park site. During the next nine hours, numerous demonstrators and onlookers were injured (one critically) by police and sheriff's deputies.

The symbolic value of People's Park was clear from the start. An article written shortly after the confrontation on May 14 states that "The Berkeley crisis was never over whether the University would be able to stop one 'people's park,' but rather over whether it would succeed in what had been a long-term strategy of eliminating the culture of protest by denying it its turf" (Scheer, 1969, p. 43). However, the university was able to maintain a fence around and authority over the park until May 1972. At that time increased U.S. bombing in Vietnam fueled the protests against institutional authority at home, and People's Park advocates successfully removed the fence and began to reestablish gardens on the site (Sommer & Thayer, 1977).

Since 1972, the park has remained unfenced, and completely open for daytime use by students, residents, and street people. Some of the original area is maintained by the University and other portions by individuals and grass-roots groups. Maintenance by the latter has been somewhat haphazard, giving the space a somewhat tattered and sometimes underutilized appearance. However, periodic announcements of university plans for development of the site have been consistently met with strong reaction from students and members of the Berkeley community. Although university administrators continue to redesign and redevelop the park (current changes include adding a sand volleyball court), it is clear that the ideals symbolized by the park will persist indefinitely. A statement made by Sommer and Thayer in 1977 suggests this possibility.

The ability of People's Park to possess great symbolic meaning has not waned, placing it strangely in the same category as battlegrounds and historic monuments in terms of significance. Although no sign spells out its historic relevance the symbolic weight of this piece of land is still captured in the local folklore. (p. 514)

Related cases: Vietnam Veterans Memorial, Barretto Street Neighborhood Park.

Symbolic values can be used in the design of a public place to enhance its meaning. But symbolic references can be both positive and negative. Association with pride, enjoyment, or nostalgia can add to the meaning of the site for users; however, some sites may be constant reminders of an old wound to an area or group – for example, Boston's West End Urban Renewal Area (Gans, 1962) or Sacramento Mall, described by Becker (1973), associated with the decline of downtown. Perceptions of the meaning of public space may differ greatly, and such differences are sometimes central to urban planning controversies. A case in point is Times Square.

Times Square in New York City is a public space that is internationally known.
(Leanne Rivlin)

TIMES SQUARE
New York, New York

*Located between Broadway and Seventh avenues from Forty-second to Fif-
tieth streets, plus adjacent side streets, Manhattan; managed by diverse
public agencies, City of New York, and private development corporations;
size, approximately 8 city blocks and adjacent side streets.*

The image of New York as a crossroads, a place of continual, high energy
activity is closely linked to the existence of Times Square (Hiss, 1990). In
fact Times Square is a bow-tie space created by the crisscrossing of Broadway and Seventh Avenue. Its boundaries are formed less by space created
by the convergence of these major avenues than by the surrounding streets
filled with their bars, discos, theaters, restaurants, fast-food shops, hotels
(including several that have housed homeless persons), clothing stores, movie
houses (some with their pornographic titles), street vendors, and "con artists" that are part of the midtown vitality.

The prominence of this area can be traced to the early 1900s when it
emerged as the city's center for theater, vaudeville, and (by the 1920s) mov-
ies, taking its name from the Times Tower, originally the home of the *New
York Times* newspaper. The facade was extensively altered although the
"moving" lights proclaiming news remain a local feature. With its bright
lights and many forms of entertainment, Times Square became a focal point
for all New Yorkers, including waves of new Irish, Jewish, and Italian immigrants. According to critic and civic activist Brendan Gill, for these immigrants Times Square was "a town square, something they had in Europe
and missed here" (Gottlieb, 1984, p. B7). He says, "That belief that there
was some heightened sense of life, of amusement, has existed for a long

time. The sense of lottery, of hope life will be better, is what is proposed by its lights."

The image of Times Square as a focal point for the city's energies and a gathering place for all its people, is reinforced by the yearly New Year's Eve celebration there. It also is a memorable place for many Americans and people in other parts of the world, even though their images come from photographs and pictures on television. The traditions of Times Square and its role as a historic site – where war victories have been celebrated along with ringing in the New Year – act to create meanings for people making it a place they want to visit when they come to New York. But there are deeper meanings that can be experienced both by tourists and New Yorkers, meanings that grow out of inspiration and delight on the one hand and fear and disgust on the other.

In his evocative descriptions of Times Square, Tony Hiss (1987) communicates the experience of going there. Unlike many other open spaces he finds that Times Square "conveys the impression that there's room enough here for all" and as a result "gives you a sense of being protected" (p. 78). He also points to the access to the sky, the "bowl of light" that is "a product of small-scale buildings, light, and sky," qualities threatened by some of the planning for the area. At night the area takes its energy from the remarkable neon lighting, the theater and movie crowds, and the hangers-out and hustlers who populate the streets.

But neither Hiss nor others who enjoy Times Square deny the many problems there, not the least of which is its dirty and deteriorating quality. In the past two decades pornography, drug dealing, prostitution, and street crime have become increasingly visible around Times Square. The eradication of undesirable activities is a major goal of a publicly sponsored controversial project to redevelop a block of Forty-second Street. This much-delayed project, along with recent zoning changes that allow for larger-scale development in the area, are likely to drastically increase the number of large, commercial buildings around Times Square.

Interestingly, both proponents and critics of this redevelopment make reference to the traditional meanings of Times Square. The chairman of the key agency sponsoring the Forty-second Street redevelopment claims that by reducing tawdry and illegal street activities, his project will "help to bring back the days of George M. Cohan when Broadway was truly the Great White Way" (quoted by Gottlieb, 1984, p. B7). Opponents of redevelopment and its large-scale office construction stress that Times Square remains the region's major low-income entertainment district. With its cut-rate movie theaters, bright lights, and vibrant street life, some say Times Square is as much a magnet to poor and working-class New Yorkers in the 1980s as it was in the 1940s. Critics contend that a proliferating wave of high-rise office construction could result in the elimination of much of what gives the Times Square area its meaning, and its continuity to the past, such as large neon signs, entertainment arcades, inexpensive movie theaters and restaurants, and studios and theaters for innovative performing artists.

Architect Hugh Hardy (1986) has offered a number of suggestions for planning that would encourage investment in the area while retaining its essential character. He has called for design guidelines that require that new buildings must be "welcoming and sprightly at the base, an armature for signage as they set back, and a celebration, both night and day, at the top" (p. 6). Hardy also suggested that zoning policies and economic incentives be used to assure that a rich mix of entertainment-related uses remains a dominant aspect of Times Square.

To some degree, Hardy's recommendations seem to be reflected in later developments. The area now has a mix of new hotels and large scale office buildings – with the major additions yet to be built. These are four huge office towers, a city and state collaboration of the Times Square Redevelopment Project. Some of the historic theaters will be renovated and restored. One feature that has been included in all of the new building is the use of exterior lighting and commercial signage, which are mandated by the zoning regulations. They reflect an attempt to recapture or restore the nostalgic qualities of the "Great White Way" by mandating some of the elements while permitting the construction of new buildings of enormous bulk. How much of the sense of roominess, light, and sky, so admired by Hiss (1987, 1990), remains is questionable. We can only hope that a new vitality, a new and playful life emerges out of the new glass towers and silver spires that will be scraping the skies of midtown Manhattan.

The varied meanings that are carried by spaces and their different functions in the lives of a heterogeneous community suggest that places like Times Square and People's Park, with their past histories somewhat clouded by present realities, will be experienced and valued in different ways, over time. Yet despite this variety they carry with them symbols of their pasts and sometimes ominous prospects for the future.

There is another category of sites with group significance, sites that symbolize historic continuity and economic rebirth, however controversial they may be. Perhaps Times Square will fall within this group at some future time. This category is represented in the approach to the design of urban public spaces used by Jane and Benjamin Thompson, for the Rouse Company. Their redesign of two waterfront areas, Baltimore's Harborplace and New York's South Street Seaport and one old market area, Boston's Faneuil Hall and Quincy Market, into a new kind of urban mall or "marketplace" draws on images of the past and people's nostalgia for the physical forms and activities reminiscent of the past. By utilizing symbols of the earlier functions of the areas and the historical significance of the buildings, the developers have fashioned a fantasy of old and new, a pseudo-historical connection that creates a sense of former times, while satisfying contemporary interests and appetites. Sometimes this is enhanced by special programming that stresses the historical ties. In the case of South Street there is a museum, a multimedia movie production on the history of the area, rehabilitated landmark buildings, a fleet of historic ships moored to the piers, antique shops specializing in nautical objects, and a panoply of boutiques, shops, and eating places both inside two large pavilions and on the surrounding streets.

FANEUIL HALL MARKETPLACE
Boston, Massachusetts

Located between waterfront and City Hall; designed by Benjamin Thompson and Associates, Architects; developed and managed by the Rouse Company; completed in 1976; size, 6.5 acres.

The redevelopment of Boston's historic wholesale food market is undoubtedly the best known of the increasingly common public–private partnerships in downtown commercial redevelopment. The overwhelming popularity and financial success of the marketplace has brought private developers and municipal officials across the country together in a rush to emulate its success – a trend the editors of *Progressive Architecture* labeled the "Faneuilization" of America (Roundtable on Rouse, 1981, p. 100).

As urban redevelopment projects are increasingly undertaken by public–private partnerships, the question of just how "public" these projects are will inevitably be raised. Ignoring the larger question of whether they serve the public interest, let us look at a more limited facet of public–private partnerships in open space planning: private management and control of public space.

In 1973, the Rouse Company was awarded the contract to redevelop the marketplace. Under the terms of the agreement, the city retained ownership of the land and the buildings, which had already been partially renovated with public funds, and the Rouse Company was given a ninety-nine-year lease. In return, the Rouse Company developed the marketplace and

The spaces between the buildings may be the most successful part of Boston's Faneuil Hall Marketplace. (Mark Francis)

The cleanup crew of Faneuil Hall Marketplace also acts as a social filter by checking out customers. (Mark Francis)

pays taxes on all improvements, as well as remitting approximately 25 percent of the gross rental receipts to the city.

The businesses chosen by the Rouse Company to locate in the marketplace must agree to submit to the company's regulations concerning signage, displays, and other aspects of merchandise control. In return, they are assured a high level of maintenance, promotion, and appropriate retail mix.

The Rouse Company manages the marketplace in much the same way a bank or a hotel manages its lobby – as private property with public access. Although anyone may enter the marketplace, once there, their behavior must conform to standards of behavior established by the Rouse Company. The company's management office is open twenty-four hours a day and is in constant communication – often by walkie-talkie – with security and maintenance personnel on the ground. As the marketplace receives no city services, the Rouse Company maintains its own security force, which has been given the power of arrest by the city.

Each of the street performers in the marketplace has been auditioned, scheduled, and licensed by the company. Nonlicensed performers, vendors, or those handing out literature are quickly but quietly asked to move on. What appears to many people to be spontaneous street life is, in fact, quite the opposite.

It is important to consider both the intent and results of this high level of control. While the Rouse Company undoubtedly had a sincere interest in creating a project that would bring life back to a decaying part of the city, success for them was inevitably measured by high levels of spending. This could only be ensured by a carefully selected retail mix and a clean, safe, attractive, and entertaining environment, which would draw suburbanites, in particular, back into the city to shop. There is no doubt that it has been wildly successful. Today, the marketplace attracts more than a million visitors a month – more than Disneyland as James Rouse has pointed out in an all too apt comparison.

It has been argued that the highly controlled atmosphere of Faneuil Hall Marketplace presents an idealized and sanitized version of city life – one that denies the real diversity of the urban environment. As the urban world becomes, or is perceived as, increasingly threatening and as funds for management and maintenance of public space are cut, people are more than willing to permit private control over public space. Although there is little doubt that such control enhances the freedom of the elderly and others to feel safe in public places, it raises a number of important questions for the future.

Ben and Jane Thompson, designers of the market, have carefully and consciously preserved elements of the original architecture in their design for the historic South Street, New York, and Faneuil Hall areas. At both sites, relatively little demolition of early structures occurred as a result of new development. In Boston, the new market is visually dominated by the bulk of historic Faneuil Hall, and the market sheds from a previous era have been retained. This leads one writer to state that Faneuil Market is "full of connections to its surroundings and to its past" (R. Campbell, 1980, p. 48). Even at Baltimore's Harborplace, composed entirely of new structures, the Thompsons tried to link their design to local maritime tradition. *Architectural Record* reports that:

In form and scale the two new buildings of the complex have a strong resemblance to the wharf buildings that once occupied the site. . . . According to Jane Thompson, "We remembered the tradition of commercial waterfront construction: shed-like warehouses and covered piers" (A new marketplace, 1980, p. 100)

On the other hand, it seems that new and essentially discontinuous uses in a historic area may detract from experiencing connections with the actual history and tradition of a place. A strong statement of this is made by Kopkin (cited in Stephens, 1978b, p. 52) in describing Faneuil Market:

Something happened to the rootedness of the old buildings when they were scrubbed and arranged and organized. (Because the buildings are related to a timeless, airless, placeless standard that exists outside any specific context, redevelopments are interchangeable in design as well as content.)

It seems clear that severing old structures and districts from their original uses (the marketing of produce and waterfront activities) and grafting on new uses (the selling and consumption of speciality items) leads to the creation of settings that may not foster connections to local tradition and history, and may drive out some of the former users of the area. The renovated areas may appeal to a new user group who can relate to the images being created, but this raises serious questions regarding the previous users or residents who may lose their connections to an area and even their homes. However, in order to weigh the importance of this loss, in comparison to any economic gains or increased use (and, presumably, enjoyment) resulting from the new developments, it is necessary to evaluate the extent to which the settings in their previous state facilitated important symbolic links. We subscribe to the notion (similar to Lynch, 1972b) that historic preservation is of great value only when the site in question has clear meaning to present populations, or is likely to have such meaning in the future. Thus, although it is clear that developments such as the Rouse/Thompson designs may sever important connections to local traditions, we perceive a need to balance the strength of such connections against the possible benefits of these projects, other alternatives possible for the site, and other resources in the general area.

On the other hand, it seems that new and essentially discontinuous uses in a historic area may detract from the experience of connections with the actual history and tradition of a place. In redeveloping Faneuil Hall Marketplace as a modern urban market, the Rouse Company and architect Ben Thompson obviously sought to build a connection to both the original use of the building and to the marketplaces and bazaars that have been the center of city life throughout history. Although the ancient marketplace undoubtedly provided recreation and entertainment, it never lost its connection to the necessities of life.

Faneuil Hall Marketplace, with its emphasis on shopping as a recreational activity and its focus on "impulse" goods and prepared food stuffs, fails to make this connection. Isolated, self-conscious, and divorced from the daily life of all but a few of the city's inhabitants, the marketplace has a way of turning everyone, native or not, into a tourist.

Unfortunately, even the restoration and redesign of the original market buildings were carried out in a way that significantly weakened the sense of connection to the past. Although architect Ben Thompson felt that the buildings' history would best be expressed by emphasizing their development over time, the city chose to follow the advice of preservation consultants who recommended restoring the building facades and roofs to their original condition. This decision, combined with Thompson's own decision to flank the central market building with glass canopies, and the "upbeat" and colorful design vocabulary, makes the buildings' historic quality difficult to distinguish except by their monumental size and distinctive roof lines.

Related cases: The Market at Citicorp Center, Haymarket, Church Street Marketplace.

———

In a similar fashion, much of the main-street development in small towns and cities represents an attempt to evoke the old functions of these commercial pathways, to bring shoppers back to downtown areas at a time when increasing numbers are drawn outside the towns. Using a variety of design and management strategies, many of these developments have been able to attract people with a mix of physical amenities, sales techniques, and an evocative image of the town as marketplace.

Finally, in considering group connections and connections to a larger society, we can examine the role of a much-neglected kind of public space, cultural and educational settings. Although these places may attract a small portion of a total population, they do function as national or local symbols, and for users they represent opportunities to connect with the cultural and educational domain of an area. College campuses function as public open spaces in many parts of the world, drawing groups together to socialize, to play games, to engage in political debate. Their context, the buildings on the campuses, refines the functions of these places as aristocratic or democratic places of learning, as containers of knowledge and the system for obtaining that knowledge, as places where members of the academic community, students and teachers, can rise within the status system of their communities. Campuses are designed to separate the institution from its surroundings and once inside there are many cues to the special status of those within – high fences, gates, statues, signs, and monumental building design, among others.

The cultural center functions in a similar way to confirm special status on users and particularly, to evoke the significance of the experience for those who partake of it. The prototype for this is Lincoln Center in New York, haughtily set off from its rather ordinary surrounds and characterized by extraordinarily monumental buildings, spaces, fountains, and the like. Apart from occasional programmed activities it also is strikingly devoid of any other activity, a negative feature that has led Dallas, Texas, and other cities to attempt to create arts districts, rather than centers, integrating cultural facilities with the life of the city. Both the cultural center and the academic center function as readily comprehended symbols for the larger society, symbols that endow an area with prestige and proclaim a value, symbols that sometimes exclude.

Sensitive public space design and management requires an ability to discern the existence and extent of symbolic links between people and places. It involves an understanding of the meaning of places beyond the superficial level. Is a vest-pocket park that is threatened by development, used by individuals or groups whose connections to the space go beyond the simple pleasure of an occasional visit? Does the site serve a special purpose for members of a social group? Do some of the park's visitors have important memories associated with the park? These are the kinds of questions that require attention in addition to instrumental concerns.

However, environmental planners and managers must not only be sensitive to the need for preservation but also for evolution and change. The

Rome is like a time cake: From the Campidoglio one can see layers from Imperial Rome, the Middle Ages, the Renaissance, and the Baroque period. (Stephen Carr)

establishment of personal and group connections often requires that a site be modified, and that it is not overly laden with connections to the past. Lynch (1972b, p. 39) stresses the need for "a world that can be modified progressively, against a background of valued remains, a world in which one can leave a personal mark alongside the marks of history."

The freedom to leave a personal mark on a site, one that can rest within the marks of history is one kind of valued modification. The photographs, notes, and flowers left at the Vietnam Memorial in Washington offer a moving image of this kind of transformation.

BIOLOGICAL AND PSYCHOLOGICAL CONNECTIONS

Up to this point, we have been discussing the role of public spaces in fostering connections between the past and present of an individual and between different members of a social or cultural group. Although much of the evidence for these connections must lie within the realm of conjecture, there is the possibility that places that stimulate associations with human spatial archetypes draw people to them and create enduring ties. Images that come to mind are the brooding Lincoln father-figure sitting in the womblike cave of his monument or, even more directly, the phallus of the Washington Monument on axis with the Capitol dome and the reflecting pool.

Perhaps as powerful as the sexual evocation of caves, obelisks, domes, and triumphal arches are the ways in which people-created places can evoke the archetypal natural settings that nurtured humankind through our millions of years of evolution. Buildings with cavelike entrances and overhanging cornices set on an open plaza speak of shelter and security, like the overhanging cliffs and caves that sheltered our forebears. Monuments and important public buildings, where possible, are raised on high not only to attract attention but also to command symbolically the surrounding landscape. One thinks of the Athenian Acropolis or the Campidoglio in Rome with its proud statue of Marcus Aurelius on horseback (now removed for preservation). Other places, enclosed and protected like canyon floors, seem right for nurturing the peaceful rituals of communal life. The agoras, the forums, and the market squares of Europe powerfully convey such associations.

In our society, these European spaces often have been used as prototypes for American public spaces. Sometimes this has worked, but more often in the wide-open, pluralistic, and continually changing environments of our cities, these archetypical associations are diminished. A public square enclosed with a single tier of buildings set in the midst of highways, surface parking lots, and gas stations cannot provide a very powerful sense of sheltered, communal gathering. A public space set in a com-

Rome's Fontana di Trevi whimsically displays the origins of culture in nature. (Stephen Carr)

manding location may command only visual chaos. American designers seldom can rely on either the social or the physical context to enhance such archetypal meanings.

Until recently, the most successful public spaces in the United States have been its great public parks. These parks, in the design tradition established by Olmsted, have borrowed devices such as axial malls, fountains, and picturesque structures from continental and British prototypes. But these more formal elements have typically been set in a landscape that is resolutely naturalistic, representing, in only slightly exaggerated ways, what one might find in the countryside. Thus, in Central Park in the center of Manhattan, we have the Sheep Meadow, the Ramble, the Ravine, the Lake, the Great Hill. This is not like the Japanese garden, which represents the natural landscape quite abstractly and at a very different scale. For all intents and purposes, these parks are that landscape itself, transposed into the city.

Perhaps all cultures have mimicked the natural landscape in some way in their architecture and open space. It seems a natural thing to do, whether consciously or unconsciously. That Americans like such natural references and find them meaningful seems clear. Even that most urbane of American public spaces in Rockefeller Center relies for its success on a formalized representation of a natural flower-lined stream, leading to the sunken "pool" of the skating rink. In the United States, there has been a history of fashioning public spaces after the natural landscape, which itself has been systematically removed from most urban areas. We have carved out our national parks and local plazas by taming the natural images before inserting them back into these recreational settings.

Against this robust tradition, the modern movement, with its liking for simple abstract geometry and clean lines and its fear of nature, set out public spaces and even parks that lack such obvious associations. If these geometric exercises have meaning, it is like the meaning of minimalist art – an insistence on an abstract notion of what are "basic" visual experiences, the studied juxtaposition of line, plane, and color.

Yet the evidence points to the fact that the presence of features found in nature – the sky, mountains, the forest, a beach, a wilderness area, water, and deserts – have special meaning for people. The bond comes from the physical quality that reaches out to individuals from their past experiences with these universal elements, perhaps from their archetypal meanings. Experience in natural settings seems to have a "restorative" value (Kaplan & Kaplan, 1990), refreshing people and sharpening their senses. In a series of studies on the effects of wilderness experiences (summarized in Kaplan & Talbot, 1983), participants reported a sense of wholeness and tranquility and improved self-esteem. This research and other work on direct contact with nature (see, e.g., R. Kaplan, 1973) document the psychological value of these experiences and raise some interesting questions concerning their stress-reducing power.

There is evidence that even passive experiences with nature may have therapeutic value. Ulrich and Simons (1986) used videotape simulation to test reaction to images ranging from natural to built environments. They found that participants recovered significantly faster and more completely from stress when exposed to natural rather than to built environments. In a related study Ulrich (1984) compared hospital recovery rates for patients with and without views of trees from their hospital beds. He found that surgical patients in a suburban Pennsylvania hospital with windows looking out at a natural scene had shorter postoperative stays, received fewer negative evaluative comments from nurses, and took fewer drugs than matched patients in similar rooms facing a brick building wall.

Another researcher (E. Moore, 1981) reported that prisoners whose cells faced natural areas used health-care facilities to a significantly lesser degree than inmates without this view. These findings document the commonsense impression that natural elements can relax, calm, and refresh the spirit, especially when one's daily experiences involve crowded conditions, overload of stimulation, and stress. The refreshment is enhanced when the natural setting removes the person, if only temporarily, from the flow of everyday events and demands. But even in urban areas natural elements – trees, water, greenery – are valued by people using public places. In our research in the vest-pocket Greenacre Park, these elements were commonly mentioned by users as important to them. There is considerable evidence that given the opportunity to choose the qualities of settings in which they spend time or on which they look out, people find natural elements to be desirable (Balling & Falk, 1982; Buker & Montarzino, 1983; Driver & Greene, 1977; Kaplan, 1983).

The many instances of incorporation of water, vegetation, and rock formations into designs for public spaces seem to reflect the importance of these elements. We see evidence of this in the internal waterfalls present in building arcades (such as Olympic Towers and Trump Tower in New York City), and the fountains dotting public spaces all over the country. Some of the best liked, such as Lovejoy and Forecourt in Portland, Oregon (see the case study in Chapter 4) mimic the natural forms of waterfalls. There is a strong movement in landscape architecture toward the revival of more naturalistic sweeps of planting, as a relief from the constructed surroundings and the constructed qualities of public places.

Concern with children's play and play areas has suggested some sound reasons for the introduction of natural and malleable elements into public spaces. The enduring power of places that enable children to manipulate, to build and rebuild, the pleasure and commitment to these areas, and the

Even in urban settings, vegetation, rocks, and water can connect children to the natural and biological world. A fishing pond in a new residential development in Delft, The Netherlands. (Mark Francis)

memories and feelings associated with them are indications of their value. Work on adventure playgrounds provides some of this evidence (see the case discussed in Chapter 5).

The Environmental Yard in Berkeley, California, provides an example of a responsive setting for children that incorporates natural elements (R. Moore, 1989). Working with the designer, Robin Moore, students, their parents, school staff, and community members transformed a schoolyard into a rich and varied play and learning environment that includes vegetation of many kinds along with other natural features such as ponds.

Whether contact with nature makes children or adults more creative or healthier in the long run is difficult to conclude; we can only say that the elements delight, and this may be enough. Although we have a fair amount of evidence regarding people's preferences in open spaces, there is less understanding of the specific contribution of natural in contrast with constructed elements. Some have suggested that preferences for nature and specific types of nature are innate (Driver & Greene, 1977) and derived from our evolutionary history (Balling & Falk, 1982). Whether this is so must still be a matter of speculation, but there is ample evidence that the more "natural" features of open spaces are noted, enjoyed, and part of what users are seeking.

Another level of biological connection can be found in the natural cycles of life, the daily cycles reflected in the passage of hours, the cycle of seasons, and the progression of birth, aging, and death. While these can be seen directly in nature – the opening and closing of flowers, the impact of seasonal changes, the life cycle of both plant and animal species, and the hourly changes marking the course of a day – they also can be components of public spaces making conscious the biological clock that is part of all life. Visible in activities such as birdwatching and safaris, as well as trips to zoos, this aspect of life can be enhanced by public spaces as well and is evident in the increasing popularity of town trails and nature trails.

CHURCH STREET MARKETPLACE
Burlington, Vermont

Located on Church Street between Main and Pearl streets; designed by Carr, Lynch Associates; managed by Church Street Marketplace District Commission; completed in 1983; 4 blocks long.

The Church Street Marketplace is designed to be a common ground for Burlington, Vermont – a place that gathers in and displays the city's special character. In an extended process of dialogue with citizens, the designers were encouraged to draw on the social and physical context of Burlington in order to make the street more meaningful. Three themes emerged: to enhance the sense of connection to the surrounding landscape; to express the rugged individualism of this mercantile city and of Vermont, often referred to as "contrary country"; and to improve the setting and atmosphere for meeting other people and for knowing merchants personally.

To reflect and interpret the striking landscape of the Burlington area became the most pervasive theme of the design. Massive boulders were embedded in pavement, which was designed to recall the bare earth in color and texture. Surrounding the boulders are clusters of irregular woodland trees. In front of City Hall, at one end of the street, is a garden of native plants and a fountain with stonework recalling a cliff or quarry face.

The architects commissioned five artists to collaborate on various elements of the design and to interpret this theme in their own ways. Bronze sculptures of deer and bears are placed in the two basin-fountains, set against the granite backdrop and naturalistic planting. Another sculpture, free-standing in the street, consists of a set of weathered aluminum pyramids, topped by cut, polished granite of various types. This piece recalls the rocky, mountainous landscape in a more abstract way than the boulders. Still another piece consists of overlapping neon outlines of mountain and lakeshore forms and is hung in the peaked glass roof of the bus shelter where many people arrive downtown. Banners, changing with the seasons, are designed to recall the rising and setting sun and other cyclic natural events.

The boulders have become a well-loved feature of the Marketplace in Burlington, Vermont. (Stephen Carr)

The sense of connectedness that the designers have sought to build through paving boulders, naturalistic plantings, and artworks operates at both the individual and the community level. The elements might remind one of a particular experience in the Vermont countryside or reinforce Burlington as a community with a special relationship to the natural environment. A local mythology has already sprung up about the varied native stones: that each represents a different county in Vermont.

The design also intends to connect one to the larger world. A granite stripe, or "Earthline," representing the longitude on which Burlington is located, is embedded in the pavement and extends the length of the street, symbolically from the North Pole to the South Pole. Granite paving blocks, inscribed with the names of all the major cities around the globe lying within 500 miles of this longitude have been placed in the pavement, at the proper scale distance. There are no explanatory graphics, so the Earthline is a mysterious element to be discovered and interpreted, adding new meaning over time.

The design also attempts to reflect the Vermont character and to help reinforce connections between people. Church Street is bordered by a wide

Exhibit "A" by Nicholas Pearson suggests, perhaps, the surrounding mountains. Burlington, Vermont. (Stephen Carr)

range of turn of the century and some more recently constructed commercial buildings. There is no unified architectural style, but rather an expression of individualism. Glass and metal sidewalk canopies and canvas awnings provide protection in inclement weather and establish a sense of continuity among these individuals, without destroying their diversity. The canopies are simple, almost industrial structures, designed to be in keeping with the straightforward, no-nonsense practicality for which Vermont residents are famous. Other street furnishings such as light poles, benches, and cast-iron flower pots are designed or selected also be a collection of compatible individuals, each straightforwardly expressing their use and special character, rather than being made subservient to a singular design statement.

To reinforce social connections, the designers worked with the future managers of the Marketplace to encourage sidewalk cafés and better merchandising by established businesses, and to create opportunities for street vendors and entertainers. An activity program was designed with seasonal festivals, appropriate celebrations of each holiday, and street sales to bring merchants out of their stores. This program continues to evolve and, as a result, Burlingtonians look to the Marketplace as the space in which their public life is displayed. Sidewalk cafés, with their easy sociability, have blossomed beyond the designer's hopes, and the Marketplace currently boasts seven in four blocks.

In a period in which pedestrian malls are falling out of favor as economic panaceas for failing downtown retail areas, Burlington's Church Street Marketplace has been a resounding economic success. Space on the street rents

The Earth-line was an idea of Kevin Lynch to anchor Church Street on the earth. Burlington, Vermont. (Stephen Carr)

at a premium and new businesses press for downtown locations nearby. Although there are reasons for this that go beyond the design of the mall, the Marketplace has undoubtedly found favor with Burlingtonians and become a point of pride in the city. It is Burlington's common ground. The many connections that the design helps people to make contribute to the economic and social success of this public space.

Related cases: Gågate Walking Street, Haymarket, Downtown Washington Streets for People.

CONNECTIONS TO OTHER WORLDS

The world of the imagination draws people to many settings. They include the fantasy places created by Disney to those appealing to the cosmic and universal connections suggested in places such as Stonehenge in England. Fantasy is built in as an attraction in some public spaces. The lights, theaters, and color of Times Square and the now-faded amusement areas of Coney Island, in Brooklyn, New York, both project people into a world that removes them from their humdrum or difficult lives. Coney Island was created out of the fabric of fantasy. Begun in the mid nineteenth century it did not attract large numbers until railroad systems reached the area. Coney Island became the "Mecca of the Millions," appealing to thousands of visitors who flocked to the beaches, the restaurants and saloons, the hotels and amusement parks – Steeplechase, Luna Park, and Dreamland. Beyond the spectacular and scary rides, roller coasters and Loop the Loops, there were various kinds of entertainments and hundreds of thousands of lights, which created a veritable fantasy land to people who flocked there. Frederick Fried, a historian of the area, describes some of the attractions of Luna Park when it opened in 1903: "In addition to A Trip to the Moon, an illusion of various aircraft racing to the moon, awe-inspiring storms, and a weird cruise over the fantastic moon land, there was Fire and Flames, a realistic rescue scene of people trapped by the burning of an entire city block" (Fried, 1990, p. 32).

Each new amusement park competed with earlier ones to create larger, more spectacular, and more unusual attractions, grandiose architectural splendors to impress the visitors. These fantasy constructions have all but disappeared with the closing and demolition of Steeplechase in 1964. There are a few rather tawdry relics of the past, some food stands, rides, and games of chance and hopes that the area will be revived and reconstructed. But the image of the world that was is fresh in many people's memories. Tourists to New York City still are drawn there partly for the amusements that remain, but largely because it represents a genre of places developed in the nineteenth century to transport people to another world.

The contemporary versions of this fantasy world are the Disneylands and Disney Worlds, prototypes for the theme and amusement parks popular today. They too transport people to other worlds through a combination of rides, historical displays, and fantasy characters, although most are rather costly expeditions. For the most part the rough edges and bawdy character that made Coney Island appealing to the masses have been replaced in these manicured settings by carefully orchestrated entertainment and heavy management.

The cosmic realm is yet another domain for connections: to the sun, the planets, the stars, the universe itself. The presence of sundials in public places signifies this influence and places like Stonehenge in England evoke this sphere. This prehistoric monument on Salisbury Plain is a large circle of huge stone posts and lintels that is presumed to be some kind of system for marking time. The scale of the stones, the mystery they evoke, and the realization that there is a universal message embodied in their arrange-

The large reflective sphere with its ethereal music, just outside the Paris Science Museum, is a recent attempt to connect people to the cosmos. (Stephen Carr)

ment all draw huge crowds of people trying to fathom the meaning of it all. It is as impressive as a cathedral or pyramid and the openness, the projection to the sky, enhances its connectedness to the area, to the past, and to the universal qualities it embodies. Many other ancient sites, such as the Mayan ceremonial centers or the Egyptian pyramids, suggest these cosmic connections. Some contemporary artists, through earthworks and "lighting fields," are attempting new connections of this sort.

THE CREATION OF MEANING

The development of meaning is an interactive process between space and person that evolves over time, a transactional process in which user and setting are both impacted. The space provides one set of stimulations while the users bring their own histories and associations. Repeated direct experience is a requirement for connections to develop, unless the place is a spiritual, ethnic, national or historic one where indirect experiences form images and meanings that are evoked by the name. In most cases the person must have a personal relationship with a place in order to develop connections to it.

Meanings do not remain the same over time. They change as the spaces and their functions change, as the context, the neighborhood changes. Over time, settings can become more or less important to people, more or less meaningful as they play different roles in their lives, or drop out completely. A precious park may become threatening as different users take it over. An important childhood space may lose its significance when it is physically altered. Even the universal and national spaces change as a person's political philosophy, personal ideology, and world view develop over time and a person's relationship to the larger world changes.

The developers, designers, and managers of public spaces can assist in the process of making places meaningful. But good intentions and understanding of the ways people seek meaning in public spaces will not automatically assure that good public space design will occur.

To make a meaningful place requires a shared understanding among designers, managers, and users. This understanding must spring from a deeper source than a personal vision, one that resonates with time and runs out along the physiographic web in which time is cradled. The structure of such a place will be given by the human purposes it serves, but its meanings will derive from the subtle poetics of time and place.

The art of public space design must allow for the creation of settings that are both evocative and flexible, responsive to changing users and uses over time. In Walzer's (1986) terms, the spaces must be "open-minded" rather than "single-minded," "designed for a variety of uses, including unforeseen and unforeseeable uses, and used by citizens who do different things and are prepared to tolerate, even take an interest in, things they don't do" (p. 470).

It is difficult to create a design with both evocative power and open-mindedness. This is particularly so in a society such as ours, which is made up of many cultural groups with differing traditions of public space use and often antagonistic views of one another.

To be most meaningful and most artful, a public space should resonate, not only with its historic antecedents but particularly with the larger landscape in which it exists. Cities develop in and from their natural and rural contexts. Rivers, harbors, lakefronts, valleys, trails, hills, and traditions of land subdivision continue to shape cities even as they utterly transform the detailed character of the landscape. In North America, a city's inhabitants are typically a polyglot gathering of people drawn for mostly economic reasons from some distance – often from elsewhere in the world – bringing with them their particular cultural traditions and environmental preferences. These immigrants have come predominantly from rural and small community settings and, at least in the beginning, settled in the relatively supportive ethnic "urban villages" described by Gans (1962) and other observers of our urban scene. Those achieving economic success have typically moved on through mixed transitional neighborhoods to suburban settings, which attempt to recreate – at a much-reduced intensity – some of the meaningful features of their rural and small community origins, such as connections to nature.

Because American cities have grown rapidly and have drawn their diverse populations from afar, and because these populations continue to be mobile, there is little deep-rooted resonance between people and their environment. Of course there are exceptions – families in Boston or Charleston or New Orleans that go back over a few generations in the same environment – but by and large we find ourselves living in and striving to adopt and adapt environments that we did not create. Usually, we are only dimly aware of who did create them. Often enough, these environments were built only for speculative gain in patterns that were felt to be "marketable" or just serviceable, given the purpose of building and particular economic conditions and building traditions of the time. The meanings that these built environments create tend to be either obscure, representing the cultural preferences of a group long gone, or blatantly utilitarian, as in a factory or a speculative office building. Sometimes, as in the "signature" erections of the corporate giants, they combine the worst features of both by absurdities such as "Gothic" spires on glass curtain-wall buildings.

In this confused and confusing urban setting, public space has veered between utilitarian neutrality and eclectic incoherence. Spatial form, sculpture, paving patterns, or some selection of plantings are often employed to give "meaning" to a space, but usually the reference is to some other time and place rather than to current users. In part, this is simply the expression of our own immaturity as a culture – that we have yet to develop a rich and broadly understood set of symbols that are our own. In part, our cultural diversity demands that we should mimic the great public places of the past that were created by the more holistic cultures from which our diverse society derives. Unfortunately such borrowings often added to the cultural confusion, as in the use of the Piazza del Campo in Siena as the inspiration for the central public space fronting the city hall of a city whose dominant population is of Irish ethnic origins. In its most extreme form, this borrowing produces "themed" environments in which the creation of exotic settings (or even a familiar but idealized setting such as "Main Street, USA") is used as part of a commercial attraction. In this Disney is the master.

In the European countries from which we derive most of our traditions and models of good public space, user populations, until recently, have been culturally homogeneous. Such homogeneity allows for considerable

Art can add meaning to public space. Ned Smyth's *The Upper Room,* Battery Park City, New York City. (Kim Drain)

economic and social mixing because the shared culture provides for shared meanings and basic rules of conduct, even across economic distances. In this country, wide-ranging ethnic, cultural, and economic differences reduce the shared meanings and rules of conduct to a level that can create insecurity and confusion in close encounters. As technological means have allowed for it, the discomfort and fear of too much human diversity has been reduced by economic segregation.

It is no exaggeration to say that the most "successful" urban public spaces created in the past few years have been in cities, or locations within them, with relatively homogeneous user populations. If not, they have been designed and managed to attract such users and exclude others. Many of the examples used in this book – the fountain in Portland, Oregon, Ghirardelli Square in San Francisco, the Church Street Marketplace in Burlington, Vermont, and the Faneuil Hall Marketplace in Boston – are of this type. Some less successful projects such as Downtown Washington Streets for People can be attributed, at least in part, to their efforts to cut across cultural and economic groupings.

That artists, public space designers included, must know their intended audience to create immediately meaningful works is no surprise. The greatest artists have been able to create works that withstand the test of time, even when they are not immediately accepted. Apparently they have been able to evoke some more universal human responses, perhaps programmed at a level deeper than cultural conditioning or at least so basic to the human experience as to be cross-cultural. Although we cannot expect every public space to reach such heights (or depths), the growing cultural diversity of our cities makes it necessary for the designers of urban public spaces to search for themes with this deeper appeal.

MAKING MEANINGFUL PUBLIC SPACES

To create settings that are meaningful in a deeper sense is the art of public space design. A space that truly meets people's needs will, by virtue of that alone, have meaning for them. By contrast, a monumental space consciously designed to be impressive and thus "meaningful" may convey little to its users apart from the discomfort of walking across it. As we have been saying, to find out what people need in a given place, the surest way is to ask them, and to do so in a context that provides for repeated exploration of possible needs they have and the means by which a given space might satisfy them.

To continue to satisfy these needs a space must be manageable. In part, this is a technical and resource question: Is management staff available and can it appropriately oversee and easily maintain the space in question? But, before that, it is a question of design: Has the space been designed to protect the rights of individual and group users and to provide supports that will assist groups in establishing their rights in nonconflicting ways? As we have seen, this politics of public space can be very complex and difficult to work out, especially when there are many conflicting demands on the same small space. But, as with identifying and meeting needs, the best way to identify and assure rights is to engage potential users in discussion of the issues prior to construction and then to set up a management structure and process in which they can continue to voice their needs and concerns.

Attention to needs and rights of public space users is the means of making public spaces civil. It creates the fundamental level of civility that prepares the way for the expression of cultural meanings. If only public space design would satisfy these basic performance dimensions, the coherence and meaning of places would be greatly increased. But beyond that, there are many choices to be made that are often thought of as the artistic prerogative of the designer. These choices in specific forms and materials greatly influence the user's experience of associative meaning. They determine how a place resonates with the cultural expectations and longings of users and, we would argue, have a great deal to do with whether it becomes a place that is loved and enriched over time.

237

As we have said, our multicultural society offers many associations with other times and places upon which the designer might draw. Almost any way we might choose to "theme" an environment could appeal to a particular group. However, such themes may be meaningless or even abhorrent to others or have only the transitory appeal of novelty. To achieve a deeper and more lasting meaning, we believe, requires that a place be richly embedded in its context. It requires a gathering in and expression of those qualities of context that make a region or a city or a neighborhood unique and give it its character.

Such qualities come first from the natural landscape that is characteristic of the surrounding region. Inspiration can come from the topography, the abundance of particular materials or colors, the presence or absence of water, or the typical vegetation to be found there. The great urban central parks have often developed these associations. A second set of contextual references may be historical, whether from the typical settlement patterns of the place or the typical qualities of the context or from the immediate history of the site itself, as are the grand monuments to immigration in the New York Harbor, the Statue of Liberty and Ellis Island.

Our examples from Lowell and the Tennessee Riverpark illustrate this idea. The line between this approach and the themed environments of Disney World (or Shopping World) is a fine one, but highly significant. The "classical quotations" by postmodern designers are a weak attempt to make connections with a commonly revered past but one that has little resonance with the lives of people today. More powerful are the whole cities such as Santa Fe, New Mexico, and Santa Barbara, California, which have chosen environmental themes for themselves derived from the way of life, cultural forms, and building technologies of earlier peoples on those sites.

Most difficult, least developed, and potentially most rewarding would be the development of qualities and associative meanings that are special to our own time and place and the experience of our emerging culture. Such work has always been the special domain of artists, often working within the context of an inspirational religion. Frequently, works that later seem a powerful distillation of the spirit of a time are not recognized as such when created because they are a step ahead and to the side of current fashions. Perhaps in our society, such work must spring from and draw its inspiration from human nature itself, if such exists. It might be inspired by insight into human spiritual needs and mythologies or it might learn from cross-cultural studies of anthropologists, or even from the tentative theories of sociobiologists. It would, by its nature, go beyond the information given to create a new synthesis with appeal to a broad cross section of people.

Making public spaces meaningful is a process involving users, designers, and space managers. As we have proposed, first, the spaces must support meaningful experiences, they must have sufficient variety for people to satisfy their needs and find pleasure, interest, and delight in using the places. The spaces themselves must fit well into their context and enable people to feel comfortable and secure in going there. The management system should be a democratic one, allowing cultural expression, temporary claiming, and change so that people feel that the space is part of their lives, an expression of their identity if only while they are using it. In order to develop a tie to a space and concern for it, a group or community should be involved in control of the space with rights and responsibilities in its management. Finally, the management should provide meaningful elements and events within the spaces, resources that resound with the users to stimulate interest, use, and commitment to the place, qualities that are the foundation of meaning.

SUMMARY

Positive public space meanings develop when people are able to form roots in an area, when settings become important parts of their lives. This occurs when spaces are well suited to their surroundings both physically and socially, when they support the kinds of activities users desire, and when they engender feelings of comfort, safety, and connections to other people. Individual connections emerge in a number of ways – from a person's life history and personal experiences, from a tradition of use of an area, and from special events in a place. But regular use of a public place by a group of loosely or strongly affiliated persons also can create connections to the site. These bonds are enhanced by the presence of natural elements and design features suggesting connections to the larger universe. Sacred and ceremonial places draw people together in the interests of historical, religious, or cosmic forces and can create symbolic connections to a site and feelings of continuity, awe, and concern. Understanding how meanings are created can offer directions for design and management policies for public spaces.

MAKING PUBLIC SPACE

In Part III, we trace the implications for design and management of the historical and social analysis of Parts I and II. The changing relationships between public life and public space, examined in Chapter 2, have led to the current proliferation of public space types described in Chapter 3. The needs served, rights offered, and meanings conveyed by public places have evolved together with the social and technological context of modern society. These human dimensions, described in detail in Chapters 4, 5, and 6, are rooted in history, supported by social research, and central to contemporary uses and expectations of public space.

To carry out an appropriate analysis of the context and requirements of a public space project, and then to draw useful conclusions for design and management, are not simple tasks. The multicultural nature of our society and its rapid rate of change require a systematic approach, with the flexibility to adapt to many particular contexts. In Chapter 7, we describe the theoretical and philosophical underpinnings of that approach, along with some practical examples.

In Chapter 8, we analyze how design and management are typically carried out and propose a more effective process. The purpose of this process is to understand the social and physical context of a public space through the eyes of its users and, thereby, to focus on its human dimensions. The touchstone of the process is the organized and in-depth involvement of existing or potential users.

In Chapter 9, we project the long-term trends in public space development into the future. These trends raise difficult issues of equity, public versus private control, and the common grounds for meaning. These issues must be confronted if public spaces are to become more supportive, democratic, and meaningful.

USING THE DIMENSIONS

The human dimensions of public space, described in Part II, provide a means for discovering what is important to space users. They can be helpful in defining a public space project, in guiding its design and management, and in evaluating its performance. They are *human* dimensions because they describe types of relationships between people and places that are important across cultures and for all public spaces in varying degrees. They become useful to design and management in light of the social and physical context of a particular place. In context, needs, rights, and meanings can be transformed into working tools to shape a public space and guide its further evolution. How to do that in our culturally plural and constantly changing society is the subject of this chapter.

THE CHALLENGE

The ecological sciences, including environmental psychology, have taught us that our physical surroundings are best understood not merely as inert supports or constraints to human action, but as part of a set of living, changing relationships between places and people. As many of the studies in Part II have shown, these relationships are often troubled by a lack of fit between a place and its users. The design of a place creates built-in programs for its use and a set of clues to its potential meaning. These programs may be tight and specific, as in a tennis court, or loose and multiple, as in a large, flat area of lawn. The users of the space bring their own programs in the form of expectations and desired activities, which may or may not be accommodated by those that are built in. If built-in programs and user-desired programs do not match, managers are left with a problem: They must either attempt to control user behavior within the constraints of the space program, which can cause conflict, or they can

Space and use often do not fit. The playground as center field and bleachers. In-wood Park, New York City. (Roger Hart)

let the users try to adapt the space to their desires, which may result in frustration or damage.

To create and maintain a good working relationship between a space and its users, designers and managers need to understand, in advance, the needs and expectations that potential users are likely to bring to the place. The more diverse the range of user groups, the more difficult it will be to develop appropriate criteria for design and management. In the United States, strong ethnic, regional, and class differences make for complex relationships between public space and the people who use it.

The task of understanding people's needs and expectations is made more difficult by the volatile nature of modern communities. A space may be designed and managed with the users' programs well in mind and be useful and meaningful to them. As the context, users, and standards of behavior change, the built-in space programs may become obsolete. Whether as a result of differing cultural heritage or of life circumstances, different groups of people, or even the same group at different points in time, can have sharply varying needs and expectations about the actions appropriate to a given setting. Management may try to adjust but be hampered by lack of understanding, by the built-in physical constraints of the original program, or by the lack of funds for change. Instead of a change in users and their needs being accommodated with modest changes in management policy, conflict develops and use may fall off. Former users may feel excluded and be accommodated elsewhere, usually at additional cost and with a loss in social continuity and meaning.

In Exposition Park in Los Angeles, twice the site of the summer Olympic games, in 1934 and 1984, a formal grass mall leads up to the entrance to the Coliseum. The Hispanic population of the surrounding neighborhood saw that this mall was about the right width for soccer and, because no other space in the park would serve that need as well, they proceeded to play. In 1983, just before the Olympics, park management responded by placing an "artwork" in the center of the mall, which consisted of a line of stones that were large enough and close enough to preclude use

Artwork installed in the mall. Exposition Park, Coliseum Mall, Los Angeles, California. (Stephen Carr)

for soccer. The former users responded by breaking bottles on the art-work, thereby gaining a reputation for being both vandals and Philistines. They moved their games to a second "inappropriate" setting in the park. Another indestructible artwork was proposed and from there the battle has raged: art versus life.

This conflict in Exposition Park shows the effect of social context and of change in context. The park grounds were designed primarily as a set-ting for various regional sports and museum facilities at a time when the surrounding neighborhoods were white and middle class. Local neighbor-hood people used the park for picnicking or strolling, mixing comfortably with museum-goers and tolerably with periodic inundations of sports fans. Use of the grounds for informal active sports was not considered appro-priate by the park administration nor demanded by users. Now the popu-lation has changed, bringing with it a new set of needs for which the park was not designed and to which management, which is narrowly focused on institutional needs, has not responded. Indeed, park administration has consistently reduced green space available for even informal use by ex-panding institutions and building parking lots. This has caused conflict with the community and dramatic reduction in informal use, which in turn has led to increased incidence of drug dealing and crime within the park.

Because of the culturally diverse and dynamic nature of our society, we cannot offer a simple set of rules for good design and management. In the United States, many cultures have come together, sharing a common dream of freedom and prosperity, but with frequent clashes of values and life-ways. Myths and rituals that have persisted have been adapted to existing spaces rather than themselves creating spaces (e.g., Italian street festivals on saint's days). Traditional mores may be modified or suppressed to adapt to the larger society. However, in the ethnic urban "villages" and in smaller communities where certain ethnic groups predominate, public life still reflects the culture of origin (Hall, 1966). Other social variables, such as age and income are important determinants of public behavior and needs in all societies, and this adds to the complexity of ethnic diversity. Al-though one cannot discount the possibility that there may be some uni-versal "deep structure" in the relations between people and public space, the overwhelming evidence of the social sciences suggests that these re-lations vary with culture. Further, as seen in the case of Exposition Park, normal processes of urban migration, in which one group in the tributary area of a space replaces another, can throw any relationship between peo-ple and place rapidly out of balance.

As a result, there can be no general recipes or patterns for a good park, plaza, or playground. Appropriate physical design and management poli-cies can only be determined with a thorough understanding of context and users, and for a particular period in the evolution of the local public life. Most design guidelines are useful for their observations of existing relations between people and space, but their attempts to generalize are limited by the particular context in which the ideas were developed (Alexander et al., 1977; Gehl, 1987; Whyte, 1980). To take account of cultural and temporal variables, a different approach is needed.

The theory and practice of public space design and management must address these questions: How can the social and physical context of a place be most effectively and efficiently analyzed? How can the human dimensions best be used in this analysis to produce working criteria? Can the needs and rights of all potential users be accounted for, or are we forced to design only for the majority? What about change? How can a space be made adaptable to change, so that each shift in users does not require that settings be reconstructed? Must adaptable space be bland? Can the same place be meaningful to diverse groups of users? Finally, given a diversity of users and shifts in their social composition and needs, how can a place have meaning over time?

THE BASIS OF DESIGN AND MANAGEMENT

Design and management are critical phases in the endless process of creating the human environment and keeping it fit for its intended uses. They are the primary means for shaping and responding to the complex and changing relationships between people and their physical environment. But while design and management may have the same overall purpose, they are different and complementary activities.

Design comes forward when resources have been gathered to make a substantial change in an existing place. Its function is to discover the purposes of that change, to organize the appropriate means of bringing it about, and to guide construction or reconstruction. It is a relatively brief and intense act of creation.

Management is the process of controlling the use of the resulting place and of maintaining and adjusting its form to satisfy changing needs. It is a lengthy endeavor, cyclic in nature, and also creative. Management may emphasize simple caretaking, with occasional bursts of activity to adjust course, like sailing with prevailing winds; or it may involve continuous active intervention, like navigating in a storm. This depends on the nature of the place and its use.

To intervene successfully in the dynamic relations between people and public space, designers and managers need a theoretical frame of reference and a way of working that helps them see these relations clearly so as to manage change effectively. The human dimensions of public space, described in Part II, are intended to provide such a framework. They focus on the *relationship* between people and places, rather than on abstract human needs or place qualities. The approach and methodology that we will describe in this chapter and the next provide the means for making these dimensions specific to particular groups of users and to each context. As the example of Exposition Park illustrates, groups with differing expectations and desires will give differing values to the dimensions of need, and to rights and meanings, in the same place. Indeed, the "same place" is not really the same for different users. In key respects, each group will see it, use it, and think about it differently.

Because the design of a place is the most important factor in shaping people's perception and use, the designer wants to be able to predict these responses. The manager needs to read and understand how people are actually using a space and why. For the designer and the manager, knowledge of other spaces, past and present, provides information about the possibilities for shaping and managing new spaces. This information is even more useful when the relationship between the design of the space and the public life of the time in which it was created is understood. More important than examples from the past, however, is direct observation of people using the space in question, or using similar spaces, if it does not yet exist. The dimensions can also provide a structure for observation.

The research and case studies reported in Part II of this book are mostly based on this kind of close study of the relations between people and space. For similar contexts and user groups, these studies and others like them may provide a useful source of understanding. Existing spaces can sometimes be close enough to the situation under study to provide a prototype. However, in searching for prototypes one must proceed with caution because the differences in context and user groups often outweigh the apparent similarities in the type of space. The case of Boston City Hall Plaza, reported in Chapter 4, provides one example among many of a failed attempt to apply an Italian prototype to a North American space.

The perceptions, responses, and visions of the existing or future users of a place provide the most telling sources of information for design and management. If users are involved in the process of analysis, design, and management, this information enters with the immediacy of face-to-face communication. Images of real people replace the vague projections of imagination or the ghosts of statistical analysis. These people, representing all users, can engage in dialogue with designers and managers to inspire, to shape, to clarify, and to test their ideas. The human dimensions can become a framework for discussion and, if the dialogue is both open and well managed, it will lead to development and refinement of these dimensions. User participation can transform them into design and management criteria that are appropriate to the environmental context and to the particular groups that are drawn from that context.

apply this to cohousing

involve users

For the dimensions to be useful in this process, they must first become an active reality, which means that they will be part of the designer's vocabulary for thinking about design, a part of the manager's framework for evaluating how a space is working and for formulating policy to deal with it, and a part of the user's vocabulary for responding to possibilities or providing information about a working space. Designers and managers can make these human dimensions their own through practice – that is, by using them in observing and analyzing existing spaces, in thinking about design and management policy, and in discussing these matters with clients and users. This framework of concepts is not arcane. It refers to common experience. User participants can easily understand and respond to the issues it raises.

The relationship between the dimensions and the participating users is complementary. The dimensions provide a comprehensive framework for organizing ideas about the social utility of a space. The user participants provide the vital energy and the special insight to bring these initially abstract ideas to life. For example, comfort may be important in all spaces, and we know most of the physical and psychological variables that affect an individual's experience of comfort or discomfort. To gain an understanding of how comfortable surroundings are best created and maintained, in a given context, requires detailed knowledge of a place, its users, and the activities they want to pursue there. While some insight will come from repeated visits to the place and by the observation of people in similar settings, in-depth understanding is best gained in dialogue with actual users. If it is a place in their community, they are more likely to be aware of the peculiarities of the existing microclimate and social context. Certainly they will know best what they want to do there. *comfort*

Even more important than understanding each dimension, in the particular way that user involvement makes possible, is achieving the right balance among the dimensions. Any design is a balancing act among competing goals and priorities. Consultation with users creates a vivid awareness of the real social diversity, which enables designers and managers to formulate this balance and decision makers to better understand the social implications of design and management policies.

By engaging in dialogue with a representative cross section of users, potential and existing conflicts among groups can be addressed and, in most cases, resolved or managed. People are skilled in the arts of accommodation, and most people want to reach a consensus when a group is working to accomplish something together. Again, careful management is required to keep the lines of communication open, to make sure that differences are brought to the surface and debated with a minimum of rancor, and to avoid premature closure. Although such disputes may be difficult, they are far less so than the acting out of differences that occurs when the design and the management policy are insensitive to social diversity.

Once a forum of involved users has been created, it can even help deal with the knotty problem of future change. The people who use a place may be more aware of problems in the relations among various groups than is management. When things are not going right, management may not see the problem until it results in physical abuse to the space or in open conflict. Users are more likely to see the problem developing, and they can therefore be very helpful to the manager. Often, a timely shift in policy or operation can avoid costly physical repair or reconstruction.

Public space design and management are processes of guided search for the set of interventions in the ongoing environment that will best produce and maintain a socially useful place. They are guided by past experience, but they also make use of the creative power of the human mind to synthesize new information and solve complex problems. In the participatory mode we advocate, design and management depend not only on professional knowledge and skills, but also on the creativity and judgment of those directly affected, and on the capacity of human groups, through political dialogue, to strike and maintain an appropriate social balance.

MANTEO NEIGHBORHOOD AND WATERFRONT PLAN
Manteo, North Carolina

Located in downtown area and along waterfront of community; designed by landscape architect Randolph T. Hester, Jr., with input from local residents; built and managed by local residents; plan was completed in 1980 and waterfront construction in 1984; the size of the planning area is approximately 41 acres and the waterfront park is approximately 800 linear feet.

The Manteo plan is an example of a participatory approach to the planning and design of communitywide public spaces. Manteo, a historic waterfront community on the North Carolina coast, was faced with economic problems. The town wanted a plan that responded to the need for economic development while respecting the values and qualities of the community. They hired landscape architect Randy Hester to develop a plan for a new waterfront park. According to Hester (1985) "it took only a few days on the site to realize that a waterfront park would be a cosmetic cover-up. With over twenty percent seasonal unemployment and a declining tax base, Manteo needed a new economy" (p. 11). Hester convinced the town to let him work with the larger economic and physical landscape of the community.

Hester used a twelve-step participatory design process to develop a community and waterfront plan (Hester, 1984). The twelve steps were:

1. Listening to local concerns and ideas
2. Setting the neighborhood goals
3. Mapping and inventory of community resources

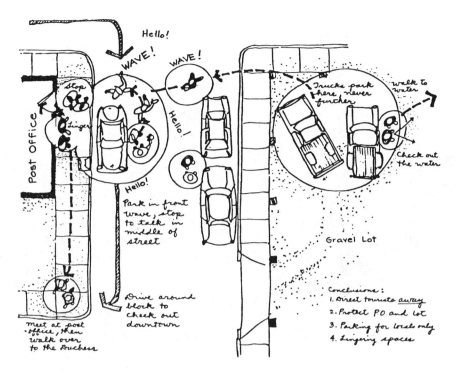

"Newsing at the Post Office" – analysis of community activity used by landscape architect Randy Hester to develop town plan for Manteo, North Carolina. (Randolph T. Hester, Jr.)

4. "Introducing the neighborhood to itself"
5. Getting a "gestalt of salient neighborhood issues"
6. Drawing anticipated activity settings
7. "Letting archetypes and idiosyncrasies inspire form"
8. "Making a conceptual yardstick"
9. Developing a spectrum of design plans
10. Evaluating costs and benefits of plans before construction
11. Transferring responsibility for the project from the designer to the community
12. Postconstruction evaluation

Participatory techniques used in the process included formal and informal user interviews and questionnaires, community surveys, observations, "ecology mapping," neighborhood forums and meetings, role playing, and brainstorming.

Hester (1985) describes his role as community designer in Manteo helping "the residents identify and preserve their valued life styles and landscapes in the face of change" (p. 10). The participatory process allowed community members to identify valued places and to understand the possible impact of changes on this "sacred" landscape of the town. It was a learning process for both the designers and the community participants.

Based on the mapping of the sacred structure of the community, Hester and the local residents developed a plan for improving the public environ-

User built boardwalk, which resulted from "sacred structure analysis" and participatory design process in Manteo, North Carolina. (Randolph T. Hester, Jr.)

ment of the waterfront. The participation process did not stop with the de-design. Local residents were responsible for actual construction of the waterfront boardwalk using community development funds to pay for materials. The completed waterfront project is a physical reflection of the values identified in the larger community design process. As Hester states (1985, p. 21), "at a recent tourist event that attracted several thousand visitors, local people were still able to walk to the post office, crab, and swim at the waterfront and have a leisurely breakfast at the Duchess diner in the section set aside for locals." Without the sensitivity to the local places and values gained from the participatory process, it is unlikely that these important aspects of the public life of the town would have been preserved.

Related cases: Barretto Street Neighborhood Park, Grand Street Waterfront Park, Gas Works Park, Boston Waterfront Park.

THE ART OF DESIGN

The art of design, in our view, is the ability to go beyond the information given to create an inclusive, unified, and durable vision for a place. Designers must often achieve this creative synthesis among conflicting needs and desires. They bring to the table their past experience, their ability to visualize and convey images, their knowledge of typical open space needs and rights, their research into the history and character of the place and its context, and their insights into its potential meanings. Other participants have their own experience of similar places and their particular points of view, but will rely on the designer's skills and judgment to assist them in visualizing and articulating their goals. An open and democratic design process is one of mutual learning and discovery. — *cohousing*

To work effectively in such a process, designers must learn to alternate comfortably times of extreme openness and responsiveness to the needs and wishes of others with periods of self-directed work leading to closure. In an inclusive design process a good listener will hear many voices, sometimes contradictory ones. The designer must discover how such a range of diverse needs may be accommodated within a space to achieve a well-functioning whole.

For instance, a new waterfront park to be built in a densely populated urban area, with both office and residential areas nearby, will have potentially conflicting demands upon its use. There will be those who wish to use it only for passive engagement – strolling, sitting, reading, taking the sun, watching other people, eating lunch. Families will want to use it for some of those purposes, but also more actively for child and adult play, especially in the late afternoons, evenings, and on weekends. This may include space-consuming games such as tossing a frisbee or shagging flies. Still others will want dedicated play spaces for young children, or for softball, basketball, handball, or tennis. Unless the park is very large, these user needs will compete for the space available. The rights of sunbathers are likely to be in direct conflict with those who want to play pickup softball. The designed balance of spaces will affect not only the rights of the users but also the meaning of the park in their lives.

The designer must be able to imagine the ways and times the park will be used by various groups and anticipate the potential conflicts. If this information is communicated clearly to participating users and the client, then many of the possible conflicts can be discussed and avoided through appropriate design and management policies. For instance, when space is limited, most settings can be made suitable for multiple uses. It requires experience and imagination to make this work, but both become more effective when grounded in direct knowledge of real people who will use the park.

Such a dialogue can be helpful in exploring and developing the subtler aspects of design, such as meaning. Good discussions with users, with examples from other times and places, can reveal the dimensions of meaning to which they will respond most strongly. Although meaning deepens and changes through experience, the grounds for this evolution are created by the initial design of a space and its management policies. The resonant connections between the place and its larger environment must be there

Citizens of Lewiston, Maine, discuss how they want their main street to be, after a slide show with examples from elsewhere. (Stephen Carr)

to be discovered, and then given personal and group meaning by future users.

Environmental design is an art that is founded in the craft of place making. Artistic creation arises from mysterious depths of the human mind, which we do not presume to be able to probe. It is this poetics of design, the opportunity for self-expression, and through that for expression of the human spirit, that motivates people to become designers and keeps them motivated through all the struggles required to bring a design project to fruition. Nonetheless, all artists must know their craft.

In the case of environmental design, this craft is often thought to involve a mastery of the technical and business skills of the profession. To practice public space design in a socially responsible way, these skills must be expanded to include those of communication, social relations, and politics. In the next chapter we will suggest ways to organize and carry out public space design so that it can become a true collaboration between designers and the people who are intended to benefit. In these public design processes, the designer's social skills will be sharpened, and much new and challenging information will become available.

In the creative synthesis of design, this information is sorted, reorganized, and put forward as design hypotheses. The participatory process provides the means for pretesting these hypotheses and refining them, before the space is built. Good management provides the mechanism for ongoing adjustment, after it is built. In both endeavors the human dimensions are a useful means for organizing design hypotheses and analyzing the human consequences of alternative spatial moves. To see how this can work, let us consider each of the dimensions in turn.

DESIGN FOR NEEDS

The generic dimensions of comfort, relaxation, passive engagement, active engagement, and discovery, discussed in Chapter 4, must be given concrete expression by the designer in a particular social and physical context. For example, the evidence suggests that the need for active engagement is a basic one that people will seek to satisfy in some way in virtually any public space. However, opportunities for active engagement in a park or a playground differ sharply from those that might be offered in a downtown plaza, and would also differ from one cultural group to another. The design challenge is to discover those types of engagement that are right for a particular space and social context, and to strike an appropriate balance with the satisfaction of other needs.

To do this, the designer can begin by drawing out from users the types of engagement that people may seek in this space: say, striking up acquaintances with strangers, socializing with friends and relatives, and active recreation. Then, based on a program analysis, the designer would think of the various potential users and imagine the type of setting that best supports a particular activity for a particular group. For instance, in the example of the waterfront park, a large level lawn area for informal organized sports like pickup softball or soccer may be needed in addition to resilient hard surfaces for court games. These same spaces, appropriately arranged, can be used for other activities, such as relaxing on the lawn, dancing, or roller skating in a court area or socializing at a group picnic or bake sale. By imagining these relations between groups, needs, and settings, the designer can begin to project the particular qualities that will make the space work well for various uses at various times. Each such projection contributes an hypothesis that can be tested through discussions with user participants.

Even conventional spaces may need to be reviewed. Although the dimensions and requirements for the creation of a basketball court are well known, important questions include whether to provide half courts for simple informal use or a full court for real team play, and whether to provide arrangements for viewing the games. The designer should be able to help people understand that if multiple use of a hard surface area is desired, then two small half courts with space between for volleyball, badminton or dancing may be much more useful for more people than a full court, which would likely be appropriated by organized teams to the exclusion of other activities. Further, if the court were recessed with tiered seating around, it could be used for informal performances as well as basketball.

Because of the different activities preferred by people of differing ethnicity, age, or income and the special space requirements of each, the potential for conflict and for failing to meet some needs is great. Zoning of various activities allows for the creation of appropriate settings in each zone, and is an obvious approach where space allows. However, because there is rarely enough space to provide a separate and appropriate setting for each desired activity, the creation of multi-use settings is a more common solution. As in the examples just given, this usually results in some compromise in the accommodation of some activities (e.g., half court for full) and careful study and discussion with users is required to make the most productive choices. Conversely, if some needs for active use are ignored, a space designed for one activity may be usurped for another, which creates greater management problems. A thoughtfully designed multiuse space, far from being bland, can be an intriguing place, rich with possibility.

In Gallery Place, in downtown Washington, D.C., the central space was designed to be, alternatively, a play fountain, a reflecting pool, and a festival space, complete with tent tie-downs. (Stephen Carr)

The tent in place for an international food fair. (Stephen Carr)

The designer must not only think about how to support multiple uses of a space, but also how this time sharing will affect the use of adjacent spaces. The possibilities can be studied by means of simple "bubble diagrams" trying out uses in several locations, which helps to think through the implications. However, this gives only crude answers, because details of design, such as the nature of perceived boundaries, can make a big difference. A good designer will be imagining mitigating details even in the diagram stage. As these alternatives are discussed with users, it will be important to describe, in an understandable way, how these boundaries and buffers can work. Pictures of other existing settings can be used to simulate the possibilities.

The accommodation of other less active needs, in settings used by several groups, may be easier. The requirements for comfort, being based in large part on human anatomy and physiology, are similar for all groups. In our culture, backless benches tend to be uncomfortable for people of all ages. However, even comfort, and certainly relaxation, are not to be achieved in public settings without the proper social and psychological as well as physical supports. It is important to understand what various groups find relaxing as well as how they perceive each other. If one group wants to relax by listening or dancing to loud music, a space should be available that is not immediately next to the sitting areas near entrances where older people like to congregate. Even if the music is not objectionable, the presence of numbers of highly active young people can create a threat to an older person whose mobility and sense of physical stability may be impaired.

Passive engagement and discovery are also needs that may not seem to produce potential conflict among different user groups. After all, people-watching is a prime form of passive engagement. Observation of differences and surprising similarities can provide delightful discoveries. However, to enjoy these popular activities, an individual must be relatively comfortable and relaxed. The setting must feel safe and provide havens for observation, close to but out of the action. The best settings, like the Fontana di Trevi in Rome, provide for graded degrees of involvement, from an overview in the complete security of a nearby restaurant to near immersion in the water. The case of the steps of the New York Public Library (presented in Chapter 4) shows how this works in a less elaborate setting. Such graded settings allow people to choose the level of engagement and openness to discovery appropriate to their needs.

As in any problem of resource allocation, the satisfaction of some people's needs through the design of public space can lead to ignoring or increasing the needs of others. Although the scarce resource of available space may be stretched by design for multiuse, this may put a strain on another scarce resource: good management. In a large park it is relatively easy to accommodate the needs of people for active recreation while still providing ample space for the passive pleasures of sitting or lying in the sun. As the park becomes smaller, the same lawn may have to do double duty, requiring that the times for the incompatible activities be scheduled. In a neighborhood park this becomes even more difficult, in principle, because the space is smaller. In practice, it may be worked out simply by neighbors accommodating one another. Achieving such a balance in a local playground can be particularly difficult because of the space-consuming nature of young children's play and the dimensional requirements of court games. The designer's ingenuity may yet find a comfortable, protected place for older people to sit in such a setting, but sometimes the decision to favor one group's needs and rights over those of another will be unavoidable. A representative process of user involvement allows such decisions to be made in open debate among the different interested parties.

PROTECTING RIGHTS

Skill in achieving and maintaining an appropriate balance between potentially conflicting needs and rights is central to both design and management. This is essentially a political skill, which must be informed by the advice and consent of representative users to be successfully employed.

In any democratic system there must be protection for the rights of minorities against the tyranny of the majority. Public space is no exception.
Although there is no public space user's Bill of Rights, we suggest that
the rights enumerated in Chapter 5 provide a very useful guide to issues
that are likely to be important in any design or management of public
space for multiple user groups. We believe that the rights of access, freedom of action, claim, change, and ownership are fundamental in a democratic society. They need not all be exercised in every case, but they must
always be considered as a potential to be exercised. We citizens do indeed
own our public spaces and have the right to change them if they don't
suit us, even though we may not wish to organize to do so just now.

People's rights in a space are not often explicitly considered in design.
Partly as a result, conflicts over access and use can become an onerous
and sometimes overwhelming preoccupation for managers. Designers may
take it for granted that if people's needs are served by a space, it will be
used. There are, however, many examples to show that perfectly "usable"
spaces are avoided because the potential users do not feel that they have
the basic right of access, or freedom of action once there. The Forty-
second Street side of Bryant Park in New York, which was claimed by
drug dealers, is a case in point. There may be a failure of management to
provide adequate security or to deal with inappropriate turf claims. As
often, the design itself fails to provide the right physical supports and visual clues to open access and use. In Bryant Park, the area of drug dealing
is raised above the adjacent sidewalk and screened from view by a balustrade and hedge.

Needs and rights are intertwined in practice. A person confined to a
wheelchair may need a suitably designed ramp and the absence of other
barriers in order to have the right of access to a place. Freedom of action
for all depends on designed freedom from both physical and psychological
barriers. The right of one group to claim a space for its short-term use may
frustrate another that needs it for some other purpose. This problem, in
an extreme form, has been poignantly illustrated by parks "taken over" by
homeless people, who are then in conflict with people from the surrounding community. The designer can delineate physical subareas within a
space, which will, by their size, shape, equipment, and boundaries, encourage or discourage temporary claims. Careful design to protect rights
can help the elderly and teenagers to coexist in the same public space,
and even discourage drug dealing, but it cannot redress the societal inequities that lead to homelessness.

The rights of permanent change, ownership, and disposition do not appear to be within the designer's prerogative to create or protect. These are
rights that, in our culture, tend to run with the legal control of the land

and to be eased or squeezed more by management than design. Supports for temporary change can be designed into the space, as when electrical outlets are provided for sound systems, or when tent tie-downs for community events are located in paved areas. Demountable shelters, stages, and bleachers, together with movable lighting and sound systems and places for storing them, provide further flexibility for short-term change. When users can readily adapt spaces to their changing needs, their *sense* of ownership increases, whatever may be its legal status. When adaptable spaces are coupled with responsive management, conflict is reduced.

In contemporary urban plazas, conflicts over needs and rights are often subtler than in parks. City squares are nearly always circulation spaces, gathering places, and resting places. Gathering for public events and performances requires visually open areas with, preferably, sloped or tiered ground planes. Desired lines of movement, often on a diagonal, may cut across the space, potentially interfering with the views of events or diverting those wishing to move through. Recessed spaces with sloped or tiered sides will make movement difficult for the elderly or those in wheelchairs. These spaces may also become unsafe, if the recess is great enough to block views from adjacent streets. People wanting to sit and rest may enjoy watching the passing flows, but will also want some seclusion and

Pioneer Square in Portland, Oregon, attempts a multi-use solution but still resembles an empty amphitheater most of the time. (Stephen Carr)

Too many planters can stifle commercial life. The "K" street pedestrian mall in downtown Sacramento before being renovated into a transit mall. (Mark Francis)

protection from crowds watching an event. Many will want shade, thus reducing the open gathering space. As with parks, if the plaza is large enough, all these needs might be accommodated with minimum infringement on the rights of others. In most cases the designer, with the help of user participants, must strike a careful balance within narrow confines. Designing to secure rights can become a process of negotiation.

Downtown shopping streets transformed into pedestrian malls pose even more dilemmas. Desires for movement and rest are often in conflict. Business people, except for café owners, typically want to keep people moving – window shopping and frequenting the shops. Designers of downtown pedestrian malls, perhaps confusing these streets with plazas or parks, have often located raised planters and other structures in the middle of the street. These may include sitting places, fountains, shelters, playgrounds, or stages. Such designs occupy the street, which may seem too wide and empty once the cars are removed, but they also block easy visual access and limit freedom to cross the street from one shop to another – even though achieving such ease of movement may have been a primary reason for closing the street in the first place.

Other conflicts will often occur over the rights of street vendors or performers to claim the street in front of established retail businesses. On conventional downtown shopping streets, with roadways and sidewalks, the width of sidewalks will often limit vending activity. Police will prevent vendors or performers from blocking the free flow of pedestrians or access to businesses. In most cities, vendors and performers are required to have permits, which often limit the choice of locations to avoid conflicts with businesses. In the new downtown mall designs, where much more space is available, accommodation of both can be achieved, especially because established business people have come to see vendors and performers, within limits, as desirable to activate streets that may otherwise seem empty. In some cases (see the Church Street Marketplace case in Chapter 6), there will be a downtown management entity that carefully regulates the types and locations of vendors and performers, often using particular designed settings within the street as spatial anchors.

Street vendors can be a colorful addition to public space helping to attract new customers downtown if their locations are managed to avoid conflict. Burlington, Vermont. (Stephen Carr)

Harborplace, on Baltimore's Inner Harbor, has drawn new development but remains primarily public. (Stephen Carr)

In shopping centers and the festival marketplaces of certain downtowns, these activities are highly formalized and regulated, with uniform carts for vendors, stages for performers, and a designed balance and schedule of activities. Some semipublic atria also feature staged and managed activity, and all regulate access. As noted in Chapter 5, this has led to protest and sometimes to public regulation to assure free access, at least during open hours. It is clear, however, that one current trend, for which the "worlds" of Disney were the vanguard, is toward commercially oriented semipublic spaces in which the visitor's experience is highly designed and in which freedom of access, action, and claim are all abandoned for the pleasure of being entertained.

Urban waterfronts also can be zones of conflict over rights of access and use. In many cities, formerly industrial waterfront areas are being opened up for other activities. Waterfronts are especially attractive for residential development and for some types of office and commercial activities. Cities are always eager for new tax-paying uses. On the other hand, there are also strong public demands for free access to the waterfront and for new open space to support a wide variety of recreational activities. Some cities, such as Boston, Philadelphia, and San Francisco, have managed to accommodate both. Others, such as Detroit, which are more beleaguered and desperate for new taxes, have allowed fenced enclaves of middle-class housing to usurp parts of the waterfronts. In still other places, including Manhattan's West Side, a battle is currently raging over whether any more private development like that at Battery Park City should be allowed on the Hudson River waterfront in order to pay for new public spaces to open up access. It is a common perception among West Side residents that no matter how well designed these spaces may be, they will never be truly open to a full range of people, so long as they are associated with luxury developments. North Park, now under construction at Battery Park City and specifically designed for use by the larger community, with their participation, will test this hypothesis as to the limiting effects of social context.

Even in community open spaces, which are designed with or by the community, such as gardens, miniparks, or playgrounds, there are important questions about rights. These spaces are typically fenced and often closed to nonmembers or open only for a few hours a week, even when they are on public land. It is understandable that those who build and maintain a space wish to keep it mainly for themselves. Further, in the case of gardens, there is a need to protect against potential vandalism or theft of produce. In playgrounds, use by outsiders can lead to unwarranted liability for those who have built them. By careful design, noncommunity members can be allowed to view activities without engaging in them. The best solution, however, is likely to be some form of cooperative ownership in which land is leased or deeded to a group, which is then in control of use for its own members. Where the land was originally public, the quid pro quo may be to require that membership must be open to all within the community.

The rules of private property which is open as a public park must be explicitly stated. (Mark Francis)

To establish and protect people's rights in public space requires close attention to both design and management. Design alone will not do it. A thorough site and context analysis and participatory program development can identify many of the possibly conflicting needs and rights at the beginning of a project. To invent a design that protects the rights of all with a minimum of conflict requires skilled and experienced designers and managers, and a participatory process that continues into use. Similar examples should be studied, and options must be explored in order to learn what the space can accommodate and how that will affect the rights of users. However, in order really to understand this and to create the right balance of supports and constraints in the physical designs, management policies should be set and a program designed at the same time. If the predicted effects on people's rights of access, use, claim, ownership, and disposition are made explicit in the design stage, there will be a baseline for evaluating the space in use and for making the necessary adjustments over time.

MAKING SPACES MEANINGFUL

Making public spaces meaningful is also a process involving users, designers, and space managers. First, spaces must support meaningful daily experiences. They must have sufficient variety for people to satisfy their needs and find pleasure, interest, and delight in using them. The spaces must fit well in their context and enable people to feel comfortable and secure in going there. The management system should be a democratic one, allowing cultural expression, temporary claiming, and change so that people feel that the space is part of their lives and an expression of their identity, if only while they are using it. In order to develop a tie to a space and concern for it, a group or community should be involved in both design and control of the space, with rights and responsibilities in its management. Finally, management should provide meaningful elements and events within the spaces, resources that resound with the user's cultural preferences to stimulate interest, use, and commitment to the place, qualities that are the foundation of meaning.

A space that truly meets people's needs will, by virtue of that alone, have meaning for them. By contrast, a monumental space consciously designed to be impressive and thus "meaningful," may convey little to its users — apart from the discomfort of walking across it. Attention to needs and rights of public space users prepares the way for the expression of cultural meanings. If public space design would satisfy these basic performance dimensions, the meaning of places would be greatly increased. People return repeatedly to a space that provides for important needs and secures

Cohousing

their rights of use, and this repeated experience results in the personal attachments that are one basis of meaning.

Beyond function, there are many choices to be made that are often thought of as the artistic prerogative of the designer. These choices of specific forms and materials, and the relations among them, greatly influence the user's experience of associative meaning. They determine how a place resonates with the cultural expectations and longings of users, and have a great deal to do with whether it is loved and enriched over time. To create settings that are meaningful in this deeper sense is the greatest challenge of public space design.

Our multicultural society offers many potential associations with other times and places upon which the designer might draw. Almost any way we might choose to create an environmental theme could appeal to a particular group, as Disney has so successfully demonstrated. The simulation of history seems to have special appeal for a restless and often rootless population, even though it is "just pretend," as on Disney's Main Street or in the latest pleasure dome shopping centers (Henry, 1986). However, this false historicism can be meaningless or even abhorrent to many, or have only the transitory appeal of novelty. Instant history, like instant coffee, may stimulate without satisfying.

One way to achieve a deeper and more lasting meaning is to emphasize the connections between a place and its context. To do this requires a gathering in and expression of those qualities of context that make a region or a city or a neighborhood unique. For central spaces, these qualities might be derived from study of the natural landscape that is characteristic of the surrounding region (Hough, 1990; Norberg-Schulz, 1980). Inspiration can come from the topography, the abundance of particular building materials or colors, the presence or absence of water, and the typical vegetation to be found there. The great urban central parks have often developed these associations, but it can be done in other types of space as well (cf. Church Street Marketplace, Chapter 6).

A second set of contextual references may be to real historical connections, whether to the typical settlement patterns of the place, the typical qualities of past architecture, or the particular occurrences. Monuments, of course, usually refer to the past, and when they memorialize truly significant people or events, they can retain their meaning for long periods of time. The "classical quotations" of columns, pediments, and the like, currently in fashion among "postmodern" designers, attempt to make connections with a commonly revered past, but they are often wildly out of context in U.S. cities. The Piazza d'Italia in New Orleans, one of the more successful examples of this trend in public space, is located in the yard of an office building, but at least has the pretext of a nearby Italian-American neighborhood. Cities such as Santa Fe, New Mexico, and Santa Barbara,

Santa Barbara, California, has maintained a Spanish colonial character in both old and new development. The El Paseo. (Stephen Carr)

California, have chosen environmental themes derived from the way of life, cultural forms, and building technologies of earlier people on those sites. These can be evocative, if often irrelevant to modern life. When the formal devices of a design recall the history of the site without creating a pastiche, they can stimulate thought. The Benjamin Franklin Park in Philadelphia memorializes his house and gardens without attempting to recreate them. The Lowell Heritage State Park Entrance Plazas (see Chapter 6) recall the train station once on the site where millworkers first entered the city, and celebrate the city's unique canal system, used for powering the textile mills.

Most difficult, least developed, and potentially most rewarding would be the development of qualities and associative meanings that are appropriate to our own time and place and the experiences of our emerging culture. In the past, such work has been produced by artists, often in the context of an inspirational religion. Works that will later seem a powerful distillation of the spirit of their time often are not recognized as such when erected, because they are a step ahead and to the side of current fashions.

In our society, which lacks spiritual unity, meaningful designs may draw inspiration from our understanding of human development and from our growing awareness of our place in the biosphere. One can see hints of this in true adventure playgrounds, community gardens, and in the new emphasis on working with nature by using native plants and meadows, in place of clipped grass. As the environmental movement develops, trees and forest may come to seem sacred in themselves. If environmental stewardship becomes our highest calling, then designers and managers alike will see their roles quite differently, and meaning will flow directly from their way of working with people and nature.

The design of a site potentially is the strongest factor in establishing connections to an area and the people in it. Each of the components of meaning – the history, the people, the groups, other buildings in the area, natural and cosmic forces – can be translated into an image by the design. Ultimately this image and a feeling for ambience is what the users carry in their minds. It is the synthesis of experiences in a place and the stage for their memories. In some cases the design may be a fairly literal translation of the connection – the Statue of Liberty, Lincoln's seated figure in his monument, the pagoda in a Chinatown plaza, the Hispanic design of a Chicano plaza. In other cases, the image may be distilled from less direct sources – the moving lights around the old New York Times Building that broadcast the centrality of that site or the St. Louis Arch, "Gateway to the West." All of these images are initially laid down by the design and are later developed by patterns of use and experiences over the years. It is these continuations of image and use that are the essential ingredients of environmental meaning.

PUBLIC ART AND COLLABORATIONS

For thousands of years the creators of public places have turned to artists to provide meaningful symbols. From the Minoan murals and the Greek and Roman friezes and statues of the gods, emperors, and battles, we have derived a tradition of artworks in public places depicting figures and events of consequence to the culture of the time. In nineteenth-century America, in civic plazas and on public buildings, the embarrassing virility of our raw commercial and industrial might was often cloaked in neoclassical garb, producing many icons that were probably meaningless to most people except as declarations of power, prosperity, and cultural striving. Parks were often graced with statues of their benefactors. When the politicians and the commercial barons of the time could resist this temptation, they

The classic nineteenth-century monument. Union Square, New York City. (Stephen Carr)

would often find a military figure who could be placed in a commanding position on horseback, upon whose pedestal their own name could appropriately be displayed. Public art was seen as a means of uplifting the taste of the masses and was not a product of a democratic process.

We have not yet broken free of this particular prejudice – that art is something to be selected by an elite of qualified judges, and then presented to the public for its enlightenment. The committees who currently select public art and artists are typically made up of museum curators, collectors, and dealers, with an occasional token community member, business person, or artist. Even in Cambridge, Massachusetts, where the process is more than usually democratic, the Arts Commission creates two parallel groups for artist selection – a citizens' committee to advise a panel of experts. These experts then vote behind closed doors. The choice is often determined by esoteric values, and it should not be surprising if public art selected by such a process is seen as meaningless or worse by those to whom it is finally exposed. At times public outcry has even forced the removal of the work, as in the well-publicized case of Richard Serra's *Tilted Arc*, which was installed in New York's Federal Plaza.

One problem for art in our time may be the shortage of inspiring universal themes, such as a religion provided. Artists can nearly always produce pleasing arrangements of shape and color and surprising figures to delight the eye, but beauty is only the promise of art. The modern works with the greatest power to move people seem to be those that memorialize atrocities, like Picasso's *Guernica,* the work of several artists at the Ardeatine Caves outside Rome (commemorating a World War II massacre), the evocative sculptures outside the Holocaust Museum in Jerusalem, or the Vietnam Memorial in Washington, D.C. Some artists, like Claes Oldenburg, have found ways to make everyday objects, like clothespins and baseball bats, into easily understandable monumental icons, poking fun at monuments while reminding us of the ascendancy of the ordinary in our lives. Far more meaningful as a cultural expression of our time might be the "walls of fire" in Hispanic East Los Angeles or other amazing creations of unknowns, like the famed Watts Towers, which dot our landscape (Wampler, 1977). Certainly they display an energy and creativity often lacking in "high culture" public art.

However selected for the task, the artist faces the same difficulty as the public space designer in discovering and expressing ideas that are meaningful to a diverse and changing audience of users. A seemingly promising "new" idea is collaboration between artists and architects, or landscape architects, in the initial stages of design. This idea is founded in the hope that artists may be in touch with deeper wellsprings of creativity than their counterparts in the applied arts, and that the design professional will help the artist become aware of the practical and technical considerations involved in the design of public space. From such alliances

North Cove, Battery Park City, New York City. (Stephen Carr)

South Cove, Battery Park City, New York City. (Stephen Carr)

are expected to come spaces of greater beauty and meaning than usual. When artist and designer select each other, out of a mutual interest in and respect for the other's work, the results can indeed be as imagined. When artists and designers are selected independently and asked to work together, the product of such an arranged marriage may be disappointing.

Designers are accustomed to being in charge of the design process, and artists to working independently on their own ideas. True collaboration is a skill that must be learned, and work on an important public commission is a charged and difficult setting for learning. When artists and designers are each determined to control the design, the results can be extremely bland, because little of interest can be agreed upon. When the artist dominates, the outcome can be insensitive to needs and rights that do not fit with the particular artistic vision, as in Serra's *Tilted Arc*. When the designer dominates, the artist may feel thwarted and produce lame decorative works, as seems to have been the case in Battery Park City's North Cove. On the other hand, South Cove, another collaboration of an artist and designers in the same development, is an interesting blend of elements that is evocative of seaside settings.

There is hope in the idea of collaboration, especially if it can be broadened to include not only an artist and a designer, but also the space manager and representative users. Because commissions for important public works are obtained on a competitive basis, teams of artists and designers might be formed prior to selection; or else, because the designer is likely to have overall responsibility for implementation, then he or she should be involved in the selection of an artist. The compatibility of designer and artist is essential to a productive working relationship. Users should also be involved in both designer and artist selection and throughout the working process. The result would be to open up the process and to sensitize both collaborators to the real purposes of their work. Attention to the human dimensions and the users of public space could yet produce a public art with meaning for our time.

THE ART OF MANAGEMENT

To achieve the proper balance of uses in a space, to secure the rights of users, and even to encourage the development of meaning requires a full and accurate understanding of the management system that will govern

Understanding the expected level of maintenance during design is very important to the choice of materials. In a plaza in central Tokyo, Japan, maintenance is typically of higher quality than in the United States. (Mark Francis)

and maintain the space. Funds for management of public space are often near the bottom of the municipal hierarchy of political demands, falling far behind such services as police, fire, waste disposal, and road maintenance. In many cases, the capability to provide continuous management or even adequate maintenance is minimal. Such a situation places severe constraints on a design. For instance, in the example of the park with conflicting user needs and limited space, multiuse spaces can resolve potential conflicts only if recreation staff is available on site to manage lawns that can be used for sunning, picnicking, or informal softball, and volleyball courts that are also striped for badminton. If staff cannot be secured for the foreseeable future, then dedicated single-use facilities are more likely to be successful, even though this reduces dramatically the range of possible uses for the space.

Involvement of managers in the design process is the best way to learn about the limitations and the potentials of the management and maintenance system. Even when new projects attract special management funding, managers are more likely than designers to have realistic expectations about future change. This change is often in the direction of reducing the available budget and staff, once a new space has become established. Sometimes such reductions can be precipitous and have drastic results, as the Downtown Washington Streets for People case illustrates. More often, there is simply a tendency to gradually expand the responsibilities of staff without increasing their number, eventually reaching the lowest common denominator typical of the city. The designer must often resist the temptation to design with a high standard of maintenance and management in mind and work within more modest expectations. Our public spaces are filled with fountains that no longer function, richly planted areas that have gone to weed, and broad sweeps of once lushly green turf that have reverted to bare ground through misuse and lack of maintenance.

DOWNTOWN WASHINGTON STREETS FOR PEOPLE
Washington, D.C.

Located on F Street between Seventh and Ninth streets, G Street between Ninth and Tenth streets, and Eighth Street between E and F streets, covering an 8-city-block area; designed by Arrowstreet, Inc.; completed in 1974; managed by the District of Columbia Department of Transportation.

By 1970, the retail core of Washington had suffered significant losses and declining retail sales as businesses failed or relocated to the city's other retail centers or to the suburbs. The Streets for People project was part of an ambitious plan to rebuild and revitalize this once thriving part of the city. The plan, which focused on the redesign and management of public space, was originally intended to encompass a sixty block area. Today, more than twenty years later, only Phase 1 of the project has been completed.

Sponsored by the city's Redevelopment Land Agency and designed by Arrowstreet, Inc., the Streets for People project was intended to create a strong identity for the retail area and to provide the physical improvements needed to encourage and support a wide range of public activities. The plan also included the development of a preliminary first-year activity program aimed at drawing a wide variety of users to the area.

Four of the blocks reconstructed in Phase 1 were designed as pedestrian-only spaces. The other four involved sidewalk improvements to vehicular streets. The center and focal point of the project is Gallery Place, a large, open plaza in front of the National Gallery on F Street between Seventh and Ninth. This space was designed to permit large public gatherings, such as fairs and festivals (see figures 7.6 and 7.7). Variable fountain displays animated the space. Adjacent to it on Eighth Street, between I and F streets, is the Vendors' Plaza, which was envisioned as a lively outdoor shopping street. Vendors' stations that provided permanent storage and display space were installed along both sides of the street. Together, Gallery Place and Vendors' Plaza were intended to be a hub for both formal and informal activities in the project area.

Library Place, on G Street between Ninth and Tenth, in front of the Martin Luther King Memorial Library, was planned for a sharply contrasting program and purpose. Designed around an extensive system of granite pools and fountains that extend the length of the block, Library Place was intended to provide a quiet sitting area that could be enjoyed by both library users and shoppers. It was also considered a memorial garden for Dr. King, with plantings selected in part for their interest, in scent and texture, to the blind.

Of particular interest was the programming and design process. The designers organized and carried out an extensive user consultation, which reached out to engage people from the area. A brief on-the-street interview identified the range of people present on F or G Street at various times of the day and week. From this larger sample, a representative cross section was contacted and engaged as user consultants. They met with the designers over an eight-week period. Initially organized in small groups, primarily by age and ethnicity, these users started by analyzing downtown's problems and developing their own solutions and ended by reviewing the designers' ideas in mixed groups. The program for the entire downtown, and especially the built spaces, was developed through this process, with additional guidance from the downtown business community and the Redevelopment Land Agency. The final designs were developed to the point of satisfaction of all these parties.

In the first year, with a strong and supportive activity program, Phase 1 was quite successful as a new downtown magnet. Today, poorly managed, undermaintained, and largely unused, the Streets for People project is a far cry from the lively "Washington Commons" envisioned by the designers. Despite the extensive participatory effort that went into planning and design, the project's current condition results from a number of unaccounted for and unforeseen circumstances: the failure of several key assumptions that were critical to the project's success; failure in the arrangement for

unintended outcomes

Streets for People was an ambitious set of new public spaces in downtown Washington, D.C. In Library Place, designed as a memorial to Martin Luther King, Jr., an extensive fountain system created an oasis of peace. (Stephen Carr)

management and maintenance; and a changing political and economic climate.

Although the city's Redevelopment Land Agency was responsible for overseeing the planning and implementation of the project, its authority

275

In the first year of Streets for People, a program of festivities and performances drew a diverse population of users. (Stephen Carr)

ceased with completion of construction. It had been assumed that Downtown Progress, a private business group, would continue to operate the activity program and push for good public maintenance and the completion of the project. However, the deteriorating downtown economy caused the organization to go out of existence just after Phase 1 was complete. At the designer's urging, the Redevelopment Land Agency tried to contract with the National Park Service, which maintains the Washington Mall, to operate Streets for People; but this arrangement fell through at the last minute as well. It would appear that too little attention had been given to building the institutions and assuring the involvement of existing organizations that could have played a more permanent managerial role.

Without an appropriate agency to take responsibility, the management and maintenance of the project fell upon the D.C. Department of Transportation, because they "owned" the streets. This agency was inadequately funded and organized to undertake the higher-than-average level of maintenance that the project required and it was not their interest. As well, there was no one to take responsibility for programming activities, which were critical to the project's success in the first year. Not only did a management group fail to develop, but several other redevelopment projects, to which

Streets for People had been designed to respond, either failed to be implemented or had considerably less impact than had been anticipated. Each of these problems was exacerbated by the severe cutbacks in federal funding under the Nixon administration, which also occurred at the time Phase 1 was completed. As a result of these declining budget allocations, inadequate maintenance and management, and the failure of the retail core to undergo substantial redevelopment, the first Streets for People now stand in a semiruined state, with empty fountains and plantings that have gone to weed.

The lesson of Streets for People is that the best of intentions, skillful design, and a design process with full public involvement cannot achieve lasting success in the absence of firm commitments to first-rate management. In another economic and political climate, the decline of these spaces might not have been so precipitous, but lacking a competent operator, it would still have occurred. Perhaps, too, the responsible agency and its designers overestimated their power to influence the local political economy. This first phase was consciously located to help strengthen the end of downtown most used by lower-income blacks, and it therefore lacked economic support. Even the recent private redevelopment of the other end of downtown for middle- to upper-income retail and office uses has failed to spur renewal of the Streets for People area.

Related cases: Church Street Marketplace, Gågate Walking Street.

On the other hand, where users are so directly involved that they actually help support the operations of a space, it is much more likely that high standards will be maintained. In the case of the Church Street Marketplace in Burlington, Vermont, described in Chapter 6, the merchants along this main street agreed to an additional charge above property taxes to operate an activity program and to maintain the streets after substantial public space improvements were made. The city's government, for its part, twice turned down a proposed regional shopping mall on the outskirts. Downtown fees are scaled to the size of business, are mandatory, and were agreed to in anticipation of increased sales, once improvements were made. This increase has occurred, and so it is really the citizens of Burlington who pay for street entertainment and upkeep of the Marketplace as they use it. The Marketplace District Commission, rather than building up a large staff of its own, uses private contractors to perform the maintenance. With a small staff it can directly arrange for street performers and for periodic fairs and festivals, as well as manage street vending. This arrangement has proved to be highly successful and durable through the first ten years of operation. Because both the merchants and the citizens of Burlington were involved extensively in the design of the street, there has never been any question that this central space belongs to the people of the city. By creating a self-funding commission to be the responsible operating entity, the city not only gained a better meeting ground for its

Good, active, well-funded management of space use and maintenance is a key to the success of the Church Street Marketplace, Burlington, Vermont. (Stephen Carr)

population but has been able to retain downtown as the dominant retail and business center. At the same time, Burlington has not given over full control of this key central space to the private sector, since the city council appoints the commissioners and oversees their activity.

The frequently disappointing history of management by conventional public agencies has caused private developers to insist on private management for the public spaces they fund or create. The privatization of downtown public space in "festive marketplaces," interior atria, and gallerias, solves the problem of operation by treating it as one aspect of good business. Spaces that are clean, well lit, and secure, with carefully maintained plantings, continuously running fountains, fresh flags and banners, and an ever-changing display of programmed activities have proved to be successful attractors of people in suburban shopping centers. Some cities have embraced and heavily subsidized these private facilities located on formerly public land, in the hope of revitalizing their failing downtowns. In the process they have created controversy over whose spaces these really are, and what purposes they are to serve.

These commercially managed spaces often provide a relatively high level of comfort and security, passive engagement and discovery. Providing for this particular array of needs supports their overall purpose, which is to transform consumption of goods and services into a profitable recreational activity. They do not provide for relaxation, since the idea is to keep people excited and moving, nor for active engagement except in the act of buying. Their physical design and management policy compromise or severely limit access, freedom of action, and the rights of claim and change. Whatever its benefits, private management should be limited to those situations where the space is under private ownership or else be made fully accountable through public oversight.

Although some aspects of maintenance and security may be efficiently provided on a contract basis, privatization is not a panacea for the problems of public space management. If it is to be accountable to provide for the full spectrum of needs and rights, management must be under public control, even if it is privately funded. The Battery Park City Authority, in New York City, provides an interesting example of such a hybrid. On filled land off lower Manhattan, the authority is building a vast complex of offices and housing, together with an extensive system of public places, mostly on the Hudson River. As a basis for creating this development it was agreed that all public space would ultimately revert to city ownership, with all normal rights of access and use guaranteed, but that the city would not have to maintain it. A parks corporation, funded by monies from ground leases to developers and controlled by a board of residents and users, manages and maintains the spaces.

As the trend toward such joint public and private development continues, it appears that there will be a growing number of hybrid spaces. Whether on public or private property, spaces such as festival marketplaces that are created with public funds, for use by the general populace, should guarantee the rights of users, even when under private management. This should also apply, as it now does in New York City, to atria created under zoning bonus provisions that allow greater density of development in return for the provision of these indoor "parks." The specific rules will likely vary from city to city and be hotly debated, especially if our cities continue to harbor large populations of homeless people who want to use these places to get out of the cold. It is, however, exactly such conflicts in needs and values that are best adjudicated through the democratic mechanism of public control.

Even more difficult than the problem of conflicting values is the problem of change. An appropriate balance may be reached for one set of groups, only to be invalidated by a change in users. This is primarily a management problem and can sometimes be resolved through changes in policy, which often have consequences for maintenance. In the example cited earlier, had the soccer players been allowed to use the Coliseum mall at Los Angeles's Exposition Park, a battle would have been avoided, but certainly at the cost of much more intensive lawn maintenance in a visually critical area. Had there been a mechanism for dialogue, a better alternative site might have been found or created. Adaptation to change through management is much more likely when users have a means to participate.

Often the design of a place for a specific set of users and needs makes it difficult to adapt the space to other needs. Various devices that have been suggested to deal with this problem include building in excess capacity to accommodate future change, which is expensive and may be wasteful in the short run; creating semibounded subspaces to allow parts to change without greatly affecting the whole, which may be quite difficult in smaller spaces; and keeping the built-in use-specific furnishings and fixtures to a minimum. The latter can be a very effective strategy where management budgets allow. For instance, an open meadow in a park can be set up alternately as a softball diamond or a soccer field, with the aid of demountable backstops, portable bases, movable goals, and the like. Part of a plaza could at one time be a reflecting pool and at another be used to set up a tent for a food fair, provided that tent tie-downs are built in. The most effective strategies for dealing with unknown future change, therefore, combine responsive management with careful attention in design to making spaces adaptable. Even then, with our limited ability to predict the future, the saving grace is often the adaptability of people.

In a good design, development, and management process there will be room for further evaluation and design adjustment after construction. Although it is rarely done, funds should be set aside in the beginning of a project for adjustments beyond routine management and maintenance. In shopping centers, theme parks, and festival marketplaces, management expects to adjust to changing user interests or to correct elements that did not work in the first place. In hybrid spaces such as the Church Street Marketplace or the open space at Battery Park City, private funding provides some latitude for postconstruction evaluation and adjustments. In truly public space, such adjustments often take a concerted effort on the part of frustrated users to force recognition of problems and action to deal with them.

When politicians, administrators, managers, and users keep talking about how a space is working, management and maintenance are likely to be better. The vehicles for this can range from publicly appointed but privately supported entities like the Marketplace Commission in Burlington, to community organizations that own and manage parks and playgrounds. In between are many varieties of advocacy groups and committees that are appointed or take it upon themselves to oversee some significant public space resource such as a large central park. These groups can be very effective in marshaling the political support necessary to increase budgets and improve the level of management and maintenance: The Central Park Conservancy played a key role in developing support for the Central Park Management and Restoration Plan and in raising private funds to assist the subsequent physical improvements and changes in management practice and policy (Barlow, 1987).

THE POWER OF A SHARED VISION

To be successful over time, public space design and management must be motivated by a shared vision among those who initiate, create, tend, and use the place. A durable vision will be both unified and inclusive. Instead of a formal geometric order in which there is an obvious congruence of similar parts, the unity that lasts through change will be more like that of an ecosystem, in which many differing parts are interdependent and connected but also have a life of their own. Distinctive natural environments – uplands, valleys, woodlands, moors, marches, lagoons, ponds – can be grasped as powerful overall images, with a great complexity of distinctive parts. Many human creations of more coherent cultures than our own seem to exhibit this sense of a deeper, almost "natural" order of things: Consider an Anasazi cliff dwelling of the American Southwest, an Italian hill town or a Japanese temple and garden complex. In public space design, parks most often achieve this strong and rich image; but there are

San Gimignano rises like a natural outcropping from the Tuscan landscape. (Stephen Carr)

281

also streets, such as the Ramblas in Barcelona, and central spaces, such as the Piazza della Signoria in Florence, that seem to achieve it as well. Their diverse parts appeal to and serve a wide range of users. Spaces with this kind of depth tend to be meaningful to each new generation of users and the meaning is enhanced by the accumulating record of past use (Lynch, 1972b).

CENTRAL PARK
New York, New York

Located between Fifty-ninth Street and Cathedral Parkway, Fifth Avenue and Central Park West, Manhattan; designed by Fredrick Law Olmsted and Calvert Vaux; managed by New York City Department of Parks and Recreation, assisted by the Central Park Conservancy; completed between 1858 and 1876, frequently modified since; size, 840 acres.

If there is a single space in America that illustrates the strength and durability of a unified vision, appropriate to its social and physical context, it is New York's Central Park. Originally designed for a competition in 1857 by Frederick Law Olmsted and his new partner, Calvert Vaux, Central Park

Central Park in New York City represents a synthesis of our principles of making a successful public space. Above all, it is a soft, natural haven in the heart of a difficult, diverse, and demanding city. (Stephen Carr)

was strongly opposed by real estate developers of the time and many have since attempted inroads. The design and management of the park have been developed and refined over many years of debate and action by politicians, administrators, and users. Through each cycle of change, the initial vision of the park has survived, and, even when severely challenged, this vision has been reaffirmed by subsequent generations of New Yorkers. Even in the late 1980s, open space advocates successfully resisted an attempt to build an office tower in nearby Columbus Circle, which would have been tall enough to cast a significant shadow across the park.

To understand this staying power, it is useful first to consider the origins of the vision and then to analyze the human dimensions of the park. Central Park was the first large public park in the United States. It was closely linked to the European municipal park movement, which began in the early nineteenth century. William Cullen Bryant and Andrew Jackson Downing both drew inspiration from European visits and began to broadcast the idea of a major New York public park in *New York Post* editorials (1849) and in *Horticulture* (1848). The first "landscape parks," such as London's St. James Park, Hyde Park, and Kensington Gardens were royal property that came into public domain by an act of royal generosity. But in Germany, central public parks were built, starting with the Friedrich-Wilhelmsgarten, in Magdeburg, in 1824 and then in Berlin, Munich, and Frankfurt. Downing cited these as prototypes. This transition from the private domains of nobility to true public parks was also important to the initial concept of Olmsted, as can be seen in the collection of his papers and other historic materials on Central Park edited by his son, Frederick Law Olmsted, Jr., and Theodore Kimball (Olmsted, Jr. and Kimball, 1973).

Olmsted, Sr., by his own admission, was more a "literary" than a "practical" man at the time. Although he was already strongly interested in the parks movement, it was somewhat by the chance of friendship with one of the early park commissioners that he was encouraged to seek the position of superintendent to manage the creation of Central Park. It is clear that the idea appealed to him greatly and he sought the post avidly. He also wasted little time agonizing over whether it was appropriate from his position to accept Calvert Vaux's invitation to join him in the design competition when it was announced later in the same year that Olmsted assumed his duties as superintendent. There is no doubt that, like the parks movement of which he was a part, Olmsted from the beginning had a powerful sense of mission. His papers reveal a spirit of noblesse oblige, nonetheless heartfelt. He considered the park to be a great democratic undertaking and was far from modest in his hopes for it: "It is of great importance as the first real park made in this country – a democratic development of the highest significance and on the success of which, in my opinion, much of the progress of art and aesthetic culture in this country is dependent" (p. 45).

While Olmsted brought to his great endeavor the eloquence and imagination of the literary man, he was also, as superintendent, concerned with management. Vaux was the already-accomplished designer that the fledgling partnership needed to render its vision for the "Greensward" in convincing drawings to complement Olmsted's eloquent words. This was a fortuitous joining of two talents, combining theoretical ability, practical concerns, democratic commitment, and artistic integrity. It is just this combination we believe is needed for the creation of fine public spaces.

In the descriptive report submitted with their winning competition design, Olmsted and Vaux laid out the theory and justification of the park's design, basing it on their accurate foresight of the future development of the city. They believed that the park must contrast with its increasingly dense urban context to provide for the needs of ordinary citizens to have access to pure and wholesome air and to scenery that would be the antithesis of streets and houses. They intended that the park would

supply to the hundreds of thousands of tired workers, who have no opportunity to spend their summers in the country, a specimen of God's [!] handiwork that shall be to them, inexpensively, what a month or two in the White Mountains or the Adirondacks is, at great cost, to those in easier circumstances. (p. 46)

To that end, they proposed that the design should interfere as little as possible with the existing "easy, undulating outlines, and picturesque rocky scenery" and in fact enhance those characteristics, which they correctly foresaw would be destroyed elsewhere by the dense urban development of the remainder of the island.

There were three principal means of accomplishing this end: first, the creation of a "woodland" on the perimeter of the Park, which would serve to screen out views of surrounding buildings (these buildings would be "twice as high as the Great Wall of China," according to Olmsted and Vaux, p. 46); second, to assign as much of the remaining grounds as possible to the cre-

In the park's pastoral landscapes one is barely aware of the surrounding buildings. (Stephen Carr)

In the Ramble, the sense of wildness is cultivated. (Stephen Carr)

ation of "tranquil, open, pastoral scenes" (p. 47); and third, to assign remaining rough areas to "passages of scenery contrasting in depth of obscu-
rity and picturesque character of detail with the softness and simplicity of
the open landscape" (p. 47). Finally, by the brilliant stroke of relegating
cross-traffic to lower level roadways, and by creating independent pathways
within the park for carriages, horsemen, and "footmen," tranquil access to
both the open areas and the picturesque passages was assured.

Although not framed in our terms, Olmsted and Vaux's theory for the
design of Central Park anticipated needs for comfort, relaxation, passive
engagement, and discovery. They took firm measures to protect the rights
of access and the claim of all to public ownership. Above all, they created a
landscape loaded with potential for the assignment of all the meanings then
current to both pastoral and wild rural landscapes, as a *psychological* relief
from confining urban conditions. It is true that their concept embodied an
elite view of the needs of the lower classes. Consultation with some of the
"hundreds of thousands of tired workers" might have led to greater emphasis on the provision for active engagement in organized games and to concern for the freedom of action of various groups, their rights to claim certain
areas and even to change them to suit. Instead, in his forty-year history with
the park, Olmsted fought, generally successfully, against the introduction
of sports fields into his meadows, as well as other changes that might dilute
the original concept. He especially opposed repeated attempts at commercial incursions, a struggle that still continues.

Fortunately, in certain respects Central Park proved more adaptable than
its creators. At the beginning of the twentieth century, the Reform Move-

ment sought and achieved increasing use of the park for programmed recreation, as one way to improve the lot of the poor. These uses, once introduced, were gradually increased, until by the 1920s the park became the
favorite setting for contests, races, regattas, meets, and derbies of every sort.
In the reign of Robert Moses as parks commissioner (1934–60), these uses
were institutionalized by the creation of many dedicated facilities, such as
baseball fields, basketball and tennis courts, an ice rink, and the Tavern on
the Green, the one solely commercial use that made its way into the park.
These brought increased recreational opportunity but were often at odds
with the original romantic concept. In the 1960s and 1970s increasing use
by large crowds, relaxation of rules, and diminishing maintenance budgets
led to serious physical deterioration. In the 1980s, major efforts were undertaken to restore the park, returning to some degree to the original concept. The Central Park Conservancy, a private group working in partnership
with the New York City Parks Department, has taken on some of the restoration and maintenance of the park.

In their great design, Olmsted and Vaux embellished their program with
natural features that made the most of existing topography, such as lakes,
rock promontories and, in one especially rough area, a "ramble." The redundant system of curving carriageways and pedestrian paths was laid out, with
through-park traffic separated by level, in order to provide the proper means
for moving about in contemplation and enjoyment of this created landscape.
Their artful blending of domestic and "wild" nature, represented by carefully organized landscape districts, seems to evoke satisfying feelings for a
great diversity of users. Olmsted himself tried to reinforce and defend his

Central Park provides for passive engagement. (Stephen Carr)

Active engagement is also provided. (Stephen Carr)

romantic structure with place names carrying associated scenographic qualities. These names and the qualities they imply suggest a preexisting natural landscape, which was in many cases not there, or the role played by these places in representing the larger natural (or at least rural) environment. We are given the "Sheep Meadow," the "Ramble," the "Lake," the "Ravine," the "Great Hill," and the "Meer."

Embedded in this naturalistic landscape, one also finds the Mall and the Bethesda Terrace and Fountain. These were the only formal elements in the original park design and were intended, in Olmsted's words, as "an artificial structure on a scale of magnitude commensurate with the size of the Park [which should] occupy the same position of importance that a mansion should occupy in a park prepared for private occupation" (p. 222). One could promenade in finery to see and be seen on the Mall and Terrace, this "mansion" of the people, and then skirt the Sheep Meadow or even venture a row about the Lake. Such a day in the park would have associations both with estate gardens in the grand manner and with the rural countryside. The Ramble, with its connotations of wilderness, might be left to the discovery of the more adventuresome.

The design of the park provides opportunities for many associative meanings for a single individual, and also the opportunity for various groups to partially claim those areas in which they feel most comfortable. This of course changes over time. The Bethesda Terrace and Fountain changed within seven years from being a quiet upper-middle-class icon, with its elegant and popular café (installed only in 1967), to the center for "action" in the park, including open drug dealing, all carried out to the lively beat of steel drums.

Bethesda Fountain draws young people. (Stephen Carr)

During this period the Mall and the Terrace were frequently used for large gatherings such as festivals and food fairs, for which they were not designed. The political and social self-expression of middle-class youth in the 1960s contributed to disorderly and sometimes destructive uses of these formal settings. Now the Terrace and the Fountain have been restored to their original designs, with a modest café, and new management policy that favors small, carefully controlled events, which will not draw large crowds. Although this effort is consistent with the thrust of historic preservation of the late 1970s and 1980s – to restore physical shells expressive of the value systems that created them – it remains to be seen whether contemporary users will adapt their behavior to the values implicit in these original forms.

In a public space as large and diverse as Central Park, it was possible to create a multitude of settings, each with its intended range of uses and users and with its appropriate poetics. Indeed the open-minded genius of this design lies in this very diversity, set within its contrasting urban frame and unified by its persuasive romantic, naturalistic themes. The scale and variety of the park landscapes, together with its extensive and often redundant system of pathways offering many choices for movement, have allowed for a constantly changing mix of users and uses, with a minimum of conflict. Interestingly, it is the most formal part of the park – the Mall, Terrace, and Fountain – that has created the most conflict, at least in recent years, as people have tried to put these popular settings to use for large informal gatherings. By and large, the size of the park and its range of settings have allowed the diverse groups who live near it, or are drawn to it from further away, to partially claim turfs without accompanying turf battles. The meanings that these settings have for those who frequent them, while no doubt reflecting Olmsted's original intentions, are now likely to be enriched by personal history with the park and by connections to valued groups and activities.

It must also be noted that Central Park is not without problems. Any public space, to some degree, mirrors the social conditions around it. Random and purposeful violence are both on the rise in our society, and especially in cities like New York, where social and economic extremes are brought together. Central Park is a meeting ground for these extremes, and this can be threatening in itself. When it is filled with people, it can be a glorious place, but at night, or even by day in the less populated areas, the hidden corners are menacing. Park management has been responsive to this and other problems of social conflict by increasing patrols, but there is a continued history of violence, including recent instances of rape and murder. Whether there is more crime in Central Park than on the adjacent streets of the city is unclear, but given New Yorkers' strong feelings for the place, the violations of people's lives that occur in the park are particularly affecting.

Overall, the design, restoration, and current management of Central Park exemplify most of the values we advocate in this book. The history of Central Park shows the power of a singular vision to create and defend a great public space. It also shows the ability of a large public space, guided by such a vision, to incorporate dramatic change in users and use. When, by the 1970s, the resulting changes in the physical setting and management had swung so far from Olmsted and Vaux's original idea that the integrity of the park was seriously threatened, an intense community effort was triggered, leading to current attempts to shift the balance of uses back toward the original design and to restore Olmsted and Vaux's vision. Although it is not problem-free, Central Park has fulfilled its cultural mission to be New York's great democratic pleasure ground and has retained its beauty, usefulness, and meaning through many social and political changes.

An inclusive but memorable vision for a place will not emerge directly from the wealth of information produced by a good participatory process. The human dimensions provide a means for organizing information and developing hypotheses, but the designer must go beyond these to create, through trial and error, a new and often surprising synthesis. This is the "magic" of design. There is no rule for how to achieve a unified vision. The hypotheses about needs, rights, and meanings, which underlie this vision, can be tested through discussions with participants. There may be conflicts in values, the resolution of which will lead to a more inclusive vision. When there is general agreement, and all the major technical and cost problems are resolved, the design will be ready for the final work leading to construction. With participatory management the vision can be further developed and refined by adjustment in use.

Designers and managers, seeking inspiration for unifying themes, will often look to prototypes from older cultures. Because our own society is an amalgam, with differing regional cultural influences, the reinterpretive use of English motifs in the Northeast, Asian and Spanish elements in the Far West, or Spanish or Native American forms in the Southwest is not wholly inappropriate. On the other hand, the growing social diversity and rate of change in our larger cities would seem to require design themes with broad appeal, together with management that is responsive to changing uses and users. Large urban parks can convey the associative power of a piece of the "country" captured within the city while providing a range of settings, adaptable to various uses. Settings that evoke experiences of the countryside seem to please most people (Kaplan & Kaplan, 1989) and, in larger parks, management is normally available to deal with the potentially conflicting values and demands on use of various social groups.

In smaller spaces, like a local park or a plaza, it is more difficult to achieve both evocative power and responsiveness. The most useful prototypes are often the simple spaces that have evolved to serve the everyday needs of people. These forms are grounded in basic human needs and

Piazza del Campo, Siena, a powerful and evocative central square, focusing and enhancing the public life of its city through both design and management. (Stephen Carr)

rights and therefore are more similar across cultures than the grand places designed as ornaments to celebrate the specialness of a society.

Central squares and shopping streets, as described in Chapter 3, have ancient prototypes in market streets and public squares that go back to the beginnings of cities and find expression in nearly every cultural group. Central squares have taken on meanings as settings for public life. They are focal points of their communities, places for casual encounter, ritual promenade, ceremonies and celebrations, uprisings and executions. In large cities, these spaces have often been made formal and grand, fronted by monumental buildings, with statues, fountains, or obelisks, as well as handsome pavements and, where resources and power have been enough, unified architectural settings. Their basic form, however, remains one of simple enclosure with level pavements where people can gather. Market streets and squares are traditionally simple and rarely embellished, gaining their character from the commercial uses that organize them in colorful ways to attract potential customers.

SUMMARY

The approach to public space design and management that we advocate brings the work out of the studio and office and into the real world of people and places. We have tried to show how the human dimensions can provide a framework to guide detailed design and management. To fill in that framework with the information necessary to create and maintain a vivid and enduring place requires a means to analyze and engage its physical and social context. Although it is not so simple as it sounds, the best means for doing this in our society is to involve space users in the process. This both empowers the users and provides a more profound understanding of the human dimensions most appropriate to a particular space. It is an effective means of reaching the insights to be embodied in a powerful guiding vision like that of Central Park. There are many ways that people can become involved in the creation of their public environment, from building spaces themselves, as in Manteo, to sitting in committees that oversee design, construction, and use. In the next chapter, we will describe in detail how the normal processes of design and management can be made more inclusive, inspirational, and effective.

THE PROCESS

Public spaces are created and maintained by a lengthy and often complex process of interaction among sponsors, designers, builders, managers, and users. This is the means by which information is gathered, evaluated, sorted, and transformed into designs and management policies. It is the vehicle for considering alternatives, making decisions, and taking action to shape a space and determine its use. In this chapter we describe a process that focuses on the human dimensions of a place, in light of its social and physical context, in order to discover what is needed for successful design and management. We will contrast this approach with the "standard" process, which often does not engage the context and therefore does not discover the dimensions of success. The key to improvement, as discussed in Chapter 7, is creative involvement of representative open space users.

THE STANDARD PROCESS

As with any other recurring activity, there is a normal sequence of steps in public space design and management in our society. This standard process determines how the design problem is defined and how design work is carried out. It also governs how the designer is selected, limits who will participate, and influences participant attitudes toward design and management of the spaces in question. In the interests of central control, and presumed efficiency and economy, this process tends to exclude many of those whose ideas and responses could be most helpful. Potential users of the space are often left out until the end, when a public hearing may be required.

It is natural for project sponsors to want to maintain close central control over the design process. Public officials are properly responsible for making decisions about the use of public funds. They are accountable for their decisions to the politicians who appoint them and, ultimately, to the voters. It is tempting for public administrators to assume that they adequately represent the public interest and that it is therefore efficient to restrict severely additional participation. Most often, the only people engaged outside of government are those with a direct economic stake or other "special interests," some of whom may have helped to promote a project and therefore insist on being consulted on its design – bankers, property owners, and merchants along a downtown mall, environmentalists interested in a park, or the abutters to a neighborhood playground.

By looking more closely at the typical process and its usual participants we can better understand how significant improvements might be made. There would be little merit to a prescription for improvement in design and management that did not take account of these typical conditions. We look first at how a project is initiated, then consider some limits on designers and designs, and finally discuss typical constraints on construction and management.

THE BEGINNING OF THE PROBLEM

The idea to create or rework a public open space may come from inside or outside of government, from an individual or group motivated by a wide range of purposes – from the preservation of wilderness to the improvement of business. Usually open space is accepted as a good in itself, but sometimes there is a perceived problem that it is expected to solve. For instance, city life is seen as unhealthy and open space is promoted for the beneficial effect of exposure to natural elements – light, air, grass, trees, water – with room to exercise and relax. Children are said to need playgrounds in order to develop physical and social skills. Public access to waterfronts is thought to be an indisputable good, simply because people are drawn to the water's edge. Standards used by planners describe open space needs in acres per thousands of people, often citing relief from urban congestion as a primary benefit. In recent years, urban leadership in America has turned back toward a more "European" image of public life, at least in downtowns, and so instead of relieving congestion, plazas and markets are planned to draw large crowds of people together to "rub elbows."

In the past decade, these social goals have become secondary to economic motivations. Even if the initiators of open space proposals have social goals in mind, they must "sell" their proposal in competition with other demands on scarce public resources. In the nineteenth century, park

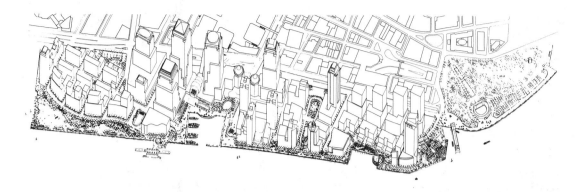

The open space system at Battery Park City in New York City is a prime example of public space being used to encourage development while at the same time being supported by it. (Drawing by James Sandell and Julie Bargman)

advocates cited beneficial effects on the health and productivity of workers and, incidentally, on property values. In our time, public space improvements are often tied directly to the promotion of private development and indirectly to the public purpose of increasing real estate tax revenues by encouraging such development. Open space proposals often are part of a renewal plan where their role is to help change the image of the city and to provide "public infrastructure" needed to encourage private development.

Symbolic values are also important. Rulers and politicians have always been mindful of the impressive image conveyed by a fine public setting. The creation of new public spaces can be a highly visible and relatively inexpensive symbol of government concerned with the people's welfare. To convince a mayor or a city council, advocates emphasize the immediate visible impact of the proposed space, together with the possible number of users and the potential economic benefits. Politicians may not be attuned to the long-term effects of public space projects. They want to see the space built in their term of office, but they may not be there to be held accountable for the longer-term results. Funds are often allocated for design and construction, with no corresponding increase in the budget of the departments that are expected to manage, maintain, and secure them. As a result, maintenance and management issues are rarely given appropriate emphasis in the problem statement or during the design process. Managers may not be included in the design team. The designer has no special incentive to consider carefully future management and may not even be informed as to the level and type of management to expect.

Frequently, public design processes are carried out under tight limits on time and money. Funding deadlines must be met, or a project must be completed within the term of a politician. Funds for public projects are

294

usually scarce. Standard fees and tight project schedules may not seem to allow for the time required to mount and manage research into user needs or for broadly based user involvement. Often, politicians who support project funding feel that they already know what the public wants, or are entitled to speak for their constituents in determining the design direction. Hard-pressed public administrators are also reluctant to commit the staff time needed to help manage an effort to reach out to potential users.

As a result, a public project often will go straight to design with little or no effort to develop a design program. The agency responsible will issue a request for proposals to designers. This request, written by a member of the staff, may be the only occasion prior to designer selection to develop the general goals of the project into more specific guidelines. However, because of the political way most projects are initiated, the rationale used for them, and the schedule and budget constraints, information on user needs will not usually be available to guide project formulation. That is the beginning of the problem.

LIMITS ON DESIGNERS AND DESIGN

Some of these same limits also constrain designer selection and design of open space. Once it is decided to build a park or other space, and funding is secured, a designer is selected. Because this is public work, selection must be made by a competitive process, which can also be "political." The selection committee may be politically appointed, with its members drawn from those who initiated the project, combined with the planning or development staff, who will fund it. Representatives of the agencies that will oversee construction and management, such as public works and parks department staff, may also be included. Although some of these committee members could be future users of the planned facility, the actual users are typically seen as being outside the designer selection process. Because responsiveness to central administrative and political authority is a key qualification for membership on the selection committee, it is also likely to be a quality sought in potential designers.

Designers are selected on some combination of reputation, perceived qualifications, the impression they make at the interview, and their specific proposal to do the work. "Reputation" may sometimes include prior personal connections with members of the selection committee. Qualifications are usually judged on past completed projects of the same type, shown to their best advantage in pictures in the proposal and at the interview. There are no research reports to prove that the smiling people shown in the pictures have remained happy with a space that has served them well over time. Selection committees seldom take the time to visit completed projects, even when they are nearby. References may be checked, but they are usually drawn from the sponsoring organization, rather than the users.

The designer's proposal may exclude or minimize user involvement, unless it is specifically requested by the sponsoring client. Clients are often reluctant to involve users because they do not clearly understand the benefits, they believe that design costs will increase substantially, and they fear losing control. Designers may have the same concerns and, in addition, are unlikely to be trained to work in a participatory setting.

Indeed, the qualities that are required for success as a designer can be difficult to reconcile, in the same person, with those needed for good participatory work. To bring any design and construction process to a successful conclusion, within tight limits of time and money, involves a powerful act of will to control or influence the actions of many disparate individuals. Even formulating the design vision requires a single-minded passion to create a unified whole. To carry that vision through to construction needs relentless attention to detail and insistence that quality be maintained against continuously eroding tendencies. On the other hand, working with users means being a good questioner and listener and giving others the room and support to articulate their needs and develop their own ideas. The openness and flexibility required for successful participatory work cuts across the grain of the designer's drive toward closure.

Starting with design education and continuing into practice, designers are expected to make a "strong design statement" and then to justify and defend it. Apparent originality in formal ideas is given precedence in design journals and among peers, but a design that closely matches the needs and preferences of its users is not likely to be a formal tour de force. A design that evolves through an open process of give-and-take among sponsors, designers, managers, and users aspires to the inclusive continuity of life, rather than a simple formal unity, which may appear "strong" to the eye while ignoring many key dimensions of human use (cf. the Freedom Plaza case in Chapter 6, among many others). In an open process, the designer works in the tradition of the medieval master builder, orchestrating the creative efforts of others, rather than that of Renaissance artist as heroic form-giver. Current training and professional reward systems do not usually support the former role.

The standard design process is often insular and exclusive. If neither the client nor the designer understands the potential benefits of user involvement, then both may be fearful of controversy and of the likely cost in additional time and money. Rather than finding a productive way to welcome citizen participation, designers and their clients may find them-

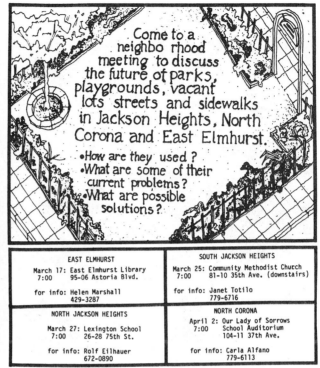

Public participation can be easily organized where there is a will to do so. Flyer for
a series of workshops in Queens, New York. (Mark Francis)

selves scheming to limit it, so that they can "get on with the work." The
real work is seen as something done in designers' offices and in meetings
with clients, whereas meetings with citizens, when required, are viewed
as painful diversions from the work.

That such isolated work is likely to result in inappropriate and unman-
ageable spaces can readily be understood from many of the examples cited
in this book. In Chapter 7 we argued that increased user involvement can
be beneficial to design and management, helping to make the human
dimensions responsive to the social and physical context of the space. The
challenge is to find a way of doing this efficiently, within the real limits
on designers and the design process.

CONSTRAINTS ON CONSTRUCTION AND MANAGEMENT

The construction and management systems for public space projects also
limit responsiveness. Because public money is usually involved, competitive bidding is required of building contractors. To make this possible,
designers must completely fix the design prior to construction, producing

Public space construction is often disruptive to existing activities, which makes it even more difficult to make midcourse adjustments. Pedestrian mall under construction in Madison, Wisconsin. (Mark Francis)

elaborate working drawings and specifications that leave as little as possible to interpretation. Sixty to seventy percent of the designer's time and budget typically goes into the creation of this documentation and monitoring of construction to see that it is followed. The designer does not have the master builder's power to make field adjustments as the space comes into being and relationships between elements can be fully appreciated. Although some minor trade-offs may be possible, if no additional cost is involved, any significant changes are likely to be costly and difficult for all parties.

Management and maintenance budgets also rarely allow for ongoing adjustments to the physical space. Operating funds are always scarce, yet public space projects frequently are conceived, funded, and designed without any analysis of the likely operating requirements and budget. No one would develop a commercial building without making such a calculation, but in public space projects this glaring omission often results from the initiating agency not being responsible for maintaining the space. Even a cursory look at park systems in our financially pressed cities will show the importance of adequate operating funds. Where active management and maintenance are lacking, spaces will frequently be misused and abused. Furthermore, the designer cannot predict all future uses from the beginning and build in all needed physical supports. Public spaces such as parks must respond to changing societal ideas about recreation and even to changing styles of play equipment. Great spaces evolve in response to use and changing perceptions based on use (cf. the Central Park case in Chapter 7). The heavy emphasis on initial capital investment, coupled with relative inability to make adjustments later, creates a crippling inflexibility.

When the construction project is completed, the space normally is placed in the care of a public works department, parks department, or a transportation (streets) department. If the operating agency has not been involved in initiating or designing the project, it is not likely to undertake its stewardship knowledgeably or enthusiastically, especially if it has not been given additional funds to deal with the increased responsibilities. Sometimes the appropriate orientation or expertise is lacking, as when a transportation agency is given responsibility for managing pedestrian spaces created from former vehicular streets because it "owns" the streets (see the Streets for People case in Chapter 7). When there is both the will and the funding, there may be a shortage of appropriate skills to deal with the broad range of activities and physical systems that make up a downtown public space network or a park system. Even when all of these ingredients are in place to do the job well, there may be no reliable means of monitoring and evaluating user response, and no funds for fine-tuning the performance of the space.

As the activities carried out in public space become more complex, more demands are made on the available management systems (Vernez-Moudon, 1987). Until recently, public space management has meant keeping cars and people moving safely on streets and sidewalks, while providing for traditional forms of active and passive recreation and for occasional large holiday gatherings or political rallies, in addition to cleaning, lawn mowing, snow removal, and standard maintenance operations. Now there is a much greater variety of programmed and unprogrammed activity in public space, including entertainment, commercial vending, celebrations of many sorts, and increasing occupancy by homeless persons. To manage such uses well requires skills akin to those of a diplomat, a public relations expert, a theater manager, and a social worker, together with an understanding of crowd control. Most agencies charged with public space management lack such expertise.

Although these restraints on responsiveness will not easily be removed, one might argue that continued problems with built spaces will inevitably

Good public space managers must have skills in activity programming and event production, as well as crowd control. "Summerthing" program, Boston. (Stephen Carr)

lead, little by little, to reformulation of the process. Certainly there are signs from the nationwide push for increased citizen involvement in development issues that this may be happening. The inherent problems that we have described are intended to help put such reform efforts in a realistic context. By understanding the motivations, attitudes, habits, and limitations of those currently involved in public space design and management, it is possible to improve the process – and ultimately the product – in ways that address their problems and concerns.

ANOTHER WAY

To create better public spaces requires another way of working. Each step of the design and management process must become more inclusive and effective, with political and financial realism. For the designer and the manager, this approach can bring a fresh flow of understanding, making their work easier and more satisfying. To users, it can mean a chance to shape their environment to meet their needs. An administrator can look forward to greater public approval and fewer operating problems. Even in the necessarily short-term view of a politician who wants to be reelected, the benefits can outweigh the costs. Sometimes politicians or public administrators are at first reluctant to consider a more inclusive process for fear that it will provoke controversy; but a public space once created is usually there for many years, and it is far better to have the controversy in the design stage than to deal with it after completion as a series of management problems.

As we explained in Chapter 7, the human dimensions of public space can provide the basis for understanding how a given space relates to its social context. The design and management process can become the means for understanding that context. By including in the process those who will use the space, the designer and the decision makers learn how people's past experiences and aspirations will shape their expectations and use of the future place. This gives place and user-specific meaning to the general human dimensions. By continuing to consult with users after completion, the manager learns how to program activities and what adjustments may be needed to keep the space functioning well. The users, on the other hand, broaden their understanding of the possibilities in response to the designer's vision. When the process goes well, it is one of mutual learning leading to collective creativity.

This process is generic, but in application it will always be different, in some or many details. To help tailor the design and management process to the specific project at hand, we offer these nine guiding principles.

The basic principle is that of *inclusiveness*. By drawing on experience of similar spaces elsewhere, coupled with demographic analysis of the context, it is possible to predict both the range and types of users. This user profile is one basis for deciding who should be engaged in the process, but potential users must be complemented by representatives of the sponsors, founders, regulators, and administrators of the project.

A second key idea is *representation.* Because all potential users cannot be identified or engaged, a representative cross section should be selected and organized into a manageable group. For a small local playground this might be as few as six to twelve people meeting on several occasions. For a large central space or park it may be necessary to engage twenty-five to fifty or more people in a longer process to have a reasonable cross section of all user groups. The process described later in this chapter will show how this can be done effectively.

A third principle might be termed *discretion*. Each group of participants must be engaged in the manner most appropriate to drawing out its true feelings and best ideas. Some decision makers, such as politicians, may need to be approached one-on-one, moving quickly to the point. Public administrators may be organized into a review group, which will likely require rather formal presentations of information. Users are best organized into discussion groups of seven to ten people, because small groups are well suited for drawing out all participants without one or two dominating.

A fourth key to success is to enable people to be *proactive* rather than simply reactive. There are many ways of doing this. Involving them in analysis of the site and of other similar projects and helping them to project their fantasy lists of desirable features or to make ideal designs are all quite useful. By doing this kind of work, especially in the early stages, participants become much better grounded in what they want and need from the project.

A fifth principle is *mutuality*. Although designers should hold back on voicing their own convictions and preconceptions about the project in the beginning, in order to encourage others to come forth with their ideas, the designers must also reveal their own views. The mutual learning that is needed for the process to be fully creative can only happen in dialogue.

Next, the process must go beyond an exchange of views to create a carefully structured and internally consistent *program*, one that spells out the desired qualities as well as the quantities of the space. Here the human dimensions are especially useful in providing a comprehensive way to organize information relating a space to its social context. The effort of writing a program will quickly reveal the inconsistencies and contradictions in people's wishes for a place and will tend to force these conflicts to be resolved, or at least to be a focus of creative management through design. The environmental program provides a first reality test for all participants.

Dialogue can best be continued through design by means of the study and discussion of *alternatives*, our seventh principle. Because design problems rarely, if ever, have only one good solution, the analysis of alternatives provides a means for gaining further understanding of users' needs, as well as of the capabilities of sponsors, designers, and managers to meet those needs.

Discussion of alternatives will sharpen people's views and prepare them for continuing *review*, through design development, of a preferred alternative. These progress reviews may themselves be structured as a consideration of more detailed alternatives. It is helpful to refer back to the program and to its specific human dimensions, which should be the guidelines for the project.

A final principle is that of continuing *adjustment*. In the best of worlds, people might directly build their own spaces, adjusting them as they go along. Sometimes this can happen, but in societies like our own with much specialization of function, it is a rare pleasure. For reasons of fiscal control, it is very difficult and costly to intervene once a public construction process is underway. However, continued involvement of users in the management process is much easier to achieve and will, if properly structured, allow for evaluation, adjustment, and even redesign, as needed.

This improved process is generic but must be tailored to the task. In application it will always be different, in some or many details. In the prescription that follows, we have assumed a project of moderate to large scale, one affecting many people and funded well enough to afford a comprehensive approach. Examples might be a park of five acres or more, a central plaza, a new recreational waterfront, or improvement of downtown streets for pedestrian use. The design process suggested here modestly increases the time and design cost over a "standard" nonparticipatory approach, but the additional time and investment are minor in relation to the life expectancy, first costs, and operating costs of a public space. User involvement typically adds no more than a month or two to the design process for a large project and costs less than 2 percent of the construction budget. Other proposals, such as the technical advisory committee, can actually shorten working and review time by bringing relevant people together in a single setting. The suggested process described at length here can be adapted to smaller projects by applying the same guiding principles and phases to the appropriately scaled effort.

VILLAGE HOMES COMMUNITY PLAYGROUND
Davis, California

Located in Village Homes neighborhood, Arlington and Russell boulevards; designed by Mark Francis, Landscape Architect, assisted by landscape architecture students, University of California, Davis; managed by Village Homes Homeowners Association; completed in 1983; size, approximately .25 acre.

In spring 1981, the parents in Village Homes neighborhood, Davis, California, asked for assistance in designing their new playground (Francis 1988b). A group of neighborhood parents had been working for over a year raising funds and holding meetings, but were in need of professional expertise to translate their ideas into a buildable plan.

The project was undertaken on several conditions, which later proved to be critical to its success. First, the parents group was asked to support an initial research study of the entire community. This was designed to gain information about existing attitudes and children's behavior in the Village Homes neighborhood. Also, both children and adults were asked to become involved in the design process. The parents agreed, with one condition. They wanted to begin construction of the project in only a few months after the research and design process began.

Village Homes provided an ideal setting for a participatory and behavioral design approach. Internationally known as a model solar community, the neighborhood was planned and developed with community involvement and interaction in mind. Many of the common areas and greenbelts in the community were designed and constructed by neighborhood residents. The parents group wanted the playground designed in the same participatory spirit,

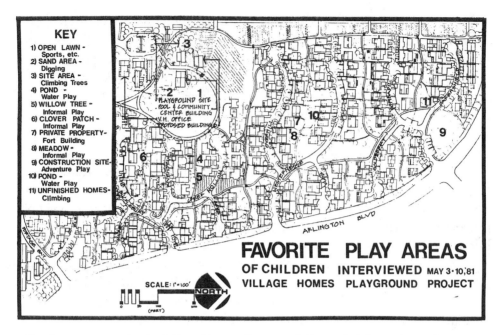

KEY

1) OPEN LAWN - Sports, etc.
2) SAND AREA - Digging
3) SITE AREA - Climbing Trees
4) POND - Water Play
5) WILLOW TREE - Informal Play
6) CLOVER PATCH - Informal Play
7) PRIVATE PROPERTY- Fort Building
8) MEADOW - Informal Play
9) CONSTRUCTION SITE- Adventure Play
10) POND - Water Play
11) UNFINISHED HOMES- Climbing

FAVORITE PLAY AREAS
OF CHILDREN   INTERVIEWED MAY 3·10,'81
VILLAGE HOMES PLAYGROUND PROJECT

SCALE: 1"=100'   NORTH

The design process for the Village Homes Playground, Davis, California, began by observing children's use of existing open spaces in the neighborhood. (Mark Francis)

so that the product would reflect the needs and ideas of the residents of Village Homes.

First, to provide information for design programming, research was conducted to find out what children did in existing open spaces, what places they valued in the neighborhood, and what ideas and concerns both parents and children had about the playground. This approach was influenced by earlier naturalistic studies with children (Hart, 1978). To keep to the tight summer construction schedule, this phase had to be completed in a two-week period.

Then, to assess children's activity, behavioral observation was done over a one-week period throughout the neighborhood. Using a simple behavior mapping form, activities were noted, including age and sex of users and whether props (such as bikes) were being used. This information was summarized on maps showing where children played as well as the locations of other frequent activities. These maps became extremely valuable in the design process, because they showed what existing activities were most popular in the community.

Finally, the design and research team worked with forty-one children in the community, involving them directly in a participatory design process. After gaining their confidence, a simple method was used to engage the children's design interest. The children were asked to lead a walking tour of their favorite places, to describe the places they valued and why. A common favorite place was house construction sites to the north of the neighborhood. The children collected scrap material to build their own "houses" in vacant lots. This later became an important design element for the play-

It then involved children in drawing ideal play environments, while at the Village Homes community pool. (Mark Francis)

ground because it showed that the children wanted to build. Another method that proved useful was asking children who gathered at the community pool to draw "ideal" playground designs on a large piece of newsprint rolled out on the pool deck.

Because children are not the only users of playgrounds, parents and other community residents were involved in the research and design process. Here, other methods were used. Structured interviews with a few parents proved useful in opening up discussions about their ideas and concerns. Then, a simple questionnaire was designed and delivered to all 175 residences in the community. Residents were asked to note demographic information, such as how many children they had, preferences for design of the playground, including ratings of design elements and materials, and future concerns. This method also served to inform the larger community of the design project.

The research findings were summarized in a report, which became the basis for developing a design program and alternative designs. The designs utilized the findings. Six weeks after the project started, a community meeting was held to review alternative designs, attended by over one hundred parents and children. Without the extensive participation and research process, such a large turnout probably would not have been possible. The response to the designs was positive with a call for starting construction as soon as possible. An additional meeting was held to develop a consensus plan, which identified first phase elements for construction.

This participatory approach did not end here but continued into construction and evaluation. Because the project was to be built by local residents, the designers had to develop materials lists, cost estimates, and details that could be handled by volunteers. The site was cleared and graded by Village Homes developer Michael Corbett. A ground-breaking party was held on a Saturday, complete with a rock band, refreshments, and newspaper reporters.

Projects that could be quickly completed were selected for initial construction. These included a roller slide made of conveyor rollers used in factories and poles and a platform for a pulley ride. Over the summer, several work parties were held on Saturdays and evenings to continue construction. A tree fort was completed and an informal children's building area sprung up on the site. Plantings and irrigation, along a slide and tot area, were installed by community work parties. The playground exists today as a well-used neighborhood play space.

A unique part of the Village Homes design approach was a commitment to evaluate and redesign the playground as it was built and used. The evolutionary nature of such community projects allows the actual use of already built elements to inform the design of future elements (Francis, 1987c). For example, in the original program, bike riding was not included as a major activity in the playground because there appeared to be adequate bike areas elsewhere in the neighborhood. The observations of use after the first phase of construction revealed that bike riding was a popular activity on one of the larger mounds in the playground. Therefore, the long-range design was adjusted to provide for this activity.

During the summer and fall, after initial construction, activity at the playground was systematically observed. Using a behavior mapping technique similar to the one used in our overall evaluation of behavior in the community, design features that were used and not used were noted. Based on the evaluation of phase 1 construction, a longer-range plan was developed that responded to the observed site use and evaluation. This plan has been used by the community for fund raising and to organize further work parties to build subsequent phases of the playground.

Related cases: Tranhytten Adventure Playground, Barretto Street Neighborhood Park.

ACTORS IN THE PROCESS

Clients and consultants must find one another and must be appropriate to the task, both in character and organization. Although it may seem easier for a designer if the client group is small and coherent, it is best for the end result if the group includes within it the full range of interested

Construction of the playground began with parents and children building a central play structure. (Mark Francis)

parties. A broad-ranging client is more likely to be able to identify the relevant issues and to test program and design hypotheses fully. Organizing the client for design can be accomplished in a variety of ways, depending on the size of the project and its social and political context. A tiered approach to engaging participants is usually the most workable, given the need to combine representation with expeditious decision making. One effective organization is outlined here.

Policy and Decision Making

Overall policy can be set and design decisions made by a small group of people who are appointed to the task by the responsible governmental authorities. Five to eight is a good size for efficient decision making with adequate breadth. This group should represent the various relevant community interests, and report to the body that appointed it – the mayor, the city council, agency head, or a neighborhood organization. For large projects, it may be set up as a commission or authority, given the legal responsibility not only to make design decisions but also to administer funds and the construction process. More often, it is an ad hoc task force or panel that manages planning and design and then turns the project over to a line agency to build. In this case, it is essential that a senior staff member from that agency be represented on the task force, normally in an *ex officio,* nonvoting role.

It is a truism that a great design requires a great client. As individuals, this decision-making group should be open to the views and concerns of users and other affected parties. At the same time, the group must be able to make timely decisions based on balanced judgments about the conflicting information that it will hear. Although it is the designer's job to provide the client group with the ideas and information it needs to make decisions, the quality and responsiveness of the people in this group will be as important to the outcome as the designer's skill and creativity.

Technical Review

It will also be necessary to review the project with public officials, including staff of constructing, operating, and regulatory agencies. For larger projects, with communitywide impact, it can be efficient to appoint an advisory body made up of the heads or senior staff members of these agencies. This might include the planning department, the public works department, parks and recreation, streets and traffic, and various utilities. The particular knowledge and expertise of such a group can be directly helpful in design. It also acts as an early warning device to flag legal, construction, or operational problems before they occur. By participating in such a group, those with implementing and management responsibilities will be fully informed about the nature and purpose of the project and thus be better prepared to take on their long-term roles. They also will be forewarned if the project will require increases in their operating budgets or staff. Individual follow-up meetings will often be necessary, as well, to discuss issues of particular interest to a single agency.

Civic Advice

Interested parties who are directly and indirectly affected by a project should be given a vehicle to participate in both its design and in its management. This, in itself, can be a broadly ranging group and needs to be carefully organized. In all cases, immediate abutters, who may be owners of affected buildings or potential building sites, as well as nearby businesses, institutions, and residences, should be notified and given the opportunity to advise. Beyond these are persons who may be affected in some less immediate way, by traffic that the space may generate or longer-term changes that it may help to spur. On larger projects of citywide import there will also be groups with special interests in particular aspects, from horticulture to bicycle paths, who can be helpful if involved early and disruptive if not. Elected officials from the project area may be another group who should be consulted as the project develops.

A good mechanism for this type of participation is a civic advisory group. Because this group will engage broad community leadership, its members must be carefully chosen, a politically sensitive task. The designer and programmer should seek the advice of public administrators and others who are familiar with these individuals, but no recruitment should be done until the policy committee has reviewed and approved the list.

User Participation

Potential users should be identified and involved, in both program development and design. Sometimes, as in a neighborhood park, it will be obvious who the users will be and there may be existing organizations who represent them. In other cases, identifying users will be part of program development. However they are selected and recruited, representative users are crucial participants in helping to make a space truly fit its social and physical context. Later in this chapter we will describe tested techniques for identifying, recruiting, and working productively with users.

Consultant Selection

Whether consultant help is sought only for design or for programming as well, selection should be done by the policy and decision-making task force. Relevant agency staff and representatives of users and others directly af-

The community workshop, such as this planning meeting for community gardens
in Seattle, is a good way to initiate user participation. (P-Patch, Seattle)

fected can advise on the selection, but the decision makers must make
the final choice. Potential consultants should be asked to respond to the
issues raised by the project and to describe their relevant experience. It
should also be broadcast in the request for proposals that the ability to
manage and work in a participatory context will be required. The ability
of the consultant to respond in a knowledgeable way to this, together with
a successful record of participatory work, will be a good test.

Certainly for designers, both creativity and the ability to deal successfully with the technical issues are necessary. Visits to completed projects,
conversations with users, and referrals from prior clients will all be useful
to the selection committee. Further, the designer's ability to relate to the
cross section of interested parties who make up the selection committee
may indicate appropriateness to the assignment.

If the designer is being selected for program development as well, then
in-depth knowledge of existing research on public space, as well as social
research skills, will be important. A few designers will have this knowledge but most will not, in which case a special consultant trained in environmental psychology or an allied field will be a helpful addition to the

team. In some states – Massachusetts is one – a history of corruption has led to a policy precluding designers who carry out program studies from doing the actual design. This is unfortunate because the understanding gained by analyzing the problem and initial interactions with users is much deeper than can be gleaned from a written program.

THE ENVIRONMENTAL PROGRAM

Writing an environmental program for a space may seem to be the logical step between identifying and organizing clients and consultants and carrying out the design. As a practical matter, the questions that programming must answer will help identify some of the key client groups, and especially the users. Like the design, the program must be appropriate to the social and physical context. The best way to accomplish that is to involve users and other key actors in the programming process, which means they must first be identified and engaged. Before describing how to do this, we will consider what the program must do.

Clarify the Purposes

Be as clear and explicit as possible about the aims of the project, including the political and economic goals and the broad social purposes that the project is intended to serve. Start with the sponsor but, if possible, canvass the likely users on this point and observe their behavior elsewhere. Imagine what these social goals might be, based on knowledge of similar places, and then test these hypotheses against the views of a small group of representative users.

List the Specific Needs

For this population and purpose, what are the user needs that the design must meet? Chapter 4 will help with this question, but the programmer must adjust the list to the particular qualities of the population and context. For a space to be used by office workers at lunch time, comfort, relaxation, and passive engagement are likely to be most important; a space designated for the use of young people is likely to emphasize active engagement and discovery. But even a "playground" will need space for the passive engagement of socializing parents. Experience in analyzing or designing a wide range of spaces will be useful in making these judgments, but for all but the simplest spaces and user profiles, consultation with representative users will be needed.

Define the Spatial Rights

For this population pursuing these needs in this space, what are likely to be the key issues of freedom and control? Although this too will emerge more clearly through the process of design, especially when users are involved, it is important to try to define these rights at the beginning, so that they can be thought about during the design. It will be especially important to think in advance about the unintended activities that are likely to occur and how they can be controlled without limiting too much the freedom of the users. For instance, will paths on a sloping site need to be designed to discourage skateboards, or can an area be set aside for them? How can a secluded area of a downtown plaza encourage relaxation without being dangerous? User consultation can be especially helpful in developing an understanding of these issues, which are seldom foremost in the minds of sponsors or designers.

Propose Meanings

In part, this step circles back to the beginning – meanings grow out of purposes. Meanings also grow out of the needs and rights being served by the design. For example, the "speakers corner" in Hyde Park in London has gained social meaning by people repeatedly exercising their right of free speech in this location. Although meaning will only emerge from the real place and its use over time, thinking about potential meanings at the beginning can greatly stimulate the design process. As we have tried to show in our chapter on the subject, public space can have deep meanings derived from its role in human evolution and the development of cultures, as well as from the history and character of its immediate context. For instance, can a neighborhood space symbolize community, as the gathering place around the well did in preindustrial societies? A good designer or artist will draw upon all of these sources, often in surprising ways, but a good programmer can start the creative engines firing by challenging the designer to be explicit about these meanings. Once again, users can and should be directly consulted on the meanings they would wish to see expressed.

Describe the Intended Activities and Settings

This is the step between learning how the human dimensions of public space apply to the project at hand and actually doing the design. This should be a generic description of the types of activities and settings required for the specified needs, rights, and meanings, together with the performance criteria that the design must meet. A list of desired activities should include a statement of how these activities would satisfy users' needs and how they might be designed or managed to avoid conflict. A proposed setting will be specified for a certain range of activities, with notes on the rights to be protected and the meanings to be fostered. The research findings we have gathered should prove useful, but as always the generalities must be adjusted to the particulars of the situation.

Describe the Intended Management System

Who will ultimately own and control the site and how will policies be set? Will there be opportunities for user comment and adjustment of the space to changing user needs? Will there be programmed activities that require support systems, such as electrical outlets or a water supply, to be built into the project? Specifying requirements for management should be an integral part of the design process. To do this the designer must know what the sponsoring agency intends from the beginning and what the constraints are on available skills and resources. Often a conscious effort can be made to change these skills and resources, but wishful thinking about management capability is a danger.

While the preceding chapters offer clues as to how to answer these program questions, each case and context is unique. Careful in-depth study of a similar case or cases is a good place to begin. To develop a program that will really help organize and inspire good design requires broad knowledge of other similar spaces as well as study of the specific place and its history and context. This work is best carried out by collaboration among designers, managers and social scientists in dialogue with representatives of the sponsor as well as users and affected third parties. Methods are likely to include demographic and historical research, observational studies, individual interviews, and in-depth focus group discussions. There is no formula or single method for writing a good environmental program. For simple spaces in socially homogeneous settings, it may be possible to develop a workable program based primarily on observation and precedent. However, it is as important to answer all of the key questions for small projects as it is for larger ones. The means for doing so and, in particular, the involvement of users can be limited to a small representative set, in scale with the project, to keep the cost at an appropriately modest level. However, note that program development is not a distinct phase but continues through the design process. Design exploration is one of the best ways of identifying the potentials of a place.

Based on our experience, the cost of programming alone, even for larger projects is typically less than 1 percent of the construction cost. This is a small price to pay to set the design process on course to develop a fully useful, manageable, and meaningful space. Such a result will bring the early success that politicians seek, as well as the longer-term success that makes a public administrator's life easier.

NORTH PARK
New York, New York

Located near Chambers and West streets in Battery Park City; designed by Carr, Lynch, Hack and Sandell, with Oehme van Sweden consulting in planting and Johansson and Walcavage on children's play areas; managed by Battery Park City Parks Corporation; completed in 1992; size, 7.5 acres.

North Park is the largest public space in the exemplary system of esplanades, plazas, small parks, and tree-lined streets that has been created as part of the Battery Park City landfill development on the Hudson River side of Lower Manhattan. It is designed to serve a wide range of users: the twenty thousand well-to-do residents of Battery Park City; the mixed-income residents of Lower Manhattan; the office workers in the World Financial Cen-

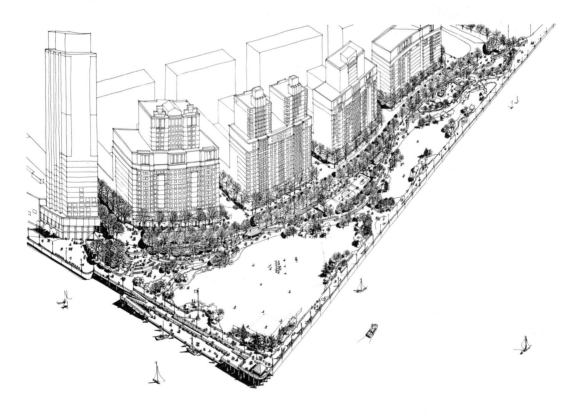

General view of North Park in New York City. (Carr, Lynch, Hack and Sandell)

The fountain and lily pool at the office worker entrance to North Park. (Carr, Lynch, Hack and Sandell)

ter and the World Trade Center; the students in the new Stuyvesant High School, one block from the site; and the mixed-income students of Manhattan Community College, just two blocks away. The project provides an extended example of a participatory programming and design process, utilizing the human dimensions of public space as organizing concepts.

The major participants, in addition to the designers, included the Battery Park City Authority, its Parks Corporation (a management entity), and Community Board no. 1, representing the residents of Lower Manhattan and Battery Park City. To keep the process manageable, it was assumed that authority staff, a large number of whom attended bimonthly meetings with the designers, could adequately represent office worker interests. Stuyvesant High School students and the community college students were closely observed and informally interviewed about their use of open space in the vicinity of their facilities, but they did not directly participate in the process. In addition, the community board requested and was granted Authority funds to hire its own liaison consultant, the landscape architect Anthony Walmsley.

The history of the project is instructive. The park was first conceived as part of an overall master plan for the north neighborhood some ten years prior to the initiation of design. As the time for design approached, the community became convinced that the authority intended to build a green and passive "front yard" for its residential development, while ignoring community needs for active recreation. At the community's urging, the authority hired a consultant to carry out a "User Survey and Community Needs Analysis." This study demonstrated the needs of young families in the area for active recreation space, but it also documented the difficulty of accommodating dedicated sports facilities within the park shape and dimensions

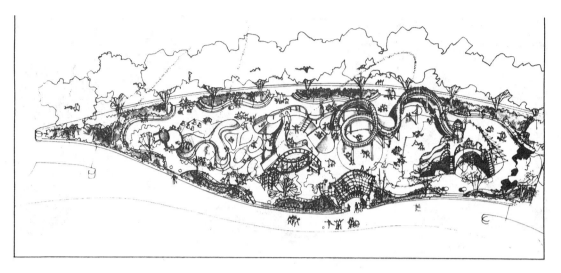

Initial design for the children's play area before being modified by comments from participants. (Carr, Lynch, Hack and Sandell)

Final play area design after modification to meet the authority's concerns for maintenance and replacement of elements. The basic ideas of the playground were maintained. (Carr, Lynch, Hack and Sandell)

dictated by the North Neighborhood plan. After diagramming how various facilities could or could not be fit within the space, the analysis concluded that a multiuse, management-intensive approach would be required to provide for a wide range of active users while creating the pervasive pastoral quality sought by the authority. Armed with this study, the community board negotiated a set of numerical but still general program requirements for the minimum amounts of soft- and hard-surface space to be provided. These were codified in a New York City Board of Estimate Resolution. Also, the authority agreed to safeguard community use by excluding school sports and to provide a full-time recreation staff to manage flexible use of facilities.

The design process that followed on this agreement had four principal meetings. These were followed by detailed review of specific design elements, such as a children's playground and the planting scheme. The designers met with authority staff for review of the design ideas every two weeks and with the community once a month. The community meetings consisted of an ideas workshop, followed by evaluation of alternative plans, then review of a preferred plan, and finally a schematic design review and approval. The ideas workshop started from the prior program analysis and agreement as a base, went on to consider possibilities shown in simulation slides, and ended with the community's wish list of elements to be included, from specific types of playfields and courts to vague concepts such as "art as play."

Based on the quantitative program analysis, ideas from the community, and discussions with authority staff, the designers prepared a detailed qualitative program for the park. This program utilized the "human dimensions" as an organizing framework. This proved to be effective with both the authority and the community, and so we reproduce it here as an example (see Table 8.1).

Table 8.1 *North Park Design Program*

GOALS AND REQUIREMENTS
1. North Park should be a predominantly green, pastoral park, open to the sun, the sky, and river views.
2. The park must provide for as full a range of needs for both active and passive use, on both hard and soft surfaces, as can be accommodated within its seven acres. Minimum requirements for the active recreation have been set in the Board of Estimate Resolution:
   • 115,000 sq. ft. of open lawn;
   • 20,000 sq. ft. of hard surface;
   • desirably, 10,000 sq. ft. of additional hard surface on site or in another area of the North Neighborhood; and
   • 5,000 sq. ft. of soft surface.
3. The park should be seen as an area facility, open to all, and not the captive of any one group of potential users. It must welcome all within range, including:
   • the residents of Battery Park City, who will live closest;
   • the residents of Tribecca and the nearby neighborhoods of Lower Manhattan;
   • office workers from Battery Park City and the Wall Street area;
   • students from Stuyvesant High and Manhattan Borough Community College; and
   • other residents and out-of-town visitors, especially on weekends.

Table 8.1 (*continued*)

4. North Park should have its own special identity, while containing elements that are consistent with the other open spaces of the Battery Park City system.
5. While being inclusive of many uses and users, the park must be strongly unified and beautiful. It should be a prototype for what can be accomplished elsewhere on the Hudson River waterfront.

DESIGN GUIDELINES

In pursuing these general goals and requirements, we will be guided by a number of design guidelines. These can be organized under four general categories:

- human *needs* that should be met;
- *rights* of use that should be protected;
- *meanings* that can be communicated; and
- *maintenance* requirements.

Many of these guidelines must be further defined by setting more specific activities or quantities. This will be done in consultation with Battery Park City staff and Community Board no. 1, as we proceed with the final phase of schematic design. The guidelines are as follows:

A. NEEDS
  1. *Comfort*
    a. Microclimate:
      1) Large open lawn areas and the esplanade in sun from late morning to late afternoon, with shade along edges.
      2) Hard surface court and children's play areas lightly shaded, late morning to midafternoon.
      3) Wind protection, especially for children's play, shaded sitting and table game areas, spectator areas near courts and softball areas.
      4) At least one rain shelter at a good observation point.
    b. Seating:
      1) Frequent benches along pathways and esplanade, facing toward sun and river views.
      2) Bench arrangements offering choice of being up front, in back, to the side, in groups, off alone, in sun and in shade.
      3) Ample seating in sight lines of all lawn and hard and soft surface play areas.
      4) Physically comfortable – wood seats with *backs*.
    c. Convenience facilities:
      1) Drinking fountains in at least three locations.
      2) Trash receptacles within 50 feet of all sitting areas.
    d. Paths, grade changes, and surfaces:
      1) Paths to be wide enough for two pairs of two people walking abreast to pass, plus benches where needed.
      2) Paths designed so that service vehicles can use them for maintenance.

3) Gentle ramps rather than steps for level changes wherever possible, wheelchair accessible.

4) Nonslip, smooth walking surfaces, suitable for prams, strollers, tricycles, skateboards, and joggers.

5) Walls to be good for leaning and sitting on (or against).

e. Lighting:

1) All pathways and sitting areas lighted to average illumination level of at least one-half foot candle (vertical) with evenness ratio of .5 (i.e., no areas on paths less than one-quarter foot candle).

2) Lighting of hard-surface play areas to be determined by residents once they are in place. Electrical lines for possible lighting of these areas to be installed at outset.

3) Special lighting to mark entrances, other key nodes, and road crossings into park.

f. Park house:

1) A single structure, centrally located, near children's play area and active hard-surface areas.

2) To contain: public restrooms with entrances visible to staff; offices for staff of two; storage for recreation equipment and a public counter; maintenance equipment storage for large riding mower, hoses, rakes, peat moss; work room.

3) Location for metering of water, electrical controls, and any pump equipment.

4) Structure should be in a location that provides good surveillance of much of the park and easy access to remainder.

5) Structure should be appropriate in form and materials to its recreational setting and consistent with overall park design.

2. *Relaxation*

a. Relation to context:

1) Sense of separation from vehicular traffic on River Terrace.

2) Contrast of openness (sky, views, sun) with high-walled, contained, shadowed streets.

3) Contrast of soft, colorful planting with hard, restrained architecture.

b. Ambience in park:

1) Pastoral retreat from city – connection to river, nature, sound of wind, water.

2) Ample sloping areas to sit or lie on grass, protected from foot traffic.

3) Opportunities for privacy, intimacy (consider movable chairs) in areas protected from high activity.

c. Security:

1) All areas of park open to surveillance from River Terrace.

2) Good views into most of park from housing.

3) Security staff present, visible.

4) Police call boxes at key locations.

Table 8.1 (*continued*)

3. *Passive Engagement*
   a. Observing:
      1) Good places to watch passing scene, people.
      2) Ample places to watch sports, children.
      3) Protected areas near entrance and on perimeter for older people to sit.
   b. Viewing:
      1) Overall views, well-framed vistas.
      2) Continuity of views down streets, across park to water.
      3) Opportunities to view artworks.
      4) Good places to watch performers.
   c. Involvement with nature:
      1) Opportunities to be close to plants (not behind fences).
      2) Contact with water (river, pond, spray pool); special opportunity to get close to water on north edge on lower platforms (possibly floating).
      3) Birdwatching opportunities.
4. *Active Engagement*
   a. Moving through the park:
      1) A walking and jogging circuit.
      2) Opportunities for small children to ride three-wheelers throughout.
      3) A good path for skateboarding and rollerblading.
   b. Communication:
      1) Entrance plazas for meeting, face-to-face communication.
      2) Social spaces for parents with sight lines to children's play areas.
      3) Social space for office workers (and others) to eat lunch/talk in groups (some with tables).
   c. Ceremony, celebration, festivity:
      1) Spaces for communal gatherings, picnics, dancing.
      2) Space for informal concerts, theater.
      3) Good places for weddings, other large family gatherings.
   d. Children's play:
      1) Protected place for supervised young children (1–6 years), including sand and water play, simple walking and climbing challenges.
      2) More open paved area for less supervised older children to run around, including equipment for active play (possible movable elements for construction) – could be subject of artists commissions.
      3) Lawn area suitable for children's games such as tag or ball play.
      4) Paved area with markings and rules for "street games."
      5) Junior basketball court.
      6) Dodge-ball area.
   e. Teens and adults play:
      1) Two lawn areas large enough to set up informal softball fields, with demountable backstops.

2) Flat area large enough for soccer or six-man football.

3) Two half basketball courts.

4) Volleyball court.

5) One or more handball and practice tennis courts.

6) Two badminton courts.

7) Game tables.

5. *Discovery*

   a. Pathways:

      1) Opportunities to observe all the different things people are doing as one moves along any path.

      2) Diversity of spaces providing changing vistas as seen from paths, so that park is not revealed in one view.

      3) Views organized to provide mystery and surprise, without loss of security.

   b. Details:

      1) Reference to history, context in walls, paving, fences.

      2) Dramatic seasonal change in plants.

B. RIGHTS OF USE

  1. *Access*

   a. Avoidance of physical barriers in approach or use:

      1) River Terrace crossings well marked, with wheelchair ramps on both sides.

      2) Spacious entrances/overlooks at the end of each approach street, including a special dignified and comfortable entrance at the foot of Chambers Street, as main entrance.

      3) All activity areas of park connected by easy to use, smooth pathways.

      4) Steps are gentle and always accompanied by ramps.

      5) All paths to accommodate emergency vehicles.

   b. Avoidance of visual barriers:

      1) Park appears open from approach streets – no high walls, fences, or dense planting to block views into park.

      2) Good visual access to areas adjacent to entries, pathways – can see that there are no muggers, drug dealers, etc.

      3) No hidden areas of park – sitting areas, entrance to restrooms open to view.

   c. Symbols of access to all groups visible from park entries:

      1) No single activity or group dominates the entrance paths.

      2) Parents can see places to go with small children.

      3) Elderly can see safe and quiet places, away from ball playing, bike riding, or other potentially dangerous activity.

  2. *Freedom of Action*

   a. Emphasize multiuse spaces:

      1) Provide several flat open lawn areas of different sizes for use by different groups.

      2) Keep paved areas flat and as free as possible from fences.

      3) Minimize activity areas useable by only a few people at a time.

   b. Zone activity areas:

      1) Noisy, active areas separated from quiet, passive ones.

Table 8.1 (continued)

2) Court games grouped to allow flexible use.

3) Areas for older and younger children separate but adjacent so that parents can oversee children of several ages.

  c. Protect special groups:

1) Secure areas for elderly use (especially in morning and early afternoon) – near flow of traffic but not in it.

2) Fenced play area for small children and their parents.

3) Comfortable locations for physically disabled – near flow of pedestrian traffic but not in it.

3. *Claim*

  a. Park provides a number of clear subspaces that can be temporarily claimed by individuals and groups:

1) Large and small lawn spaces.

2) Small, well-differentiated sitting areas.

3) Seating that groups can claim (perhaps movable).

4) Clear but penetrable boundaries of subareas.

  b. Programming and active supervision to promote use by variety of groups and prevent exclusive claim by any one:

1) Time sharing of spaces (e.g., picnicking, softball, football, volleyball on lawns).

2) Use of courts for special gatherings, events, free play.

4. *Change*

  a. Short-term:

1) Provide space for large gatherings such as a political rally, major speech, celebration, or concert.

2) Provide spaces that can seem separated for group events such as picnics.

3) Provide equipment for special games or uses.

  b. Longer-term:

1) Locations where artworks might be added over time.

2) Space to add children's play equipment.

3) Surfaces that can be painted for different games.

4) Changing plantings – perennials and areas for annuals.

5) Means for expressing concerns or requesting changes and funds for making them.

C. MEANING

  1. *Legibility*

  a. A simple clear path system, well connected.

  b. Social nodes where paths converge.

  c. Clear subareas, each with its own appropriate identity.

  d. Distinct but permeable boundaries at edges of park and between areas.

  e. Landmarks at key park extremities.

  2. *Relevance*

  a. Congruence between cultural norms of users and character of place.

  b. Formal qualities of park are compatible with other Battery Park City open spaces and North Neighborhood.

c. Park design and management conveys positive, caring attitude toward users.

d. Names for subspaces reflecting context.

3. *Individual Connections*

a. Provide anchors for personal attachment (e.g., uniquely located benches, special plants, intimate spaces).

b. Play elements for children have symbolic or narrative content (e.g., Alice in Wonderland sculpture in Central Park).

c. Places for important personal events – family outings, proposals, weddings.

d. Good strolling circuits to create familiar paths with meeting places along the way.

e. Nurturing places – places to eat, communal spaces.

4. *Group Connections*

a. Good social spaces for repeated contact of loosely affiliated groups (e.g., office workers, parents supervising children, elderly).

b. Good places for ethnic or club gatherings.

c. Spaces for group sports.

d. Art works with special group significance.

5. *Connections to Larger Society*

a. "Sacred" places.

b. Symbols of historic continuity (e.g., old waterfront).

6. *Biological and Psychological Connections*

a. Connections to natural world (e.g., references to Hudson River ecology in planting, riverbank meadows, bluff).

b. Park should have a "head" – commanding the surrounding landscape.

c. Should have soft, enclosing, protecting places, especially for children.

7. *Connections to Other Worlds*

a. Views of the Hudson as connection to the West, the wider world – how to make this even more powerful?

b. Cosmic connections to the sun and the stars – possible solar clock, star charts.

D. MAINTENANCE

1. *Programming*

a. Spaces capable of being programmed for uses in varying locations to minimize wear and tear.

b. Rules that allow recreation staff to prohibit active use of soft surface areas in wet seasons and on wet days.

c. No cleats on soft surfaces.

d. Staff can limit usage of hard surface areas by rationing equipment.

2. *Materials*

a. Durable, capable of contact without injury.

b. Capable of easy replacement when they wear out or are damaged.

c. Easy replacement of lighting and other critical elements.

d. Familiar materials to New York and other parts of Battery Park City.

e. Moderate-maintenance natural materials.

Table 8.1 (*continued*)

3. *Irrigation and Drainage*
   a. All planting beds with irrigation systems.
   b. Playfields to be watered from perimeter sprinklers.
   c. Playfields to be well drained in directions that minimize standing water on play areas.
   d. Safety grates or other arrangements to minimize injury.

This program, reviewed by the authority and Community Board no. 1, provided the base for three alternative plans. The three schemes varied in the relative amounts of hard and soft surface, the amount and distribution of tree cover, the type and disposition of court games, and the pathway structure. The pros and cons of these alternatives were separately debated by authority staff and by the community, assisted by its consultant. Each produced a long series of comments, stating its preferences and challenging the designers to produce a synthesis. Although these comments reflected the initial preferences of each constituency, there was strong overlap.

Looking at the program statement and alternatives, the community saw that the authority and its designers really did want to create a park serving a full spectrum of people and interests, as space allowed. The authority saw that the community was also strongly interested in a beautiful pastoral park, and not simply in a collection of dedicated sports facilities. The major disagreement was over tennis courts, which the authority and the designers considered too large and intrusive and serving too few people to take up precious area in this small park.

Within a month the designers were able to develop a synthesis plan with a working balance of desired elements and qualities. This design, shown in the accompanying plan and sketches, includes a fountain and lily pool at the southern end, catering to the needs of office workers for a tranquil, transporting setting; a children's play area, zoned to present appropriate challenges to toddlers, three to five years old, and six to nine; a terrace for play by older children and young adults, including swings, a large rope climb, a handball or practice tennis court, and a large multiuse space designed and striped to accommodate half-court basketball, volleyball, badminton, or roller hockey. Another terrace to the north is to be a quiet sitting area with game tables, but also incorporating a dispersed, playful bronze sculpture by the artist Tom Otterness, which is oriented to the fantasy life of young children.

These terraces are organized close to the curving street that bounds the park and are separated from it by a low wall and planting. Since the street is set above the level of the waterside esplanade and rises from north to south, the terraces establish a middle zone of hard surface activity, below the street but above and looking out over the lawn areas.

The lawns, shaped in part by the dimensions suitable for use for informal games (softball, football, soccer, and volleyball) create an open, flowing pastoral landscape adjacent to the river. They are bounded by a mix of deciduous and evergreen trees, and are edged on the river side by large drifts of perennials, roses, low evergreens, and waterside ornamental grasses. Overall, the planting scheme grades from woodland, shade-loving species on the terraces to waterside, sun-loving varieties along the esplanade. Aquatics populate the lily pool and provision is made for community gardening plots, as part of a large and colorful sun garden at the foot of the main entrance steps at the north end of the park.

Linking all elements within the park is a winding, undulating path between the terraces and the lawns. Connecting to this path at each approaching street is a combined overlook and entrance, which always incorporates ramps providing wheelchair access. At the main entrance, at the end of Chambers Street, is a grand flight of stairs which can also serve as informal seating for a small performance. Another entrance overlook is sheltered by a pavilion, which doubles as a kind of bandstand for performances to groups sitting on the lawn. On the central terrace is the park house, providing space for recreational and maintenance staff, public restrooms, work and storage areas.

The programming and design process for North Park was evolutionary, running from broad concepts through general alternatives to the detailed design development of each feature of the preferred approach. Intensive involvement by the community board members, authority staff, and the future park managers contributed to a design synthesis that, on paper, is both comprehensive and manageable. Community members who participated feel, justifiably, that they had a strong influence on the result and, therefore, have a sense of authorship that should translate into a special attachment to this park.

The designers and their client believe that North Park will be a successful and well-loved *community* park, broader in its appeal and use than it would

The proposed park house, in the tradition of pastoral parks. (Carr, Lynch, Hack and Sandell)

have been, absent such an inclusive process. Once the park is complete and in use for two or three years, a good postoccupancy evaluation would show whether this design lives up to its promise.

Related cases: Boston Waterfront Park, Village Homes Community Playground.

IDENTIFYING AND ENGAGING THE USERS

For both programming and design, and later for management, identifying and engaging the users are essential but often difficult steps in the process (Hester, 1990). Although public spaces should by definition be open to all, in practice users are more narrowly drawn. For a given city, users of a place can be predicted based on the location, size, and overall purpose of the space. For neighborhood parks, most vest-pocket parks and downtown plazas, residential streets, playgrounds, and all community-created spaces, the principal users will be drawn from those who live or work nearby. For other spaces such as a central park, commons or square, a marketplace, a pedestrian mall on the main shopping street, most waterfronts, or a town trail, the intention may be to draw on a much larger area or even a citywide population. In fact, some groups will be more likely than others to use these central spaces, but this too is predictable. For instance, the income or the ethnicity of those using a new space in downtown may be strongly influenced by traditional shopping patterns in the area, by proximity to public transportation, or by other characteristics of the near environment. For some types of spaces, such as specialized sports parks, certain public–private spaces such as atria, or spaces that are tourist attractions, likely users can be more easily defined.

For most spaces of more than local import, it is helpful in predicting use both to analyze the existing situation carefully and to apply judgment based on experience with similar spaces in other cities. Economic consultants analyze "comparables" to estimate the market for a proposed commercial development. The case studies in this book provide some guidance to complement study of local conditions. Accessibility to various populations of potential users is key, and, for other than neighborhood spaces, this will be a combination of walking distance and location in the street and public transportation networks. A large park may be geographically near the center of the city, but it is not central to the full population unless served by public transportation at times such as evenings and weekends, when it is most likely to be used. Its actual use may be limited to those who can drive, if parking is available, or who live or work near enough to walk.

The character of the immediate context is also critical to use. An inner-city office development, which won an urban design prize from an architectural journal, proposes to build a green space referred to as a "commons" and said to be for the use of people living in the surrounding working-class neighborhood. However, the space will be lined by office buildings, for which it will be the front yard, and will be managed by the developer. It is not likely to be hospitable either by character or management policy to parents with young children, teenagers, or older residents, who constitute typical users of neighborhood parks.

The question of user identity is not merely one of prediction but also of prescription. What users are wanted and for what purpose? Public spaces, when large enough and strategically located, do have some ability to influence the processes of physical and social change that are continually occurring in communities. In recent years, many cities in the United States have built parks, together with other recreational attractions, to help revive districts that have become abandoned or underutilized as local economies have changed. Prediction and prescription of users in these cases are functions of the larger planning and redevelopment scheme of which open space is a part. In any such undertaking, the planners have a responsibility to consider those already living or doing business in the area and to help them deal with change in positive ways. The design of the

In the Downtown Washington Streets for People project a cross section of users was identified and recruited by means of a random on-the-street survey. (Stephen Carr)

327

open space, and the identification of users to work with the designers, will need to include these existing residents and workers, as well as future users.

If users are to be drawn from a larger area than the immediate surroundings, predicting the particular population, or "market," will be a combination of project goals, demographic analysis, transportation availability, context analysis, and judgment based on knowledge of how similar spaces have been used in other places. For most neighborhood spaces, one can analyze census data on the area within easy walking distance to determine the potential user population. The size of the space and the range of facilities to be provided will give a further indication of the particular groups within this population who will actually use it. For a central park or a waterfront, the principle is the same, but if the facility is unique, the projected users must be adjusted to reflect the population who can easily reach it by public transportation or private car. Consideration must also be given to nearby office workers who may use the park briefly at lunchtime or after work and to visitors from out of the city.

For other types of downtown spaces, such as pedestrian malls or markets, the best starting point would be an on-the-street survey of those who are currently there, adjusting the demographic results by experience from other cities. Once again, accessibility will be a key factor, together with the predominant income and ethnicity of existing populations in the nearby area. Because it is so easy to engage in wishful thinking about the power of public space improvements to change the image of an area and to draw new people, it is important to make a careful study of experience elsewhere. In doing so, it will be necessary to find cities with similar populations and competitive alternatives to downtown.

More specialized spaces such as plazas, vest-pocket parks, and atria will usually have easily predictable user populations, based primarily on nearby office workers supplemented by visitors and, depending on location, a few shoppers and nearby residents. These spaces often provide havens for homeless persons and tempting markets for drug dealers. A questionnaire survey of nearby office workers can provide an understanding of the base population and its likely use of the space, but these other potential frequenters must not be forgotten. If the space has a commercial basis, as in festival marketplaces, the developer will usually do a market analysis to determine the particular balance of office workers, visitors, and residents that can be anticipated.

The means of contacting and recruiting users to participate in a programming and design effort will depend on the nature of the project and the resources available. In the simplest case, say a community playground or small park, the programmer and designer can usually work through an existing organization to reach the most likely user groups, who will be the friends and neighbors of organization members. Self-interest will often provide enough incentive for voluntary participation and a local church or school will offer a meeting space. The designer must be careful that no significant groups, as indicated by census analysis of the vicinity, are excluded because they are not currently represented in the organization. Most community organizations are interested in building their memberships and are usually open to some outreach effort by means of flyers and telephone or door-to-door canvassing. When resources permit, a brief questionnaire, mailed to the entire neighborhood and asking for basic demographics and about interest in participation, is the most effective means.

For downtown spaces, if a survey can be done either by questionnaires distributed to office workers or on the street, respondents can be asked whether they would be willing to come to a few meetings to discuss the proposed space. A small cross section of those contacted, based on representative demographic characteristics, can then be called and asked to participate. In this case, self-interest may not be strong enough to gain consistent participation of all, especially if any economic hardship is involved. At a minimum, the recruiter may wish to offer assistance with baby-sitting or travel costs. It may be best, however, simply to pay participants a modest stipend to serve as "user consultants," a practice similar to paying people to serve as members of focus groups in marketing studies. This will likely guarantee a more representative cross section, as well as better attendance over a sequence of meetings.

For projects of larger scope, say the reclamation of a waterfront or a large central park, several means of reaching users will be needed. As always, it is best to begin with those nearby, contacting existing organizations within adjacent communities and asking them to recruit a cross section of participants corresponding to the demographic analysis for the project. Citywide civic organizations can provide representation of the broader user population. In case strong organizations are lacking, direct recruitment can be done by telephone canvassing or by contacting people in the streets. In most cases, interest in such a development should be strong enough to engage participants on a volunteer basis, but if not, payment can be offered.

THE PARTICIPATORY DESIGN PROCESS

Once all the client groups have been identified and organized, a designer selected, and a preliminary program prepared, the proper design process can begin. The structure for a participatory design process, involving the groups that we have described, can be tied to the normal phases of design from concept through construction. Although it will vary with the size and civic importance of the project, this process is likely to have the elements outlined in this section.

Meeting with Key Actors

Usually, politicians, business leaders, and other "key actors" in initiating or funding a project are best approached individually. Presentations to city councils, chambers of commerce, and the like may also be necessary in the course of a project, but these public meetings, with the press often in attendance, are rarely a good format for open discussion. In one-on-one meetings, even if brief, the designer has an opportunity to probe and address each individual's ideas and interests. A public design process must reconcile the interests of those who have the authority or the "clout" to make or strongly influence decisions, with the expressed needs of people who will actually use the space. An appropriate balance can be struck only when these interests are understood. Public design often becomes, at least in part, an exercise in diplomacy.

Decision Meetings

Meetings with the task force or other direct client group will be the most frequent, often scheduled on a monthly basis. The designer must get to know this group and its views well, both as individuals and as a whole. It is therefore wise at the beginning also to have an individual discussion with each group member. The balance, leadership, and dynamics of such a group can be critical to the success of a project.

Technical Advice

For public administrators, barring some major disagreement with what is being proposed, it will usually be enough to meet once in the beginning to elicit views and concerns and then to report back near the end of each phase of work. When administrators can be assembled into a "technical advisory committee" the review process will be both more efficient and productive because this format allows for exchanges among various departments. In any case, adequate time must be allotted in the process for officials to review drawings and reports in more detail and to comment before next steps are taken. Individual meetings may be necessary to address special concerns, and particularly to discuss the design with those individuals (usually from public works or parks departments) who will have management and maintenance responsibility. The better the designer understands their procedures and constraints, the more manageable will be the result.

Civic Advice

If there is a civic advisory committee to represent the views and interests of various advocacy organizations, it can meet on a schedule like that of the technical advisory group. Individuals in this group as well are likely to have particular knowledge and ideas to contribute to a project, even if they do not have longer-term responsibility. They might be environmentalists, fitness experts, arts activists, historic preservationists, bicycle enthusiasts, or financial experts, each with expertise in their field of interest that could help the project. If large group sessions are difficult because of this range of interests, breaking up into subcommittees may prove more effective.

User Participation

The usual mechanism for user and nonuser participation is a public hearing, but this forum does not provide adequate representation (Hester, 1990). Many people who may have an interest do not hear about it, usually it comes too late in the process, and it is not a good setting for informed discussion. As a supplement to these hearings, which are often required by law, a series of less formal meetings – or "workshops" – should be held at each design stage of the project. These can be organized to allow for small group discussion, following presentations to a larger group. For larger projects, a series of meetings with small groups can precede the workshops, allowing participants to gain in-depth understanding of the issues.

Once assembled, a good initial way of organizing people for small group discussion may be by age, ethnicity, or income, because people open up more when they are with those with whom they feel they share common goals. Depending on the project, it may also be appropriate to organize groups by special interest or geographical location. In some cases, there can be value in mixed groups from the start, because different facets of issues emerge, but if social class or age differences are too great, people may have difficulty speaking their minds. Later in the process people can gather in larger mixed groups to share ideas. However organized, people in meetings of about seven to ten seem to feel most comfortable asking questions and voicing their opinions. When large-group presentations are needed, they can be followed by small-group discussions. In these small groups each participant can get adequate "airtime," and it is possible to have productive discussions among designers, managers, and users.

Users can be consulted on the same schedule as public officials and civic committees, but the style of the interaction will be different. Public officials will often be reluctant to voice their opinions in meetings, asking for time to review issues with their staffs. Those chosen for civic advisory groups usually have particular issues or points of view that they represent. User participants chosen by demographics are likely to be more open to dialogue, both learning and giving opinions freely. As in any process of group discussion, a few talkative people can dominate if the format is not controlled. While breaking up into small groups will mitigate this problem, the designers who are facilitating the discussion must take care to draw out the views of all present. A group process resource person can be very helpful to facilitate the meetings and make sure each voice is heard.

Groups of user participants will not often produce follow-up written comments. It is best to design agendas so all that is needed can be learned at the meeting and recorded by the facilitator for the next session. A useful technique is to write conclusions on large newsprint pads so that the group can verify or correct them at the time. It can sometimes be helpful to vote or to have people fill out a simple questionnaire at the end of a meeting, if a quantitative sense is needed on certain key issues.

Meetings should be scheduled with the policy panel, technical and civic advisory groups, and users at each phase of the design process. Each set

A neighborhood process might best begin with small groups organized by area, age, and ethnicity. (Carr, Lynch Associates)

Later, as people's ideas and feelings become clear, exchanges between different groups can be productive. (Stephen Carr)

of participants can be helpful in analyzing existing conditions, developing the design and management program, considering alternative conceptual and schematic designs, and reviewing the final design and management plan.

The process must be carefully laid out in advance, and the roles and responsibilities of the various participants clearly understood. Each participant should know who will make the decisions and what decisions will be taken at each stage of work. The professionals guiding the process will need to explain at each meeting what has been decided to date, what is currently being asked of participants, and who will act on the information received. It is especially important that those guiding the process report back promptly on what was heard and how it was acted upon. Few participants will expect all of their ideas to be accepted, but they will want them to be seriously considered.

In the beginning, a visit with users to the site and to existing spaces similar to what is being proposed can be very useful. People can be given throw-away cameras to record their impressions and can talk with users of the place as well as with the designer and programmers about what they observe. Immediate follow-up meetings are important to discuss observations before they fade in memory. Further insights can be stimulated by looking together at slide images of other related spaces. In this process

Sometimes design meetings can be held on site. Workshop for Central Park Master
Plan, Davis, in Central Park on a Saturday morning. (CoDesign, Inc.)

the designer and programmer not only learn about participants' initial
preferences and perceived needs, but also gain a sense of empathy with
them. Such shared experience can make later representations of the future space – whether by photographic analogies, drawings, or word pictures – much more understandable and easier to analyze and discuss.

Prior to the next meeting, these initial perceptions can be developed as
specific program alternatives to be discussed. Once again, dialogue can
be assisted by simulation slides of similar places and simple sketch images, together with diagrams to show how the various program elements
might be arranged in space. Program ideas may also come from the project sponsor, a civic advisory group, a user survey, or the designer and
programmer. Sometimes it can be helpful to participants in gaining an
understanding of what can be accommodated if they move around blocks
of paper, scaled to various activities, on a map of the site. User-drawn
"ideal" designs can also be useful in stimulating discussion on goals and
desires. The designer and programmer can guide discussion to focus on
the needs, rights, and meanings that can be addressed by the program
elements and arrangements. The professionals should be forthcoming about
the opportunities and constraints that they see in the site, as well as limi-

tations deriving from the sponsor's resources and technical or legal realities. After these meetings a proposed program can be written, as previously described, for review by all parties. In developing this program, designers and programmers will need to test further the preferred alternatives by analyzing their fit with the site and with each other, keeping in mind the sponsor's goals and the users' feelings. This is really the beginning of design.

After a general program has been agreed to by the sponsor's decision-making group, most likely with some alternatives for parts of the project, the process moves on through the various phases of design. Here the user's role becomes less proactive and more reactive. Although there have been many examples of community spaces, such as gardens and playgrounds, that have been designed and built by users, in most cases a designer's skill and experience is required to project workable solutions, based on the program information and criteria.

At each stage of refinement, the designer can present alternatives with the implications spelled out. Guided discussion can focus on how each alternative, for the whole or for parts, addresses people's needs, protects their rights, and conveys desired meanings, as set forth in the program objectives. Here the designer's challenge is to draw out people's true feelings rather than to "sell" a personally preferred solution. Because designers tend to become attached to their ideas, this is not a simple task. Once again, a group process specialist can be helpful in taking the designer off the spot, but a confident designer can have a favorite idea rejected, learn from it, and move on to a better design.

As the designer moves forward through the process toward closure, among the most difficult issues to resolve is likely to be how to accommodate diverse user groups within the same space. To determine the proper balance among various competing user needs and rights, the designer and manager must be able to imagine correctly the various types of individuals and groups that will use the space and how they are likely to relate to one another. It is extremely helpful in visualizing activity in a place to work with a cross section of the people who will ultimately use it. It is the designer's responsibility to invent the solution, or alternative solutions, to the problem of competing demands on the same space. If the consequences of these alternatives are appropriately displayed, users can then comment on which seems to be the best balance for them. These responses can give comfort to decision makers in choosing among alternatives.

Discussed in the abstract, this process may seem daunting. The number of meetings can be large and the opportunities for disagreement and conflict may seem to multiply as a result. Yet any significant public space initiative, in our pluralistic society, is certain to involve controversy arising from different desires and demands on the space. If these differences are not faced in the beginning, they will arise later, in the actual use of the space. That is why competitions are an especially poor design method, as Boston's Copley Square has twice demonstrated. Any public design project will also involve many meetings, which can expand rapidly as various groups push to enter and have their say. What is proposed here is an orderly and systematic process for gathering pertinent information, for surfacing and dealing creatively with differences, and for assuring that those who need to be involved can be included at appropriate times and in appropriate ways to contribute their knowledge and opinions. By applying the principles described in the beginning, the process can be scaled down to fit more modest projects. Through such a process, design can reach conclusions that will be accepted by the affected parties and will stand the test of use over time.

BETTER MANAGEMENT

There is a growing trend, illustrated in some of our examples and case studies, toward more comprehensive environmental management of public space. Often, this results from public and private cooperation in creating the space, but sometimes, as in the case of Central Park, it springs from action by concerned citizens' groups. In the long run, good management of a space is as important as good design in determining user satisfaction. Good management must start with a full understanding of the purposes for which a place was designed, the intended or actual users, and the needs, rights, and meanings they seek there.

For new spaces, the intended activities, management, and maintenance should be specified as a management program. As a basis for this, the initial environmental program can be updated to reflect the learning that took place in the design process and the specific intentions of the final design. This management program should be prepared by the designer at the end of the construction phase and should be reviewed by the manager. It should describe the activities envisioned and how the settings are designed to accommodate them, including provisions made for changes in use. It should also be explicit about potential conflicts and describe how the design and management can provide for the rights of individuals and groups. The program can show how good management will enhance meaning by keeping the place secure, clean, and comfortable and by encouraging activities with communal and artistic significance.

Above all, the management program should describe the level of management and maintenance required to make the space function well over time, given the expected uses. A proposed staff and budget for this also should be included. Procedures should be suggested for annual reevaluation and updating of the program. If the process was structured properly, the designer writing the program will have worked out the general requirements in advance with the responsible management entity.

It is ideal if a knowledgeable public space manager can be part of the design process. If the future manager of the space has not yet been hired, another manager could be engaged as a consultant to the team. The best result will occur when space and management program are designed together.

Many of the same qualities needed in a good public space designer should also be sought in a public space manager (Whyte, 1980, 1988). Knowledge about how people use space is as important as technical mastery of management and maintenance procedures. An ability to reach out to users and engage them in the management process is also important. A good manager should be able to work with many different types of people and to empathize with their wishes and problems.

Technical expertise is increasingly important for managers. There are many new strategies for mounting and managing activities in public space and in keeping it well cared for. This is a developing field, and there is a need for special training programs. Perhaps the most skilled practitioners currently are to be found in the semipublic arenas of the regional shopping malls, the downtown festival marketplaces and gallerias, or at attractions such as Disney World. However, there are also some excellent managers currently working for parks departments and managing downtown streets. Despite generally lower salaries than in the private sector, public space management can attract able people if there is a clear public commitment to the task and a means for evaluating and rewarding success.

Although little can be done in the public arena to build more flexibility into the construction process itself, everything possible should be done to secure a substantial operating budget so that flexibility can be provided in operation. For beloved spaces such as Central Park, private funds have been raised to supplement scarce public funds. Several public funding devices, ordinarily used to support capital bonding for construction, can also be used to generate ongoing funds for operation and maintenance. These include tax-increment financing, special assessment districts, ground rents from related development, and user fees as well as the usual – and increasingly difficult to secure – support from a city's general tax revenues.

It is helpful in securing and maintaining management funds if the task force or commission that acts as client for the design continues to oversee management. The Church Street Marketplace Commission in Burlington,

Vermont, is one example (see Chapter 6). Often there will be a change in the makeup of this group at the completion of construction because the project tends to lose glamour at that point. Those willing to serve in a continuing capacity are likely to have a direct self-interest in the place, such as business people along a pedestrian shopping mall or neighbors to a park. However, these management entities are typically appointed by mayors or city councils, and so there is usually an effort to supplement locals by individuals who have broader interests and influence.

When special operating entities do not exist, line management through traditional city agencies can be supplemented by citizen advisory groups. Advisory groups can be drawn from the same people who participate in a broad-based design process. They have a stake in success and are already sensitized to the purposes of the design and to the likely management issues. As time goes on, and the space matures and use changes, citizen groups can assist in the process of reevaluation of user needs and space performance and can form a key element of the client group for redesign and policy change. If they feel a sense of responsibility for the space, they will keep the pressure on politicians to provide the necessary funding. The continued presence of an advisory group is very much in the interest of managers.

Management of the Church Street Marketplace in Burlington, Vermont, has allowed for continuous adjustment of the space by commercial users, while protecting the public purpose. (Stephen Carr)

By being outside the bureaucracy and advocating for the smooth functioning of the space, a citizen advisory committee can maintain an objectivity that is difficult for the harried manager. The group can make or seek independent evaluations when necessary. By working closely with management, the group comes to understand the limitations of the system and is more likely to see problems to be overcome rather than "failures." From the manager's perspective, the advisory committee can maintain a perspective on the situation, as well as constructive criticism and support when change is needed. From the participants' point of view, there is an opportunity to contribute to the evolution of public places that are important in their daily lives.

In small neighborhood spaces, management and oversight may be combined. Increasingly in cities, users of a park or playground are given management control of the space, with maintenance often done by contract to a private provider or by a public agency. This can be abused when gates are locked to members of the public not in the core working group, but more often it simply increases the likelihood that there will be concerned eyes on the space and shortens the path to needed improvement. Because such monitoring is typically done on a volunteer basis, the responsibility is rotated among different members. One very successful example is Washington Market Park in Lower Manhattan which, like many such parks, was the result of a long struggle by the community to secure much needed open space (Francis, Cashdan, & Paxson, 1984). Space that was hard-earned is usually treasured and well cared for.

When committee members are also users of a space, as they often are, they will provide an early warning system for problems and will also have their own ideas for new uses or physical improvements. If their presence is made known to the general public, they will be used as a conduit for complaints and suggestions. In cases of extreme difficulty, as when a public park is taken over by an "undesirable" group, the advisory committee can hold public meetings on what to do about the problem, make recommendations, and then form a special task force to follow up with public officials and mount lobbying efforts to see that the recommendations are implemented. A citizen advocacy effort in Boston resulted in the appointment of a new parks commissioner, a comprehensive study of the conditions, repair, and maintenance needs of the city's parks, and a commitment from the mayor to an increased capital and operating budget.

EVALUATION AND ADJUSTMENT

It will be helpful to management if, from time to time, postoccupancy evaluations are made of the effectiveness of the place and its management

(Cooper Marcus & Francis, 1990; Francis, 1987c). A thorough and objective approach combining observation studies with questionnaires or structured interviews will provide the most complete information. A simple evaluation approach can also be useful. A good manager will be able to understand much from daily on-the-job experience, if he or she is thinking about the dimensions explained here. Systematic observation of use, which can be done by on-site recreation and maintenance staff, together with a few simple questions of users can give great insight. If there is a continuing advisory committee, including users, feedback is likely to be constant. Lack of resources will often be a greater obstacle to improvement than lack of information.

When a space is not working well, and has physically deteriorated due to misuse or neglect, a plan for its improvement will be needed. Improvement plans are best prepared by teams consisting of a manager, a designer, and an environmental researcher. This team should report to a citizens' task force as well as to the responsible public administrators. It must evaluate not only existing conditions, and what is required to repair them, but also existing use and how it relates to the present design and management of the facility. The human dimensions can be used as a mea-

The angular concrete forms of the first Copley Square competition winner seemed to many Bostonians to be antithetical to the graceful landmark buildings that surround it. (Stephen Carr)

Boston's Copley Square today, after a second competition, is merely bland. (Stephen Carr)

surement system for evaluating performance. Recommendations will likely include proposals for changing the space and the management policy and operating procedures, as well as a budget and staffing for doing so. New York City's Central Park Management and Restoration Plan (Barlow, 1987) is an excellent example of such an effort.

Sometimes citizen action and study of the deficiencies in existing conditions and use can lead to substantial redesign of a space. In Boston, a group of corporate neighbors in the vicinity of Copley Square became concerned about the use and character of the space. Copley Square had been the subject of a national design competition in 1964. The winning design included a large area around a fountain, which was depressed some eight feet below the level of the adjacent main street. The base of the wall along that edge of the space became a favorite hangout for street people because it was out of view from passing observers. The space was also seen by these new neighbors to have been designed with angular forms and built with poor quality materials, inappropriate to its context. As a result, a group from MIT was engaged to analyze the space and prepare a detailed program for redesign. Unfortunately, a new competition was held, rather than a participatory design process, but this time designers were required to follow the program closely. The corporate sponsors shared the cost of the redevelopment with the city and the reconstruction is now complete, awaiting a new evaluation. Initial reviews have not been favorable, and Copley Square may yet become a monument to the liabilities of competitions as vehicles for designing important spaces.

SUMMARY

In this chapter, we have advocated some modest reforms to the programming, design, and management process for public space. In general, our prescription is for greater inclusiveness at each step. Just as we argue, in the book as a whole, for attention to all of the human dimensions of public space, so we suggest that the best design and management are to be obtained by working with all those responsible for and affected by a space.

We offer specific ideas about whom to include in client groups, how to select designers and programmers, how to develop a program, how to identify and recruit participants, and how to organize and conduct an effective and efficient participatory process. We do not assert that this is the only way to carry out this work and to make good spaces. However, from our collective experience and observation of planning and design in practice, we believe it is an approach that works well and which seems to be quite helpful in making public spaces responsive, democratic, and meaningful. For those already attuned to the benefits of an inclusive design process, these suggestions for incremental change will not be radical departures from their own practice.

Our process recommendations address the social – some would say the ethical – basis of public space design, without intending to inhibit the more personal and playful aspects of the art. This formal play, which is one of the joys of design, can serve users in another way by bringing surprise and delight into their daily lives. We do believe, however, that lasting beauty is more than at the surface, and that it will shine forth most strongly from those spaces that are the continually evolving, collective products of all those who decide about, design, tend, and use them.

THE FUTURE OF PUBLIC SPACE

At the beginning, we took note of the striking proliferation of new public spaces dedicated to human use and enjoyment. In many of our older cities, the existing stock of open space is also being renovated and improved. Although some social critics, such as Sennett (1977), have decried the *Fall of Public Man,* this movement suggests something else: that Americans are in the midst of creating a new public space culture.

The relationship of public space to public life is dynamic and reciprocal. New forms of public life require new spaces. Consider, for instance, the present demand for jogging trails and bicycle paths. New spaces, when they are more than corporate emblems or institutional symbols, create opportunities for increased public life. As the two develop together, the culture of public space evolves.

In this chapter, we speculate on the future of public space in the United States, and with it on the future of public life. We view this future through the framework of our own values and close the chapter by asking how public space and public life can become more responsive, democratic, and meaningful. We examine three key issues that stand in the way: equity, control, and cultural diversity.

THE CULTURAL MISSION OF PUBLIC SPACE

Each new public space directly affects the public culture. A large intervention such as Haussmann's Parisian boulevards, New York's Central Park, or Boston's "Emerald Necklace" of Olmsted designed parks can have a dramatic effect on the life and development of a city. A community-built garden or playground can greatly enrich the social life of a neighborhood. When public spaces are successful, in the ways that we have advocated, they will increase opportunities to participate in communal activity. This

People gather to appreciate each other's efforts and socialize at the Clinton Community Garden in Manhattan, New York City. (Trust for Public Land)

fellowship in the open nurtures the growth of public life, which is stunted by the social isolation of ghettos and suburbs. In the parks, plazas, markets, waterfronts, and natural areas of our cities, people from different cultural groups can come together in a supportive context of mutual enjoyment. As these experiences are repeated, public spaces become vessels to carry positive communal meanings.

In good public spaces, one can see the social world and other individuals in a culturally favorable light. In the often stressful realms of daily life, including poorly designed and managed public spaces, individuals erect a self-protective shield about themselves, which focuses and narrows their perceptions. Utilitarian purpose and self-protection become centrally important in determining how one responds to others. Stereotypes can seem to be an efficient means of simplifying a complex and threatening social world, placing entire groups of people into the class of "the others," with whom one does not need or want to have contact. In well-designed and well-managed public spaces, the armor of daily life can be partially removed, allowing us to see others as whole people. Seeing people different from oneself responding to the same setting in similar ways creates a temporary bond. There may be a spontaneous exchange of smiles and, perhaps, a conversation. Even if there is no direct communication, good public space supports what developmental psychologists call peaceful parallel activity: Individuals may pursue their interests but women are not harassed; older children allow young ones to play; the elderly are not bothered; and so on. Such a space encourages cross-group socialization and tolerance and can be thought of, in Michael Walzer's term, as being "open-minded" (Walzer, 1986).

Looked at in this way, public space design and management has a cultural mission. Our parks and plazas and Main Streets can be precious social binders, which help create and sustain a coherent and inclusive public culture. Well-functioning public spaces provide vivid examples of a society more egalitarian than we normally experience. When people wish to demonstrate their support for greater freedom and equality, they invariably choose a central public space as the most appropriate setting to join together and make their feelings known. Sunday in Central Park, or any great park, provides an opportunity, to observe how the family life and shared pleasures of others, whose cultural history and circumstances may be different, can have much in common with one's own. A neighborhood playground can also be a fine common ground. Even when differences are great, people can peacefully coexist. These experiences foster a sense of community of the whole and reinforce cultural norms of tolerance across the economic and social distances of our society. In these ways, the public space movement can be a force in improving our public culture.

CREATING NEW SPACES

If public space is to play such a valuable role in shaping and maintaining public culture, how can that mission be accomplished in the future development of our cities? In utopian visions such as Ebenezer Howard's influential *Garden Cities of Tomorrow* (1945), regional open space systems were seen as a crucial balance and limit to urban development, and they were typically described in loving detail. Open space has always held a prominent place in the dreams of regional planners. "Greenbelts" shape and bound planners' pictures of the future city, and green parks are spaced rationally across them. What is the likely prospect for regional open space systems in our future cities?

In a few places, regional agencies have actually been empowered to carry out the planners' dreams, and in most other cities there is potential to develop regional open space. Boston's Metropolitan District Commission created and now manages thousands of acres of diverse open space and is still adding to its inventory. Where the political will exists, regional open space agencies can become important tools in the struggle to preserve and create open space against the pressure of metropolitan growth.

Other agencies that operate regionally, such as state departments of transportation, mass transit authorities, and port authorities routinely create "landscaped" space as an adjunct to their primary responsibilities. They have the power to do much more if they can see it as part of their charge. Los Angeles has some four hundred miles of freeways, often flanked by landscaped green space. Instead of treating this space merely as a pleasant setting for the roads, it could have been (and in places still could be) designed to accommodate pedestrians and cyclists, and expanded to serve local neighborhoods. In contrast, Boston's Massachusetts Bay Transportation Authority has created linear parks above and alongside the newest extensions of its mass transit system, serving local needs by regional action. The New York State Department of Transportation is about to rebuild the formerly elevated West Side Highway as an urban boulevard. The city and state are cooperating to create a Hudson River waterfront park, four and one-half miles long, as a part of this roadway project (West Side Waterfront Panel, 1990). Under pressure from the open space and environmental movements, these regional agencies will be an important means of developing new open space in large cities. Although their actions will not result in coherent regional open space systems, they can help to connect local areas rather than divide them as they have done so often in the past.

The Hudson River waterfront in New York City, shown here in the West Village area, awaits its transformation. (Carr, Lynch, Hack and Sandell)

The proposed Hudson River Esplanade Park in New York City's West Village.
(Carr, Lynch, Hack and Sandell)

For the most part, the creation and tending of public space will continue
to be the responsibility of local jurisdictions within metropolitan areas. In
addition to parks departments, cities already have development agencies
with the power to create public space in order to spur desired private development. Wherever the development market is strong, private developers will be required to create public space as a *quid pro quo* for gaining
development rights. Office and light industrial developments now routinely create parklike settings, often decorated with large sculptures or
other art works, and these "parks" in the future will provide exercise courses
and playfields for health-conscious workers and open them to neighbors
on weekends. Mixed-use developments in cities will continue to create
focal indoor and outdoor spaces with required public access and will carefully landscape the streets on which they front. New waterfront developments will be required to create pleasant means of public access and useful public spaces on the water.

With the aid of these various public and private agencies and actions,
cities now compete with one another on the basis of the "quality of life"
they offer. The completion of the interstate highway system, generally
improving local air service, and the advent of modern telecommunications
make businesses "footloose" in choosing locations for new investments in
regional offices or manufacturing plants. Choices are significantly influenced by the attractions a city can offer to management and professional

347

staff. The ideal city for this key economic group will be green and pleasant overall, with close and affordable suburban housing, an extensive sports-oriented park system, and an ample array of cultural and entertainment facilities, with their related urban open spaces.

Governmental and business leadership drawn primarily from this group – or cooperative with it – is now setting the agenda for the next quarter century of urban development, including public spaces. To compete for the knowledge-based and service-related industries, which are the growing edge of our economy, these leaders will attempt to transform or further develop cities in the ways that are attractive to decision makers in this sector. Projects will be favored that have the potential to draw attention to a city and improve its image – projects such as large waterfront developments with ample public space. Because people still seek pleasant, walkable downtowns with retail activity, cultural opportunities, and lively entertainment, much effort will continue to go into reviving or recreating these older centers, with particular emphasis on downtown residential neighborhoods. Citizen groups will seize the opportunity to turn these urban enhancement projects to local purposes by means of community involvement in their planning. Cities will also invent strategies for coordinating public and private actions, often by means of new quasi-public entities designed to facilitate the desired development. Chattanooga's RiverCity Company, which grew out of an extensive community planning process, is a recent example of this trend. It is charged with developing the Tennessee Riverpark along twenty miles of the river as it passes through Chattanooga (Carr, Lynch Associates, 1985).

Urban waterfronts will continue to be fertile ground for the creation of new open spaces that are both community enhancing and community serving. The success of waterfront developments in the United States and Canada will lead to more of them in the future, so long as centrally located, underutilized waterfront land still exists. Water bodies and waterways, once thought of as obstacles to be overcome or as resources to be exploited for industrial use, are now seen as recreational opportunities and strongly attractive settings for new urban development. Influenced by successful examples in Boston, Baltimore, San Antonio, and San Francisco, other cities including Philadelphia, New York, Pittsburgh, Washington, D.C., Detroit, Indianapolis, Toronto, Minneapolis-St. Paul, Portland (Oregon), Seattle, Memphis, and Chattanooga all have made efforts to revive and transform their waterfronts.

Sometimes these waterfronts will offer opportunities to preserve natural areas, but more often they will be sites for major new open spaces with citywide appeal, comparable to building the great central parks of the nineteenth century. Strong public pressure will mandate continuous public access to the water's edge. Typically, there will be an esplanade or trail

Urban waterfronts will continue to be fertile grounds for the creation of new public spaces. Waterfront walkway in False Creek, Vancouver, B.C. (Gary Hack)

along the edge or near it for strolling, jogging, and resting. Cycling and even horseback riding will usually require a separate path. There will be one or more public parks of the pastoral sort with "meadows" for relaxation and informal play, wooded areas, and special gardens. There will also be piers for getting out in the water and for fishing, and marinas for pleasure boating. There may be active urban plazas, especially at the ends of important streets. The reuse of these waterfronts will be celebrated in annual festivals.

There will be increasing debate, as there is now in New York City, about the use of waterfront lands for private purposes, such as office and retail development, housing, and institutions. In some cases, private development will be needed to bring people to the waterfront and make it safe for public use. There are good examples in Boston, Baltimore, and San Antonio to show that public access can be preserved and even improved through commercial and institutional development. In many other cases it will be asserted that development is needed to pay for the new public spaces and, on that point, the argument will rage, because it is the openness of water-fronts that is most treasured. However accomplished, what will be sought is that balance of activity in new public spaces and on the water itself that can bring together a broad range of people, ready to rub elbows and enjoy themselves in these peaceful open settings.

Cities not favored with existing waterfronts ready to be made into large-scale playgrounds may attempt to create them or make use of more limited opportunities (Girot, 1988). San Antonio and Austin, Texas, through flood control and public works projects, were able to transform inconsequential but occasionally flooding waterways into recreational waterbodies of great importance to those cities. Dallas and Phoenix are attempting to follow their lead by creating town lakes from largely dry riverbeds. The proposed Rio-Salado project in Phoenix, perhaps the most ambitious of its kind, would create a fifteen-mile-long water-based linear park in the bed of the Salt River (Carr, Lynch Associates, 1984). In the desert of Phoenix, so the theory goes, these new parks and lakes could draw enough private development to their edges to pay for themselves through new taxes; but the start-up infrastructure cost is high. Even in landscapes where there are no rivers, cities are looking to their neglected drainage systems for opportunities to create greenways, parks, and development opportunities while also solving flooding problems. Oklahoma City and Davis and San Jose, California, are examples.

The Salt River in Tempe (Phoenix), Arizona, today. (Carr, Lynch, Hack and Sandell)

The vision of Rio Salado as a braided chain of lakes. (Carr, Lynch, Hack and Sandell)

At the same time, whether or not linked to waterfront development, cities will continue to try to revive their central areas. As an initial response to suburban business and population shifts, many cities mounted joint public and private efforts to transform their too-wide, automobile-oriented downtown shopping streets into something more attractive and competitive with the suburban malls. City planners and business people hoped to attract suburbanites back downtown. In some of our colder and hotter large cities, a secondary system of "skyways" or subways was built, linking commercial activities above or below the streets and allowing people to move about without exposure to the weather. Many small to medium-sized cities mimicked the suburbs directly by creating parking lots or structures and then excluding cars from central shopping streets, replacing them with landscaped malls that their designers hoped would prove attractive to people on foot. Most of these efforts were only marginally successful in countering the larger trends toward decentralization of middle-class housing and work places. Many downtowns have become local shopping areas for downtown workers and nearby residents, who are often minority groups with limited incomes.

In the future, downtown public space improvements will be one part of a more comprehensive strategy. Typical of such strategies will be support for specialized retail, entertainment, and cultural institutions, together with

The Santa Cruz Mall in California provided an excellent model for a successful integration of retail uses with pedestrian space, planting, and room for the automobile until destroyed by the 1989 earthquake. (Stephen Carr)

an effort to increase middle- to upper-income housing downtown. The greening of downtown by adding trees and creating small parks will continue to be a key feature of these revitalization attempts. Fully pedestrian downtown malls are likely to be replaced by shopping streets that still carry traffic but have wider sidewalks with trees and festive lighting, accented by small activity spaces. Some old malls are already being redeveloped along these lines. Private developers will continue to build indoor shopping malls downtown and to increase rentable ground-floor space by providing enclosed atria in office buildings, rather than open plazas. There will be continuing efforts to protect the rights of all users in these semi-public spaces.

Other more powerful forces will help to transform many central cities once again. The rising cost of new suburban housing makes older center city housing more attractive. As both husbands and wives have entered the workforce, the journey to work has become a more important variable in determining residential location. Those who work in the city often want to live there. The resulting gentrification of some older neighborhoods close to downtown has created new demands for central open space. Interest from this group in unprocessed foods has led to a revival of green markets. With luck, true public markets like the Pike Place Market in

Seattle will thrive in place of "festival marketplaces." As the suburbs themselves become more dense and urbanized, there is growing pressure to reserve or create spaces for sports and nature experience. In both center and suburbs, the gradual increase in homework utilizing computers, phone lines, and cable will likely result in new demands for nearby recreational open space.

In old gentrifying neighborhoods, the newcomers are ready to form coalitions with their less affluent neighbors to pressure cities to revive older parks, playgrounds, and other central spaces and to make them useful again. Cities eager to attract and hold middle-class residents will be more likely to invest in tree planting and park and playground improvements in these neighborhoods than in others. Where funds are scarce, as they usually are, cities will set up programs to allow residents to purchase trees. In higher density areas where private space is scarce or nonexistent, combined groups of new and old residents will continue to create community gardens and to build playgrounds on vacant sites acquired or appropriated by local people. As new development reaches these neighborhoods, opportunities for community gardening will be increasingly incorporated into new residential complexes.

As a result of these trends and countertrends, it may be that a new public space form – neither "urban" nor "suburban" – will evolve in the United States and Canada. This new combined form will blend landscape qualities of the park with those of the traditional European square or pedestrian street. This blend can be shaded in either direction, depending on the uses to be accommodated. Downtown shopping streets and civic plazas have increasing numbers of trees and other plants, and industrial and office developments in the suburbs are beginning to create true parks, actually useful for recreation. This integration of plants with the urban landscape of buildings and paving may satisfy a particular need of North Americans to soften the city and make it remind us of its origins in smaller towns and countryside. It may also be seen as part of the larger greening of cities movement, which has been gaining ground in Europe and other more developed countries and is certain to accelerate in response to global warming. As larger cities develop dispersed multiple centers of dense activity, and populations both stratify and partially reintegrate, the old distinctions between "urban," "suburban," and "rural" places will become less meaningful. These green spaces, particularly in the renewed central areas of cities, will once again become meeting grounds for a wide range of people.

We foresee that the environmental movement will reinforce these trends in many ways and contribute substantially to the growth of public space in American cities. Public space has long been promoted for its benefits to the health of city dwellers by giving them access to fresh air, sunlight, physical activity, and tranquil settings (Kaplan & Kaplan, 1989). These goals will continue to be important, but people will see that open space is essential to cities in other ways as well. The conservation, creation, and design of open space can enhance drinking water quality, offer new waste treatment options, moderate wind effects due to high buildings, and reduce air pollution on city streets. In can reduce erosion and increase the presence of wildlife. Anne Whiston Spirn (1984), in her fine and influential book *The Granite Garden*, and Michael Hough (1984), in his useful *City Form and Natural Process*, outline these and other benefits, while making the case that although the city as a whole is our greatest artifice, it remains steadfastly a part of nature.

There is a new popular awareness of the consequences of development for our water supply, air quality, waste disposal, and the overall health of the biosphere. Although there have been recent setbacks in a continuing struggle, federal and state environmental laws provide a framework for before-the-fact review processes that can sometimes prevent or "mitigate" the most negative consequences of proposed development, at least for the physical environment. In the future, planners and designers will attempt not only to protect the environment but to enhance it by working with natural processes. Already, green space is preserved and even designed in suburban developments to provide for on-site water retention, creating water features that are not only attractive but useful. Many suburban office developments, which would have once created substantial runoffs from paved parking areas and might have tried to bury on-site drainage, are now designed around landscaped retention basins and natural drainages as central features of the site, creating more pleasant environments for workers and wildlife havens. Some even incorporate gardens to raise flowers and vegetables, as an alternative to the heavily irrigated and costly corporate landscape (Francis, 1989b). Even tertiary treatment of waste water – exposing it to air and sunlight – can become an attractive landscape feature. Spirn describes a series of pools and waterfalls built into the landscape of a resort near Santa Fe that provide such treatment to ready waste water for use in irrigation.

Following a long-established tradition in Holland, there will be increasing interest in the United States in "nature parks." Instead of planting the usual ornamental species requiring high maintenance, native plants will be used and allowed to develop in natural succession. At its simplest, this can be the creation of wildflower meadows instead of clipped lawns in areas such as nature preserves, institutional settings, the fringes of neighborhoods, or along roadways, where there is not likely to be intensive human use. Such plantings require less maintenance than ornamentals (al-

"Nature parks" and greenways, often utilizing drainage areas and former urban wastelands, can provide access to natural elements. Mission Creek in San Luis Obispo, California. (Mark Francis)

though they are not maintenance-free) and can help to restore a sense of nature to the city in a more direct way than more manicured parks. At the same time, there will be more support for educational public gardens, including arboretums and botanical gardens.

Certainly there has been a long history of efforts to bring rapidly vanishing countryside near cities under public ownership. In Raleigh, North Carolina, Denver, and Davis, California (Dawson, Francis, & Jones, 1990), groups are currently working to create integrated "greenway" systems of public lands (Little, 1990). Now, as slowly but surely the open countryside has disappeared under development, a new value is assigned to the leftover spaces, the real wastelands. Often these spaces are associated with natural stream beds or drainage systems that have not been piped and buried. Here one finds remnants of ecosystems struggling to survive despite trash dumps and the petroleum, lead, and other pollutants from urban runoffs. These urban wilds, in vacant lots, wetlands, or on slopes too steep for building, are already gaining appreciation as natural resources and habitats within the city, especially as cities are hard-pressed to raise the funds to acquire land and create new parks. The protection and conservation of these lands – especially wetlands – has been legislated in many areas and will become more prevalent in the future. Children will use these areas extensively, if accessible, and they can be quite important for child development. If made visible and accessible to other nondestructive human use, these wilds help to keep urban populations connected to nature and remind us that indeed the city still is a part of nature.

One notable urban wilds project involves a highly industrialized six-square-mile section of New York City's Staten Island, dominated by wetlands. As the water quality of this area has gradually rebounded since the passage of the Clean Water Act, these wetlands have become one of the Northeast's major urban nesting and breeding grounds for colonies of wading birds, including herons, egrets, and ibises. Utilizing these birds as a vital symbol for the regeneration of urban natural areas, the Trust for Public Land and the New York City Audubon Society are spearheading an effort to preserve and restore the Staten Island wetlands – dubbed "the Harbor Herons Wildlife Refuge."

Like historic preservation, conservation of undeveloped land can be taken to an extreme. There is often strong resistance from conservationists to any measures that would assist in human use of such lands, even for nature walks. Although it could be said that these areas have value in and of themselves as remnant ecosystems and should be preserved for that reason alone, it is not necessarily the case that they will be destroyed by human use. The fact is that these are usually rugged plant and animal communities, with their members well adapted not only to the specific conditions of the site and local climate but also to the conditions imposed by the surrounding urban uses. Simple public walkways, located and designed to protect the more fragile environments, such as wetlands and riverbanks, can create nearby opportunities for public enjoyment of nature at very low cost compared with creating new parks. Gas Works Park in Seattle is a well-known example, combining the transformation of a wasteland and an abandoned gasworks into a useful site with both natural and historic merit (see Chapter 4).

We have attempted to project the future of public space based on present trends, and have tried to relate this future to its urban context and to changes in culture and public life that drive public space development in a particular direction. We have suggested by example some of the images of success that will serve as models for this development. We see a new overall form of public space emerging – one that increasingly combines, as do our cities overall, qualities that were once thought of as distinctly urban or suburban. This is part of a process of acculturation, helping to create an integrated urban culture across the many social and economic distances in our society.

As we see it, the typical urban open spaces to be found in most cities will include large-scale linear systems, located principally along paths of movement and waterways; networks of smaller open spaces in functional areas such as retail and office districts and even in some industrial areas; focal spaces carrying on and reinterpreting the long tradition of central squares, markets, and parks; neighborhood spaces including the small parks, playgrounds, and community gardens that are easily accessible to residential areas; former urban wastelands that become valued and protected found spaces; and special attractions, such as public markets, occurring in any accessible location and designed to draw people for the quality of their offerings, as well as fun and profit. These recurring types of public space will have many variations, reflecting regional and local differences, to be discovered through participatory design and management.

Like any other attempt to predict the future, ours is pure speculation. All trend lines are subject to abrupt breaks in apparent continuity. We have selectively focused on some of the most visible and attractive features of our emerging urban society, but just out of this picture and pushing into the edges of the frame are the more troubling issues that are only beginning to be addressed. Foremost among them are pressing problems of equity and social justice, public versus private control, and the search for shared meanings. These are fundamental problems in most twentieth-century societies and they will be solved, if at all, mainly in other realms than public space. But unless they are addressed here as elsewhere, we shall not achieve a public environment that is responsive, democratic, and meaningful.

EQUITY IN PUBLIC SPACE

The decisions that will create future public space will be an expression of the political economy that governs the growth of American cities overall. This political economy is increasingly challenged to confront the issue of equity. The general history of cities in the twentieth century has been one of increasing segregation by residence and workplace. The most striking dimensions of this separation in America have been economic and racial.

The plight of homeless people in America is nowhere more poignant than in Washington, D.C. (Mark Francis)

Although overt segregation of public schools and facilities has been largely overcome, and excluded minorities have gained voting rights, this has only prepared the way for the creation of an integrated society. So far, economic and social integration into the "mainstream" has been possible for only a minority of African-Americans and Hispanics. Against the success of these few must be set society's failure adequately to nurture, educate, and provide work opportunities for the poor in general and for minorities of color in particular. In our increasingly technical society, we are creating a large, mostly urban, "underclass" of virtually unemployable people. The appalling problems of homelessness, undernourishment, drug abuse, and crime that our economic and political system creates or augments must become central issues for urban and national politics in the immediate future. When not addressed elsewhere, these problems become highly visible in public space, leading to daily conflicts over appropriate use.

Not surprisingly, the same pattern of neglect can be seen in the development of urban public space. Those types of spaces that serve the middle class and wealthy have been on the increase, whereas those that serve the working class and the poor have been in decline. Inner cities across America are littered with neglected neighborhood parks, broken playgrounds, and dead street trees. For those already oppressed and depressed by the shortage of suitable employment, adequate housing, schools, and other social supports, the limited number and poor condition of existing parks, playfields, and playgrounds constitute just one more message that the majority society does not care. This is an especially damaging message for young children and youths, for whom these facilities are most important. The "vandalism" that often is blamed on inner-city youth is, at least in part, the result of competition for the few existing spaces and often a specific protest against the inadequacy of city provision, management, and maintenance of open space.

In some older cities where the problem has been greatest, including New York and Boston, modest efforts at real improvement have begun. Whether in the next twenty years cities will turn substantial resources in the direction of creating new parks and playgrounds, and to repairing and maintaining the existing stock in the poorer neighborhoods, remains to be seen. The answer may be linked to the even more pressing need to increase the supply of affordable housing, especially for families. As new housing becomes more expensive to produce, and therefore even more restrained in unit size, there will be an ever stronger need for readily available parks and playgrounds. As housing in older neighborhoods is rehabilitated that too will be done with minimum space standards in order to control costs. Additional public funds will be needed to create or improve open space in or near affordable housing developments.

Often, public space improvements are promoted for their ability to stabilize a neighborhood or to "upgrade" it. Stabilization may mean retaining younger people who grew up in the neighborhood but now seek a better environment. "Upgrading" usually means attracting young people of higher income, a policy known as "gentrification." In either case, there is a corresponding responsibility to existing lower-income residents who can be bid out of a rising housing market. It is therefore necessary to understand not only the public space needs and expectations of the rising middle class, whether indigenous or not, but also how these aspiring young families can coexist with older and poorer residents. Both in older neighborhoods and in cities as a whole, an inclusive public space policy will complicate programming, design, and management. But the costs of exclusionary policies and designs will be to encourage intergroup conflict and hostility, with public space as a battleground.

Self-help is part of the answer. A community planting for urban greening. Jungle Hill, Oakland, California. (Trust for Public Land)

Reliance on a participatory design process, with full and representative involvement of the potential users of neighborhood spaces, will assure that the interests of less affluent residents are considered. Because more affluent participants are likely to be more vocal about their needs, and may be more politically powerful, special efforts will be needed to determine and protect the rights of minorities. Such protection is a necessity in any working democratic system and is a hallmark of a caring government.

Self-help will be important as well. A part of the answer to the needs of poor communities may lie in an expansion of the community garden movement, with its economic and nutritional benefits. Cities could more directly support community self-help efforts to build small parks and playgrounds on vacant lots or to create local play streets, by providing simple landscape materials, fences, and barricades, as well as staff assistance and modest funding.

Self-help alone cannot create the diverse and substantial open spaces and management programs that are needed, nor make up for the many years of neglect that have ravaged existing park systems. Significant investment of public resources in less affluent neighborhoods will be needed. This will most likely come as part of a renewed political movement to address the larger social inequities of which inadequate open space is one symptom.

PUBLIC VERSUS PRIVATE

The question of equity is related to a second major issue: private versus public control in the creation and management of open space. Increasing private control, because it tends to put space in the hands of those who view the physical environment as a means for creating profits, will tend to focus attention on people with money to spend, and ignore or exclude the poor. By the same token, a primary concern for profits has not been conducive so far to environmental protection. Nonetheless, it appears certain that the future development of public space will require increasing private sector participation, both in providing the political justification for its creation and in securing adequate funding and management. Cities and developers will cooperate, in their joint self-interest, and the mechanism for control of design and management will be crucial.

As businesses and the middle class left older cities for the suburbs, revenues declined and the cost of services went up, resulting in higher property taxes. Politicians were forced to campaign against increased taxation and thus against their own ability to perform once in office. As cities increasingly became the refuge of poor and minority groups, with limited political influence, states and the federal government could safely withdraw support. Maintenance of infrastructure, schools, parks, and other

In Toronto, Canada, private development which was initially so important to opening up the waterfront, now threatens to overwhelm it. (Gary Hack)

San Antonio's Paseo del Rio provides an example of a fine balance, where commercial uses enliven the public space without dominating it. (Stephen Carr)

public facilities was deferred and new facilities seldom were built. The overall level of expectation for service delivery by the public sector declined drastically. Some cities, most notably New York, teetered on the edge of bankruptcy.

As a result, cities began to take a new attitude toward developers and development. The "public–private partnership" was born, allied closely with the phenomenon of gentrification. Cities that still had appeal to the young, two-wage-earner, middle-class couples began to act more and more like businesses. They hired managers with an entrepreneurial bent and charged them with making conditions good for business. Cities could use tools such as urban renewal and eminent domain together with bonding authority to acquire property, build streets and plazas, and otherwise support the types of urban development that would bring back white-collar jobs, reverse the image of decline, and appeal to the young middle class and "empty nesters." These public actions are normally part of a "development compact" with the private sector, which frequently involves private management of spaces created with public dollars. This arrangement relieves the public partner of an ongoing cost and assures the private partner that management will actually be done. This is the model for many developments such as festival marketplaces, but also for high-cost ventures such as Battery Park City in Lower Manhattan. In most of the newer cities of the sunbelt, it has always been understood that a central purpose of local government is to make conditions good for business and, because there is less need in these cities for business to support public improvements, "partnerships" are more one-sided.

As desirable as these arrangements are for cities seeking development to increase their tax bases and attract middle-class residents, they can limit or distort other important public powers. Cities that are actively courting developers are unlikely to adequately defend their residents against the negative consequences of development. Rampant gentrification drives up real estate values and puts affected housing out of reach of the poor. Disruption of neighborhood streets by traffic generated by intense development reduces the ability of these streets to serve as settings for family life, socializing, and children's play. When a city creates a public space and then turns over its management to a developer to rid itself of the responsibility, it is in a weak position to restrain that developer from excluding "undesirable" people from its use. When the developer creates the spaces as settings for office buildings and hotels, it is unlikely that they will be designed to welcome people from nearby neighborhoods or to address their needs. There is typically a perceived conflict and often a real one between the developer's interest in bottom-line profitability and the publicness of public space.

This idea of private involvement in the creation of the public environment is really nothing new. Even in the nineteenth century, there was private participation in the creation of some of the great central parks through special benefit taxes levied on abutters, although the extent of reliance by cities on private initiative to create the public environment is perhaps reaching new heights. From the Middle Ages onward, wealthy and powerful individuals have created public spaces fronting their palaces to enhance their dominance. In our times, the construction of Lever House and the Seagram Building on Park Avenue revived this tradition and began a trend in the creation of plazas as empty gestures. More recently in New York and elsewhere, developers have been granted bonuses in building area allowed by zoning in exchange for creating plazas. Many of these have been inappropriately located and designed for public use, and close public scrutiny is required to prevent them from being empty, windswept places.

Now we find special public authorities and even private companies being set up by public initiative, with the full cooperation of private enterprise, to create the public space and conditions necessary to spur development in certain areas or to attract people back into a city. As this cooperative strategy evolves and is adapted to the particular political realities and conditions of various cities, there will be many different forms of "partnership." From our perspective in assuring that design and management will address the critical dimensions of public space and in light of the special issues of social equity and environmental sensitivity, it will be best if private initiative remains under public control. This is most easily done when a public agency creates and manages the space with public funds, not only to make a better setting for development but also to serve a larger social purpose and public clientele. An example of this is North Park, created by the Battery Park City Authority to provide an attractive setting for the development of the north neighborhood, but also with the intention of serving residents of Lower Manhattan and with the direct participation of this nearby community (see this case in Chapter 8).

In other cases, where the public funds are not available or cannot be generated by the development, as they are in Battery Park City, public control will be more difficult to achieve. Much will depend on how badly the city wants the development and on the political will of its citizens. The source of the funding is crucial. When new spaces are created through private contributions of funds, labor or both, those who have invested will want to stay in control. As we have pointed out in Chapter 5, this has created problems of access in some community gardens and parks, even when built on public land. The problems are multiplied in larger private developments such as festival marketplaces. In most cities, however, there will be enough public funds involved to require that there be a mechanism for continuing public oversight through design and management. Active involvement of the city parks department or a public space commission can serve this essential purpose, even when land is the only public contribution.

MEANING

Both of the foregoing issues must be addressed by citywide policies, but for the designer one of the greatest challenges is to learn how to create meaningful spaces in our diverse and segmented culture. Meaning results from the interpretation given to a place by those who use it. The place itself can provide clear and explicit clues to the meanings intended by the designer or it can be visually reticent and confused. Chapter 6 and examples in Chapter 7 describe some of the ways public space can be meaningful and how such meaning can be communicated. More important than how to convey meaning, however, is the question of what meaning to convey.

In this chapter we suggest that public space design in our society can and should have a cultural purpose. We believe that the overriding mission of public space should be to assist in the creation of a free and democratic public life. To do so, design and management should be carried out with participation of users and in the light of the human dimensions.

The resulting spaces will provide for freedom of use by the actual users, while at the same time protecting the rights of individuals and minorities. When spaces are designed in this way, they will also become meaningful to their users. That meaning will be the direct result of the social success of the spaces. As environments in use, they will express the cultural values of freedom and democracy.

The art of public space design is not only to provide the basic physical supports for these values, but also to make visible and heighten their expression. Here, the visual language of form becomes important. Designs that make use of a neoclassical formal vocabulary, even when that vocabulary is used whimsically, harken back to past environments designed to reinforce authoritarian social control. The axes, allées, triumphal arches, encircling colonnades, rigidly symmetrical plantings, and carefully controlled vistas of past landscapes are vivid expressions of human fantasies of domination. It is not merely the presence or absence of physical supports, such as benches and shade, or of active and responsive management that fully determines the meaning of such spaces. Essential as these factors are, they provide only the bare bones frame for action. The specific forms given to these elements create the pattern of associations that can make a place seem democratic and free or domineering and rigid. Returning to the classical traditions of architecture and landscape architecture, as they are currently being revived, is counterproductive because they were developed in the service of authoritarian dominance and carry the emotional load of that heritage. This is not only a question of historical connotations. The forms themselves are rigid and limiting, forcing living things, whether people or plants, into the straight lines of the draftsman's T-square and triangle. Not only nature but human nature is to be brought under the control of reason and set upon the proper path of humility and awe in the presence of higher authority. That such formal devices are now most often to be found in the plazas and gardens of corporate headquarters is no accident.

On the other hand, romantic, flowing pastoral landscapes of the sort that Olmsted and Vaux created are well suited to the expression of freedom and democracy. Perhaps on some atavistic level, we associate such landscapes with our long heritage as hunter gatherers, in which humankind was more obviously a part of nature. More directly, the redundant paths, ups and downs, and varied spaces of a large pastoral park can allow for a relaxed, meandering, plural pattern of use that accommodates the needs of diverse groups and individuals with a minimum of conflict, and seems conducive to an attitude of tolerance. The many explicit formal references to pastoral landscapes evoke the harmonious settings and natural rhythms of the well-tended countryside, a release from the rigid structure of space and time imposed by cities.

Because of their size, natural character, and the social diversity of their spaces, nearly all large central parks have the potential to be experienced as free and democratic places. Yet this is only possible if fear is not one's constant companion. Recent events in Central Park remind us that social antagonisms can erupt into violence, even in these generous spaces. So long as the conditions of economic and social inequity which lead to crime and violence continue to be ignored, these great parks will retain their positive meaning only when they are filled with people and well secured.

Although their user populations are frequently less diverse, smaller central spaces such as pedestrian malls, central plazas, and marketplaces can also carry the message of democratic pluralism, if they are properly designed and managed. To do so, such spaces must accommodate the full range of user needs rather than being single-purpose and simplistic. There must be comfortable places to sit under various conditions, but also more sheltered places where real relaxation is possible. There should be plenty of opportunity to watch others, but also things and activities with which to get actively involved. There should be significant aspects of the places that do not reveal themselves on first visit, but that allow for discovery over time. There must also be free access for all and freedom to act in all the ways that the larger society allows. In many cities, special efforts will

For a space to be responsive, democratic, and meaningful requires the right combination of design, management, and use. (Stephen Carr)

be needed to assure that older shopping areas do not continue to become racially segregated, and these efforts must go beyond public space to transportation, housing, and economic policies. At the same time, it still should be possible for particular groups to lay temporary claim to parts of these spaces and to feel that there are means available for change, if the place is not functioning properly. Use under those conditions will build up the associations with personal history, to valued groups and to the culture as a whole that can convey lasting social meaning.

Community parks, playgrounds, play streets, and gardens are usually modest and functional. Their sponsors and designers do not normally aspire to the creation of meaning for the society at large. Often they are designed by the users themselves, to serve local populations that are fairly homogeneous and whose needs are straightforward. Sometimes, as neighborhoods change, there can be conflict in the use of these spaces and they can be taken over at times by particular groups such as teenagers or dog owners, to the exclusion of others. Such places are managed by their neighbors and users, if at all, with occasional prompted interventions by police or parks departments. By and large, these local spaces offer freedom of access and use to those who live nearby and are managed in a reasonably democratic manner.

There is basic social meaning to the mere provision of open space to meet the needs of all groups within the society, whether it is for local communities or for the city as a whole. Yet, public space design has tended toward the monumental or the minimal, evoking the glories of past autocracies or simply the functional requirements of the activity at hand. Except in our few great parks, one is hard-pressed to find spaces that convey by their form the relaxed freedoms of a working, pluralistic democracy. Ironically, some of the best examples are provided by "found" spaces such as the steps of the New York Public Library, too steep streets reused as gardens on San Francisco's Telegraph Hill, or formerly vacant lots in many cities, appropriated and modified for community use. Perhaps designers and managers, enthralled by history or burdened by a narrow functionalism, are less able than others to act on the ideals of our society.

Why should the design and management of public space not further those ideals by providing settings that inspire a free and democratic public life? If public space truly meets people's needs and protects their rights, that in itself will go far toward making it meaningful. Beyond that lies the challenge to the designer as artist and the manager as impresario. What is the appropriate form and operating policy for each different setting to put its users at ease and allow them to enjoy themselves and each other's company, even when they are socially diverse? We suggest putting these questions to the users themselves. Participatory design and management can make public space more accessible and welcoming to people, with great effect on whether or not a place is taken to heart and becomes a meaningful part of an individual's life.

In the burgeoning of public space that can be seen about us, there are many partial models for the creation of democratic meaning. We have attempted to provide some of the information needed to develop a new design and management synthesis from these fragments. We see a promising approach evolving, one that is grounded in the fundamental questions of people's needs and rights, as determined by them, and goes on to invent a poetics of space that is proper to our pluralistic public life. There will be a full recognition that the city is a part of nature, a special concern for social equity, and a firm resolve to keep private initiative under public control. We look toward a future public environment that is in all senses barrier-free, with public spaces that are both open-minded and open-hearted.

THE AUTHORS

Stephen Carr is an architect, urban designer, and public space designer. He is president of Carr, Lynch, Hack and Sandell, an environmental design firm. His public space designs have included parks, plazas, and pedestrian streets. He has prepared participatory plans for a 25-mile regional park for Phoenix, Arizona, a 20-mile river park in Chattanooga, Tennessee, and a four-and-one-half-mile esplanade park on the Hudson River waterfront in Manhattan. In 1991, his firm won an open international competition to redesign the central waterfront of Perth, Australia. He is author of *City Signs and Lights*.

Mark Francis is Professor of Landscape Architecture at the University of California, Davis, and design principal of Codesign, Inc., landscape architects and architects. He has designed public space projects in California, New York, Massachusetts, and in Europe. He is editor of *The Meaning of Gardens* (with Randolph T. Hester, Jr.) and author of *Community Open Spaces* (with Lisa Cashdan and Lynn Paxson).

Leanne G. Rivlin is Professor of Environmental Psychology at the City University of New York Graduate School. Her current work centers on the history and experience of homelessness and policies concerning homeless persons. She is editor of *Environmental Psychology* (with Harold M. Proshansky and William H. Ittelson), author of *An Introduction to Environmental Psychology* (with William H. Ittelson, Harold M. Proshansky, and Gary H. Winkel) and author of *Institutional Settings in Children's Lives* (with Maxine Wolfe). In 1990 she was recipient of the career award of the Environmental Design Research Association.

Andrew M. Stone is Director of the New York City Program of the Trust for Public Land, a national land conservation organization. Previously he worked with the Council on the Environment, the Mayor's Open Space Task Force, and the Department of Parks and Recreation, all in New York City.

BIBLIOGRAPHY

Ariès, P., & G. Duby (Gen. Eds.). 1987, 1988, 1989, 1990. *A History of Private Life*. Vols. 1–4. (A. Goldhamer, Trans.). Cambridge: Harvard University Press. (Original work published 1985, 1986, 1987 as *Histoire de la vie privée*. Paris: Sevil.)

Alexander, C., S. Ishikawa, M. Silverstein, M. Jacobsen, I. Fiksdahl-King, & S. Angel. 1977. *A Pattern Language*. New York: Oxford University Press.

Alexander, C., H. Neis, A. Anninou, & I. King. 1987. *A New Theory of Urban Design*. New York: Oxford University Press.

Altman, I., & D. Stokols. 1987. *Handbook of Environmental Psychology*. 2 vols. New York: Wiley.

Altman, I., & J. F. Wohlwill (Eds.). 1983. *Behavior and the Natural Environment*. Vol. 6 of *Human Behavior and Environment*. New York: Plenum.

Altman, I., & E. Zube (Eds.). 1989. *Public Places and Spaces*. Vol. 10 of *Human Behavior and Environment*. New York: Plenum.

Anderson, L. M., B. E. Mulligan, L. S. Goodman, & H. Z. Regen. 1983. Effects of sounds on preferences for outdoor settings. *Environment and Behavior* 15: 539–66.

Anderson, S. (Ed.). 1986. *On Streets*. Cambridge: MIT Press.

Anthony, K. 1979. Public and private spaces in Soviet cities. *Landscape* 23: 20–5.

Aoki, Y., Y. Yasuoka, & M. Naito. 1984. Assessing the impression of streetside greenery. *Landscape Research* 10: 9–13.

Appleton, J. 1975. *The Experience of Landscape*. New York: Wiley.

Appleyard, D. 1977. Understanding professional media. In I. Altman & J. F. Wohlwill (Eds.), *Advances in Theory and Research*, pp. 47–89. Vol. 2 of *Human Behavior and Environment*. New York: Plenum.

1979. The environment as social symbol. *Journal of American Planning Association* 45: 143–53.

1981. *Livable Streets*. Berkeley: University of California Press.

Appleyard, D., & M. Lintell. 1977. The environmental quality of city streets: The residents' viewpoint. *American Institute of Planners Journal* 43: 84–101.

Appleyard, D., K. Lynch, & J. Meyer. 1964. *The View from the Road*. Cambridge: MIT Press.

Bacon, K. 1981. Festivals: Hooking into the rhythm of city life. *Livability* 3: 3–4.

Balling, J. D., & J. H. Falk. 1982. Development of visual preference for natural environments. *Environment and Behavior* 14: 5–28.

Banerjee, T., & M. Southworth (Eds.). 1990. *City Sense and City Design: The Writings and Projects of Kevin Lynch*. Cambridge: MIT Press.

Barlow, E. 1972. *Fredrick Law Olmsted's New York*. New York: Praeger.

1987. *Restoring Central Park*. Cambridge: MIT Press.

Bassett, T. J. 1981. Reaping on the margins: A century of community gardening in America. *Landscape* 25, 2: 1–8.

Beardsley, J. 1981. *Art in Public Places*. Washington, D.C.: Partners for Livable Places.

1984. *Earthworks and Beyond: Contemporary Art in the Landscape.* New York: Abbeville Press.

Becker, F. 1973. A class-conscious evaluation: Going back to Sacramento's pedestrian mall. *Landscape Architecture* 64: 295–345.

Bengtsson, A. 1972. *Adventure Playgrounds.* London: Crosby Lockwood.

Benn, S. I., & G. F. Gaus (Eds.). 1983. *Public and Private in Social Life.* New York: St. Martin's Press.

Berdichevsky, N. 1984. Gågade, the Danish pedestrian street. *Landscape Journal* 3: 115–23.

Berman, M. 1986. Take it to the streets: Conflict and community in public space. *Dissent* 33, 4: 476–85.

Biederman, D. A., & Nager, A. R. 1981. Up from smoke: A new improved Bryant Park? *New York Affairs* 6: 97–105.

Biesenthal, L., & J. D. Wilson. 1980. *To Market, to Market: The Public Market Tradition in Canada.* Toronto, Canada: Peter Martin Associates.

Boehm, E. 1980. Youth Farms. In P. F. Wilkinson (Ed.), *Innovation in Play Environments,* pp. 76–84. London: Croom-Helm.

Borchert, J. 1979. Alley landscapes of Washington, D.C. *Landscape* 23: 3–10.

Bosselmann, P. 1983a. Shadowboxing: Keeping sunlight on Chinatown's kids. *Landscape Architecture* 73: 74–6.

1983b. Simulating the impacts of urban development. *Garten und Landschaft* 93: 636–40.

1987. Times Square. *Places* 4, 2: 55–63.

Boston Urban Gardeners. 1979. *A City Gardener's Guide.* Boston: Boston University Press.

Brambilla, R., & G. Longo. 1977. *For Pedestrians Only: Planning, Design and Management of Traffic-Free Zones.* New York: Whitney Library of Design.

Breines, S., & W. Dean. 1974. *The Pedestrian Revolution: Streets without Cars.* New York: Vintage.

Brill, M. 1989a. Transformation, nostalgia and illusion in public life and public place. In I. Altman & E. Zube (Eds.), *Public Places and Spaces,* pp. 7–30. Vol. 10 of *Human Behavior and Environment.* New York: Plenum.

1989b. An ontology for exploring urban public life today. *Places* 6, 1: 24–31.

Broadbent, G. 1990. *Emerging Concepts in Urban Space Design.* New York: Van Nostrand Reinhold.

Brower, S. 1973. Streetfront and sidewalk. *Landscape Architecture* 63: 364–9.

1977a. The design of neighborhood parks. Baltimore: Baltimore City Planning Commission.

1977b. A year of celebration. Baltimore: Baltimore City Department of Planning.

1988. *Design in Familiar Places.* New York: Praeger.

K. Dockett, & R. Taylor. 1983. Residents' perceptions of territorial features and perceived local threat. *Environment and Behavior* 15: 419.

Brown, D., P. Sijpkes, & M. MacLean. 1986. The community role of public indoor space. *Journal of Architectural and Planning Research* 3: 161–72.

Brown, J., & C. Burger. 1984. Playground designs and preschool children's behavior. *Environment and Behavior* 16: 599–626.

Bryant Park Restoration Corporation. 1981. Annual Report. New York.

Buker, C., & A. Montarzino. 1983. The meaning of water. Paper presented at the Fourth Annual Conference of the Wilderness Psychology Group. Missoula, Mont., August.

Burden, A. 1977. Greenacre Park. New York: Project for Public Spaces.

Burns, J. 1978. Evaluation: A classic recycling after 11 years. *AIA Journal* 67: 50–9.

Buttimer, A., & D. Seamon (Eds.). 1980. *The Human Experience of Space and Place.* New York: St. Martin's Press.

Campbell, C. 1973. Seattle's gas plant park. *Landscape Architecture* 63: 338–42.

Campbell, R. 1980. Lure of the marketplace: Real-life theater. *Historic Preservation* 63: 46–9.

Carmody, D. 1983. Proposal for restaurant in Bryant Park disputed. *New York Times,* May 16, p. B3.

Carr, S. 1973. *City Signs and Lights.* Cambridge: MIT Press.

Carr, S., & K. Lynch. 1968. Where learning happens. *Daedalus* 97: 4.

Carr, S., & K. Lynch. 1981. Open space: Freedom and control. In L. Taylor (Ed.), *Urban Open Spaces,* pp. 17–18. New York: Rizzoli.

Carr, S., & D. Schissler. 1969. The city as a trip. *Environment and Behavior* 1: 7–36.

Carr, Lynch Associates. 1984. Rio Salado Master Plan. Phoenix: Rio Salado Development District.

1985. Tennessee Riverpark Master Plan. Chattanooga: Moccasin Bend Task Force of the Chattanooga/Hamilton County Regional Planning Commission.

Chabrier, Y. U. 1985. The greening of Copley Square. *Landscape Architecture* 75: 70–6.

Chidister, M. 1986. The effect of context on the use of urban plazas. *Landscape Journal* 5: 115–27.

1989. Public places, private lives: Plazas and the broader public landscape. *Places* 6, 1: 32–7.

CitiCorp Center: A megastructure that ties into the street. 1978. *Urban Design* 9 (Spring): 23–5.

City of New York. 1897. Report of the Committee on Small Parks. Department of Parks.

1914. Annual Report. Department of Parks.

1960. Twenty-six years of Park Progress: 1934–1960. Department of Parks.

Cobb, E. 1959. The ecology of imagination in childhood. *Daedalus* 8: 537–48.

Cooper, C. 1970. Adventure playgrounds. *Landscape Architecture* 60: 18–29, 88–91.

Cooper Marcus, C. 1978a. Environmental autobiography. *Childhood City Newsletter* 14: 3–5.

1978b. Evaluation: A tale of two spaces. *AIA Journal* 67: 34–8.

1978c. Remembrance of landscapes past. *Landscape* 22: 34–43.

1990. The garden as metaphor. In M. Francis & R. Hester (Eds.), *The Meaning of Gardens*, pp. 26–33. Cambridge: MIT Press.

Cooper Marcus, C., & C. Francis (Eds.). 1990. *People Places*. New York: Van Nostrand Reinhold.

Cooper Marcus, C., & W. Sarkissian. 1986. *Housing as If People Mattered*. Berkeley: University of California Press.

Corbett, M. 1981. *A Better Place to Live*. Emmaus, Penn.: Rodale Press.

Corbin, A. 1986. *The Foul and the Fragrant: Odor and the French Social Imagination*. (Miriam Kochan, Trans.). Cambridge: Harvard University Press. (Original work published 1982 as *Le miasme et la jonquille*. Paris: Aubier Montaigne.)

Correll, M. R., J. H. Lillydahl, & L. D. Singell. 1978. The effects of greenbelts on residential property values. *Land Economics* 54: 204–17.

Cranz, G. 1978. Changing roles of urban parks: From pleasure garden to open space. *Landscape* 22: 9–18.

1980. Women in urban parks. In C. R. Stimpson, E. Dixler, J. J. Nelson, & K. B. Yaktrakis (Eds.), *Women in the American City*. Chicago: University of Chicago Press.

1982. *The Politics of Park Design*. Cambridge: MIT Press.

Crouch, D. P. 1979. The historical development of urban open space. In E. Taylor (Ed.), *Urban Open Spaces*, pp. 7–8. New York: Rizzoli.

Cullen, G. 1961. *Townscape*. New York: Van Nostrand Reinhold.

Dalton, D. W. 1987. Harvey Fite's Opus 40: The evolution of meaning from private garden to public art work. In M. Francis & R. Hester (Eds.), *The Meaning of Gardens*, pp. 198–205. Cambridge: MIT Press.

Dawson, K., M. Francis, & S. Jones. 1990. The Davis Greenway. In *Contemporary Landscape Architecture: An International Perspective*, pp. 232–3. Tokyo: Process Architecture.

Degnore, R. 1987. The experience of public art in urban settings. Ph.D. dissertation, City University of New York.

Driver, B. L., & P. Greene. 1977. Man's nature: Innate determinants of response to natural environments. In *Children, Nature and the Urban Environment: Proceedings of a Symposium-Fair*, pp. 63–70. USDA Forest Service General Technical Report NE-30. Washington, D.C.: Government Printing Office.

Erickson, A. 1985. *Playground Design*. New York: Van Nostrand Reinhold.

Eubank-Ahrens, B. 1985. The impact of woonerven on children's behavior. *Children's Environments Quarterly* 1: 39–45.

Fein, A. 1972. *Frederick Law Olmsted and the American Environmental Tradition*. New York: George Braziller.

Feinberg, R. A., B. Scheffler, & J. Meoli. 1987. Some ecological insights into consumer behavior in the retail mall. In *Proceedings of the Division of Consumer Psychology*, pp. 17–18. Washington, D.C.: American Psychological Association.

Feiner, J. S., & S. M. Klein. 1982. Graffiti talks. *Social Policy* 12: 47–53.

Filler, M. 1981. Art without museums. In L. Taylor (Ed.), *Urban Open Spaces,* pp. 86–7. New York: Rizzoli.

Firey, W. 1945. Sentiment and symbolism as ecological variables. *American Sociological Review* 10: 140–8.

1968. *Land Use in Central Boston.* Westport, Conn.: Greenwood Press. (Original work published 1947.)

Fischer, C. 1976. *The Urban Experience.* New York: Harcourt Brace Jovanovich.

1981. The public and private worlds of city life. *American Sociological Review* 46: 306–16.

Ford, L. R., & E. Griffen. 1981. Chicano Park. *Landscape* 25: 42–8.

Forrest, A., & L. Paxson. 1979. Provisions for peoples: Grand Central Terminal/CitiCorp Study. In L. G. Rivlin & M. Francis (Eds.). New York: Center for Human Environments, City University of New York.

Fowler, G. 1982. Crime in Bryant Park down sharply. *New York Times,* August 10, p. B1.

Fox, T. 1989. Using vacant land to reshape American cities. *Places* 6, 1: 78–81.

Fox, T., & T. Huxley. 1978. Open space development in the South Bronx: A report on a demonstration project. Washington, D.C.: Institute for Local Self Reliance.

Fox, T., I. Koeppel, & S. Kellam. 1985. *Struggle for Space: The Greening of New York City.* New York: Neighborhood Open Space Coalition.

1990. *Urban Open Space: An Investment That Pays.* New York: The Neighborhood Open Space Coalition.

Francis, M. (Ed.) 1979. *Participatory Planning and Neighborhood Control.* New York: Center for Human Environments, City University of New York.

1984. Mapping downtown activity. *Journal of Architectural and Planning Research* 1: 21–35.

1987a. The making of democratic streets. In A. Vernez Moudon (Ed.), *Public Streets for Public Use,* pp. 23–39. New York: Van Nostrand Reinhold.

1987b. Some different meanings attached to a public park and community gardens. *Landscape Journal* 6: 100–12.

1987c. Urban open spaces. In E. Zube & G. Moore (Eds.), *Advances in Environ-ment, Behavior and Design,* Vol. 1, pp. 71–106. New York: Plenum.

1988a. Changing values for public spaces. *Landscape Architecture* 78: 54–9.

1988b. Negotiating between children and adult design values in open space projects. *Design Studies* 9: 67–75.

1989a. Control as a dimension of public space quality. In I. Altman & E. Zube (Eds.), *Public Places and Spaces,* pp. 147–72. Vol. 10 of *Human Behavior and Environment.* New York: Plenum.

1989b. The urban garden as public space. *Places* 6, 1: 52–9.

Francis, M., L. Cashdan, & L. Paxson. 1984. *Community Open Spaces.* Washington, D.C.: Island Press.

Francis, M., & R. Hester (Eds.). 1990. *The Meaning of Gardens.* Cambridge: MIT Press.

Francis, M., & A. Stone. 1981. Neighborhood residents and environmental researchers and planners. In A. E. Osterberg, C. P. Tiernan, & R. Findlay (Eds.), *Proceedings of the 12th Environmental Design Research Association Conference.* Washington, D.C.

Franck, K. A., & L. Paxson. 1989. Women and urban public space: Research, design, and policy issues. In E. Zube & G. Moore (Eds.), *Advances in Environment, Behavior and Design,* Vol. 2, pp. 122–46. New York: Plenum.

French, J. 1978. *Urban Space: A Brief History of the City Square.* Dubuque, Iowa: Kendall-Hunt Publishing.

Fried, F. 1990. *Built to Amuse: Views from America's Past.* Washington, D.C.: Preservation Press.

Fried, M. 1963. Grieving for a lost home. In L. J. Duhl (Ed.), *The Urban Condition: People and Policy in the Metropolis,* pp. 151–77. New York: Basic Books.

Fried, M., & P. Gleicher. 1961. Some sources of satisfaction in an urban slum. *Journal of the American Institute of Planners* 27: 4.

Frieden, B. J., & L. B. Sagalyn. 1989. *Downtown, Inc.* Cambridge: MIT Press.

Frost, J. C. 1985. History of playground safety in America. *Children's Environments Quarterly* 2, 4: 13–23.

Gans, H. 1962. *The Urban Villagers.* New York: Free Press.

Gas Works Park. 1981. *Landscape Architecture,* September, 71: 594–6.

Gehl, J. 1987. *The Life between Buildings.* New York: Van Nostrand Reinhold.

———. 1989. A changing street life in a changing society. *Places* 6: 8–17.

Girot, C. 1988. Captive waters. Master of Landscape Architecture thesis, Department of Landscape Architecture, University of California at Berkeley.

Girouard, M. 1985. *Cities and People.* New Haven: Yale University Press.

Glazer, N., & M. Lilla (Eds.). 1987. *The Public Face of Architecture: Civic Culture and Public Spaces.* New York: Free Press.

Global Architecture. 1977. *Centre Georges Pompidou, Paris.* Tokyo: A.D.A. Edita.

Godbey, G., & M. Blazey. 1983. Old people in urban parks. *Journal of Leisure Research* 15: 229–44.

Goffman, E. 1963. *Behavior in Public Places: Notes on the Social Organization of Gatherings.* New York: Macmillan.

Gold, S. 1972. Non-use of neighborhood parks. *AIP Journal* 38: 369–78.

Goldberger, P. 1989. Can architects serve the public good? *New York Times*, June 25, II, 1: 2.

Goldfarb, W. 1945. Psychological privation in infancy and subsequent adjustment. *American Journal of Orthopsychiatry* 15: 247–55.

Goldman, E. 1955. *Rendevous with Destiny.* New York: Vintage.

Goldstein, S. 1975. Seeing Chicago's plazas: Delight and despair. *Inland Architect* 19, 8: 19–23.

Goodey, B. 1979. Towards new perceptions of the environment: Using the town trail. In D. Appleyard (Ed.), *The Conservation of European Cities*, pp. 282–93. Cambridge: MIT Press.

Gottlieb, M. 1984. The magic is faded, but the ghosts of Broadway past haunt Times Square. *New York Times,* August 30, pp. B1, 7.

Greenbie, B. B. 1981. *Spaces: Dimensions of the Human Landscape.* New Haven: Yale University Press.

Haag, R. 1982. It's a gas. *Outreach,* Department of Landscape Architecture, Ohio State University, 4: 3–6.

Halbwachs, M. 1980. *The Collective Memory.* New York: Harper and Row. (Original work published 1950.)

Hall, E. T. 1966. *The Hidden Dimension.* New York: Doubleday.

Halpern, K. 1978. *Downtown USA: Urban Design in Nine American Cities.* New York: Whitney Library of Design.

Halprin, J., & J. Burns. 1974. *Taking Part: A Workshop Approach to Collective Creativity.* Cambridge: MIT Press.

Hardy, H. 1986. Make it dance. *The Livable City* 10: 6–7.

Hart, R. 1974. The genesis of landscaping. *Landscaping Architecture* 65: 356–63.

———. 1978. *Children's Experience of Place.* New York: Irvington.

———. 1987. Children's participation in design and planning. In C. S. Weinstein & T. David (Eds.), *Spaces for Children: The Built Environment and Child Development*, pp. 217–39. New York: Plenum.

Hartig, J., M. Mang, & G. W. Evans. 1991. Restorative effects of natural environment experiences. *Environment and Behavior* 23: 3–26.

Hayden, D. 1984. *Redesigning the American Dream.* New York: Norton.

Hayward, D. G., M. Rothenberg, & R. R. Beasley. 1974. Children's play and urban playground environment. A comparison of traditional, contemporary and adventure playground types. *Environment and Behavior* 6: 131–68.

Hayward, J. 1989. Urban parks: Research, planning and social change. In I. Altman & E. Zube (Eds.), *Public Places and Spaces*, pp. 193–215. Vol. 10 of *Human Behavior and Environment.* New York: Plenum.

Hayward, J., & W. Weitzer. 1984. The public's image of urban parks. *Urban Ecology* 8: 243–68.

Heckscher, A., & P. Robinson. 1977. *Open Spaces: The Life of American Cities.* New York: Harper and Row.

Hedman, R. 1985. *Fundamentals of Urban Design.* Chicago: Planners Press, American Planning Association.

Helphand, K. 1976. Environmental autobiography. Eugene: Department of Landscape Architecture, University of Oregon. Unpublished manuscript.

Henry, G. M. 1986. Welcome to the pleasure dome: Canada's Ghermezians create Disney-style shopping playground. *Time,* October 27, p. 75.

Heritage Conservation and Recreation Service. 1979. *Urban Waterfront Revitalization.* Washington, D.C.: U.S. Department of Interior.

Heroz, T. R. 1985. A cognitive analysis of preferences for waterscapes. *Journal of Environmental Psychology* 5: 225–41.

Hester, R. T. 1983. Labors of love in the public landscape. *Places* 1: 18–27.

1984. *Planning Neighborhood Space with People.* 2nd ed. New York: Van Nostrand Reinhold.

1985. Subconscious landscapes in the heart. *Places* 2: 10–22.

1987. Participatory design and environmental justice. *Journal of Architectural and Planning Research* 4: 301–9.

1990. *Community Design Primer.* Mendocino, Calif.: Ridge Times Press.

Hill, M. R. 1984. Stalking the urban pedestrian: A comparison of questionnaire and tracking methodologies for behavior mapping in large scale environments. *Environment and Behavior* 16: 539–50.

Hiss, T. 1987. Reflections: Experiencing places. *New Yorker,* June 22, pp. 46–68 and June 29, pp. 73–86.

1990. *The Experience of Place.* New York: Knopf.

Hitt, J., R. Fleming, E. Plater-Zyberk, R. Sennett, J. Wines, & E. Zimmerman. 1990. Whatever became of the public square? *Harpers* 281: 49–60.

Horwitz, J. 1986. Working at home and being at home: The interaction of microcomputers and the social life of households. Ph.D. dissertation, Environmental Psychology Program, City University of New York.

Horwitz, J., & S. M. Klein. 1977. *Lunatics, Lovers and Bums: A Look at the Unintended Uses of the New York Public Library Entrance* [Ten minute Super 8 sound and color film]. New York: Graduate School, City University of New York.

Hough, M. 1984. *City Form and Natural Process.* New York: Van Nostrand Reinhold.

1990. *Out of Place: Restoring Identity to the Regional Landscape.* New Haven: Yale University Press.

Hough, M., & S. Barrett. 1987. *People and City Landscapes.* Toronto: Conservation Council of Ontario.

Howard, E. 1945. *Garden Cities for Tomorrow.* London: Faber and Faber.

Howett, C. 1985. The Vietnam Veterans Memorial: Public art and politics. *Landscape* 28: 1–28.

Iacofano, D. 1986. Public involvement as an organizational development process: A proactive theory for environmental planning program management. Ph.D. dissertation, Department of Landscape Architecture, University of California at Berkeley.

Im, S. B. 1984. Visual preferences in enclosed urban spaces. *Environment and Behavior* 16: 235–62.

Israel, T. 1988. The art in the environment experience: Reactions to public murals in England. Ph.D. dissertation, City University of New York.

Iwasaki, S., & J. Tyrwhitt. 1978. Pedestrian areas in central Yokohama. *Ekistics* 273: 436–40.

Jackson, J. B. 1981. The public park needs appraisal. In L. Taylor (Ed.), *Urban Open Spaces,* pp. 34–5. New York: Rizzoli.

1984. *Discovering the Vernacular Landscape.* New Haven: Yale University Press.

1985. Urban circumstances. *Design Quarterly* 128: 1–32.

Jacobs, A. 1985. *Looking at Cities.* Cambridge: Harvard University Press.

Jacobs, J. 1961. *The Death and Life of Great American Cities.* New York: Vintage.

Janowitz, M. 1967. *The Community Press in an Urban Setting.* 2nd ed. Chicago: University of Chicago Press.

Jensen, R. 1981. Dreaming of urban plazas. In L. Taylor (Ed.), *Urban Open Spaces,* pp. 52–3. New York: Rizzoli.

Joardar, S. D., & J. W. Neill. 1978. The subtle differences in configuration of small public spaces. *Landscape Architecture* 68: 487–91.

Johnson, T. 1982. Skid row parks: Derelicts' needs vs. business interests. *Landscape Architecture* 72: 84–8.

Kaplan, R. 1973. Some psychological benefits of gardening. *Environment and Behavior* 5: 145–61.

1983. The role of nature in the urban context. In I. Altman & J. Wohlwill (Eds.), *Behavior and the Natural Environment,* pp. 127–62. Vol. 6 of *Human Behavior and Environment.* New York: Plenum.

1985. Nature at the doorstep: Residential satisfaction and the nearby environment.

Journal of Architectural and Planning Research 2: 115–27.

Kaplan, R., & S. Kaplan. 1989. *The Experience of Nature*. Cambridge: Cambridge University Press.

Kaplan, R., & S. Kaplan. 1990. Restorative experience: The healing power of nearby nature. In M. Francis & R. Hester (Eds.), *The Meaning of Gardens*, pp. 238–43. Cambridge: MIT Press.

Kaplan, S., & J. Talbot. 1983. Psychological benefits of a wilderness experience. In I. Altman & J. Wohlwill (Eds.), *Behavior and the Natural Environment*, pp. 163–201. Vol. 6 of *Human Behavior and Environment*. New York: Plenum.

Karp, D. S., G. Stone, & W. Yoels. 1977. *Being Urban: A Social Psychological View of Urban Life*. Lexington, Mass.: D. C. Heath.

Knack, R. 1982. Pedestrian malls: Twenty years later. *Planning* 48: 15–19.

Korosec-Serfaty, P. 1976. Protection of urban sites and appropriation of public squares. In P. Korosec-Serfaty (Ed.), *Appropriation of Space*, pp. 46–69. Proceedings of the Architectural Psychology Conference, Strasbourg, France.

1982. *The Main Square: Functions and Daily Uses of Stortorget, Malmo*. AIRS-Nova Series NRI. Lund, Sweden: University of Lund Press.

Kostoff, S. 1985. *A History of Architecture: Settings and Rituals*. New York: Oxford University Press.

Kowinski, W. S. 1985. *The Malling of America*. New York: William Morrow.

Ladd, F. 1975. City kids in the absence of . . . In *Children, Nature and the Urban Environment: Proceedings of a Symposium-Fair*, pp. 77–81. USDA Forest Service General Technical Report NE-30. Washington, D.C.: Government Printing Office.

1978. Home and personal history. *Childhood City Newsletter* 14: 18–19.

Lady Allen of Hurtwood. 1968. *Planning for Play*. London: Thames and Hudson.

Lang, J. 1987. *Creating Architectural Theory*. New York: Van Nostrand Reinhold.

Laurie, I. C. 1978. Overdesign is the death of outdoor liveliness. *Landscape Architecture* 68: 485–6.

(Ed.). 1979. *Nature in Cities*. New York: Wiley.

Leavitt, J., & S. Saegert. 1989. *Housing Abandonment in Harlem: The Making of Community Households*. New York: Columbia University Press.

Lee, R. G. 1972. The social definition of outdoor recreation places. In W. Burch (Ed.), *Social Behavior, Natural Resources and the Environment*, pp. 68–84. New York: Harper and Row.

Lennard, S. H. C., & H. Lennard. 1984. *Public Life in Urban Places*. Southhampton, N.Y.: Gondolier Press.

Levine, C. 1984. Making city spaces lovable places. *Psychology Today* 18, 6: 56–63.

Linday, N. 1977. Drawing socio-economic lines in Central Park. *Landscape Architecture* 67: 515–20.

1978. It all comes down to a comfortable place to sit and watch. *Landscape Architecture* 68, 6: 492–7.

Lindsey, R. 1986. A patchwork of rulings on free speech at malls. *New York Times*, February 10, p. A12.

Little, C. 1990. *Greenways for America*. Baltimore: Johns Hopkins University Press.

Lofland, L. 1973. *A World of Strangers: Order and Action in Urban Public Space*. New York: Basic Books.

1983. The sociology of communities: Research trends and priorities. Paper presented at the meeting of the American Sociological Association, Detroit, Michigan. September.

1984. Women and urban public space. *Women and Environments* 6: 12–14.

1989a. Social life in the public realm: A review essay. *Journal of Contemporary Ethnography* 17, 4: 453–82.

1989b. The morality of urban public life: The emergence and continuation of a debate. *Places* 6, 1: 24–31.

Love, R. L. 1973. The fountains of urban life. *Urban Life and Culture* 2: 161–209.

Low, S. 1986. The social meaning of the plaza. Unpublished grant proposal.

1987. Advances in qualitative methods. In E. Zube & G. Moore (Eds.), *Advances in Environment, Behavior and Design*, Vol. 1, pp. 281–306. New York: Plenum.

1988. Urban public spaces as reflections of culture: The plaza. Unpublished paper. Environmental Psychology Program, City University of New York.

Lyle, J. T. 1970. People-watching in parks. *Landscape Architecture* 60: 51–2.

Lyman, S. M., & M. B. Scott. 1972. Territoriality. A neglected sociological dimension. In R. Gutman (Ed.), *People and Buildings*, pp. 65–82. New York: Basic Books.

Lynch, K. 1963. *The Image of the City.* Cambridge: MIT Press.

1972a. The openness of open space. In G. Kepes (Ed.), *Arts of the Environment*, pp. 108–24. New York: George Braziller.

1972b. *What Time Is This Place?* Cambridge: MIT Press.

1981. *A Theory of Good City Form.* Cambridge: MIT Press.

1984. Reconsidering *The Image of the City.* In L. Rodwin and R. M. Hollister (Eds.), *Cities of the Mind: Images and Scenes of the City in the Social Sciences*, pp. 151–61. New York: Plenum.

Machlis, G. E. 1989. Managing parks as human ecosystems. In I. Altman & E. Zube. (Eds.), *Public Places and Spaces*, pp. 255–76. Vol. 10 of *Human Behavior and Environment.* New York: Plenum.

Madden, K., & E. Bussard. 1977. Riis Park: A study of use and design. New York: Project for Public Spaces.

Maitland, B. 1985. *Shopping Malls: Planning and Design.* Essex, England: Construction Press.

Martin, D. 1987. Behemoth on the Prairie. *New York Times,* January 4, 5: 19.

Marx, L. 1964. *The Machine in the Garden: Technology and the Pastoral Ideal in America.* New York: Oxford University Press.

McCabe, J. D., Jr. 1984. *New York by Gaslight.* New York: Crown. (Original work published 1882 under the title *New York by Sunlight and Gaslight.*)

Meining, D. W. (Ed.). 1979. *The Interpretation of Ordinary Landscapes.* New York: Oxford University Press.

Melville, H. 1961. *Moby Dick.* New York: New American Library. (Original work published 1851.)

Milgram, S. 1970. The experience of living in cities. *Science* 167: 1461–8.

Mooney, R. T. 1979. Waterfronts: Building along the Mississippi. *AIA Journal* 68, 2: 47–53.

Moore, E. O. 1981. A prison environment's effect on health case service demands. *Journal of Environmental Systems* 11: 17–34.

Moore, G. T. 1985. State of the art in play environment research and applications. In J. Frost (Ed.), *When Children Play*, pp. 171–92. Wheaton, Md: Association for Childhood Education International.

Moore, R. C. 1978. Meanings and measures of children/environment quality: Some findings from Washington Environmental Yard. In W. E. Rogers & W. H. Ittelson (Eds.), *New Directions in Environmental Design Research*, EDRA 9, pp. 287–306. Washington, D.C.: Environmental Design Research Association.

1980. Collaborating with young people to assess their landscape values. *Ekistics* 281: 128–35.

1986. *Childhood's Domain: Play and Place in Child Development.* London: Croom-Helm.

1987. Streets as playgrounds. In A. Vernez-Moudon (Ed.), *Public Streets for Public Use*, pp. 45–62. New York: Van Nostrand Reinhold.

1989. Playgrounds at the crossroads: Policy and action research needed to ensure a viable future for public playgrounds in the United States. In I. Altman & E. Zube. (Eds.), *Public Places and Spaces*, pp. 83–121. Vol. 10 of *Human Behavior and Environment.* New York: Plenum.

Moore, R. C., S. Goltsman, & O. Iacofano. 1987. *The Play for All Guidelines: Planning, Design and Management of Outdoor Settings for All Children.* Berkeley, Calif.: MIG Communications.

Moore, R. C., & D. Young. 1978. Childhood outdoors: Toward a social ecology of the landscape. In I. Altman & J. Wohlwill (Eds.), *Children and the Environment.* Vol. 3 of *Human Behavior and Environment*, pp. 83–130. New York: Plenum.

Morris, A. E. J. 1979. *History of Urban Form before the Industrial Revolution.* 2nd ed. New York: Wiley.

Mozingo, L. 1989. Women and downtown open spaces. *Places* 6, 1: 38–47.

Muller, P. 1980. Improvement of children's play opportunities in residential areas through traffic reduction schemes. *Garten und Landschaft* 90: 108–12.

Mumford, L. 1961. *The City in History: Its Origins, Its Transformation.* New York: Harcourt Brace and World.

1970. *The Culture of Cities.* New York: Harcourt Brace Jovanovich.

Nager, A. R., & W. R. Wentworth. 1976. Bryant Park: A comprehensive evaluation of its image and use with implications for urban open space design. New York: Center for Human Environments, City University of New York.

Nasar, J. L. (Ed.). 1988. *Environmental Aesthetics: Research, Theory and Application.* Cambridge: Cambridge University Press.

Newman, O. 1973. *Personal Space.* New York: Macmillan.

1980. A new marketplace with the vitality of an old landmark: Harborplace in Baltimore. *Architectural Record* 168, 5: 100–4.

Newton, N. T. 1971. *Design on the Land.* Cambridge: Harvard University Press.

Nicholson, S. 1971. How not to cheat children: The theory of loose parts. *Landscape Architecture* 62, 1: 30–4.

Norberg-Schulz, C. 1980. *Genus Loci: Toward a Phenomenology of Architecture.* New York: Rizzoli.

O'Donnell, P. M. 1981. Houghton Park extension: User survey report. Paper presented at the meeting of the Environmental Design Research Association, Ames, Iowa, April.

Organization for Economic Cooperation and Development. 1974. *Streets for People.* Paris.

Olmsted, F. L., Jr., & T. Kimball. (Eds.). 1973. *Forty Years of Landscape Architecture.* Cambridge: MIT Press.

Partners for Livable Places. *The Economics of Livability.* Washington, D.C.

Pateman, C. 1970. *Participation and Democratic Theory.* Cambridge: Cambridge University Press.

Perez, C., & R. Hart. 1980. Beyond playgrounds: Children's accessibility to the landscape. In P. F. Wilkinson (Ed.), *Innovations in Play Environments,* pp. 252–71. New York: St. Martin's Press.

Pitt, D. G. 1989. The attractiveness and use of aquatic environments as outdoor recreation places. In I. Altman & E. Zube (Eds.), *Public Places and Spaces,* pp. 217–54. Vol. 10 of *Human Behavior and Environment.* New York: Plenum.

Place debate: Piazza d'Italia. 1984. *Places* 1, 2: 7.

Plattner, S. 1978. Public markets: Functional anachronisms or functional necessities? *Ekistics* 273: 444–6.

Poulton, M. 1982. The best pattern of residential streets. *Journal of American Planning Association* 4: 466–80.

President's Commission on Americans Outdoors. 1987. *Americans Outdoors.* Washington, D.C.: Island Press.

Pressman, N. (Ed.). 1985. *Reshaping Winter Cities.* Waterloo, Ontario: University of Waterloo Press.

Program on Public Space Partnerships. 1987. Report. Winter/Spring. Cambridge: Kennedy School of Government, Harvard University, 1987.

Project for Public Spaces, Inc. 1977. Greenacre Park study. 48 pp. New York.

1978. Plazas for people: Seattle's First National Bank Plaza and Seattle Federal Building Plaza – a case study. 44 pp. New York.

1979. *Film on User Analysis.* 72 pp. Washington, D.C.: American Society of Landscape Architects.

1981a. Bryant Park: Intimidation or recreation. New York.

1981b. What people do downtown: How to look at mainstreet activity. Washington, D.C.: National Trust for Historic Preservation.

1982a. Designing effective pedestrian improvements in business districts. 60 pp. Chicago: American Planning Association.

1982b. User analysis: An approach to park planning and management. Washington, D.C.: American Society of Landscape Architects.

1984. *Managing Downtown Public Spaces.* Chicago: Planners Press, American Planning Association.

Proshansky, H. M. 1978. The city and self-identity. *Environment and Behavior* 10, 2: 147–69.

Proshansky, H. M., A. K. Fabian, & R. Kaminoff. 1983. Place identity, physical world socialization of self. *Journal of Environmental Psychology* 3, 1: 57–83.

Proshansky, H. M., W. H. Ittelson, & L. G. Rivlin. 1970. Freedom of choice and behavior in a physical setting. In H. M. Proshansky, W. H. Ittelson, L. G. Rivlin (Eds.), *Environmental Psychology: Man and His Physical Environment,* pp. 173–82. New York: Holt, Rinehart & Winston.

Pruis, R. 1987. Developing loyalty: Fostering purchasing relationship in the marketplace. *Urban Life* 15: 331–66.

Rapoport, A. 1982. *The Meaning of the Built Environment: A Nonverbal Communication Approach.* Beverly Hills, Calif.: Sage.

Relph, T. 1976. *Place and Placelessness.* London: Pion.

1987. *The Modern Urban Landscape.* Baltimore: Johns Hopkins University Press.

Reps, J. W. 1965. *The Making of Urban America.* Princeton: Princeton University Press.

Richardson, M. 1982. Being in the market versus being in the plaza: Material culture and the construction of social reality in Spanish America. *American Ethnologist* 9: 421–36.

Riis, J. A. 1957. *How the Other Half Lives.* New York: Hill and Wang. (Originally published in 1890.)

Riley, R. 1987. Vernacular landscapes. In E. H. Zube & G. T. Moore (Eds.), *Advances in Environment, Behavior and Design,* Vol. 1, pp. 129–50. New York: Plenum.

1990. Flowers, power and sex. In M. Francis & R. Hester (Eds.), *The Meaning of Gardens,* pp. 60–75. Cambridge: MIT Press.

Rivlin, L. G. 1982. Group membership and place meanings in an urban neighborhood. *Journal of Social Issues* 38, 3: 75–93.

1987. The neighborhood, personal identity, and group affiliations. In I. Altman & A. Wandersman (Eds.), *Neighborhood and Community Environments,* pp. 1–34. Vol. 9 of *Human Behavior and Environment.* New York: Plenum.

Rivlin, L. G., & M. Francis (Eds.). 1979. Provisions for people: Grand Central and Citicorp study. New York: Center for Human Environments, City University of New York.

Rivlin, L. G., & A. Windsor. 1986. A study of found spaces. New York: Environmental Psychology Program, City University of New York. Unpublished report.

Rivlin, L. G., & M. Wolfe. 1985. *Institutional Settings in Children's Lives.* New York: Wiley.

Roundtable on Rouse. 1981. *Progressive Architecture* 62, 7: 100–6.

Royal Dutch Touring Club. 1978. Woonerf: Residential precinct. *Ekistics* 273: 417–23.

Rudofsky, B. 1964. *Architecture without Architects.* New York: Museum of Modern Art.

1969. *Streets for People.* New York: Doubleday.

Rustin, M. 1986. The fall and rise of public space. *Dissent* 33: 486–94.

Rutledge, A. J. 1976. Looking beyond the applause: Chicago's First National Bank Plaza. *Landscape Architecture* 66: 22–6.

1986. *A Visual Approach to Park Design.* New York: McGraw-Hill.

Ryan, M. P. 1981. *Cradle of the Middle Class: The Family in Oneida County, New York, 1790–1865.* Cambridge: Cambridge University Press.

Sale, Kirkpatrick. 1990. *Dwellers in the Land: The Bioregional Vision.* San Francisco: Sierra Club Books.

San Francisco Department of City Planning. 1985. *The San Francisco Downtown Plan.* San Francisco.

Sandels, S. 1975. *Children in Traffic.* London: Paul Elek.

Scharnberg, C. 1973. *Bornenes jord* (Children's earth). Arhus, Denmark: Forlaget Avos.

Scheer, R. 1969. Dialectics of confrontation: Who ripped off the park. *Ramparts* 7, 2: 42–9, 52–3.

Schonberg, H. D. 1982. Where the real world meets the artists' world. *New York Times,* September 8, p. C24.

Schroeder, H. W. 1989. Research on urban forests. In E. H. Zube & G. T. Moore (Eds.), *Advances in Environment, Behavior and Design,* Vol. 2, pp. 87–113. New York: Plenum.

Schroeder, H. W., & L. M. Anderson. 1983. Perception of personal safety in urban recreation sites. *Journal of Leisure Research* 16: 178–94.

Scott, M. 1969. *American City Planning.* Berkeley: University of California Press.

Seamon, D., & C. Nordin. 1980. Marketplace as place ballet: A Swedish example. *Landscape* 24, 3: 35–41.

Sennett, R. 1977. *The Fall of Public Man.* New York: Random House.

Sijpkes, P., D. Brown, & M. MacLean. 1983. The behavior of elderly people in Montreal's indoor city. *Plan Canada* 23: 14.

Sime, J. 1986. Creating places or designing spaces. *Journal of Environmental Psychology* 6: 49–63.

Sommer, B., & R. Sommer. 1985. *A Practical Guide to Behavioral Research.* 2nd ed. New York: Oxford University Press.

Sommer, R. 1980. *Farmers' Markets of America.* Santa Barbara, Calif.: Capra Press.

——— 1981. The behavioral ecology of supermarkets and farmer's markets. *Journal of Environmental Psychology* 1: 13–19.

——— 1983. *Social Design.* Englewood Cliffs, N.J.: Prentice Hall.

——— 1989. Farmers' markets as community events. In I. Altman & E. Zube (Eds.), *Public Places and Spaces,* pp. 57–82. Vol. 10 of *Human Behavior and Environment.* New York: Plenum.

Sommer, R., & F. Becker. 1969. The old men in Plaza Park. *Landscape Architecture* 59: 111–13.

Sommer, R., J. Herrick, & T. Sommer. 1981. The behavioral ecology of supermarkets and farmers' markets. *Journal of Environmental Psychology* 1: 13–9.

Sommer, R., M. Stumpf, & H. Bennett. 1982. Quality of farmers' market produce, flavor and pesticide residues. *Journal of Consumer Affairs* 16: 130–6.

Sommer, R., & R. L. Thayer. 1977. The radicalization of common ground. *Landscape Architecture* 67: 510–14.

Sommer, R., M. Wing, & S. Aitkins. 1980. Price savings to consumers at farmers' markets. *Journal of Consumer Affairs* 14, 2: 452–62.

Sommers, L. 1984. *The Community Garden Book.* Burlington, Vt.: National Gardening Association.

Sorensen, G., T. Larsson, & S. Ledet. 1973. Byggelegepladser I Storkobenhaun (Adventure playgrounds). Copenhagen. Unpublished report.

Spirn, A. W. 1984. *The Granite Garden: Urban Nature and Human Design.* New York: Basic Books.

——— 1988. The poetics of city and nature: Towards a new aesthetic for urban design. *Landscape Journal* 2: 108–26.

Spitz, R. A. 1945. Hospitalism: An inquiry into the genesis of psychiatric conditions in early childhood. *Psychoanalytic Study of the Child* 1: 53–74.

Spivack, M. 1969. The political collapse of a playground. *Landscape Architecture* 59: 288–92.

Spring, B. F. 1978. Evaluation: Rockefeller Center's two contrasting generations of space. *AIA Journal* 67: 26–31.

Stearn, J. 1981. *Towards Community Uses of Wastelands.* London: Wastelands Forum.

Stephens, S. 1978a. At the core of the apple. *Progressive Architecture* 59: 54–9.

——— 1978b. Introversion and the urban context. *Progressive Architecture* 59: 49–53.

Stewart, J., & R. L. McKenzie. 1978. Composing urban spaces for security, privacy and outlook. *Landscape Architecture* 68: 392–8.

Stilgoe, J. 1982. *Common Landscapes in America.* New Haven: Yale University Press.

Stokols, D., & S. A. Shumaker. 1981. People in places: A transactional view of settings. In J. H. Harvey (Ed.), *Cognition, Social Behavior, and the Environment,* pp. 441–88. Hillsdale, N.J.: Lawrence Erlbaum Associates.

Stoks, F. 1983. Assessing urban environments for danger of violent crime: Especially rape. In D. Joiner et al. (Eds.), *PAPER: Proceedings of the Conference on People and Physical Environment Research.* Wellington, New Zealand: Ministry of Work and Development.

Stone, A. 1986. A history of open space in New York City. New York: Open Space Task Force.

Storr, R. 1985. Tilted Arc. *Art in America* 73: 90–7.

Strauss, A. L. (Ed.). 1961. *Images of the American City.* New York: Free Press.

Suttles, G. 1968. *The Social Order of the Slum.* Chicago: University of Chicago Press.

Suzuki, P. 1976. Germans and Turks at German railroad stations. *Urban Life* 4: 387–412.

Talbot, J. F., & R. Kaplan. 1984. Needs and fears: The response to trees and nature in the inner city. *Journal of Arboriculture* 10: 222–8.

Taylor, L. (Ed.). 1981. *Urban Open Spaces.* New York: Rizzoli.

Tishler, W. (Ed.). 1989. *American Landscape Architecture.* Washington, D.C.: National Trust for Historic Preservation.

Trancik, R. 1986. *Finding Lost Space.* New York: Van Nostrand Reinhold.

Tuan, Y. F. 1974. *Topophilia.* Englewood Cliffs, N.J.: Prentice-Hall.

——— 1978. Children and the natural environment. In I. Altman & I. F. Wohlwill (Eds.), *Children and the Environment,* pp. 5–32. New York: Plenum.

1980. Rootedness versus sense of place. *Landscape* 24, 1: 3–8.

Tyburczy, J. 1982. The effects of California state certified farmers' markets on downtown revitalization. M.A. thesis, University of California at Davis.

Tyburczy, J., & R. Sommer. 1983. Farmers' markets are good for downtown. *California Agriculture* 37: 30–2.

Ulrich, R. S. 1979. Visual landscapes and psychological well being. *Landscape Research* 4: 17–19.

1984. View through a window may influence recovery from surgery. *Science* 224: 420–1.

Ulrich, R. S., & D. L. Addoms. 1981. Psychological and recreational benefits of a residential park. *Journal of Leisure Research* 13: 43–65.

Ulrich, R. S., & R. F. Simons. 1986. Recovery from stress during exposure to everyday outdoor environments. In J. Wineman, R. Barnes, & C. Zimring (Eds.), *The Cost of Not Knowing: Proceedings of the 17th Environmental Design Research Association Conference*, pp. 115–22. Washington, D.C.

Untermann, R. 1984. *Accommodating the Pedestrian*. New York: Van Nostrand Reinhold.

van Andel, J. 1985. Effects on children's outdoor behavior of physical changes in a Leiden neighborhood. *Children's Environments Quarterly* 1: 46–54.

1986. Physical changes in an elementary school yard. *Children's Environments Quarterly* 3: 40–51.

Van Dyke, J. C. 1909. *The New New York: A Commentary on the Place and the People.* New York: Macmillan.

Van Vliet, W. 1983. An examination of the home range of city and suburban teenagers. *Environment and Behavior* 15: 567–88.

Vance, B. 1982. Adventure playgrounds: The American experience. *Parks and Recreation* 17, 9: 67–70.

Verwer, D. 1980. Planning residential environments according to their real use by children & adults. *Ekistics* 281: 109–113.

Vernez-Moudon, A. 1986. *Built for Change: Neighborhood Architecture in San Francisco.* Cambridge: MIT Press.

Vernez-Moudon, A. (Ed.). 1987. *Public Streets for Public Use.* New York: Van Nostrand Reinhold.

Veyne, P. 1987. The Roman empire. In P. Veyne (Ed.), *A History of Private Life*, pp. 5–233. Vol. 1 of *From Pagan Rome to Byzantium.* (A. Goldhammer, Trans.). Cambridge: Harvard University Press. (Original work published 1985.)

Violich, F. 1983. Urban reading and the design of small urban places. *Town Planning Review* 54: 41–62.

Von Eckardt, W. 1981. Reclaiming our waterfront. In L. Taylor (Ed.), *Urban Open Spaces*, pp. 48–9. New York: Rizzoli.

Wachs, J. 1979. Primal experiences and early cognitive intellectual development. *Merrill-Palmer Quarterly* 25: 3–42.

Walzer, M. 1986. Pleasures and costs of urbanity. *Dissent* 33, 4: 470–5.

Wampler, J. 1977. *All Their Own.* Cambridge, Mass.: Schenkman Publishing.

Wandersman, A. 1981. A framework of participation in community organizations. *Journal of Applied Behavioral Science* 17: 27–58.

Ward, C. 1978. *The Child in the City.* New York: Pantheon Books.

Warner, S. B. 1962. *Street Car Suburb.* Cambridge: Harvard University Press.

1987. *To Dwell Is to Garden.* Boston: Boston University Press.

Webber, M. 1963. Order in diversity: Community without propinquity. In L. Wingo, Jr. (Ed.), *Cities and Space: The Future Use of Urban Land*, pp. 23–54. Baltimore: Johns Hopkins University Press.

Weinstein, C. S., & T. David (Eds.). 1987. *Spaces for Children: The Built Environment and Child Development.* New York: Plenum.

West Side Waterfront Panel. 1990. A Vision for the Hudson River Waterfront Park. New York: A Report to Governor Mario M. Cuomo and Mayor David N. Dinkins.

Westin, A. F. 1967. *Privacy and Freedom.* New York: Atheneum.

Whitaker, B., & K. Browne. 1971. *Parks for People.* New York: Schocken Books.

White, R. W. 1959. Motivation reconsidered: The concept of competence. *Psychological Review* 66: 313–24.

Whitzman, C. 1990. Design guidelines towards a safer city. Draft Report. City of Toronto Planning and Development Department.

Whyte, W. H. 1980. *The Social Life of Small Urban Spaces.* Washington, D.C.: The Conservation Foundation.

Whyte, W. H. 1988. *City: Rediscovering the Center*. New York: Doubleday.

Wilkinson, P. F., & R. S. Lockhart. 1980. Safety in children's formal play environments. In P. F. Wilkinson (Ed.), *Innovation in Play Environments,* pp. 85–96. London: Croom-Helm.

Wiedermann, D. 1985. How secure are public open spaces? *Garten und Landschaft* 95: 26–7.

Wuellner, L. H. 1979. Forty guidelines for playground design. *Journal of Leisure Research* 11: 4–14.

Wurman, R., A. Levy, & J. Katz. 1972. *The Nature of Recreation*. Cambridge: MIT Press.

Zeisel, J. 1981. *Inquiry by Design*. Cambridge: Cambridge University Press.

Zube, E. H., J. L. Sell, & J. G. Taylor. 1982. Landscape perception: Research, application and theory. *Landscape Planning* 9: 1–33.

Zube, E. & G. Moore (Eds.). 1987, 1989, 1991. *Advances in Environment, Behavior and Design*. 3 Vols. New York: Plenum.

Zucker, P. 1959. *Town and Square: From the Agora to the Village Green*. New York: Columbia University Press.

NAME INDEX

Name index

SUBJECT INDEX

Subject index

Subject index

walking streets, 7, 41, 142–4
wall activity, high-style, 114–15
walled towns, 53–4
Washington, D.C.: Downtown Washington Streets for People, 273–7; Freedom Plaza, 18, 208, 210, 211–12; historical monuments, 47; L'Enfant's plan for, 59; Mall, 68; monuments, shrines, 207–8; Pershing Park, 95–6, 149, 180, 212; Redevelopment Land Agency, 274, 275–6; Vietnam Veterans Memorial, 171, 208–10; waterfront, 348
Washington Market Park (Manhattan), 339
Washington Monument, 224
Washington Square (New York City), 145
wastelands, urban, 355–6, 357
water, 42–3, 50, 114, 116, 226, 238, 266; connection to, 191–2; contact with, 123–4; importance of, 103
water retention, on-site, 354
waterfalls, 95, 103, 226; Greenacre Park (New York City), 99, 102, 113, 122
waterfront development, 36, 347, 348–50, 351
Waterfront Park (Boston), 96, 118, 191–2, 252, 326
waterfronts, 8, 42–3, 118; access to, 263–4, 293, 348, 349–50; Boston, 77; conflict over rights of access and use, 263–4; users of, 326, 328
waterfront esplanades, 67
Watts Towers, 270
Westside Community Garden (New York City), 182
wetlands, 8, 79, 356
wilderness areas, 123
wildlife habitat, 79, 354
women, 210–11, 345; crime against, 33; freedom of movement, 155–6; safety concerns, 48, 97
woonerf, woonerven (Delft, the Netherlands), 70, 121, 139–42, 144, 164, 198
work at home, 28–30, 353
working class, 4, 5, 35, 64, 137, 359; and parks, 63, 67
workshops, 331
World of Strangers, A (Lofland), 25–6

Yokohama, Japan, 116

zoning, 256
zoning incentives, 74–5, 177, 178, 279, 363